THE ARAB
AWAKENING

A SABAN CENTER AT THE BROOKINGS INSTITUTION BOOK

THE ARAB AWAKENING

America and the Transformation of the Middle East

KENNETH M. POLLACK

AKRAM AL-TURK

PAVEL K. BAEV

MICHAEL S. DORAN

KHALED ELGINDY

STEPHEN R. GRAND

SHADI HAMID

BRUCE JONES

SUZANNE MALONEY

DANIEL L. BYMAN

JONATHAN D. POLLACK

BRUCE O. RIEDEL

RUTH HANAU SANTINI

SALMAN SHAIKH

IBRAHIM SHARQIEH

ÖMER TAŞPINAR

SHIBLEY TELHAMI

SARAH E. YERKES

BROOKINGS INSTITUTION PRESS
Washington, D.C.

Library of Congress Cataloging-in-Publication data

The Arab awakening : America and the transformation of the Middle East / Kenneth M.
Pollack . . . [et al.].
     p.   cm.
   Includes bibliographical references and index.
   Summary: "Analyzes key aspects of the 2011 Mideast turmoil, such as Arab public
opinion; socioeconomic and demographic conditions; the role of social media; influence
of Islamists; the impact of political changes on the Arab-Israeli peace process; and
ramifications for the United States and the rest of the world. Also provides country-by-
country analysis of Middle East political evolution"—Provided by publisher.
   ISBN 978-0-8157-2226-7 (pbk. : alk. paper)
  1. Arab countries—Politics and government—21st century. 2. Democratization—Arab
countries—History—21st century. 3. Protest movements—Arab countries—History—
21st century. 4. United States—Foreign relations—Arab countries. 5. Arab countries—
Foreign relations—United States. 6. Arab countries—Foreign relations—21st century.
I. Pollack, Kenneth M. (Kenneth Michael), 1966– II. Title.
   JQ1850.A91A73 2011
     956.05'4—dc23   2011038375

9 8 7 6 5 4 3 2 1

Printed on acid-free paper

Typeset in Minion

Composition by Cynthia Stock
Silver Spring, Maryland

Printed by R. R. Donnelley
Harrisonburg, Virginia

We only have one fear, that the revolution will stop. Nothing else.

Twenty-five-year-old Syrian activist
Beirut, July 2011

Contents

PREFACE

Why Should You Read This Book?

What happened in the Arab world in 2011 was stunning. Wondrous things happened. Tragic things happened. Other things happened that only time will tell if they were good, bad, or something else entirely. The result is that the Middle East will never be the same. And because the Middle East—through its energy supplies and central location—affects every other part of the world, neither will anything else. As breathtaking as the events of 2011 were, they are only the beginning of the changes that will likely take place in the region in the decades ahead. They are the start of what will doubtless be one of the major developments of the twenty-first century: the reemergence of the Arab world after decades of political stagnation.

An event as big as this, that has only just begun to unfold, cannot possibly be covered in every aspect by a single volume—and certainly not one written so soon after the first acts have played out. That said, there is a crying need for sober analysis of the events of 2011. The media have shown us what happened, but done little to explain why, or what it all means, or how all of the pieces fit together in a larger picture.

That is why we wrote this book. We wanted to provide an overview of the Arab Spring, the dynamics driving it, and what these dynamics suggest for the future. We wanted to explore the events in each of the various states of the region and how they are interacting. We wanted to take a look at how the broad patterns affecting the entire region are mingling with the specific, idiosyncratic features of each state to produce a set of events that in some ways seems remarkably similar in, and in other ways entirely unique to, each country. We also wanted to help policymakers in the United States and elsewhere make better decisions in reaction to the revolutionary changes occurring.

To do all this, we have written chapters that look at key issues that have affected the entire region and will be critical themes in the years ahead—from the Arab economies to their militaries, from the role of the Islamists to the role of new media, and from terrorism to the Arab-Israeli conflict. But we have also provided concise assessments of how the Arab Spring has played out in virtually every country of the region so that readers looking for a better understanding of what happened or what may happen in key states can find that too. We have chapters on non-Arab regional actors—Israel, Iran, and Turkey—because they exert important influence on events in the Arab world and will themselves be deeply affected by the unfolding course of the Arab Awakening. Finally, it is impossible to understand what is happening in the Middle East, what is likely to happen there in the future, and how what is happening there will affect the rest of the world without looking at how global powers like the United States, China, Russia, Europe, Brazil, and India have viewed and reacted to the Arab Spring.

Taken together, we hope that this approach provides something for everyone. For readers looking to get their arms around just what happened in the Middle East in 2011, we hope this book will help you see the big-picture issues as well as the country-specific developments, both today and looking out into the years ahead. For those who simply want to know more about certain things that caught their eye while watching the drama of the Arab Spring, the many concise chapters of this book ought to allow them to focus on what they feel matters most. For those looking to understand how the events of the Arab Spring fit into 2011's global trajectory, there are discussions of both the meta trends and the more specific impacts on key actors within the global order. We deliberately wrote it so that it could be enjoyed either as a whole or à la carte.

This Is NOT an Edited Volume

Now, we know what you are thinking: you think this is an edited volume by the scholars of the Saban Center at Brookings as well as a number of other well-versed Brookings experts. Well, not really. Although this book is not quite a fully coauthored work, it is not an edited volume either. Instead, it is a collaborative work among all of the authors.

We generally don't like edited volumes. They tend to be very uneven. They lack a narrative arc. Most of the chapters don't relate to one another in any way. There are rarely any common threads among the various essays—no common perspective or set of ideas being developed. Most edited volumes are, at best, a collection of decent, independent essays about a general topic.

This book is not that. We could not have eighteen people coauthor a book; Saban Center scholars disagree in their interpretations of many key issues, and to force agreement would mean describing events or interpreting them at such a high level of generality as to be useless. However, we approached writing the book very much as a unified project. The scholars of the Saban Center—including those located at the Brookings Doha Center in Qatar—met on several occasions to hammer out the basics of the book. We agreed on a common framework, a common set of themes that we wanted all of the chapters to explore, a common vocabulary, and a common methodology. But more than that, in the course of those meetings and from e-mails and comments on one another's drafts, we also formulated a common set of ideas about the Arab Spring: what has happened in the region, why it happened when and in the way that it did, what the various scenarios for the future are, and of greatest importance, how the United States should react to events in both the near and longer terms. As noted, we all read one another's chapters and commented on them, which led to decisions to have some chapters that began as single authored pieces coauthored, and to add several more chapters that we all felt were necessitated by our discussions and the ideas that percolated from them.

During the course of this process, we found that our views on how American interests were engaged by the developments in the Arab world and what policies the United States should pursue toward the Arab Spring were remarkably in sync. Indeed, the final chapter, chapter 36 on the United States and the Arab Spring, is effectively a collective essay by nine of the permanent fellows of the Saban Center (Ken Pollack, Dan Byman, Bruce Riedel, Suzanne Maloney, Mike Doran, Steve Grand, Salman Shaikh, Shadi Hamid, and Shibley Telhami), along with Sarah Yerkes (formerly of the Saban Center), regarding how the United States should approach the Arab Spring and its aftermath. We had some differences of opinion about whether some additional topics should be included in that chapter—and what the United States should do about them—and because of those differences, we felt we could not make it a coauthored chapter. So, Ken Pollack, who drafted it, signed his name alone. That said, it reflects a near consensus among us on how the United States should be thinking about the Middle East in the years to come.

Moreover, we spent a great deal of effort trying to weave the chapters into a coherent whole with a consistent set of themes that built from one chapter to the next, and that explicitly referenced foundational and related ideas found elsewhere in the book. Thus, all of the chapters "speak" to one another and create a narrative flow that begins with the broad, overarching themes of the origins and dynamics of the Arab Spring, before moving on to look at how nearly every country in the region experienced this period (and how the United States should be interacting with that country in the future), followed by key countries outside the region and what the Arab Spring has meant for them.

Nevertheless, because there were small, but in some cases important, differences that remain among us on a number of issues, in the end we let the chapters stand as the work of their specific authors—and the rest of us should not be blamed for their foolishness!

We decided to break up the Middle Eastern states into several groupings as a way of helping the reader understand what has gone on in the region. So the organization we employed was not the traditional geographic categories, but instead categories based on the experiences of the states during the Arab Spring and the challenges they face. The point we sought to make by doing this was that what matters today in the Middle East is really a country's political development; whether it is pursuing a course intended to address the political, economic, and social grievances that caused the unrest and revolts of the Arab Spring; and if so, how. Our contention is that, in general, the states of the Middle East (excluding Israel) fall into three broad categories: states where the autocratic regime has fallen and most people there hope to build a democracy; states where the autocratic regime is still in power but needs to move down the path of reform to accommodate the demands and grievances of the population to avoid unrest or even overthrow in the future; and states where protests against the government have led not to regime change, but to civil war. Of course, each state is unique in its particulars, but we believe these categories present similar patterns and challenges that can help us think better about the region.

This is a different way of thinking about the Middle East than Americans traditionally have in the past. That's good. This year, the Middle East began a process of change that will likely take a generation or more, but will leave the region profoundly different from what it was. To start coming to grips with the scope of that change will mean changing our ways of thinking about it too. We hope that this book gives you a good start at finding a new perspective on the new Middle East.

The Authors
The Brookings Institution
September 2011

ACKNOWLEDGMENTS

This book was a work of almost epic proportions. Because of its size—thirty-six chapters written by eighteen different authors—and the speed with which we put it together to get it out while it still had relevance, it became all-consuming for a number of people on the staff of the Saban Center at Brookings. As the U.S. military likes to say, "Fast, good, cheap: you get to pick two." We wanted fast and good and that meant a lot of people had to invest a lot in it.

The place to begin thanking those who worked so hard to bring this project to fruition is with Ariel Kastner, the terrific assistant director for publications at the Saban Center. More than anyone else, Ariel breathed life into this book. He herded the cats, keeping the authors on schedule, negotiating with the Brookings Press, and constantly rejiggering the timeline when new developments in the Middle East made it necessary to change things—something that happened on an almost daily basis. He did yeoman work editing this volume, taking eighteen different voices and weaving them into a unified chorus. More than that, Ariel is an expert on the region in his own right, and he provided excellent insights and important caveats to all of the authors that made the book much better than it otherwise would have been.

As always, we were ably assisted by a pack of exceptionally talented researchers. First among equals was Irena L. Sargsyan, who not only helped with a number of the chapters but, along with Zachary Ruchman and Heba Tellawi, collected, sorted, and analyzed reams and reams of data to craft the appendix of indicators to the book. Such a compilation of basic statistics is always an extremely helpful tool for readers, and Irena and her team have our great gratitude for all of the work they invested in pulling that together. In this effort, Laura Mooney was a tremendous help, tracking down sources to put together such a complex appendix.

Zack Gold, Carmiel Arbit, Mehrun Etebari, and Eran Sharon each provided valuable research for many of the authors as well as comments on various sections of the book. Eitan Paul provided research assistance on chapter 22, "Morocco: The Model for Reform?" Vicky Macintyre reviewed the text and played an instrumental role in the editing process.

Bob Faherty and Chris Kelaher at the Brookings Institution Press were, as usual, absolute pleasures to work with. Their encouragement and flexibility were invaluable in making this project a reality, and they demonstrated to us once again why we are so fortunate not only to have a Brookings Press, but to have the press we do, manned by the people we do. Likewise, Janet Walker and Larry Converse at the Brookings Press kept the project on track, despite several last-minute additions to the text. Their patience, creative suggestions for expediting the publication process, and commitment to this endeavor ensured that the book was printed in a timely manner. Susan Woollen and Sese-Paul Design always do a great job with our cover designs, but this one was above and beyond the call of duty: having to deal with eighteen authors, all of whom had a very different idea of what should be on the cover and at least half of whom wanted to pick up a pen or a Photoshop program and do it themselves, was more than the usual amount of frustration. We are thrilled that they came up with such a lovely and evocative design, and that they refrained from killing any of the authors in the process.

Martin Indyk, the vice president of Foreign Policy at Brookings deserves our thanks for suggesting the idea for this volume. At that time, we might have wanted to do much bodily harm to Martin for challenging us to produce a book like this in the time we did it in. But having done so, and having read the final product, we all recognize that, once again, Martin was spot on. We are all very proud of this work and never would have tried had it not been for Martin's typically keen insight.

Finally, we would like to publicly thank one another. When we started out on this project, we were all somewhat skeptical of what we might produce. However, at one of our meetings after we had the first draft of all the chapters, everyone of us realized that we had done something quite remarkable, and far more valuable than I think any of us (except Martin Indyk) believed it would be. Reading and discussing one another's work helped each of us to refine his or her own thinking. All of us grew intellectually in the process of writing and discussing this book. All of us learned things we had not known before. All of us gained perspective we had lacked before. In the end, it was a great project for all of us, and we are grateful to one another for sharing those insights, that knowledge, and these ideas. Now, we hope you feel the same.

1

INTRODUCTION

Understanding the Arab Awakening

KENNETH M. POLLACK

The Arab Spring is dead. Long live the Arab Spring.

The events that began in Tunisia in January 2011 and spread to Egypt and then Libya, Jordan, Morocco, Bahrain, Syria, and beyond, shook the political, social, and intellectual foundations of the Middle East. The tremors can still be felt, and no one is quite certain when the aftershocks will end, or when another shock wave of popular unrest might occur.

Nevertheless, enough time has passed to try to make sense of what has happened so far and, perhaps, gain an inkling of where the region is headed. Because we are still too close to the events to understand the meaning of all their complexities, our assessment can only be preliminary. In fact, many of those affected still do not understand the full extent of the ways in which they themselves and their circumstances have changed. Others have not yet taken the actions that history may record as having been produced by the Arab Spring.

Unfortunately, the United States does not have the luxury of waiting to make sense of what occurred. Although the shock of the initial events of the Arab Spring has ebbed, many of the miseries that gave rise to it persist and remain compelling motives for many people across the region. The changes that the initial wave of revolution left in its wake are barely half-formed. How they develop will be critical in shaping the longer-term effects, as will actions today of the United States and its allies, which remain important forces in the region. While these revolutions were not made in America, American actions may have an outsize impact, perhaps even on their ultimate success or failure. The storm of unrest that spread from the Atlantic to the Persian Gulf may have subsided, at least in some parts of the region, but its story has just begun.

THE CAUSES OF THE ARAB SPRING

Like all great social upheavals, the Arab Spring was long in the making, and born of many intertwined causes.[1] It might have happened at any time over the past two to three decades, but each passing year brought new developments that made it that much more likely. Economic problems, social problems, political problems, juridical problems, and diplomatic problems all contributed to a furious sense of grievance across the Arab world that finally boiled over in the winter and spring of 2011.

The best way to understand what happened in the Arab world in 2011 is to start with the stagnation of the Arab economies—as Suzanne Maloney explains in chapter 8—because that is where the frustration began for the vast majority of Arabs, although that is certainly not where it ended. While other countries in the world evolved from agrarian economies to industrial economies to information economies, the Arab world lagged far behind. In particular, the educational system of the Arab world remained stuck in a pre-modern era. As the United Nations' *Arab Human Development Report* first warned almost ten years ago, the educational method of the Arab world hindered young Arab minds from thinking critically, producing knowledge, and mastering many technical fields.[2] While there has been no shortage of education in the Arab world in recent years, Arab schools and universities have not prepared their students for a modern, information-age global economy. With so little human capital available, relatively few entrepreneurs have invested in the Middle East, other than to harvest the region's plentiful oil and gas resources—investments that have benefited the regimes and their cronies, but not the vast majority of the people.

Even with economics as a starting point, one cannot get very far in explaining the origins of the Arab Spring without bringing in politics. Before 2011 the Middle East was a democratic desert: only Iraq, Lebanon, and the Palestinian territories could lay any claim to democracy, and all three efforts were deeply imperfect.[3] These autocratic regimes added to the misery of their people by tolerating, and even encouraging, widespread corruption and sketchy legal systems that frightened away legitimate investors. As a result, foreign investment and development were replaced by those looking to exploit the region in cahoots with its semi-criminal elite.

The net effect has been a raft of ulcerous economic liabilities: unemployment (especially among the outsized youth population); underemployment (especially among the middle class, whose education and status make them believe that they deserve managerial or clerical jobs, rather than driving a taxi or working in a restaurant); yawning wealth gaps; low levels of direct foreign investment outside the energy sector; meager non-energy exports; disproportionately low levels of international trade; excessive dependence on the public sector for employment;

rapid urbanization coupled with inadequate infrastructure development; and heavy outflows of capital, both human and financial. In short, the economies of the Arab world (and Iran) have been failing their people for a very long time.[4]

Inevitably, people unhappy with their economic status look to their governments for help—in the Middle East no less than in the American Midwest. But in the Arab autocracies, the poor, the working classes, and the middle classes met only callous indifference, corruption, and humiliation when they sought redress from their governments. Indeed, the massive, bloated, corrupt government bureaucracies did nothing to alleviate the suffering of their people and a great deal to make it more painful. They cared nothing about the lives of their people, only about perpetuating their own advantages. "Good governance" was a bad joke in most of the Middle East—a taunt of what so many Arabs wanted and raged that they would never have. The monolithic regimes were not merely inert bodies unwilling and unable to make the situation better, but vast dead weights that pressed down on the people, holding the exploitative systems in place. And so, personal unhappiness grew into political discontent.

For their part, the regimes mostly reacted to burgeoning popular unhappiness with a combination of fear and contempt, which translated mostly into repression coupled with superficial (often deeply cynical) pseudoreforms. Repression can often succeed in controlling popular unhappiness, but, over time, if those grievances are not defused by somehow being addressed, repression typically acts as a pressure cooker: keeping the unhappiness bottled up but magnifying its volatility such that an unexpected event can produce a sudden explosion. No one could have predicted that the match struck by Mohammed Bouazizi to set himself afire in Sidi Bouzid on December 17, 2010, would ignite the entire Arab world, but the kindling had been laid and was there for all to see years before.

CHARTING THE ARAB SPRING

We still do not know for certain why Bouazizi's sacrifice caused so many Tunisians to take to the streets to demand the regime's ouster. Perhaps it was simply the poignancy of the gesture. Certainly, the frustrations and humiliations that drove him to this final deed resonated with a great many of his countrymen. But when thousands of Tunisians succeeded in forcing their dictator, Zine al-Abidine Ben Ali, to flee for his life, it was a watershed for the rest of the Arab world. Suddenly, Arabs everywhere saw people just like themselves, angry about problems just like their own, defying vast autocracies just like those they lived under, and toppling regimes that had once seemed impregnable.

Even those who had long feared that the growing frustration of so many Arabs would inevitably result in explosions of popular unrest never imagined that a revolt in one country, especially a small state, would cause dominoes to topple across the entire region. It was for this reason that the regimes themselves, and not just the rest of the world, were taken by surprise not only when Ben Ali fell, but also when his fall served as the earthquake that sent shockwaves from one end of the Middle East to the other.

As Shadi Hamid describes in chapter 12, Egyptian president Hosni Mubarak and his top advisers were also caught off-guard by the passion of the protesters and, as Mike Doran discusses in chapter 5, by their sophisticated use of new social media to mobilize and capture the sympathy of the wider international audience. More surprising for Mubarak was the fact that his own military had developed a corporate identity independent from his own rule. This meant that its leaders believed their own perks and privileges could best be guaranteed by sacrificing Mubarak in hope of holding on to the key aspects of his system that benefited them the most. Indeed, ironically, it was Mubarak's own past decision to try to meet the material demands of his officer corps by encouraging them to delve into Egypt's civilian economy that severed his "power of the purse" and gave the army an independent economic base, enabling and encouraging it to separate itself from the figure of the autocrat.[5]

With the strong dictatorships in Tunisia and Egypt overthrown, it was perhaps inevitable that the dysfunctional dictatorship lying between them—Libya— would face a similar challenge. Events in Libya demonstrated that what had happened in Egypt and Tunisia were not cookie-cutter models that could and would be applied across the region. The underlying set of political, economic, and social grievances were similar across the region, and in every one of the Arab states (and in Iran in 2009) they caused large numbers of urban, mostly secular, people to take to the streets and demand the overthrow of the regime and its replacement with a democracy. However, once these protest movements began, in every case they engaged the other, preexisting rifts in each country. Thus when Libyan crowds took to the streets to try to emulate the Egyptians in Tahrir Square, their protests against the regime immediately engaged Libya's long-standing geographic and tribal divisions, resulting in an outcome very different from that in Egypt and Tunisia. In Libya, the most important geographic rift is between Cyrenaica, comprising the eastern part of the Libyan coast, and Tripolitania, the western part of the coast. Since Cyrenaica had always opposed the Tripolitanian Muammar Qadhafi, it not surprisingly declared for the protesters, along with a number of tribes who decided their interests would be best served by Qadhafi's fall. Tripolitania remained more loyal to Qadhafi, as did a number of powerful tribes in other parts of the country.

Similar phenomena were found elsewhere across the region. In Bahrain, for instance, the protests immediately engaged the country's deep Sunni-Shi'i divide, to the point where it became unclear how much the new opposition was merely the old Shi'i opposition in a new garb and how much a different, more ecumenical protest movement (one driven more by class grievances) that embraced a wider spectrum of the Bahraini populace. In Yemen, the protests immediately became bound up in preexisting fights between north and south, between Houthi Shi'ah and Sunnis, and between various pro- and anti-Saleh tribes. It is this mixture of common grievances coupled with country-specific rifts that has made the unrest across the Arab states very similar in certain ways, while nevertheless taking on unique characteristics in each country.

Each regime also responded differently. Where Ben Ali and Mubarak stepped down, Bashar al-Asad and Qadhafi dug in and proved willing, again, to slaughter their own citizens to try to hold on to power. Bahrain's leaders even turned to their ally, Saudi Arabia, asking Riyadh to dispatch troops across the causeway linking the two countries to suppress the protests. The Saudis, for their part, threw money at their own problems and helped bankroll other Arab monarchies to do the same.

In retrospect, part of the reason the protests in Tunisia and Egypt resulted in relatively quick and clean revolutions that succeeded in overthrowing the leaders seems to be the relative homogeneity of their populations.[6] While societal divisions certainly exist in Egypt and Tunisia (divisions that have, in some cases, been enflamed by the success of the revolutions), the protests actually brought disparate groups together in these states, while they tore people apart elsewhere in the region. This made Ben Ali's and Mubarak's regimes more vulnerable to a seemingly unified public outpouring against them: their security forces were less willing to fire on their own people, and the regimes did not have a significant section of the elite automatically behind them. Elsewhere, the deep, preexisting societal divisions have allowed the regimes to call on segments of the wider population to support them by claiming that the protesters represented their traditional rivals, just marching under different banners—Cyrenaicans in Libya, Palestinians in Jordan, Shi'ah in Bahrain, and so on.

Moreover, as others have observed, the Arab monarchies demonstrated much greater staying power than the secular dictatorships (euphemistically styling themselves "republics"). Several factors seem to be responsible for this. The monarchies often enjoy greater legitimacy than the republics.[7] Many can count on religious justifications, long-standing historical associations between the state and the ruling family, and a degree of popular affection—even pride—in the ruling dynasty. Because the monarchs technically stand above politics, they can divert popular ire from them to the governments by replacing the current cabinet as a sop to popular unrest. Although the term "monarchy" conjures up an image of a small family running the show, in reality many ruling families are vast clans that have forged marital, business, and political alliances with other major families. Some of the monarchs are even popular and respected by their people, as is King Abdullah of Saudi Arabia, at least in part because of their ability to stand above politics.

Ultimately, while powerful protest movements rocked virtually all of the regimes of the region, relatively few fell. Most found ways to cling to power until the wave receded. They did it by relying on the inherent strengths of monarchical government. They did it by manipulating preexisting divisions in their society to mobilize support for themselves and opposition to the opposition. But they also did it by employing old-fashioned repression, sometimes in new-fashioned ways.

One critical, lingering question today is what did the regimes and the demonstrators learn? Did the regimes realize that they all sit on top of time bombs—populations furious at their misrule and looking for any opportunity to overthrow them? Or did they learn that repression, once again, works? That if repression is dressed up with a few hollow promises of reform to take the edge off, crushing popular opposition is a successful tactic and a perfectly viable long-term strategy. For their part, did the protesters learn that they have the power to topple governments under the right conditions? Or that no matter what they do, no matter how many risks they take, government repression always prevails? How these various groups answer these questions will go a long way to determining the fate of the Middle East in the years to come.

Did the Arab Spring Matter?

Inevitably, scholars will debate the impact of the 2011 Arab Spring for decades, if not centuries, to come. A first impression suggests that what happened may not have overturned the political order of the Middle East but was nonetheless profound. More of the ancient regimes of the Arab world may or may not fall in the next few months (or even years); but regardless, what happened will have profound consequences for the future of the region, and beyond.

Perhaps the most obvious lasting impact of the Arab Spring will be the changes in governments, especially in North Africa. Mubarak's Egypt, Ben Ali's Tunisia, and Qadhafi's Libya are gone. Saleh's regime in Yemen will never be the same, even if it finds a way to cling to power. These changes have fundamentally altered the geopolitical map of the Middle East. If Egypt, Libya, and Tunisia eventually emerge as stable democracies—perhaps joined by a similar kind of state in Iraq—they will exert a profound influence on the internal politics of the region, by demonstrating successful alternative models to the autocracies and theocracies that have previously been the only choices on offer. They could also reorient the strategic balance of the region, perhaps by creating a new bloc of states that might stand apart from the monarchies, the dictatorships, and the Iranian theocracy.

The Arab Spring also shattered several important myths that had previously held sway both in the region and outside it. The first of these was that the Arab populations were largely apathetic. The Arab Spring (arguably, along with the birth of the Green Movement in Iran in 2009) demonstrated, across the region, that the people of the Middle East are no longer willing to simply accept their misery. Rather, they are willing to take to the streets and risk their lives to demand change. Indeed, a critical corollary is that the Arab people themselves have, in many cases, found that when they take action, they can change their own circumstances. That new activism alone will transform Middle Eastern political dynamics.

The second myth that the Arab Spring shattered is that the Arabs do not understand or want democracy. This claim was always spurious, and there was tremendous evidence to the contrary long before the crowds gathered in Tahrir Square.[8] But it persisted until the people took to the streets and proclaimed their demands for democracy, not just in name but also in practice and in all its particulars. This realization will be important both for the regimes of the region and for the West. Neither will be able to hide behind the convenient fiction anymore that the Arab people do not want democracy. In particular, the United States will no longer be able to claim that its short-term interest in partnering with autocratic regimes does not conflict with its long-term strategic interest in (and national value of) promoting democracy.

For all of these reasons, even if another Arab regime does not fall in the near term, the impact of the Arab Spring will persist. The Middle East will never be the same. The forces that have been unleashed are likely to remain critical drivers in regional politics for decades to come. Unless the regimes of the region respond effectively to the underlying grievances that motivated the Arab Spring, it is highly likely that the autocracies that withstood the 2011 wave of unrest will face future waves. Indeed, the region continues to face widespread internal unrest from the first series of protests, and some of the states that survived this round may fall in future rounds unless they are willing to make many of the changes that animated the authors of the Arab Spring to begin with. In that sense, the full impact of the Arab Spring may not be felt for years to come.

AMERICAN INTERESTS AND THE ARAB SPRING

For a very long time, the United States has defined its principal interest in the Middle East as "stability." It never was. America's primary interest has always been in the free flow of the region's oil—preferably at low prices, although U.S. efforts to influence the price itself have been of a much more subdued nature. In addition, the United States has always had friends in the region that it wanted to see remain free and secure, Israel first among them since the 1970s. If the Middle East had been a roller-coaster of instability (which it mostly was), but the oil had flowed (which it mostly did), American interests would have been satisfied (which they mostly were).

Of course it is true that instability could menace those real interests, and from time to time it did so. The Arab-Israeli wars, the Iranian Revolution, the Iran-Iraq

War, Saddam Hussein's invasion of Kuwait, and other instances of instability did either threaten or cut into the region's oil exports. Unfortunately, Americans were misled by our mistaken fixation with "stability." We have misinterpreted it first of all to mean stability among the nations of the region—no wars among them. But we also have misinterpreted it as an interest in the status quo, both among the states of the region *and within them*. Washington wrongly assumed that the regimes of the region understood their domestic situations perfectly, and that their stagnant autocracies could last in perpetuity. Indeed, a critical element in America's approach to the Middle East over the past fifty years has been the assumption that the internal politics of the Arab states and Iran are irrelevant to American interests. The Iranian Revolution should have been the first clue that this was misguided, and 9/11 should have been another, but the United States is good at missing clues when it is not particularly interested in seeing them.

Hopefully, the events of the Arab Spring will finally shatter the cracked lens through which the United States has been seeing the Middle East and allow Americans to finally see it as it is. The anger and frustration that exploded onto the streets of Tunis, Cairo, Sana'a, Manama, Amman, Dara'a, Hama, and countless other cities across the region should make clear that change is coming to the Middle East, whether the United States likes it or not. The question is not whether, but when . . . and how.

In that sense, the Arab Spring may be the opportunity to end the tension between America's interests and its values in the Middle East, or more properly the tension between its short- and long-term interests in the Middle East. America has long espoused an interest in seeing democracies flourish and has embraced national self-determination, both because it is ethically right and because doing so is an important means of avoiding wars that could threaten our vital interests. But in the Middle East, Washington set those values and interests aside, both because it feared that their application to the Middle East would produce Arab states inimical to American interests and because we always had immediate concerns in the region that required the cooperation of America's Arab allies. The price for that cooperation was to disregard American values as well as our longer-term interests in seeing the region change gradually and peacefully.

Nevertheless, in the years ahead, there will doubtless remain a tension between short-term and long-term interests. Just because it is clear that the "unreformed" Arab states are unlikely to endure forever, it is equally unlikely that they will all be swept away as quickly as Mubarak's reign, or that the regimes will not endure in an altered form. Indeed, the best outcome for these states would be a gradual process of evolutionary reform that would eventually produce different, more democratic governments, but that might still include important elements of the current regimes.

Consequently, the United States cannot possibly dismiss the current Arab regimes. Many of those governments are hesitant to begin the process of reform, and will resist American pressure to do so. In addition, the United States may need the help of some or all of those regimes to achieve other American goals in the region—stabilizing Iraq, Egypt, Tunisia, and Libya; pressuring Iran to give up its nuclear program; keeping down the price of oil; containing spillover from civil wars in Yemen and Syria; and pushing forward peace negotiations between Israelis and Palestinians. Inevitably, those near-term needs are going to impose trade-offs with America's long-term interest in seeing peaceful, gradual change to head off future waves of violent, unpredictable change.

Even in light of the truth revealed by the Arab Spring, those trade-offs will not be easy, as many of the chapters of this book discuss in various respects. What Washington must avoid, however, is to fall back into its accustomed, wrong-headed pattern of assuming that change will never come to the Middle East. It cannot allow itself to believe that the Arab Spring really did not matter, or perhaps that it never really happened at all. It happened, and if the United States does not learn its lessons, it will happen again and again, and perhaps next time it will not be so kind.

PART I

The Dynamics
of the Arab Spring

2

ARAB PUBLIC OPINION

What Do They Want?

SHIBLEY TELHAMI

It was hardly surprising to discover that Arabs were angry with their rulers. In fact, every year, after conducting the Annual Arab Public Opinion Poll in Egypt, Saudi Arabia, Morocco, Jordan, Lebanon, and the United Arab Emirates, the question that leapt from the findings was not "When will Arabs have reason to revolt?" but "Why haven't Arabs revolted yet?"[1]

ARAB PUBLIC OPINION IN THE INFORMATION AGE

The most striking feature of the Arab uprisings, certainly in Tunisia and Egypt, was that they were not led by major political parties or well-established leaders. This had seemed theoretically improbable. But we are in a new world where there is an information revolution whose impact is not yet fully understood. This revolution has empowered the public, reduced its information-dependence on governments, and provided new instruments of mobilization without the need for traditional political organizations. As Mike Doran discusses at greater length in chapter 5, satellite television, the Internet, social media, and other information technologies have robbed governments of their monopoly on information. To get a sense of how rapid the growth of new media has been, note that in the 2010 Arab Public Opinion Poll, most respondents said that their first source of news is a satellite television station from outside their own country (with the Qatari-based Al Jazeera leading the way).

This expansion of regional and global television has taken away the government's ability to control the political narrative. It also has reflected the loss of credibility of the local, government-controlled media. In the case of Egypt, which had historically invested heavily in state-sponsored media that dominated the news, the transformation was hard to miss, as more Egyptians flocked to external sources of news such as Al Jazeera and Al Arabiya. This was particularly noticeable during the 2008–09 Israeli war with Hamas, when the public was far more sympathetic to Hamas than were the government-sponsored Egyptian media.

FIGURE 2-1. *Media: How often do you use the Internet, if at all?*

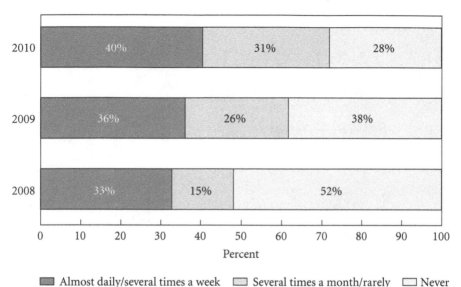

Almost daily/several times a week   Several times a month/rarely   Never

More Egyptians turned to Al Jazeera not only because it provided more extensive coverage of the war but also because the public identified with its narrative.[2]

It is also notable that following the Egyptian and the Tunisian revolutions, the Libyan, Yemeni, Bahraini, and Syrian governments had little success in selling the narrative that the uprisings were the work of foreign parties, including the West, Israel, and al-Qaeda. Even where Arab governments prevented satellite networks from covering the uprisings, particularly in Bahrain and Syria, footage of hundreds or thousands of protesters found its way on air or online, undermining the claims of government-controlled media that the protests were made up of only a dozen or so individuals.

While the transformation of the regional television market has been the single most powerful factor in the loss of governments' ability to control the narrative, the dramatic expansion in the use of Internet and social media over the past five years has also played a role.[3] As illustrated in figure 2-1, in just two years (from 2008 to 2010), the number of people who said they never used the Internet dropped from 52 percent to 28 percent.

WHAT ARABS SAID

The widening gap between governments and publics in the Arab world was noticeable in public opinion polls conducted over the previous decade. One survey question asked which leaders respondents admired most outside their own countries. It was striking that not a single Sunni Arab leader was among those named. And those most admired were often the ones Arab governments generally opposed, or those who, unlike many Arab rulers, were seen as standing up to Israel and the United States: Hassan Nasrallah of Hizballah after the 2006 Israel-Hizballah war; Hugo Chavez, after his support of Hamas in the 2008–09 war; Jacques Chirac, after he stood up to George W. Bush on Iraq in 2003; and Recep Tayyip Erdoğan, following his 2009 confrontation with Shimon Peres at the World Economic Forum.

Yet the surveys also found that few Arabs wanted either an Iranian-style theocracy or a Salafist caliphate, demonstrating that Arabs admired these figures for their willingness to confront the status quo and those who enforced the status quo—namely, their own leaders and the Americans behind them. Similarly, among those who admired any aspect of al-Qaeda, for instance, most identified its confrontation with the United States and its stand on issues like Palestine as being the reason for their support. Fewer than 10 percent of respondents expressed admiration for the group's overall aims.

The overwhelming majority of the Arab publics, even (sometimes, *especially*) in countries whose governments were particularly close allies of the United States (Egypt, Jordan, Morocco, Saudi Arabia, and the United Arab Emirates), identified the United States as one of the two most threatening states to them, after Israel. And even as their governments were highlighting what they perceived as a growing Iranian threat, polls indicated that the Arab publics were far less worried about Iran. In the decade after 9/11, most polls indicated that the negative Arab views of the United States (which increased particularly after the Iraq war in 2003) were not the result of a clash of values, but rather anger over U.S. policies—particularly toward Iraq and the Israeli-Palestinian conflict. Arabs would often cite Europe and the United States as attractive places to live and places to study, and when asked to identify places where they thought there was most freedom and democracy for their own people, the overwhelming majorities repeatedly identified Western countries. The lives they yearned for were not so profoundly different from those of citizens of the countries whose policies they despised. And this was also recorded in their media behavior: while most watched Arab satellite networks as a source of news, most also watched Western programs for entertainment.

The seeming paradox of the decade was that the leader they disliked most was the one who outwardly advocated freedom and democracy in the Arab world as a priority of American foreign policy: George W. Bush.[4] But the paradox virtually disappears when one considers that in every year since the Iraq war, Arabs have expressed skepticism about stated American intentions. The general perception was that the Bush administration used the slogans of democracy and freedom to cover the absence of weapons of mass destruction in Iraq. One reason America's message did not seem genuine was that despite what the United States said about democracy, people saw little change in their own freedoms (in fact, many sensed that their own security services had actually tightened control behind the façade of America's "war on terror"). The bottom line, therefore, was not a rejection of democracy as much as a rejection of American foreign policy and suspicion of American intentions.

The net result during the Bush years was mixed. The American position on democracy actually hampered the work of local democracy advocates. They were implicated in a Bush administration agenda that the public had rejected. Pictures of anarchy in Iraq also played into the hands of governments by enabling them to exhibit warnings about what might happen in Cairo and Amman should the government loosen its grip.

While the Arab public is open to democracy and aspires to freedom, the picture is of course more complex. As Steven Kull has described well, receptivity toward democracy in Arab and Muslim societies is often accompanied by deeply held religious beliefs.[5] While polls indicate that only minorities support religious parties, such as the Muslim Brotherhood in Egypt, most people profess to being religious and see Shari'a law as the basis of the law of the land. This tension is already present in the ongoing debates in Egypt about the nature of the political system, where even secularists and Christians have accommodated themselves to references to Shari'a law as long as the rights of people of other faiths are protected.

"Raise Your Head, You Are an Egyptian"

Many Arab demonstrators said that they sought "dignity and freedom" above all else. This pursuit of dignity is in the first place about citizens' grievances with their own rulers on matters small and large. But while foreign policy issues were not the most prominent aspect of the slogans in the Arab street, it is a mistake to underestimate the importance of these issues in how the Arab public sees its dignity. A good place to understand this is Egypt.

A week after Hosni Mubarak fell from power, millions of Egyptians packed the streets to celebrate their revolution. One dominant chant stood out: "Raise your head, you are an Egyptian." That this was a revolution about dignity is hard to miss. But that this dignity had a regional dimension is sometimes harder to identify.

Egyptians have long had a strong sense of their state identity and have generally seen Egypt as a regional leader. Affectionately, they viewed Egypt as *Um al-Dunya* (Mother of the World). But the fact that, in their moment of celebrating an internal revolution against their own regime, they were asserting their

FIGURE 2-2. *Identity: Which of the following is your most important identity?* *(Egypt)*

Percent

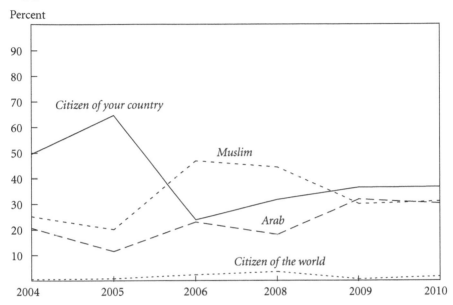

Egyptian identity with pride was particularly telling. Over the past decade, Egyptians had come to see themselves less and less as Egyptian (see figure 2-2). In part, this is a symptom of conflating Egypt the state with Egypt the ruling regime. Over the years, Arabs have found it hard to differentiate between state and government; in fact, in popular discourse, the word *dawla* (the state) has often referred to the rulers.

ARAB PUBLIC OPINION SINCE THE AWAKENING

A number of opinion polls have been conducted in the wake of the revolutions, especially in Egypt, giving early hints about how Arab public opinion has been affected by the sweeping change in the region. An International Republican Institute poll released in April 2011 found that the vast majority (89 percent) of Egyptians believe things are going in the "right direction."[6] A Zogby poll released in July found more ambivalence about the current state of affairs, but still considerable optimism about the future.[7]

In examining specific ways Egyptians would like the government reformed, a Gallup Center poll released in June 2011 found that 92 percent of Egyptians would include free speech as a part of the new constitution, 67 percent say the same regarding freedom of religion, and 55 percent say the same about freedom of assembly.[8] Sixty-four percent of Egyptians say the country should rely on a democratic system of government to solve the country's problems, whereas 34 percent believe a strong leader would be more effective.[9] Fewer than 1 percent of Egyptians believe the country should adopt an Iranian model of government; instead, 69 percent believe religious leaders should advise those in authority rather than have full authority themselves.[10]

One of the most striking findings, however, has been the extent to which the Arab Spring has not changed public attitudes toward the United States. Arab attitudes toward the Obama administration were warm when the president first took office in early 2009 but had become highly negative in 2010, even before the Arab Spring. Given the Arab openness to Western intervention in Libya, and the assumed shift in regional priorities, there was some expectation that attitudes toward the United States would move in a positive direction. The Zogby poll found the opposite: favorable attitudes toward the United States among people in Morocco, Egypt, Jordan, Saudi Arabia, and the UAE have dropped since 2008 and 2009, and have remained stagnant among people in Lebanon.[11]

With the exception of Saudi Arabia, people in all of these countries named the United States the least favorable entity out of Turkey, China, Iran, France, the United States, and the United Nations.[12] When asked, the majority of people in each country disagreed that the United States "contributes to peace and stability in the Arab world."[13] In fact, people in Egypt, Lebanon, and the UAE view American policy as a cause of many of their challenges, feeling that "U.S. interference in the Arab world" is "very much" an obstacle to peace and stability in the region (people in Morocco and Jordan rated this as the second highest obstacle).[14] When asked to choose the single greatest obstacle to peace and security in the Middle East, people in Lebanon, Saudi Arabia, and the UAE chose U.S. interference in the Arab world, while people in Morocco, Egypt, Jordan, and an equal number in Saudi Arabia named the occupation of Palestinian lands the greatest obstacle.[15] The majority of respondents in Morocco, Egypt, Jordan, and the UAE named "resolving the Palestinian issue" the most important issue for the United States to address in order to improve ties with the Arab world.[16] The Gallup poll shows similar displeasure with the United States, with Egyptians' approval of American leadership at or below 20 percent.[17] About two-thirds of Egyptians "disagree that the U.S. is serious about encouraging democratic systems of government" in the Middle East and North Africa, and 68 percent believe that the United States will try to "exert direct influence over Egypt's political future."[18]

Taken together, these early polls suggest that the Arab Spring has not significantly altered the Arab public's views of the West, particularly the United States. People continue to be suspicious of American foreign policy, concerned about American aims, and angry over Washington's approach to the Palestinian-Israeli conflict.

FIGURE 2-3. *Perceptions of Uprisings: Do you think the popular uprisings in the Arab world are:*

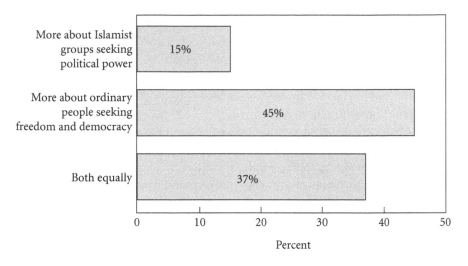

VARIATIONS AND PROSPECTS

While it is fair to speak of an "Arab Spring" and "Arab public opinion," it is also important to recognize the differences across the Arab world in both opinion and priorities. Tunisian and Egyptian societies are largely homogeneous, for example, whereas others, such as those of Yemen and Syria, are diverse in a manner that gives rise to conflicting views about the shape of the government they want. Similarly, while most Arabs profess to care about the issue of Palestine, it is far more of a priority for Israel's neighbors than for others. And while most of the Arab world is struggling economically in a manner that adds fuel to the fire, there are also rich countries, such as Saudi Arabia, that can mitigate possible revolt through generous spending. In the end, the outcome of the uprisings will vary from country to country. But one thing is clear in every place: no government can afford to ignore public opinion.

This can also be said of Western governments, most of which have been struggling to adjust their policies to accommodate Arab public empowerment. The most striking case has been that of France, which after initially inviting Arab public anger by expressing support for Tunisian dictator Zine al-Abidine Ben Ali, reversed course, fired its foreign minister, and took the lead by militarily supporting the uprising in Libya. The United States, too, had struggled with its posture, particularly in its reaction to the Egyptian uprising, where responding to public aspirations ultimately trumped the commitment to its loyal ally, Hosni

Mubarak. But one of the fascinating aspects of Arab public empowerment has been the impact on American public opinion.

American public attitudes toward Arabs and Muslims had been colored for a decade by 9/11, which gave rise to popular assumptions about Arabs, their culture, and their dominant religion. But following the Tunisian and Egyptian revolutions, there was evidence that American public opinion was shifting. According to an April 2011 poll, one reason for this shift is that Americans were finding Arab public motivations to be more connected with the pursuit of freedom than with Islamist ideology (figure 2-3).[19]

These perceptions may account for the fact that in the same poll most Americans expressed positive views of the "Arab people," and 70 percent expressed a positive view of the Egyptian people in particular. These views can of course change as Americans reinterpret the Arab Spring, and if violence becomes prevalent. But it is fair to say that the mostly peaceful behavior of the Arab public in the early months of the uprising and the universal aspirations expressed have already transcended the post-9/11 American views of the Arab world.

3

DEMOCRATIZATION 101

Historical Lessons for the Arab Spring

STEPHEN R. GRAND

More than anything else, the Arab Spring has been about a yearning for democracy. A number of Arab states have succeeded in taking a first step toward democratization, either by overthrowing an autocratic regime or by forcing it to start to change. But democratization is not easy, and it is not quick. To glimpse where the politics of the Middle East may travel, the best guide is the experience of other regions of the world that have gone down the path of democratic reform.

In a 1991 book, the late political scientist Samuel Huntington identified three waves of democratization that have swept the globe in modern history. The first, he argued, began with the expansion of political suffrage in the United States in the 1820s and ran up until the rise of fascism some hundred years later. The second coincided with European decolonization following World War II and ran through 1962. What he termed the "Third Wave" of democratization began in the Iberian Peninsula in 1974, with negotiated transitions to democracy first in Portugal, then in Spain, and soon Latin America and later East Asia. The fall of the Berlin Wall precipitated a wave of popular revolutions in Eastern Europe that resulted in the fall of communism and the eventual disintegration of the Soviet Union. Democratic fervor spread thereafter to sub-Saharan Africa, hastened by the collapse of apartheid in South Africa.[1] The Third Wave crested in the 1990s and then came to a halt the following decade. Before the events in Tunisia and Egypt, some analysts spoke of a "democratic recession" as a number of countries, including some long-established democracies, seemed to be reverting to authoritarianism.[2]

The one region bypassed almost entirely by these three successive waves of democratization was the Arab world. Up until the Arab Spring, not a single Arab regime could be said to be fully democratic. Lebanon came the closest, particularly before its 1975 civil war, though its confessional power-sharing arrangements have included some decidedly undemocratic elements. In Iraq, the U.S.-led invasion and occupation in 2003 initiated a controversial and highly volatile democratic experiment that continues to this day. In the West Bank and Gaza, the Palestinian Authority—in response to American pressure—called parliamentary elections in early 2006, which had the consequence of handing Hamas, a militant group with an uncertain commitment to democracy, a plurality of the votes.

That all changed in Tunisia. The Arab Spring has raised hopes that the world may be witnessing the start of a fourth wave of democratization, one with the Middle East at its epicenter. Whether or not that proves to be the case, it is worth considering the lessons the Third Wave holds for democratization efforts in the Arab world, as well as our understanding of the phenomena of democratization and development more generally.

Democracy has acquired the status of a near-universal norm. In public opinion surveys, the majority of citizens in most countries around the world express a preference for democracy over other forms of government.[3] That represents an important shift from decades past in which other political models—such as socialism, authoritarianism, and even totalitarianism—held broad popular appeal in various corners of the globe.

PATTERNS OF DEMOCRATIZATION

Democratization has tended to occur in geographic clusters. Both a demonstration and diffusion effect appear to contribute to the spread of democracy from one country in a region to the others.[4] When one of them becomes democratic, many—though not necessarily all—of its neighbors have a tendency to follow, eventually. Language and culture may play a role. When one country overthrows a dictator, citizens in other countries that share a common language—or at least commonalities in language and culture—are more likely to hear about it, view the example provided by their neighbor as relevant to their own condition, and feel empowered to take action because of it. Improvements in communications technologies have only accelerated these effects.

With increasing frequency, democratic breakthroughs have been driven from the bottom up, rather than the top down. In the countries that were an early part of the Third Wave—Portugal, Spain, and parts of Latin America—democracy developed in large measure as the result of bargains between reformers and more moderate elements within the previous regime, which paved the way for a set of founding elections and the adoption of democratic institutions. However, beginning with the People Power movement in the Philippines that swept strongman Ferdinand Marcos from power in 1986, democratic change more and more has come not from elites, but from the people.[5] Indeed, the story of the Arab Spring to date has been one of ordinary Arabs finally finding their voice and pressing their demands for change.

In fact, cases of autocratic leaders initiating a transition to democracy are quite rare. Democratic breakthroughs have at times occurred as a result of some combination of top-down and bottom-up factors—for instance, public protests on the streets putting pressure on elites to reach some sort of new political accommodation—but seldom solely at the volition of the reigning autocrat.

Over the past century, different theories have been advanced regarding prerequisites for democracy.[6] Over time, every one of these notions has been debunked. One of the most enduring claims within the social sciences since Barrington Moore wrote his seminal study of democratic transitions in 1966 was that "democracy has required a middle class."[7] But the Third Wave witnessed a number of lower-income countries—defined as countries with average per capita income below $4,000 per year—successfully becoming consolidated electoral democracies.[8] In fact, one of the more surprising developments during the Third Wave was the number of poor countries that succeeded in holding regular elections and becoming "consolidated democracies," at least in the Huntingtonian sense of power rotating at least twice among political leaders as a result of elections.[9] Other theories of democratic prerequisites include having a past democratic experience, or a certain kind of political culture. But what matters in terms of prospects for democratization increasingly appears to be not the state of the country at the time that transition occurs, but the nature of the transition and whether a set of attitudinal changes among the citizenry occurs—shifts that are typically easier, but not assured, with higher levels of income.[10]

In general, democratization has proven to be a more long-term, complex, and perilous process than initially thought. The early democratization literature, which drew heavily from the Iberian and early Latin American experiences, assumed that once a democratic breakthrough had occurred—once elites agreed to move toward democracy—the path from breakthrough to democratic consolidation was largely a straightforward technical one, a matter of organizing elections that were free and fair and putting in place proper democratic political institutions.[11] On the contrary, the path from democratic breakthrough to consolidation has often been full of twists and turns. The process has also been highly political, and much more uncertain and contingent than imagined.

The example of the former Eastern Bloc is noteworthy here. Twenty years after the collapse of communism, democracy has a mixed record in Eastern Europe and the former Soviet Union. Today, Freedom House categorizes only thirteen of that region's countries as "free," eight as "partly free," and seven as "not free."[12] All had very similar institutions to start. All proceeded to craft what were, at least on paper, democratic constitutions. All put in place a set of putatively democratic political institutions, including elected parliaments and independent judiciaries. And all gave some space for independent civil society groups and independent media—with quite varying results, however. Certainly, the prospect of European

Union membership was a powerful incentive for some states to democratize, but of at least equal importance was the existence, or non-existence, of a political constituency for democracy.

Political change began in the Middle East in much the same manner as it did in the closed societies of the former Soviet Bloc. The Arab popular revolts of 2011 did not begin with someone putting up a Facebook page any more than the popular revolutions that convulsed the Eastern Bloc two decades ago began with televised images of the fall of the Berlin Wall. Both had much longer historical antecedents. But, in both cases, technological change gradually eroded the regime's monopoly on the flow of information and hence its control of the national narrative. These changes enabled citizens to see for themselves, more vividly than they ever had before, how their society compared with that of others. At the same time, a new generation came of age that was better educated, more exposed to the outside world, and more tightly networked together—and with higher expectations. Through trial and error, they began to learn how collectively to challenge the regime and to have their voices finally heard.

The conditions that make for successful popular revolt and those required for successful democratization bear some similarities, but they are far from identical. The ouster of an autocratic leader is not on its own sufficient for democracy to flourish. As Barrington Moore observed so astutely over a half century ago, people revolt in response to a deeply felt sense of injustice, usually emerging out of concrete grievances experienced in their everyday life. These grievances often have to do with the perception that the dominant group within society has violated the implicit or explicit norms that hold society together.[13] Revolt is generally spontaneous, reactionary, and short-lived. Its success hinges on the mobilization of broad segments of the population, often including parts of the security establishment, against the regime. Democratization, on the other hand, requires a positive vision, not of what was but of what could be. It takes much longer to evolve and includes the convening of free and fair elections but also the creation of a set of democratic political institutions and an accompanying democratic political culture. It requires a set of political ideas about how society could be better ordered and the organizational power to see them realized. And it entails a much longer-term engagement by citizens, not only to help enshrine those ideas in a concrete set of political institutions, but also to ensure that these new institutions function as intended and indeed reflect the will of the people and safeguard their individual rights as citizens.

PITFALLS ON THE PATH TO DEMOCRACY

As experience has shown, initial breakthroughs can get hijacked in many ways en route to a stable democracy. The ouster of an authoritarian regime can swiftly degenerate into civil war if contending factions within society cannot agree on a new set of rules of the game. Popular revolutions are also vulnerable to cooptation by regime insiders—as witnessed in many successor states of the former Soviet Union—or to continued domination by a single political party—as was the case for many years in Mexico. The siren song of silver-tongued populists may hold powerful appeal for citizens of newly emerging democracies; so, too, may the religion-tinged political programs of Islamists attract people in the Middle East. Even in relatively functional democracies where power rotates among different political parties, the parties themselves can be weak and ineffective at governing—a condition that Tom Carothers describes as "feckless pluralism"; or they can be too strong, such that the state tramples on individual rights—in a manner that Fareed Zakaria has labeled "illiberal democracy" and academics increasingly refer to as "pseudodemocracy," or "competitive authoritarianism."[14] What was once envisioned as a single path of democratic transition has in fact proved to be multiple paths.[15]

Recent years have witnessed the emergence of "hybrid regimes" that are neither democratic nor autocratic, but occupy a murky grey area in between the two.[16] They possess many of the institutional trappings of democracy—constitutions, electoral systems, nominally independent judiciaries and legislatures, a somewhat independent press, and civil society organizations—but political life is tightly controlled by a single ruler or party. Some hybrid regimes have come into existence because countries get stalled along the path toward democracy (for instance, the dominant party refuses to cede real power); others because authoritarian rulers implement limited reforms (which stop short of democracy) in the interest of legitimizing their continued stay in power. The heightened appeal of democracy globally and its growing normative acceptance as the "least worst" form of government has perversely provided rulers of all stripes with strong incentives to "look" democratic in order to garner greater legitimacy with their citizens and the international community.[17]

The prevalence of such hybrid regimes has added to the debate about the ultimate objective of democratization efforts. It has raised questions as to whether the "two-turnover rule" (a country is considered a democracy after two peaceful changes of power) is the right metric for determining whether a democracy is in fact consolidated and whether regular elections are even sufficient to count a country as fully democratic. Is a country that holds regular elections, in which incumbents are occasionally rotated in and out of power, truly democratic if its rulers do not feel bound by the law and routinely trample on the rights of their citizens? Increasingly there is a recognition that the quality of democracy matters, not just a country's adherence to a procedural rule of periodic elections. Therefore, democratization efforts should be directed toward creating stable democracies that not only hold regular elections, but that are also anchored in the rule of law.[18]

Corruption is one of the deadliest enemies of democratization, and success in the latter typically requires success against the former. For some time, the scholarly literature on corruption has emphasized the importance of both institutional checks and balances (horizontal mechanisms of accountability) and public demand (vertical mechanisms of accountability) in curbing malfeasance by government officials.[19] International institutions now fund advocacy groups in developing countries that target corruption by promoting transparency and accountability. This reflects a recognition that institutions will only alter the behavior of political leaders if they are backed up by public pressure.

Similarly, the success of democratization efforts in the Middle East over the long term will depend in good measure on the existence of public demand for reform and democracy. Well-designed constitutions are important, as are effective democratic institutions that help structure political life, but they will be rendered meaningless if the public is not willing to stand behind them to ensure they function as intended. Transitions to democracy are more likely to remain on track and be successful with the help of an empowered and engaged citizenry, capable of reminding politicians that there will be a price to pay should they deviate from the new rules of the game. All else remaining equal, one can expect countries with citizens who are more educated, more exposed to the outside world, and more highly networked together to fare better than those whose citizens are not.

HELPING DEMOCRATIC TRANSITIONS FROM THE OUTSIDE

If democratization is difficult and uncertain to undertake, so too is it for a state—or foreign entity—to help another do so. Certainly, it has been done: the United States was instrumental in German and Japanese democratization, and may eventually get credit if Iraq successfully makes the same transition. Numerous states helped the Philippines, Chile, and other countries build democracy in a variety of ways. International organizations, including the World Bank and the European Union, played important roles in Eastern Europe after the fall of communism, albeit with very mixed results and records. An equally wide range of nongovernmental organizations have played smaller, but often instrumental, roles in helping countries fashion the nuts and bolts of democratic institutions and practices. Despite a long history, however, such assistance is not always the difference between success and failure.

The mixed results of American efforts to promote democratic transitions abroad yield some important lessons about what the United States should and should not do. Large-scale grant and contract programs that have sought to impose a parochial, American vision on another society, for example, have done much harm and little good. The practice of dispatching waves of high-priced American consultants with little familiarity with the local context has not worked well either. Overall, Washington cannot look at democracy promotion abroad as a largely technical exercise in designing U.S.-style political institutions.

Instead, the United States should consider the importance of the attitudinal aspects of democracy. Washington should provide assistance in rewriting constitutions and helping craft new democratic political institutions where warranted. But more critically, it should seek to accelerate the cultural and perceptual changes that have brought a new Arab generation into politics and upended political discourse in the region, as this emerging political constituency for democracy will be the ultimate guarantor of these institutions' success. As Ralph Waldo Emerson once observed, "The wise know . . . that the form of government which prevails, is the expression of what cultivation exists in the population which permits it."[20] The United States should assist with the cultivation.

The United States has more tools at its disposal than it may recognize when it comes to building political constituencies for democracy. American technologies, American music and film, American universities, and the American example of democracy all played some part in the dramatic cultural and attitudinal changes that have taken place in the Middle East. They can be used to help accelerate these changes.

At a certain level, such an effort entails helping to open what have been in recent years relatively closed societies. Openness will speed the cultural and attitudinal changes already under way. The United States should be encouraging "brain circulation"—the flow of people and ideas in, out, and across the region. For example, Washington should continue to support greater Internet access and Internet freedom, and find more ways for Arab and American youth to connect via social and virtual media.

Also, Washington should look for ways to get as many Arab youth and professionals as possible *out* to other parts of the world—through exchanges, study tours, and professional development opportunities—so that they can experience other cultures and observe firsthand how citizens mediate relations with political authority in other settings. And, for the same reasons, Washington should be encouraging as many people as possible from outside the region to come *in*—as volunteers, as English-language instructors, as educators, as administrators, and as technical advisers.

In addition, Washington should seek to help develop indigenous educational institutions that are capable of providing a world-class education and nurturing a new generation of informed citizens. Citizens who are capable of thinking critically and acting independently are the bedrock of a successful democracy, not to mention a successful economy.

Equally important, financial support is needed for civic initiatives that bring like-minded citizens together for common public purposes. Building a political constituency for democracy requires not only informed citizens but also those who have the skills to work collectively for shared public ends. Washington should help underwrite citizen-inspired initiatives to address pressing political and economic problems, large and small, with the understanding that such initiatives will allow citizens to learn and grow more confident working together, while building enduring networks of cooperation. The aim should be to help create a new generation of citizens who are more educated, more open to the world, and more connected to one another. If the past is any guide, this will be the best guarantor of democracy's long-term success.

In this effort, certain principles should guide U.S. assistance. First, the United States should be patient and focus on the long term. It is attractive to evaluate performance with metrics, but Washington should not allow the desire for short-term results to skew its longer-term priorities. At times the most important variables—things like behavioral change—are the most difficult to measure. To reiterate, democratization in the Middle East is going to require time and patience, and the United States needs to be in it for the long term if it is to be helpful and successful.

Second, U.S. assistance efforts need to be locally driven. It would be a mistake to try to impose U.S. visions and institutions on other societies. It will simply not work. Democracy needs to emerge organically if it is to flourish over the long term.

Third, the United States should be strategic in how it delivers assistance, particularly in a time of constrained budgets. Often small amounts of money targeted at the right individual or organization can be far more effective than large, expensive, top-down programs. In a moment of tremendous change, assistance needs to be delivered swiftly and nimbly, which is not something governments always do well. This task may be better performed in many instances by private foundations and civil society groups.

Fourth, Washington needs to recognize that democracy promotion is as much a political as a technical endeavor. The best-designed institutions will not endure unless they have strong public support. Moreover, many of the issues with which political and civic activists on the ground are now grappling—whether or not to engage in dialogue with an existing authoritarian regime, how to ensure a credible transition, how to deal with injustices committed in the past, whether constitutions should be rewritten before or after founding elections, how to assert civilian control over the military, and so on—are questions more of political strategy than of institutional design. In such instances, the best form of assistance the United States can provide may be connecting these activists with others who have grappled with similar strategic challenges in other parts of the world.

Fifth, and most broadly, U.S. assistance should be guided by lessons learned from experiences with democratization elsewhere. The United States has a long history of democracy promotion around the globe. Along the way it has had many successes, but also many failures, from which hard lessons have been learned. Washington would be well served to remember that history.

4

ISLAMISTS AND THE BROTHERHOOD

Political Islam and the Arab Spring

SHADI HAMID

For the members of Egypt's Muslim Brotherhood—the oldest and most influential Islamist political party—the Arab Spring may not have been entirely of their making, but it surely was the answer to their prayers. As recently as December 2010, the group's members were routinely rounded up by security forces. The regime of President Hosni Mubarak had manipulated the November 2010 elections even worse than usual, leaving the Brotherhood with zero seats in parliament (compared with their previous share of eighty-eight seats, or 20 percent). The regime seemed bent on erasing the Brotherhood from Egyptian political life altogether.

In Tahrir Square, the Muslim Brotherhood ordered its members to avoid using any Islamic slogans. ʿAbd al-Rahman Ayyash, at the time a young Brotherhood activist, explained, "If it's ever perceived that this revolution is an Islamic one, the U.S. and others will be able to justify a crackdown."[1] For this reason, the Brotherhood purposely downplayed its participation in the protests. But behind the scenes, it provided significant support, offering food and medical services to protesters, protecting them from regime thugs, and generally keeping order.

Less than a month later, on March 4, 2011, Egypt's interim prime minister, Essam Sharaf, addressed a raucous crowd in Tahrir Square. Standing by his side on the stage was prominent Brotherhood leader Mohammed al-Beltagi, capping what amounted to a remarkable reversal of fortune for the long-banned group. The political ascendance of the Islamists was confirmed on March 19, 2011, when the constitutional amendments they had aggressively supported passed overwhelmingly in a referendum, with 77 percent of the vote.

After the revolution brought down Mubarak, the Brotherhood found itself in an enviable, if delicate, position. The movement, founded in 1928, had long defined itself as an opposition movement, with a history of mass arrests and extended spells of imprisonment under successive regimes.[2] Up until February 2011, the prospect of legislating or governing always seemed too remote, allowing the Brotherhood to postpone confronting difficult questions over the role of Islamic law in public life. Today, the Brotherhood has a newfound power and responsibility, putting it in an unprecedented position. These new realities have provoked dissension within its ranks, as prominent youth activists have defied the group's leadership by forming their own political party, al-Tayyar al-Masri (the Egyptian Current). A handful of well-known Brotherhood "reformists," including presidential candidate Abdel-Moneim Abul-Futuh, resigned their positions within the organization. All in all, thousands of Brotherhood activists have defected, had their memberships frozen, or been expelled altogether.

ISLAMISTS AND THE ARAB SPRING

One of the greatest question marks hanging over the Arab Spring has been the role of Islamists—those who believe that Islam and Islamic law should play a prominent role in public policy. The Arab world is generally quite religious, and even people who do not consciously associate with groups seeking an Islamic form of government nevertheless believe it acceptable, even necessary, for religion to have a role in politics. In part for that reason, Islamist groups like the Muslim Brotherhood (referred to simply as the Brotherhood, or Ikhwan, across the Arab world) have been among the most popular opposition groups in the region. Before the Arab Spring, regimes feared the Ikhwan and their ilk. But, at times, they tolerated them as a (much-constrained) opposition, partly to shut out other, more secular and liberal opposition groups.

Not surprisingly, the revolutions and revolts of the Arab Spring have brought the Islamists back to the fore. Initially, the Arab revolutions seemed "secular" and non-ideological. This was true to the extent that the protesters in Tunisia and Egypt were not raising Islamic slogans or demanding Shari'a law. Over time, however, Islamist groups, with their organization and large numbers of loyal adherents, began to make their presence felt. In April, Syria's exiled Brotherhood leadership made an official declaration of support for the Syrian protest movement. This gave Syrian demonstrations a significant boost, particularly in the former Islamist stronghold of Hama. Their long pedigree, extensive grassroots networks, and experience as semi-legal opposition to the autocracies have allowed Islamist groups to emerge as the single most powerful political force in virtually every one of the Arab states. Indeed, in Egypt and elsewhere, Islamists have had to work hard *not* to capture the government.

For a great many people, it is not clear whether Islamists will be a productive or destructive force in politics. There is considerable debate over how compatible Shari'a is with democracy. An older generation of Islamists saw the two as fundamentally incompatible, although Islamists today have insisted on the opposite. As former assistant secretary of state for Near Eastern affairs Edward Djerijian once famously remarked, "We do not support 'one person, one vote, one time.'"[3] The basic problem is that Islamists in Arab countries have rarely been given a fair role in politics, let alone the opportunity to rule, so it is difficult to know how they would act if they ever were.

Unfortunately, simply throwing up their hands and walking away from Islamists is not an option for U.S. policymakers. Because of their organizational strength and popular support, Islamists are and will continue to be a critical force in the politics of both democratizing and reforming countries. Indeed, Islamists, by virtue of their willingness and ability to mobilize large numbers of people against any Arab regime, will remain key centers of opposition even in those states where the regime refuses to do either.

ISLAMISTS UNDER AUTOCRACY

Because they have not yet seen a functioning Arab democracy, scholars of the region have had little choice but to focus on Islamist political behavior under authoritarian conditions.[4] Repression and restriction of Islamist groups—fairly constant across the Middle East—did not, as many analysts and policymakers had expected, lead to the radicalization of mainstream Islamist groups. If anything, the opposite occurred, with the Brotherhood and like-minded groups revamping their political platforms in the 1990s, minimizing explicit references to *tatbiq al-Shari'a* (application of Islamic law), and advocating for political pluralism and greater democracy.[5] By contrast, in the 1980s major Islamist movements in the region were effectively single-issue parties, preoccupied with imposing Shari'a by segregating the sexes, prohibiting interest, and banning alcohol. However, as regimes launched unprecedented crackdowns in countries as varied as Egypt, Jordan, and Tunisia, Islamist groups soon concluded that little else mattered as long as they were denied basic freedoms.

Freedom to move, act, and associate is, in some respects, more vital for Islamist movements than participating in the political process. To understand why, it is important to recognize that electoral participation is just one facet—albeit the one most visible to Western observers—of their wide-ranging work. In Egypt, Jordan, Morocco, and Iraq, mainstream Islamist groups operate as a kind of state within a state with their own set of parallel institutions, including hospitals, schools, banks, businesses, cooperatives, day care centers, social clubs, facilities for the disabled, and even boy scout troops.[6] Millions of people across the region depend on these vast social infrastructures for anything from access to jobs and affordable healthcare to small grants for opening up businesses and even financial support to get married.

In addition to an extensive social services apparatus, these organizations usually have a preaching, or *da'wa*, wing, which is, in some ways, the foundation
upon which everything else is built. The Muslim Brotherhood and its regional
affiliates are concerned with strengthening the religious and moral character of
their members through an extensive educational process with its own structured
curriculum. Unlike most traditional parties, becoming a member is a choice that
brings with it a series of obligations and strict standards of moral conduct.[7]

Because they are "mass" organizations whose raison d'être is furthering Islamization, Islamist groups and parties need the space and freedom to pursue their
nonpolitical activities with as little government harassment as possible. This
helps explain why the Brotherhood, despite its oppositional orientation, has been
more than willing to cut deals with regime authorities. This tendency has been
most pronounced in Jordan, where the Jordanian Brotherhood has maintained
a cooperative, if tense, relationship with the Hashemite regime through much of
its more than sixty-year existence. In post-revolution Egypt, Islamists have been
accused of conveniently allying themselves with the Supreme Military Council
while whitewashing the council's undemocratic practices.

Note, too, that despite having plentiful reasons to disregard the views of the
United States and the West, Islamists have been surprisingly sensitive to international opinion. At the height of the Mubarak regime's repression, the Brotherhood recognized how critical U.S. pressure on Mubarak was to allowing them,
and the rest of the opposition, a margin of freedom to operate. In 2006, while
discussing the George W. Bush administration's pro-democracy efforts in Egypt,
Abdel-Moneim Abul-Futuh, at the time one of the Brotherhood's most prominent figures, observed that "everyone knows it . . . we benefited, everyone benefited, and the Egyptian people benefited" from Washington's pressure.[8] Around
the same time, the group made a concerted effort to reach out to Western audiences, launching its official English language website as well as an internal initiative under the title "Re-introducing the Brotherhood to the West."[9]

The Islamists under the Revolutions

Nearly all mainstream Islamist groups and parties in the Arab world are branches
or descendants of the Muslim Brotherhood. While they share a similar ideological orientation, they adopt widely varying policies and positions, suggesting that
belief is not necessarily an accurate predictor of behavior.

In Tunisia and Morocco, Islamists, after initially resisting, have made peace
with progressive social policies that grant women enhanced rights. In relatively
"secular" Tunisia, the rapid rise of the al-Nahda party—which, while not a Brotherhood affiliate, shares a similar orientation—is more surprising. The group was
brutally suppressed in the early 1990s and had no organized presence in the

country, with its leaders either imprisoned or exiled. Despite this, al-Nahda, with longtime leader Rachid Ghannouchi at the helm, has played a central role in post-revolution Tunisia in helping bring down two interim cabinets, forcing the dissolution of the former ruling party, and calling for early elections.[10]

In Egypt, which has a more conservative electorate and influential right-wing groups, the Brotherhood has repeatedly stated its opposition to allowing a woman or Christian to be president.[11] Syrian Islamists, meanwhile, diverge from other Islamists in the realm of foreign policy, having consistently opposed Iran and Hizballah's growing regional influence.[12] In Algeria, the Brotherhood-linked Movement of Society for Peace (MSP) is not even an opposition party. Since 1997 it has been part of the government, serving as junior partner in the "Presidential Alliance." This is all to say that context matters. For groups that are often portrayed as ideologically rigid, mainstream Islamists are surprisingly pragmatic—some detractors would say, *too* pragmatic.

Generally, the main determinant of Islamist behavior is the level of repression they face and, more broadly, the nature of their relationship to the autocratic regimes. As authoritarian systems in countries like Egypt, Tunisia, Yemen, and Libya are dismantled, the political calculus of Islamist groups will inevitably change in important ways. For example, high levels of regime repression tend to bind opposition groups together. The unprecedented (although short-lived) unity on display in Tahrir Square during the Egyptian revolution is only the most obvious example. Before that, the Brotherhood forged an unlikely alliance with former International Atomic Energy Agency (IAEA) chief and Nobel laureate Mohamed ElBaradei, a staunch secularist, gathering more than 800,000 signatures for his reform petition. With memories of Tahrir fading—and without a hated president to unite them—the Brotherhood and Salafis on one hand and the liberals and leftists on the other have increasingly come to see each other as opponents rather than coalition partners.

Signs of these rifts can be seen across the board. The Syrian Muslim Brotherhood's engagement in a series of opposition conferences outside the country has been treated with wariness by some liberals. In Tunisia, al-Nahda has felt the need to reassure secular parties and civil society organizations that see its outward rhetoric as masking the more hard-line vision of its grassroots base. The decision of al-Nahda to withdraw from the Higher Council for the Realization of the Revolutionary Objectives, in protest over a further change to the date of constitutional assembly elections, is representative of these growing divisions.

What Islamists Want

The question of what Islamists actually want is a difficult one, as even Islamists struggle to answer it. At the most basic level, however, their raison d'être has always been the promotion of Islamic values throughout society. The means of reaching that end have varied across the region but have generally included a combination of social services, preaching, education, and, more recently, electoral participation.

Within Islamist organizations, there are those who seek the application of Islamic law from above, those who are content to Islamize society from below, and a smaller group that would like to emulate Christian Democrats in Europe or, say, the Justice and Development Party in Turkey. The gap between what many Islamists would want in an ideal world and the goals they pursue in the give-and-take of everyday politics can be quite wide, making it difficult to judge their ultimate intentions.

When in government, mainstream Islamists are likely to settle for largely symbolic gestures of Islamization—such as gender segregation in schools, restrictions on alcohol consumption, and an enhanced role for religious institutions. How far they go in this direction will depend on factors largely outside their control—such as the relative power of liberal groups, the "tea-party effect" of Salafist groups (how effective the far-right will be in dragging the center-right further rightward), and the leverage of Western powers and international institutions.

Much of the debate over what Islamists want focuses on democracy, minority and women's rights, and foreign policy, despite the fact that the number one issue for voters in Arab countries is the economy. Yet, aside from vague calls to root out corruption and ensure social justice, Islamist groups have not been known to emphasize economic policy. However, the Brotherhood in Egypt has broken the mold recently. Despite the populist mood in the country, the Brotherhood's newly formed Freedom and Justice Party (FJP) released a surprisingly detailed and free market–oriented economic program, advocating cutting the deficit, adjusting subsidies, and facilitating an investor-friendly business environment. This seems to confirm the notion that how Islamists act in opposition could differ widely from the (more pragmatic) way they may act when forced to actually govern.[13]

AN UNCERTAIN COMMITMENT TO DEMOCRACY

Most Islamist groups have publicly embraced democracy, although there is skepticism regarding their sincerity. Importantly, the Islamist "base"—the grassroots rank and file that form the core of most Islamist groups—has not been visibly supportive of its leaders' reorientation away from a Shari'a-centric agenda. Specifically, the Brotherhood's recent adoption of more "moderate" positions on women's political participation and the rights of non-Muslims has been met with skepticism or indifference by the base.

This is in line with surveys of Brotherhood members that indicate a divergence of opinion between the group's official positions and those of rank-and-file activists. According to one such survey in Egypt conducted by Khalil al-Anani in 2007, only 27 percent of respondents supported the right of Copts to hold the position of prime minister, and just 40 percent believed women should be members of parliament.[14] This is at odds with the Brotherhood's official position that non-Muslims and women can assume any post except head of state. As early as 1994, in its "statement on women," the group affirmed the right of women to stand for parliamentary elections.[15]

The Egyptian electorate is similarly conservative on a number of issues. For instance, a December 2010 poll of Egyptians found that 82 percent favored stoning adulterers and 77 percent supported cutting off the hands of thieves.[16] These are positions that accord much more closely with the religious views of Salafis, who advocate uncompromising adherence to the letter of the law.

THE SALAFIST ALTERNATIVE

Over the past few years, Muslim Brotherhood leaders across the region have warned that the alternatives to mainstream Islamists are not liberals or leftists, but rather radical Islamists. In Egypt, Salafist groups typically were content focusing on preaching, but since Mubarak's ouster, they have increasingly made their political presence felt. Believing that God is the sole lawgiver ("divine sovereignty"), Salafis have generally stayed away from parliamentary politics. With the political arena wide open, however, Salafis in Egypt have sensed an opportunity to push for the implementation of Islamic law and move toward their long-held goal of establishing an Islamic state. Far from a monolithic movement, several Salafist groups, representing various trends, have formed political parties. Some Salafist preachers have sounded ambitious notes. The prominent Salafist preacher Mohamed Abdel Maqsoud told an Egyptian newspaper: "The Brotherhood said they would run for one-third of parliamentary seats, why shouldn't Salafis run for the rest?"[17]

In Tunisia, a newly expanded political arena has seen the Salafist movement emerge to the consternation of al-Nahda. Ghannouchi and others have sought to distance themselves from these more hard-line groups, which they see as having prospered under the repression of Ben Ali while their own organization was barred from any public activity. Elsewhere, Salafis have sought to ride the wave of the Arab Spring to push their own demands. In April 2011, Jordanian Salafis took to the streets of Zarqa, their traditional stronghold, to press for the release of members of their movement.[18]

Ambitious as they are, Egypt's new Salafist parties will have difficulty translating their considerable grassroots support into electoral success. They are political novices, having virtually no experience running parliamentary campaigns or getting out the vote. That said, the Salafis have proven to be quick learners. In

Kuwait, they were able to displace the Islamic Constitutional Movement—the political arm of the Kuwaiti Muslim Brotherhood—as the dominant bloc in parliament in 2006, winning an impressive seventeen seats out of fifty.[19]

Pragmatism cuts both ways, and the rise of the Salafis is likely to drag mainstream Islamist groups—and the electorate—further to the right. With the proliferation of Islamist groups, competition over who is authentically "Islamist" will only intensify. In Western Europe and Latin America, the desire to maximize votes pulled ideological actors to the center. In Egypt and other Arab countries, it may push them to adopt "radical" positions that they may or may not actually believe in. Either way, it feeds the doubts that many have over whether the mainstream Islamist groups will prove as committed to democracy in practice as they have been in theory.

LEARNING TO WIN

Unlike Salafis, mainstream Islamists grasp the importance of international opinion. Esam al-Erian, deputy leader of Egypt's Freedom and Justice Party, noted: "Even if you come to power through democratic means, you are facing an international community that doesn't accept the existence of Islamist representation. . . . I think this will continue to present an obstacle for us."[20] Islamists in the region call this the "American veto." The fear of U.S. and European intervention draws on the memories of Algeria in 1991–92 and the West Bank and Gaza in 2006, when Islamist parties rose to power through free elections only to face international resistance. This, along with the fear of regime repression, has led to a certain ambivalence, or even aversion to power, among Islamist groups. "Our phobia is Algeria," Ishaq Farhan, a leading Jordanian Islamist, said.[21]

Belying their image as power-obsessed, the region's Islamist groups have a history of losing elections on purpose.[22] They rarely contest the total number of parliamentary seats, opting instead to run "partial slates" in countries as varied as Yemen, Jordan, and Kuwait. The case of Jordan is instructive. In 2007 the Islamic Action Front (IAF) contested only 20 percent of the total seats, the lowest percentage in the party's history. It adopted an unlikely campaign motto for a political party—*musharika wa laisa mughaliba*—which literally means "participating but not seeking a majority." In a series of interviews in 2008, senior IAF figures readily admitted that their reason for contesting so few seats was to avoid offending the regime and to demonstrate that the party had no interest in escalating tensions.[23]

This self-limiting strategy makes sense in authoritarian and semi-authoritarian settings. In democratizing contexts, however, the electoral calculus of Islamists will inevitably change. In Egypt, when Mubarak first fell, the Brotherhood said it would contest only one-third of the seats. Growing more emboldened, the leaders of the newly established FJP (who were also senior Brotherhood officials) increased the number to 49 percent several weeks later. At the same time, the group has insisted it has no interest in dominating Egyptian politics and that it will not run a candidate in presidential elections. Similarly, in Tunisia, al-Nahda has tried to alleviate the fears of secular groups. "We want to work with others in a kind of national unity alliance," Rachid Ghannouchi said. "No single party can lead during this period, not even Nahda."

But these sorts of self-limiting electoral strategies are unlikely to continue indefinitely. Once Islamists become "normalized" within the political arena— and assuming the United States and Europe shake off their long-standing fears, or perhaps even if they don't—Islamist groups will eventually begin to consider contesting, and winning, majorities.

Learning to Live with Political Islam

Political Islam is here to stay. In Egypt and Tunisia, Islamists have only grown stronger in the wake of the revolutions. The opening of political space means that Islamist parties will proliferate and that non-Islamist parties, if they want to win, will need to adopt policies and positions that more closely align with the conservative sentiments of voters.

Even if Islamists underperform in elections, they will invariably play a major role in the future of their societies. If they are not leading governments, they will be part of them. If they are not part of them, they will influence the course governments take in the coming critical years. In a positive step, the United States has begun formally engaging with Brotherhood and Nahda officials in Egypt and Tunisia, respectively, after more than fifteen years of avoiding contact. Unfortunately, this may be an example of doing the right thing but waiting until the very last moment to do it. The United States today has considerably less leverage with such groups than it might have had several years ago. Groups like the Muslim Brotherhood that now find themselves in a powerful position have less to gain from dialogue with American officials (while the latter arguably have more to gain).

In any case, current engagement efforts remain embryonic, and it will take time to build trust on both sides. The challenge will be to move from ad hoc contacts to a more strategic dialogue, focused on an exchange of interests and discussion of controversial issues such as peace with Israel.[24]

In countries where pro-American regimes are increasingly pitted against an emboldened Islamist opposition, the challenge is for the Obama administration to get ahead of the curve and develop stronger relations with Islamists; after all, it is better to have leverage with opposition groups before they come to power, rather than afterward. Afterward is often too late. Of course, pursuing such a strategy of "preemptive" engagement is no easy task as regimes will loudly protest any such move. At the very least, then, the United States should pursue a strategy of "do no harm" and refuse to buy into allied regimes' rhetoric that it is either them or the Islamists. Such logic, which has held sway in Washington policymaking circles for decades, is now outdated and counterproductive. Before the Arab Spring, the United States was never quite willing to resolve its "Islamist dilemma." But now the spread of revolution—and the subsequent rise of Islamists to unprecedented influence and perhaps even power—has rendered it moot.

5

THE IMPACT OF NEW MEDIA

The Revolution Will Be Tweeted

MICHAEL S. DORAN

On February 11, 2011, when Egyptian president Hosni Mubarak fell from power, thousands of demonstrators celebrated his departure in Tahrir Square. Meanwhile, CNN's Wolf Blitzer discussed the dramatic events with an ecstatic Wael Ghonim, the Google marketing executive who had played a key role in organizing the protests against Mubarak via the Internet. Ghonim thanked the founder of Facebook, Mark Zuckerberg, for transforming Egypt, and then he told Blitzer:

> This revolution started online. This revolution started on Facebook. This revolution started in June 2010 when hundreds of thousands of Egyptians started collaborating content. We would post a video on Facebook. It would be shared by 50,000 people on their walls within a few hours. I always said that if you want to liberate a society just give them the Internet. If you want to have a free society, just give them the Internet.[1]

Call this the Ghonim thesis. It contains two distinct but related arguments: (1) that the spread of social media was a primary cause of the Arab Spring; and (2) that the Internet, by its very nature, undermines dictatorship and promotes democracy.

Both of these are certainly defensible claims, but neither one is self-evidently true. Can one really say for sure that Facebook was a primary cause of upheaval in the Arab world? Is it not possible that a revolutionary wave would have swept the Middle East even without cyber activism? After all, many other factors were obviously at work: oppression, corruption, poverty, unemployment, the rising cost of food, and the feckless efforts of a sclerotic regime to solve these problems—all these and more were underlying causes of the revolution and alone had been enough to spark revolutions in other countries at other times. It is equally plausible, therefore, to argue that an explosion of some kind would have been inevitable even if the Internet had yet to make its debut in the Middle East.[2]

Cyber activism may or may not have been a primary cause of the Arab Spring, but it was undeniably one of its more prominent features. Almost every part of the Arab world felt the insurgent power of Facebook and YouTube, and authoritarian regimes were obviously thrown on the defensive as a result. The spread of the Internet has provided new and effective instruments for mass political mobilization. The crowds on the streets across the Arab world were often summoned thanks to the Internet. The new media raised expectations, taught atomized individuals that they shared exactly the same thoughts and feelings, and created a mechanism for coordinating opposition activities—something Middle Eastern governments have labored hard for years to suppress.

The authoritarian regimes suffered a setback, but the game is not over. The contest between freedom and authoritarianism in the Middle East will continue for many years to come, and the ultimate victory of democracy is by no means a forgone conclusion. Dictators have the capacity to learn, and the clever ones find ways to exploit the Internet to their advantage. In the coming years, therefore, the regimes can be expected to develop cyber-savvy countermeasures to address the vulnerabilities that the Arab Spring revealed.

The Advent of the Smart Mob

In the Middle East, it is risky to criticize the ruler. Consider the case of Saad Eddin Ibrahim, a famous Egyptian academic and human rights activist who was jailed in 2000. Ibrahim's reformist activities had long annoyed the authorities, but, as a friend of Mubarak's wife, he had enjoyed protection from prosecution. Until, that is, he told a joke in the wrong company. While relaxing at a social club with friends, Ibrahim let down his guard and made fun of the ruler. Someone recorded the conversation and took the tape directly to Mubarak. Incensed, the president unleashed the secret police, who threw Ibrahim in prison, where he was denied adequate medical care.[3] His health deteriorated. Three years later he emerged with his spirit intact but his body broken. He went into exile.

Saad Eddin Ibrahim was lucky. Politically connected, famous abroad, and the holder of an American passport, he got away with his life. The same cannot be said of countless others, including Khaled Said, a twenty-eight-year-old man from Alexandria who was dragged by the security services from a cyber café in June 2010 and brutally beaten to death. Pictures on the Internet of his battered head, his teeth knocked out and blood dripping from his ears, tell a gruesome tale of pain. His crime? He reportedly posted on the Web evidence of petty police corruption.

Those who are skeptical about the political power of the Internet point to the phenomenon of "slacktivism," slacker activism. Armchair militants, the skeptics claim, "like" a political cause on Facebook and then congratulate themselves for having changed the world. Their action, so the argument goes, carries no more political impact than playing Pac-Man. The skeptics certainly have a point, but it is important not to overstate it, especially when analyzing developments in the Middle East. In countries where even mild criticism of authority can elicit onerous punishment, online activism does in fact help to compensate for the absence of participatory political institutions. To be sure, cyber protest is no substitute for flesh-and-blood opposition. But it does make at least one crucial contribution to a freer political life: it facilitates the formation of an opposition culture. Thanks to the relative safety of the Internet, grievances get aired, agendas coalesce, and, importantly, symbols spread far and wide. Therefore, one of the most significant political achievements of the Internet activists in Egypt was seemingly the most mundane: creating a relatively safe space for expressing opposition to the existing order.

The paradigmatic example of this phenomenon is the Facebook site "We Are All Khaled Said," created and maintained by none other than Wael Ghonim.[4] In the pre-Internet days, Said's torture and death would have gone unnoticed by the wider society. The local authorities would have covered it up, as they had routinely handled such practices many times before. The regional cable media would never have reported on it. Wael Ghonim, however, recognized the potential of the Internet to circumvent censorship. In addition, he understood the emotive power and political resonance of Khaled Said's story. Operating out of the United Arab Emirates, safely beyond the reach of the Egyptian secret police, Ghonim turned Said into a symbol of opposition to an oppressive political system. In Said's native Alexandria and all across Egypt, protesters marched while holding his picture. Thanks to the Internet, analogous symbols of oppression simultaneously appeared in many other countries. The establishment of this virtual opposition culture introduced a small measure of accountability into Arab political life.

Small, but nonetheless meaningful. The authoritarian rulers of the region were totally unaccustomed to popular participation in politics. Syria's president, Bashar al-Asad, revealed as much in an interview in the *Wall Street Journal* published at the end of January 2011. At a moment when Tunisia and Egypt were already in a state of upheaval, Asad was asked whether the Arab Spring, which had yet to hit Syria, might force him to accelerate his supposed reform agenda. "If you were to alter your priorities," Asad explained, simply "because of what happened in Tunisia and Egypt, then it is going to be a reaction, not an action; and as long as what you are doing is a reaction you are going to fail."[5] Clearly, Asad felt that it was beneath his dignity to even acknowledge a role for public opinion in official decisionmaking. A month and a half later, protests erupted in Syria, and Asad was soon on the ropes.

But it was Zine al-Abidine Ben Ali, the Tunisian president, who produced the most stunning image of the blindsided dictator. This awkward scene took place at the bedside of Mohammed Bouazizi, the fruit vendor whose self-immolation in mid-December 2010 first generated the revolutionary wave that swept the region.

As Bouazizi lay dying in his hospital bed, wrapped in bandages like a mummy, Ben Ali came to his side to demonstrate his concern. The visit, contrived and insincere, was too little too late. A fortnight later, the dictator was forced to flee.

Before the advent of the Internet, Bouazizi's story could not have reached so many households so quickly. Nor could it have had the same explosive impact. His story was able to rouse thousands of people to immediate action because it fit seamlessly into a preexisting narrative—one that had been woven over the years by "slacktivists" such as the Tunisian blogger known as Astrubal. Back in August 2007 Astrubal cleverly recorded the misuse of public funds, scouring the Web for pictures of the presidential jet, painstakingly documenting its movements as it crisscrossed Europe.[6] The jet often ferried Ben Ali's wife, famous for her extravagant lifestyle, from expensive shopping destinations to elite resorts and then back again. Several years later, the American diplomatic cables published by Wikileaks spread more details about the profligate antics of the ruling family. Consequently, the moment Tunisians learned of Mohammed Bouazizi's story, the contrast with the regime's lavish living caused them to take to the streets. Once the first demonstrations started, the Internet helped to spread the news like wildfire. In the past, coordinated protest on such a scale would have required a hierarchical organization. Social media, however, had eliminated the need for a leader.

It was the book *Smart Mobs,* published in 2002, that first explored the idea that user-generated mass communications technologies enable leaderless groups to organize collective action.[7] The concept of the smart mob is helpful to explain just how it was that Ben Ali was forced into exile less than one month after the self-immolation of Bouazizi. The dictator's ubiquitous secret police were too busy looking for subversive organizations to understand that the most dangerous opposition network actually had no leader and no organization. Ben Ali was on the plane into exile before he could even correctly identify his true enemy.

From Tunisia, smart mobs spread across the entire region, and Bouazizi instantly became an Arab symbol. Thus in mid-March, Ghassan Aboud, the Syrian owner of Orient TV, expressed his gratitude to the Tunisian martyr. Though headquartered in the United Arab Emirates, Orient TV broadcasts in Syria, where Aboud was frustrating the Asad regime by reporting on the demonstrations against it. In retribution, Asad's secret police contacted Aboud's Syrian employees in the UAE and threatened the lives of their relatives back home unless the station stopped its broadcasts. Some of Aboud's employees quit their jobs in order to protect their families, but Aboud himself remained defiant. He stood up to the regime and lost his business as a result. In explaining his newfound rebelliousness he evoked Mohammed Bouazizi: "I too am a child of fear raised in the soil of fear. This sense of freedom came to me only after Mohammed Bouazizi burned himself. This is what gave me a spirit of freedom and broke all the walls of fear inside me."[8]

If the Internet made Bouazizi famous around the world, it also heightened awareness, in general, of the Arab Spring, particularly in the West. As a consequence, the authoritarian regimes were subjected to a new level of scrutiny. The case of Syria is particularly illustrative because Asad expelled the international media from the country precisely to shield himself from foreign audit. The effort failed. Through a deft use of satellite phones and social media tools, the Syrian opposition broadcast a continuous account of events that was much more credible in the eyes of the outside world than the Syrian regime's counterfeit narrative.

Unfortunately, this flow of information failed to prevent the regime from behaving with great brutality. However, it did force Asad to avoid the sledgehammer strategy that his father deployed in February 1982 when he leveled an entire residential quarter with artillery in Hama to put down a Muslim Brotherhood insurgency. At that time, the Hafiz al-Asad regime had been successful in limiting the flow of information about the atrocity. It took a full eight days before the first, sketchy reports from Hama made it into the *New York Times.*[9] When Bashar al-Asad laid siege to the city of Dara'a in late April, however, video clips spread around the globe instantaneously. The *New York Times* reported on the event immediately, and within five weeks Human Rights Watch published an extensively researched report on the operation.[10] According to the organization, the Syrian authorities killed 418 people—a horrendous number, certainly, but nothing like the tens of thousands who died in Hama in 1982.

Did the information tactics of the opposition force Asad to moderate his behavior? Perhaps. But whatever the case, they certainly made him pay a price internationally. The Americans backed away from their policy of engaging the Syrian regime. Together with the Europeans, they issued new economic sanctions on the leadership in Damascus. Meanwhile, Qatar and Turkey also distanced themselves from Syria—a surprising development, given that Doha and Ankara had for years been close to Damascus. Public opinion probably played a role in this development, particularly in Turkey, where the images of carnage broadcast by Syrian oppositionists stirred popular anger against the Asad regime. In the past, Doha and Ankara might have tried to hide the atrocities from their own publics in order to protect relations with the Syrian government—but now they, too, cannot control the images that are emerging from the Arab world.

An Uncertain Future

What, then, of the second prong of the Ghonem thesis? Should the Internet, in general, be regarded as a great liberator? Here the evidence is mixed. To accept this view is to see the Arab Spring as a major step forward on a road that leads directly to freedom and democracy. The events of the Arab Spring permit another interpretation, however. While the revolutionary wave was undoubtedly a setback to the dictators, it was also one from which many of them can recover. The great destabilizing power of the Internet may have derived as much from its newness and unfamiliarity as from its innately democratizing nature. The regimes were caught off guard, and they may yet learn to mitigate the dangers of the digital world.

Indeed, the limits of the power of the smart mob are already in evidence. Qadhafi's forces would almost certainly have crushed the Libyan opposition had NATO's air power not arrived in the nick of time. Furthermore, for all that the Internet did in generating greater international scrutiny of the Syrian security forces, it nevertheless failed to stay the hand of the regime. There is simply no escaping the fact, as Clay Shirky writes, that digital tools "have the most dramatic effects in states where a public sphere already constrains the actions of the government."[11] Thus in Egypt, where the military was reluctant to fire on civilians, the protesters succeeded in persuading the armed forces to push Mubarak aside. In Syria, by contrast, the readiness of the military to kill with impunity vastly reduced the power of the keyboard.

When skeptics dismiss cyberactivism as slacktivism, their analysis is over-wrought, but it is based on a real insight: lasting political change requires action by people on the ground. The Internet can facilitate the activities of vibrant organizations, but it is not a complete substitute for them. In Egypt, the reformers succeeded because they managed to occupy Tahrir Square and thereby transform their struggle into a contest that played itself out on a stage before the entire world. A prime reason that so many went to Tahrir Square was the Mubarak regime's mistake in shutting down most Internet access when the initial protests began in late January, leaving Egypt's urban youth without an online outlet and forcing them to express themselves the old-fashioned way. In the absence of this physical standoff in the middle of Cairo, it is unlikely that President Barack Obama would have felt compelled to urge Mubarak to step down. By contrast, in Syria the protesters' cause suffered from their inability to similarly dramatize their competition with Bashar al-Asad. When they attempted to emulate the Egyptians by occupying a square in downtown Homs in May, for instance, the Syrian military cleared them out with live fire in the middle of the night.

For all that the protests in Tahrir Square seemed a Facebook phenomenon, one should not forget the influence of the traditional media—the regional satellite channels such as Al Jazeera and, above all others, the American networks gave the protests saturation coverage. As a result, on the critical dates of February 10 and 11 all eyes were on Washington, waiting expectantly for President Obama's reaction to events. Facebook alone could not have generated such expectation from an American president.

If the American media were an important factor in the outcome in Egypt, so was the American military, which strongly encouraged the Egyptian military to hold its fire. By contrast, the Syrian military had no influential foreign advisers pressuring it to stand down and allow the dictator to fall. On the contrary, the Syrians' closest allies, the Iranians, supported the harsh crackdown. Asad understood that to stay in power he would have to do whatever it took to prevent the opposition from controlling physical space. He was helped by the absence of a real, not a virtual, relationship with powerful outside actors.

The smart mob is therefore not always more powerful than the gun. Nor is it necessarily effective in a prolonged and complex political fight. By its very nature, the smart mob is a classic protest coalition, a group that is much more effective at defining what it opposes than what it seeks to build. In both Syria and Egypt, the most common protest slogan has been: "The people demand the fall of the regime." OK, but then what? The protesters are drawn from diverse backgrounds, and they entertain radically different visions of the Arab future—visions that, ultimately, are totally incompatible. As a result, once the dictator is ousted, the coalition disintegrates.

This fact found poetic expression in Egypt just one week after the ouster of Mubarak. On February 18, Sheikh Yusuf al-Qaradawi, a conservative cleric who has strong links to the Muslim Brotherhood, conducted Friday prayers in Tahrir Square. Hundreds of thousands of Egyptians assembled in central Cairo as he spoke, many more people, in fact, than ever camped out in Tahrir Square during the protests. Wael Ghonim came to the event expecting to sit on the stage in a place of honor next to Qaradawi. Perhaps Ghonim even planned to address the assembled multitude. As he mounted the stage, however, the sheikh's guards turned him away. This was Qaradawi's moment of glory, and he was not about to share it with the Internet whiz kid. Ghonim, visibly unnerved, "left the square with his face hidden by an Egyptian flag."[12]

The episode raises a painful question: When the dust finally settles, will Ghonim's Internet activism have furthered his own democratic agenda, or the agenda of third parties, sly operators schooled in the arts of traditional politics? Qaradawi, though no democrat, is nevertheless very tech-savvy and fully capable of summoning his own smart mob to sideline his opponents. At the same time, he understands the value of old-fashioned political muscle. The Syrians (and the Iranians before them) have reportedly hacked into opposition social media, often with the help of passwords extracted through torture. The dictators are able to use this information to arrest key opposition leaders, disrupt efforts to organize smart mobs, and sow dissension online. The next decade, therefore, will likely see the advent of Arab Dictatorship 2.0. The new authoritarianism, however, will not operate on the same tired model as the old one. There is no denying that the

cyber optimism of Ghonim and his cohort helped to introduce elements of liberty that will not quickly disappear. At the very least, there will be a race between
the forces of control and repression and those of expression and freedom. A
contest has been enjoined and there is no telling how it will end.

The United States is no bystander. It has a vital interest in promoting liberty, and the Internet is one tool for doing so. On February 15, 2011, four days
after the ouster of Mubarak, Secretary of State Hillary Clinton gave an important speech on Internet freedom. In fact, it was her second such address. "For
the United States," she said, "the choice is clear. On the spectrum of Internet
freedom, we place ourselves on the side of openness."[13] This policy is certainly
laudable. Note, however, that Clinton has given two major addresses on Internet freedom, but she has not given any on democracy. Although an unfettered
Internet is valuable, it is but one part of a loftier cause. Therefore, it is only fitting
and proper that it be so treated in authoritative statements of American policy.

6

THE IMPACT ON
THE PEACE PROCESS

Peacemaker or Peacebreaker?

KHALED ELGINDY AND SALMAN SHAIKH

The popular rebellions across the Middle East are rooted almost exclusively in local grievances related to decades of political, economic, and social stagnation, but they have major implications for every other aspect of international relations in the Middle East, not least of all the Israeli-Palestinian conflict and the broader quest for Arab-Israeli peace. The timing of the Arab Spring, which coincides with the collapse of U.S.-led negotiations between Israelis and Palestinians, suggests that both the region and the conflict are now entering a new phase, marked by both challenges and opportunities for the pursuit of peace.

Uncertainty over the future of the transitions under way in the region, along with the Palestinian decision to seek membership in the United Nations in September 2011, has prompted calls for a new approach to Israeli-Palestinian peacemaking. Yet the possibility of such an initiative seems increasingly difficult precisely because of the overall uncertainty. The Arab Spring has complicated an already troubled peace process, though the added hurdles are not necessarily insurmountable.

BEFORE THE WORLD CHANGED

Well before the Arab Spring, both the nature of the conflict and the regional landscape had undergone dramatic changes that made a negotiated settlement to the Arab-Israeli conflict seem ever more difficult. In particular, the decade since the collapse of the 2000–2001 Camp David–Taba negotiations witnessed major changes to the internal political situations in both Palestine and Israel. The Palestinian Authority (PA), plagued by years of corruption and mismanagement under Yasir Arafat, was decimated by Israel's response to the Second Intifada (al-Aqsa Intifada), which left the PA's security and governance institutions in tatters. The process of rebuilding the PA and reinvigorating a negotiating process were each hampered by the political ascent of Hamas, which won a decisive electoral victory in 2006 and went on to take control of Gaza in 2007. The result was a political and geographical division between Hamas and Fatah that stymied Palestinians and Israelis alike. Meanwhile, Palestinian rejectionists continued to mount attacks on Israel, and Israel continued to build settlements in the West Bank, eroding popular support for compromise on both sides.

Indeed, Israel's electorate underwent a distinct rightward shift during this period. This change came about in response to political and security developments in the West Bank and Gaza, Israeli perceptions of Palestinian bad faith in past negotiations, broader changes in the regional landscape after 9/11, and the launch of the American "war on terror." In addition, two security threats to Israel affected the public's view: the proliferation and increased sophistication of weapons used by militant groups, most notably Hamas and Hizballah, as well as the dramatic rise in Iranian influence in the region, particularly after the 2003 U.S.-led invasion of Iraq.

On the ground, this political shift was manifested in a growing Israeli emphasis on unilateralism and an increasingly heavy-handed security response to internal and external threats. It began with the establishment of the West Bank separation barrier under Prime Minister Ariel Sharon in 2002, continued with Israel's disengagement from Gaza in 2005, and culminated in two conflicts—in Lebanon in 2006 and Gaza in 2008–09 (the latter referred to by Israel as Operation Cast Lead). Both of these wars complicated prospects for a viable diplomatic peace process.

Even before Israel's Operation Cast Lead offensive, Israeli and American leaders appeared to recognize that the status quo was not tenable. This realization, coupled with the Bush administration's growing problems across the Middle East, prompted Washington to renew the negotiating strategy. The Annapolis talks held throughout 2008 did make modest progress in a few limited areas, namely on borders and security, but made little or no headway on Jerusalem, refugees, and water. Ultimately, they collapsed in the face of Cast Lead, which began at the end of that year. These developments pushed the Israeli electorate even farther to the right, resulting in the election of Benjamin Netanyahu and his hard-line government. Meanwhile, the Obama administration took office amid great rhetorical support for a renewed peace process that never materialized. Consequently, even before the events of the Arab Spring turned the region upside down, the peace process had virtually ceased to exist.

AFTER THE ARAB SPRING

One of the paradoxes of the events of 2011 is that they made peace between Israel and the Palestinians both more necessary and more difficult. For the most part, the rebellions across the region did not turn into anti-Israeli protests. On the other hand, the protests were not entirely devoid of a foreign policy dimension, notably in expressing the underlying resentment of most Arabs toward Israel. A refrain heard among Egyptian protesters, for example, was that the path toward the liberation of Jerusalem had begun in Cairo.

Removing Israel from the list of Arab grievances would help Israelis and Arabs alike, but that can only come from a final resolution of the Israeli-Palestinian dispute. With the Arab world in turmoil and the Israelis "circling the wagons" to wait out the storm, neither party seems likely to take the kinds of actions that might mollify an already rancorous situation.

Israelis and Palestinians Less Flexible

Among the greatest challenges to emerge in the wake of the Arab uprisings has been the hardening of Israeli and Palestinian positions alike. For their part, Israelis are frightened by the dramatic changes they see all around them. The regime of Hosni Mubarak, Israel's most dependable Arab ally, collapsed in a matter of weeks. The situation in Jordan remains tentative while Syria is lurching toward chaos. All of a sudden, none of Israel's borders seem so secure. Israelis worry about an Islamist takeover in any of these countries, and about the possibility of newly empowered Arab publics pressuring their governments to abrogate their peace treaties or cease-fires with Israel.[1] While Egypt's new military rulers have vowed to uphold their treaty with Israel—as will, in all likelihood, any future government— they have already begun to modify its policies in ways that Israel finds troubling, most notably by brokering a reconciliation agreement between Fatah and Hamas, easing restrictions along Gaza's Rafah border crossing, and breaking the ice on a new relationship with Iran.[2] The growing frequency and size of mass protests by Palestinians, both inside the occupied territories and along Israel's borders, have only deepened Israel's sense of isolation and insecurity, posing new and unique challenges for an Israeli government more accustomed to dealing with traditional terrorist and armed threats than with large-scale nonviolent civic action.[3] All of this has left Israelis even less inclined to want to take risks for peace.

Prime Minister Netanyahu's government has consistently taken a hard-line position on peace negotiations, and the apprehension felt by his constituency has removed any popular pressure he may have felt to make meaningful concessions. In a May 2011 address to the U.S. Congress, Netanyahu praised the "courageous Arab protesters" but then devoted more time to warning that the promise of democracy could yet succumb to "powerful forces" that oppose it, including Iran and other elements of "militant Islam."[4] Still, there are signs that Israel may be coming to terms with the region's new uncertainty, and looking for a diplomatic path forward.[5] But Netanyahu's rejection of President Barack Obama's call for negotiating borders "based on the 1967 lines with mutually agreed swaps" (a formula that has guided negotiations and was unofficial U.S. policy for at least a decade) makes a return to negotiations anytime soon highly unlikely.

Arguably, the Palestinians felt the impact of the Arab Spring even more directly, both at the popular level and within the political leadership. Inspired by events in Tunisia and closer to home in Egypt, young Palestinians began to organize their own protests. Initially, these were directed at their own political leaders, demanding an end to the four-year division between Fatah and Hamas. Increasingly, however, since the signing of the Egyptian-brokered reconciliation agreement on May 4, 2011, the protests have turned toward Israel and the occupation. On May 15, the date that simultaneously marks Israel's creation and the displacement of the Palestinians, which Palestinians refer to as the *Nakba*, thousands of Palestinian refugees in neighboring Arab states attempted to march on Israel's borders in a symbolic gesture of "return." The mobilization of refugee communities, long neglected by both the peace process and the Palestine Liberation Organization (PLO), put this issue back on the political agenda in dramatic fashion. Likewise, on June 5—a day Palestinians mark as the start of Israel's occupation (the *Naksa*) of the West Bank and Gaza strip—Palestinians organized parallel protests on Israel's borders and inside the occupied territories. Roughly thirty protesters were killed and hundreds of others wounded in these marches, and initial reports (since disputed) placed the blame on Israeli security forces, deepening Palestinian and Arab anger. In August coordinated terrorist attacks launched from Egypt into southern Israel killed six and wounded twenty-five Israelis, triggereing a skirmish between Israeli and Egyptian security forces. On September 9, Egyptian crowds responded to the passivity of the Egyptian military government toward this incident by breaking into the Israeli Embassy in Cairo and setting it on fire. Meanwhile, Syrian efforts to divert their own popular anger away from the Asad regime and onto Israel by encouraging and even facilitating these marches further complicated matters.

As discussed in chapter 15, the Arab Spring has exposed the political vulnerability of the PLO/PA leadership on both the domestic and diplomatic levels. The combination of changes in the regional balance of power and mounting domestic pressure led to a shift in Palestinian president Mahmoud Abbas's political calculus in two crucial ways. Internally, Abbas found it untenable to continue the status quo with regard to Hamas, and by extension the Gaza blockade. He therefore authorized the May 4 Hamas-Fatah reconciliation agreement, despite the strong possibility of political or economic sanctions, or both, by Israel, the United States, and other countries. At the diplomatic level, Abbas has seen the Arab Spring narrow his options even further. Although the PLO/PA leadership had already despaired of U.S.-led negotiations, the Arab Spring affirmed its conviction that the "peace process is over."[6]

Even before the dramatic events of 2011, Abbas could no longer afford to engage in a process viewed by most Palestinians as not only having failed to produce benefits but in fact having yielded a great many losses. Recent opinion polls demonstrate the extent to which Palestinians have lost faith in both the peace process and U.S. stewardship of it. One such poll found that two-thirds of Palestinians believe there is little or no chance of a Palestinian state being created alongside Israel in the coming five years. An even higher proportion (69 percent) oppose America's current role in the peace process.[7]

The Palestinian leadership is in a particularly vulnerable position. Unlike public grievances in other countries of the region, which are almost exclusively domestic in nature, those in Palestine stem from both internal and external pressures. Thus in addition to the PLO/PA leadership's own democracy deficit and lack of representation, the ongoing Israeli occupation (settlements, closures, demolitions, and so on) and the inability of the U.S.-led peace process to bring about an end to it take an added toll on the Palestinian leadership's legitimacy.

Feeling that the U.S.-led peace process had become untenable, Abbas turned to the United Nations, submitting a formal application to the Security Council that requested that Palestine be admitted as a full UN member.[8] Although the measure was staunchly opposed by the United States and Israel, Abbas has doggedly pressed forward, riding on a wave of popularity that he had not enjoyed before. Tellingly, while a majority of Palestinians do not believe the UN bid will be successful, it has remained extremely popular back home.

Diminished U.S. Role

While it is widely understood that active U.S. involvement is essential to Israeli-Palestinian peacemaking, the Obama administration has so far done little to make good on its early pledges to pursue a Middle East peace agreement. The Arab Spring threatens to reinforce that unfortunate record. On the list of U.S. priorities in the Middle East, stabilizing Egypt's rocky transition, repairing relations with the Saudi monarchy, working to oust Asad in Syria, and starting a transition in Yemen—to say nothing of the wars in Afghanistan and Iraq and the ongoing fight against al-Qaeda—have all outranked the quest for Israeli-Palestinian peace.[9] The danger for Washington is that its failures in Israeli-Palestinian peacemaking threaten to undermine whatever goodwill the United States might otherwise accrue from its efforts to aid popular protests throughout the Arab Spring.[10] Furthermore, a lengthy confrontation with Abbas at the UN will likely erode Washington's standing in the Arab region, and could weaken him and his PA to the point of collapse.

Even before the outbreak of popular unrest and revolutions across the Arab world, the United States had evinced no discernable strategy or vision for breaking the prolonged impasse. To a great extent, the peace process had collapsed long before the Ben Ali or Mubarak regimes. President Obama's major speech on the Arab Spring on May 19, 2011, did little to counter perceptions that the United States was behind the curve. Despite his insistence that regional upheaval

made peace "more urgent than ever," the president failed to delineate any concrete steps for moving the process forward. Nor did his support for "the moral
force of nonviolence" elsewhere in the Arab world appear to extend to Palestinians in their own struggle for self-determination. The "new" items to emerge in
the speech were calls for negotiations on the basis of the 1967 lines with agreed
swaps, and for tackling borders and security first—both of which had been
unstated U.S. policy for some time.

The administration's inability to dissuade either party from continuing along
their respective unilateralist paths is a sign and a consequence of America's
waning leverage with both Israelis and Palestinians. In late 2010 Netanyahu
successfully resisted American appeals to extend a partial "moratorium" on
the construction of Israeli settlements in the West Bank, even in exchange for
a multibillion-dollar incentives package.[11] Likewise, in February 2011, despite
immense U.S. pressure, Abbas refused to back down from his push for a UN
Security Council resolution condemning Israel's settlement enterprise, forcing
the United States into the embarrassing position of vetoing the measure.

The Arab Spring has also cost the United States some of its leverage with
other key Middle Eastern states, particularly Saudi Arabia and Egypt, which can
no longer be relied upon to support American peacemaking efforts unquestion-
ingly. Although Egypt remains a key U.S. ally, and American military aid will
likely continue to flow to the tune of about $1.3 billion annually, a post-Mubarak
Egypt will invariably seek a more independent foreign policy, one more in line
with popular sentiment.[12] Its strong private and public backing for Abbas's UN
bid is already a break from the country's past under Mubarak. Similarly, as Bruce
Riedel describes in chapter 18, U.S.-Saudi relations have deteriorated sharply
since the Egyptian uprising, and the United States will find it more difficult to
gain Saudi cooperation. Indeed, Prince Turki Al-Faisal's opinion piece in the
New York Times in September was a not-so-subtle warning from the former
Saudi ambassador that a U.S. veto of the Palestinian bid at the UN would lead to
a downgrading of Saudi relations with the United States.[13]

Eroding International Consensus

While the Arab Spring and the Obama administration's prior inaction have
both diminished Washington's role in the region, the international consensus
regarding the peace process has also begun to evaporate. In particular, there are
growing divisions within the "Quartet"—the United States, the European Union,
the United Nations, and Russia—over how, when, and even whether to proceed
with peace talks. These divisions were laid bare by the Palestinian UN bid, with
the United States actively opposing the move, Russia openly supporting it, the
EU deeply divided, and the UN serving as the venue where it all took place. The
latest Quartet statement hurriedly agreed upon after the speeches by Abbas and

Netanyahu proposed timelines for negotiations but offered no substance that could push the Israelis and Palestinians back to the negotiating table.[14] Most disturbingly, and for the first time in Obama's presidency, there was no reference to Israeli settlement construction. The obvious question, then, is how can the Quartet convince Abbas and Netanyahu what is good for them when they can not agree themselves on the basic conditions for peacemaking?

At the center of this divide is a growing gap between the United States and Europe, the two most influential third parties in the peace process. The European Union has grown increasingly frustrated with U.S. inaction on the peace process and has signaled that it may be prepared to pursue a more independent course. French foreign minister Alain Juppe's June 2011 invitation to host Israeli-Palestinian talks underscored the collapsing consensus regarding American leadership of peace efforts.[15] And while there is also some apprehension in Europe about the Palestinian plan at the UN, the EU was far less hostile to the move than the United States. President Sarkozy's address to the General Assembly—which came soon after President Obama spoke—forcefully presented a "third way" to realize Palestinian membership at the UN and revitalize negotiations. It was significant in that he directly challenged the decades-old U.S. monopoly on Arab-Israeli peacemaking (and the role of the Quartet) by stating that the "methods used up to now . . . had failed" and asked all to "change the method. Change the mentality."[16] Several European states, including France and Spain, have said they would consider supporting a General Assembly resolution upgrading Palestine's status to that of a nonmember state if negotiations are not resumed.

Europe has already shown a willingness to part ways with the United States over the Palestinian reconciliation agreement by showing more flexibility regarding the Quartet "principles"—the three conditions imposed on the PA following Hamas's election in 2006, which require it to recognize Israel, commit to nonviolence, and uphold past agreements. Both the United Nations and Russia have welcomed the unity deal, thus challenging the viability of those principles, and perhaps even that of the Quartet itself. Indeed, the Quartet had been in a state of paralysis since its February 2011 meeting over how to jump-start stalled peace talks. Its meeting in July failed to even produce a common statement, apparently under heavy U.S. pressure to include language that opposed the UN vote and Palestinian reconciliation.[17]

IMPACT OF THE UNGA

September at the UN delivered a critical blow to the U.S.-led peace process as we know it. Abbas's decision to go to the UN Security Council—by all accounts a decision made by him alone—has directly challenged the United States and threatened its decades-old monopoly on Arab-Israeli peacemaking. By internationalizing the process, Abbas has sought to level the playing field in any future negotiations. His gambit at the UN stems from his belief that negotiations with Israel under exclusive American supervision will not be possible. With elections scheduled in the United States, Palestine, and perhaps Israel in the next twelve months, it is hard to imagine that any meaningful negotiations can overcome the domestic political constraints on all three leaders, whose UN speeches spoke as much to their audiences at home as they did to each other.

At the time of this writing in the fall of 2011, no one can predict what will ultimately happen at the UN. The Palestinian bid for membership will ultimately elicit a U.S. veto, as Washington has made clear. But the chance of that vote coming soon seems improbable, as the Palestinian application will likely be subjected to procedural haggling and committee deliberations. If the vote were to come, there is uncertainty that the Palestinians would be able to garner the nine votes in favor of their bid, and thus "win" a U.S. veto. At some point, therefore, it is likely that the Palestinians will turn to the General Assembly and cash in on the backing they have to win an upgrading of their status to that of a nonmember state. This would give them the ability to join international bodies, including, most worrisome for the Israelis, the International Criminal Court.

Just as important will be how all of the major players respond to the UN bid. Israeli and U.S. congressional threats to punish the Palestinians could ultimately harm Israeli and American interests at least as much as—if not more than—those of Palestinians. Should Israel carry through with its threats to annex large swaths of West Bank territory, cancel the Oslo Accords, or withhold tax revenues to the Palestinian Authority, any or all of these could easily backfire by hastening the Palestinian Authority's collapse, which could mean the end of the two-state solution itself. Congressional threats to cut off aid to the PA may be equally self-defeating and lead to the same end. Diplomatically, the question remains whether the current period of uncertainty leads to a new way forward or a complete breakdown in relations between the United States and Israel on the one hand, and the Palestinians and its Arab supporters on the other. The latter would not only harm the chance of reaching peace, but would likely heighten tensions in the region and undercut broader U.S. interests.

POTENTIAL FOR VIOLENCE

It may only be a matter of time before there is a resurgence of Israeli-Palestinian violence. Palestinian anger with the United States and Israel, as well as with their own leaders, has thus far remained limited in scope and largely nonviolent in nature. Israel's continued use of lethal force against unarmed Palestinian protesters, whether inside the occupied territories or along its borders, is a potential source of heightened conflict. The potential for clashes between armed Israeli settler groups and Palestinians has become a real concern. Meanwhile, sporadic flare-ups in cross-border violence in Gaza could well escalate into full-blown conflagrations that could have a dangerous spillover effect in neighboring Egypt. Palestinian attacks from Egypt itself, like those in August 2011, and the inevitable Israeli responses are even more troubling. Potential "spoilers" like Iran, Hizballah, and especially Syria might also be tempted to escalate a violent confrontation with Israel to deflect local or international attention from their own atrocities. The deleterious effects of renewed Israeli-Palestinian violence could send powerful ripples across the rest of the Arab world. The hallmark of the Arab Spring has been the empowerment of Arab populations across the region. Renewed Israeli-Palestinian fighting will undoubtedly capture the sympathy of those same Arab masses that demanded an end to corruption and bad governance and bring them back out into the streets to demand that their governments act more forcefully toward Israel and provide more direct support to the Palestinians. In a world of nascent democracies and frightened monarchies, these governments may be far more willing—even compelled—to act on such popular sentiments than in the past. Demagogues in the democratizing states and desperate rulers in the ancien regimes might even see it as in their own personal and political interests to act more aggressively toward Israel. In such a scenario, Israel would probably be keen to convince all comers of its deterrent military capabilities, raising the risk of the kind of unintended escalation that preceded the Six-Day War in 1967.

FROM CRISIS TO OPPORTUNITY

Whether the current period is more like the one that preceded the June 1967 war or the one that led to the October 1991 Madrid Conference—or something else entirely—is still to be determined. What is becoming clear is that the Arab Spring is refashioning a new order in the Middle East. Its implications should not be seen as entirely dire regarding the possibility of forging a real and genuine peace between Israelis and Arabs, particularly Israelis and Palestinians. With the momentum for change coming from the people of the region, however, an entirely new process for peacemaking is required. Much as the 1991 Gulf War and the al-Aqsa Intifada created new initiatives and opportunities like the Madrid Conference and the creation of the Quartet, the Arab Spring warrants a fundamental shift in how the United States and the international community approach Arab-Israeli peace. The key is to be open to the possibilities and willing to think well outside of what has become a rather old and unhelpful box. With this in mind, a new strategy should include the following elements:

—*Reset the principles for Arab-Israeli peacemaking.* At a time of dramatically changing dynamics in the region, there is a need to nail down key principles for Arab-Israeli peacemaking. Central among these must be the principle of land for peace, the basic formula established at the Madrid Conference. Second must be entrenching the principle of two states, Israel and Palestine, on the 1967 borders with agreed-upon land swaps. The status of Jerusalem and the Holy Sites must be resolved to the satisfaction of both sides. The parties must be willing to accept the end of the conflict between them based on the realization of the two-state solution.

—*Embrace regional actors.* Despite its inadequacies, the process started by the Madrid Conference fostered cooperation and reconciliation between the countries of the Middle East. This was a key goal of the George H. W. Bush administration, which initiated the talks. As Ken Pollack discusses in chapter 31, the Arab Spring will undoubtedly reorder regional alliances and balances of power. It has already accelerated the emergence of a broader range of independently minded regional actors. The sense of empowerment created by the uprisings means that these actors—Egypt, Turkey, Saudi Arabia, Qatar, and perhaps Syria—will demand a greater role in the peace process. Egypt's reemergence, in particular, will doubtless change the dynamics of the process. The key will be to find a suitable role for Egypt and these other states that will be critical in forging a new international consensus on how best to move forward on Israeli-Palestinian peace. Conversely, having these states remain outside the process would likely complicate any efforts as they would be "wild cards" in a process that necessitates reducing the "unknowns" as much as possible.

The U.S. Role: "First among Equals"

While American leadership remains essential to effective peacemaking in the Middle East, it may no longer be possible (or even desirable) for the United States to retain exclusive control over the process. Although this dominance was questioned even before the Arab Spring, recent changes in the region and in the international environment only underscore the need for a different approach. The Palestinian push for UN membership makes this all the more salient.

As a result, the United States needs to champion a multilateral approach that broadens the circle of involvement beyond the largely ineffectual and discredited Quartet to include the regional actors discussed in the preceding sections. In short, the United States should adjust its posture from dominance to a leadership role that allows other actors to play important, autonomous roles, and to fashion approaches to peace more collectively than in the past.

This does not mean that the United States should avoid taking an active role in the peace process. Quite the opposite. As Israel's principal ally, as a key partner of many Arab states, and still the dominant power in the Middle East, the United States needs to remain fully engaged in the process. This is especially important to reassure Israel's leaders and citizens that the path to peace and security is through negotiations.

All of this speaks to the need for the United States to act with far greater urgency than it has thus far. It is not enough for U.S. officials to observe that the current situation is "unsustainable." One way to further this approach would be for the United States to engage in the UN discussions rather than just attempt to shut them down. Sixty-four years after UN Resolution 181 (the 1947 Partition Plan), a new UN General Assembly resolution that revives the goal of a Palestinian state alongside Israel has become a necessity. Such a resolution should upgrade the status of Palestine at the UN and articulate the commonly known parameters on the core issues, such as the borders of a future Palestinian state and the contentious issues of refugees and Jerusalem. It should also recognize Israel's security concerns, while demanding a halt to Israeli settlement building.

Such a resolution would bind all Palestinians and Arab countries to the internationally agreed-upon goal of two states and offer Israelis and Palestinians, once again, a historic opportunity to choose peace. It would also acknowledge the inherent (if not organic) link between the goals of the Middle East peace process and the broader struggle for Arab freedom and self-determination.

Meanwhile, American policymakers must help foster greater urgency for peacemaking in Israel. They must help the Israeli people see that the present is a moment when Israel can and should take risks for peace. Simultaneously, Washington must work with other elements of the international community to bolster Palestinian state-building, which should also extend to Gaza and include efforts at reconciliation and cohesion, while encouraging all Palestinian factions to act responsibly. To this end, the United States and its international partners should work to prevent escalations in violence by all sides, and to quickly resolve them when they do break out. American engagement will also be crucial in working with Arab countries to forge an agreement that is acceptable to all sides.

7

THE ARAB MILITARIES
The Double-Edged Swords

KENNETH M. POLLACK

In 1932 the British granted Iraq its (nominal) independence. Four years later, frustrated with the inequities of Britain's continued behind-the-scenes rule, the Iraqi military mounted the first coup d'état in the Middle East's modern history. It was hardly the last, in Iraq or elsewhere in the region. Over the next forty years, coup after coup wracked Arab states. Some states experienced military takeovers on a nearly annual basis. Few escaped without a military overthrow at some point, and even those that did typically faced numerous plots and near misses.

In the 1970s and 1980s, however, this pattern abruptly ended. The rulers of the Middle East, many of them military officers (or former military officers) who had themselves taken power by coup d'état, devised a complex machinery of governance to prevent further coups and to stave off the threat to their rule by others just like them. While building their militaries, they devised a system of rule that James Quinlivan has described as "coup-proofing."[1] This protected their regimes against the threat of military coup d'état for forty years.

At its core, this approach has meant politicizing the military to ensure its loyalty to the autocrat. In practice, it has meant skewing senior officer promotions and assignments to favor those loyal to the autocrat; creating multiple military and intelligence organizations that can watch one another and act against one another should one attempt a coup; restricting the freedom of action, and at times even the development of capabilities, to ensure that military units cannot move against the government; and centralizing, to the extent possible, all information and command authority with the political leadership. With only a handful of exceptions, this approach virtually eliminated the coup d'état (although not necessarily coup plotting) from the Arab world by the 1980s.

Meanwhile, just to the north of the Arab world, the Turkish military took a somewhat different tack.[2] There the military became the repository and guardian of Mustafa Kemal Ataturk's legacy—the political system he had bequeathed to the nation. The Turkish military portrayed itself as the apolitical guardian of

Turkey's secular, democratic tradition, mostly standing outside or above politics, but intervening whenever necessary to ensure that all of the participants continued to adhere to Ataturk's principles and so could not subvert the system.

The reality proved quite different. The Turkish military intervened frequently in the country's politics in favor of its own prerogatives (and corrupt practices) and the captive politicians who toed that line, and against any who opposed the military's various interests. Although in theory the Turkish military intervened only to ensure the sanctity of the secular, democratic system, in practice it frequently intervened in ways that undermined those very same principles. Indeed, at times the military subverted democracy in favor of secularism, and often its intentions were not even that principled.

All of this history speaks to the critical role that Middle Eastern militaries can, may, and should play in the transformation of the Arab states. The militaries of the Arab world (and Iran, for that matter) all have the capability to move decisively against their own government or in support of it. Thus their actions are absolutely critical in ensuring positive transitions throughout these states. The militaries are all strong enough to effect any political change (at least in the sense of bringing down a government) or to prevent any political change. Indeed, a principal conclusion of the scholarly literature on the subject is that revolutions only succeed when the state loses the capacity or the willingness to employ violence—a capability that resides in its armed forces. In short, when it comes to fulfilling the promise of transformation embodied in the Arab Spring, a great deal rests on the shoulders of the region's militaries.[3]

The dichotomous capability of militaries to preserve or overturn political order creates a critical dilemma for Arab countries undergoing transformation. It creates a need to balance the strength of the military and the strength of the civilian leadership. Getting that balance right is very difficult but historically is an important element in why some states succeed in making major political transformations and why so many others fail.

Praetorianism versus Commissarism

Good civil-military relations result from properly balancing civilian power and military power.[4] If the military is too strong and becomes contemptuous of the civilian leadership, it can overthrow the government and establish a military dictatorship in its place. This kind of imbalance played an important part in bringing the Middle East to its current woeful state of affairs. It is a problem typically referred to as "praetorianism," a term derived from Rome's Praetorian Guard, the emperor's personal bodyguard, which frequently chose and deposed emperors in the centuries after Augustus and Tiberius.

On the other hand, if the civilian leadership is too strong and too fearful of the potential role of the military, it can emasculate the armed forces, politicize them, and prevent the military from playing any role—positive or negative—in the political development of the country. Joseph Stalin was arguably the first modern leader to demonstrate how effectively this could be done as he brutally bent the Red Army to his will. Consequently, this aspect of politicization is best referred to as "commissarism," after the political commissars Stalin used to control the Red Army.[5]

The fear of praetorianism, an inalienable threat resident in any military absent a pervasive culture of civilian control, can lead the civilian leadership to indulge in commissarism, or coup-proofing. This eliminates the military's ability to play a negative role (overthrowing the government), but also eliminates its ability to play a positive role (as the guardian of a democratic transition). Moreover, commissarism takes time and is never perfect, and invariably antagonizes many members of the military, who resent the heavy-handed control, distorted rewards and promotions, and denigration of military efficiency inherent in commissarism. Military leaders may well be inclined to move against the government in response to efforts to coup-proof the armed forces. Thus commissarism can provoke praetorianism.

Back to the Future?

It is something of a truism that militaries dislike instability. For that reason, they are often uncomfortable with rapid, far-reaching political transformations—especially if those transitions unfold chaotically and the end-state is unclear. Military personnel typically see these circumstances as threatening, and it may also be that the well-ordered military mind detests the "untidiness" of difficult political transitions. Of course, the events of the Arab Spring have hardly been stable, gradual, or predictable. In most cases, they have also forced the military into the political realm far more than most would like—either to support government repression of the people as in Bahrain, Syria, and Libya, or to allow the fall of a government that the armed forces swore to defend, as in Egypt, Tunisia, and Yemen.

Moreover, for those countries that fought recent civil wars, whether provoked by the Arab Spring or preceding it, their militaries have already been politicized, and may well have emerged as the strongest institution in the country, one that was forced to take on many civilian tasks by the vicissitudes of that conflict. Thus the Iraqi military found itself involved in countless areas of civilian life by the requirements of a counterinsurgency war. This bleeding of the military into the civilian also has the potential to politicize Arab militaries.

It is unfortunately likely that many of the new civilian governments that have taken power, or will take power—as a result of the Arab Spring or future rounds of popular upheaval in the Arab world—will probably fail. The vast, intertwined problems of the Arab world will not magically disappear when the old regimes fall and new ones take their places. In fact, their falls will likely exacerbate those problems, perhaps by orders of magnitude. It is going to be very hard for any new government to succeed and very easy for it to founder, and historically this has been the most common cause of military coups d'état. The generals move in most frequently when they believe that the civilians do not know what they are doing and are imperiling the strength of the nation, the security of the state, or the safety of the people.

For all of these reasons, coups may return to the Middle East in the wake of the Arab Spring. Indeed, some have questioned whether the changes in Egypt should be seen as a popularly encouraged coup rather than a true popular revolution. The best way to prevent a recurrence of coups lies in building strong civilian institutions able to maintain order on their own, while developing a strong culture of democracy both within the military and without. But those are also tall orders.

INSTITUTIONS: THE PROMISE AND THE PROBLEM OF THE TURKISH MODEL

As discussed at greater length in chapter 10, transitioning to a stable, mature democracy requires not only the transformation of a country's political culture to embrace democratic principles but also the creation of strong institutions that can create checks and balances and preserve the rights of the people—both as individuals and as members of groups—against the power of other groups and institutions. Although social scientists continue to debate these questions, a good case can be made that strong institutions must come first, although a democratic culture is the ultimate determinant of success.[6] Culture typically takes generations to evolve, whereas strong institutions can be built more quickly, and by preserving a democratic system before new norms have taken root, they can create the necessary circumstances for that more gradual cultural change.[7]

Because the states of the Middle East lack both the democratic culture and the strong institutions necessary for democratic success, many have looked for a single entity—an individual or institution—that could effectively oversee the democratic transition, safeguarding the system while the strong democratic institutions are developed and the cultural transformation is under way.[8] The role of that guardian would be to guarantee the sanctity of the political process, enforce the rule of law, fight outside spoilers seeking to wreck the transition altogether, and ensure that all actors play by the rules of the game. In some historical cases, a monarch or charismatic leader has played that role; in others, a benign military.

Across the Middle East, people are asking whether the militaries of the Arab world can and will play this part. If so, there is reason to hope that the democratic transitions can succeed. If not, the hoped-for democratic transitions are likely to prove even more challenging.

Thus everything comes back to the Turkish model, and the role that the Turkish military *claimed* to be playing in the development of Turkish democracy. In effect, what many inside and outside the region hope is that the Egyptian, Tunisian, and perhaps other Arab militaries will become the ideal type, the platonic "form," of the Turkish military: disinterested, dedicated only to preserving the principles of a democratic system itself without trying to benefit any particular actors within that system, but willing to enforce the rule of law and defeat any efforts to subvert the system.

The problem is that while this is a reasonable expectation in theory, it has proven rare in practice. Indeed, the Turkish military itself seldom lived up to this ideal. It intervened frequently in politics to advantage different parties— always those most committed to acting as the Turkish military desired. In the Arab states, even if the military leadership begins with the best of intentions, impatience alone may push it to intervene unnecessarily; most new governments suffer through many missteps before they find their way, and a military that has consciously adopted the role of guardian of the political system may be unable to resist stepping in and taking matters into its own hands in the belief that the generals will do better than incompetent politicians.

Thus without a strong democratic ethos, a military set up as the guardian of a political system can easily become its bane. Unfortunately, it is just not clear whether the Arab states will be able to build strong, civilian institutions able to protect a nascent democracy while a democratic culture grows, unless the military is willing to play that role.

POLITICAL CULTURE: AN ISRAELI MODEL FOR THE ARABS?

If a Turkish model is challenging to employ in practice, an Israeli model would be impossible even in theory. But there are important aspects of what Israel did with its armed forces that could be very helpful to the Arab states and worthy of their emulation.

Like many of the Arab states, Israel at its founding was populated by a fractious hodgepodge of races, nationalities, sects, and linguistic groups. In response, Israeli leaders recognized a pressing need to knit these widely varied groups into a more cohesive nation and to inculcate in the entire population a common democratic ethos. Part of the rationale for conscripting all young men and women into the military was that the powerful socializing aspects of military service could forge a common bond and culture within society—an endeavor that proved highly successful.

Virtually all of the Arab states could benefit from a similar approach. Military service could help bridge the many ethnic, religious, tribal, geographic, and linguistic differences in their societies. It could also hasten the spread of democratic ideals and values. In short, it could help forge mature, stable, democratic Arab nations from the current Middle Eastern cacophonies.

Yet as desirable as this may be to replicate in the Arab world, it, too, seems unlikely—and not just because the Israelis thought of it first. To begin with, many civilians tend to assume that universal conscription somehow works to the advantage of the military by "militarizing" society, leaving the populace more easily susceptible to the machinations of the army leadership. Although there is no empirical basis for this fear, it is widespread in the Middle East nevertheless. Second, in most of the developed world, the trend is heavily toward all-volunteer militaries and away from conscription. Given that most of the Arab militaries want to emulate their counterparts in the developed world, and that much of their citizenry consciously seeks to be more like the developed world in general, it seems unlikely that new Arab governments would want to move in the opposite direction on this important issue. Moreover, most of those who are agitating for political change in the Arab world today—the reformists, the opposition, the revolutionaries, whatever they are called in any given country—typically want to give the government less and to receive more. Thus the idea of universal conscription runs squarely counter to what those looking to take power want from their states.

THE AMERICAN ROLE

It is important to be blunt about the U.S. relationship with the Arab militaries. Washington can, should, and must use its extensive ties with many of the security establishments of the Arab world to help the processes of democratization and reform that have begun, or need to begin, as a result of the events of the Arab Spring. The United States *can* do so because the U.S. military and intelligence communities have considerable influence with many of their counterparts in the Arab world. The United States *should* because, as just discussed, the Arab militaries can be a powerful, constructive factor in ensuring a stable, orderly transition and preventing bad actors from subverting or hijacking that process. And the United States *must* do so because inaction will inevitably be construed by many Arabs as tacit American support for continued repression by the existing regimes.

America's relationships with the Arab security establishments can be a source of positive assistance in seeking to bring about the peaceful, stable change that would most benefit American interests. The United States has significant influence with many of the Arab armed forces (and their intelligence services), and typically more influence with them than any other state. Like everything about

America's involvement with the Arab Spring, it is a role that should not be over- or understated. Egypt is the most useful and important case in point. Throughout the run-up to Mubarak's ouster in Egypt, the constant conversations between Egyptian senior officers and their American counterparts had an impact on the decision of the Egyptian military not to employ violence against the protesters and to allow Mubarak to fall. Whether that stemmed from a fear of losing American military aid, a desire to be like the United States military because it is the most respected in the world, or some assimilation of the values of America's own military culture is impossible to know. However, it is also true that the Egyptian military had its own unique motives for making those choices, and it may be that the American conversations simply helped the military's leadership see those incentives more clearly.

In most cases, the United States will have some ability to influence Arab militaries—as a donor, a threat, or an exemplar of how the best militaries act. It is critical for the United States to develop and employ these military-to-military and intelligence ties to try to ensure that the Arab security organs do the right thing and not the wrong. Still, Washington must remember that the ultimate decisions will be made in the capitals of the Arab states, whatever weight they may attach to American views.

Thus what the United States ought to be trying to persuade Arab militaries to do during the long process of transformation that is under way is easy to describe, at least in terms of being straightforward. The United States should encourage them to:

—Refrain from employing violence, either against protesters or the governments themselves.

—Embrace democratic principles of representative government, transparency, accountability, rule of law, and basic civil rights, and insist that the country as a whole abides by those same principles.

—Act like impartial guardians of the political process, ensuring an orderly and peaceful transition—whatever that transition may entail—rather than picking specific sides.

—Oppose any individual, party, or institution that tries to employ violence or otherwise subvert the process of change.

The hard part is turning encouragement into concrete behavior, and there the United States has nothing but weak tools. The United States can and should:[9]

—Continue to provide aid to Arab militaries wherever possible—the more the better—but tie that aid to their adherence to the foregoing principles.[10]

—Encourage training and education of Arab officers in American schools. Doing so builds relationships among American and Arab military officers, endears them to the United States (mostly), and can allow some American values to rub off.

—Protect the Arab states from external threats lest these threats become excuses for the governments to shut down the process of change in the name of manning the ramparts against a foreign foe—an excuse that Arab regimes have frequently used to ignore pleas for change in the past.[11]

The militaries of the Arab world have a crucial role to play in the transformation inaugurated by the Arab Spring, even if this means standing aside and refusing to take up arms against their citizenry. The United States has some influence with many of these militaries, and it is imperative that Washington use whatever *wasta* it has to ensure that the militaries become part of the solution, not part of the problem. But American influence is ultimately modest, and Washington should not delude itself that it will be the ultimate arbiter of the Arab world's fate. Ironically, given the limitations on the influence that military-to-military ties can have, many Arabs assume that the United States, through these military ties, pulls all of the strings in their countries. For that reason, whether Washington likes it or not, Arab publics are watching what the United States does with its military (and intelligence) relationships. If these relationships are not seen as actively encouraging change, people across the region will assume that the United States is actively seeking to thwart it.

Although the U.S. Fifth Fleet headquarters in Bahrain had no interest in the popular unrest there and had no capacity to do anything about it one way or the other, Arabs across the region cite its presence—and the fact that Washington made no move to evacuate it—as proof that the United States supported the government crackdown. It is untrue and unfair, but it is undeniable and painfully commonplace. Consequently, in addition to finding ways to use security ties to encourage democratization or reform, or both, the United States may have to think about what circumstances would lead it to cut military assistance and even close U.S. bases in the Middle East, either to disassociate the United States from repressive actions by a friendly regime or to try to goad such a regime into doing the right thing. Washington has already begun to do this in Lebanon, where it cut back on military assistance after Hizballah took over the Lebanese government. Such a Hobson's choice will inevitably be painful, but it is crucial to understand that America's military engagement with the Arab world is never neutral: if it is not seen as helping, it will be seen as hurting, and in turn will inflame anti-Americanism in a region that has finally demonstrated that what its publics think really matters.

8

The Economic Dimension

The Price of Freedom

Suzanne Maloney

Seldom do street peddlers make history. So when Mohammed Bouazizi set himself on fire on December 17, 2010, in a tragic and spectacular act of protest against the confiscation of his cart, he could have had little idea that his action would not only result in the ouster of Tunisia's long-ruling autocrat but would also inspire a wave of protests that would reshape the entire Middle East.

The movement that Bouazizi inspired was initially dubbed the "Dignity Revolution," a tacit acknowledgment that his outrage transcended the simple assault on his livelihood but emanated from the sense of humiliation and indignation that had become pervasive across the region as a result of political and economic stagnation.[1] As the underlying political imperative of the protests became apparent, their intention came to be defined as regime change. In this way, the mobilization of millions across the Middle East became identified primarily as a pro-democracy, anti-autocracy crusade.

The movement's deep resonance and catalytic impact cannot be fully appreciated without considering the genesis of the whirlwind that continues to sweep the region. Bouazizi's cart represented the sole source of income for a family of eight, and his frustration at the manifold challenges of making ends meet appears to have struck a chord in a way that eclipses the profound political and social grievances of the region's population.

In other words, the Arab Spring was born of economic grievances, and it will be economics as much as any other factor that shapes the outcomes in individual states. For this reason, policies that successfully address the pocketbook will be equally, if not more, essential than elections to ensuring that the transitions to democracy are stable and durable.

Roots of Discontent

To a considerable extent, the upheaval of the Arab Spring was the product of the prevailing economic order that characterized the region for the previous sixty years. With its traditional place in international commerce, an unrivalled resource base, and a vast young labor market, the Middle East is endowed with the building blocks for prosperity. Yet the performance of the region's diverse economies in the post–World War II era has been for the most part profoundly disappointing. This underperformance is rooted in part in the aftereffects of colonialism; persistent war, civil violence, and superpower competition; the intellectual marriage of Arab nationalism and socialism; and volatility and market distortion caused by massive influxes of externally generated rents.

Poverty per se has never been the region's real economic challenge, although there is considerable poverty in virtually all of the Arab states, including major oil producers like Saudi Arabia, Iraq, and Algeria. The epic influx of wealth after the 1973 oil boom facilitated massive investment in physical and social infrastructure, and corresponding progress on basic development indicators. Rather, the fundamental problems have centered on unequal wealth distribution (greatly exacerbated by the distorting effects of massive oil revenues), corruption, bloated and noncompetitive economies, inadequate educational systems, unimpressive growth rates, highly subsidized and unproductive non-oil sectors, and a declining share of world trade. Meanwhile, the ranks of the region's have-nots have been growing; resource revenues have been on a permanent decline in countries such as Syria, Yemen, and Bahrain; and in Iran, sanctions and self-imposed limits on foreign investment may reduce the country—endowed with the third largest reserves of oil in the world—to the status of a net *importer* of oil.

In the 1990s, Arab economies grew by less than 1 percent on a per capita basis, and the ratio of foreign direct investment to gross domestic product (GDP) was less than half the global average.[2] Knowledge dispersion withered and educational attainments stagnated; according to the *Arab Human Development Report* of 2002, the region as a whole had translated approximately the same number of books into Arabic since the ninth century as Spain does into Spanish in any given year.[3] As of 2003, the entire region exported fewer manufactured goods than the relatively small economy of the Philippines.[4] Overregulation and the lack of functioning capital markets stymied entrepreneurism, while corruption drained an estimated $1 trillion in the second half of the twentieth century.[5] The sense of stagnation and failure was overwhelming, as an investment analyst told *Newsweek*: "The Arabs are going the way of Africa. You only have to draw a straight line from where the Arab economies were a century ago to where they are now to get an idea of where they're going—and the answer is very worrisome."[6]

The only real growth industry in the Middle East has been population. Rising life expectancy, declining infant mortality, and some of the highest birth rates on the planet have contributed to a disproportionately young population across the Arab world. Approximately two-thirds of the population of the region is under the age of thirty, a demographic anomaly that puts enormous pressure on infrastructure, education, labor markets, and social stability. To absorb this boom, regional states will have to create eighty million new jobs by 2020, nearly all in the private sector. At the same time, the countries will have to implement the sort of comprehensive educational expansion and reforms necessary to produce a trained work force that can take on these jobs.

ECONOMICS AND REVOLUTION

As the Bouazizi narrative suggests, the relationship between economics and uprising is an important one, although ultimately the dynamics tend to be more complex than they might appear at first. Most of the theoretical work on revolution—from the classic studies of Alexis de Tocqueville and Crane Brinton to Samuel Huntington's emphasis on the destabilizing impacts of modernization, to Theda Skocpol's work on the structural effects of economic crisis on state capacity—has posited some direct causal relationship between economic pressures and popular rebellion.[7] The series of events that prompted the uprising in Tunisia and the ensuing regional unrest provides considerable evidence that economic conditions and grievances factored heavily into the eruption of protests and the subsequent developments.

On the surface, at least, contributing factors would appear to include the aftereffects of the global economic slowdown that began in 2008, popular frustration over rising food prices and the associated inflation, anger over perceived corruption, and the lack of employment prospects among the region's disproportionately young population. Some observers suggest an alternative interpretation, consistent with historical analyses by Brinton as well as the relative deprivation thesis advanced by Ted Robert Gurr. In this view, it is global progress, and the growing gap in expectations of a better life and a more modest reality, rather than mere poverty that sparks revolutionary mobilization. Unquestionably, the Egyptian and Tunisian embrace of circumscribed economic liberalization in recent years had created unmet expectations of continuing and more evenly distributed gains. Still others point to the influx of foreign investment that boosted the Tunisian and Egyptian economy during the 2000s, but also alienated traditional business elites at a crucial juncture.[8]

Parsing out how the specific aspects of the Arab world's problematic economies prompted the Arab uprisings will have to wait for future historians and politicians. Although few hard data are yet available on the demographic composition of the crowds that thronged Tahrir Square, the Libyan rebels, or Syrian opposition, the early evidence suggests that all have skewed young. At some level, this is unsurprising because of the region's demographic balance and the fact that the overwhelming majority of the unemployed in countries such as Egypt are young and well-educated.[9] It reinforces the notion that economic considerations were central to the upheaval, given the younger generation's resentment over the difficulty in obtaining adequately paid work and achieving the accompanying milestones of independence and marriage. However, future research will be needed to analyze which aspects of the broader economic grievances were particularly troublesome, or how the broad underlying economic causes fed into the proximate triggers of the revolts.

CHALLENGES FOR A REGION IN TRANSITION

Whatever way various economic factors served as initial catalysts, it is clear that the economy will have an enormous impact on the outcomes of the Arab Spring and the more general transformation of the Middle East that is likely to follow. In Middle Eastern states undergoing democratic transitions or in countries moving toward top-down reform, the expectation of rapid economic progress will loom large. Indeed, the fate of political liberalization may rest heavily, if not almost entirely, on the capacity of new leaderships and institutions to achieve tangible progress on unemployment, corruption, and living standards. The grumble of an Egyptian tentmaker to a Western reporter—"We went to Tahrir Square and now we don't have any customers"—and the prevalence of small-scale protests over the transitional government's handling of economic policy underscore the centrality of economic performance to the longevity of the fledgling Egyptian and Tunisian democracies.[10] Similarly, Iraq's own "Day of Rage" amid the Arab Spring was specifically focused on the failures of Iraq's new political leadership to produce any improvement in the provision of basic services and basic economic factors.

The strength of public demand for government performance and accountability will be an important foundation for the cultivation of democratic polities and institutions in Arab states that are undergoing transitions. In the best-case scenario, successful economic policy in Egypt can sustain a broader national narrative of rebounding regional leadership.[11] However, growing expectations impose an enormous burden on new leaders and embryonic systems in dealing with the considerable economic challenges. It simply may not be possible for new governments struggling to establish a new polity to simultaneously fix deep-seated structural problems in the economy, and their failure to do so could undermine overall support for a liberal democratic system of government. Certainly, there are groups waiting to make such claims, and to channel public discontent into calls for different systems of government or different leaderships.

Economics will shape the outcome of the Arab Spring in a variety of other ways. Resources and the distribution of economic rewards offer useful—if not impenetrable—mechanisms for insulating governments from the full force of popular demands or regional upheaval, or both. As the tempo of uprisings escalated, the Gulf states indulged in a massive distribution of direct subsidies to their populations and other large-scale social spending—the political equivalent of hush money, intended to quell demands for greater political participation and social freedoms. Although there are good alternative explanations as to why Saudi Arabia, Qatar, Kuwait, and the United Arab Emirates did not experience the same levels of popular unrest as occurred elsewhere in the region (see chapters 18 and 20), the subsidies undoubtedly had some impact.

While economics has been a powerful incentive for action, it can also serve as a powerful disincentive, as in Bahrain, where the government has reportedly engaged in mass firings to penalize people who participated in general strikes that were called in sympathy with the February and March 2011 pro-democracy protests. Elsewhere, crony capitalism serves as a bulwark against societal dissatisfaction. Syria's largest and most influential urban centers remained largely quiet throughout the first few tumultuous months of the upheaval in that country, thanks in large part to the reliance of the merchant and middle classes on their relationships with the Asad regime for their economic well-being.[12]

Economic instruments also represent a crucial part of the Western toolbox for fostering reform as well as cooperation on vital U.S. interests. For example, Washington has sought to nurture the democratic transition in Egypt through various forms of economic support, while advancing the cause of political change in Iran and Syria by leveling new sanctions on individual human rights abusers in both countries. Note, too, that the West has an array of vital interests at stake in the changes under way in the Middle East, but ultimately the region's importance to the functioning of the global economy by virtue of its role in the production and transportation of energy represents the strategic imperative that underpins policy decisions and options.

Undoing the Damage

Predictably, nearly all of the countries that have experienced full-fledged uprisings are also experiencing intensified economic pressures as a result of the instability and uncertainty, whereas the resource-rich autocracies have by and large succeeded in placating social pressures through increased spending. The Tunisian and Egyptian uprisings are the success stories—they were relatively brief, were largely nonviolent, and satisfied immediate popular demands for political change. However, even these relatively gentle experiences with regime change have proved devastating, at least on a temporary basis, to the economic well-being of the country. The Institute of International Finance (IIF) predicts a 1.5 percent drop in Tunisia's GDP and 2.5 percent for Egypt's GDP in 2011, as compared with robust growth of 2010 in both countries (3.4 percent and 5 percent, respectively).[13] Foreign investors have been forced to shutter enterprises and lay off or evacuate employees.[14] In Egypt, manufacturing fell by 12 percent during the early months of 2011, and the increasingly profitable information technology sector will likely suffer even more as a result of the cutoffs and reassertion of government control over communications technology.[15] Tourism—a vital source of foreign exchange—effectively evaporated during the unsettled months of protests and curfews. By April visitors were back, but the volume of tourism remained at least one-third below that of previous years, and the decline will cost Egypt at least $2 billion in crucial foreign exchange revenues.[16] Both countries have launched splashy promotional campaigns to lure back tourists, whose spending amounts to 11.5 percent of Egypt's GDP.

The scope and persistence of unrest in several countries will entail large costs for the successor regimes, the region, and the international community. The economies and state structures of both Libya and Yemen have already crumpled under the weight of fierce internal violence as well as the NATO-led air campaign in the case of Libya. These two conflicts have become immediate humanitarian emergencies, with millions suffering from a lack of food, water, power, and other supplies. In both countries, a steady tempo of insurgency is destroying infrastructure and imploding the institutions of the state and the economy, and other states such as Syria may devolve in similar fashion (in Libya, Muammar Qadhafi's shelling of the UNESCO World Heritage site of Ghadames in June 2011 caused incalculable damage). Yemeni officials estimated that the first several months of instability had robbed the economy of 17 percent of GDP and placed the country "on the verge of an economic catastrophe."[17]

ECONOMIC PROBLEMS AND THE TRANSFORMATION OF THE MIDDLE EAST

It would be easy to presume that Egypt and Tunisia will rebound, and that Yemen and Libya are isolated crises. However, the reality is that the costs of regime change ripple across the region, in the form of higher oil prices, reduced tourism, more skittish investors, and lowered remittances. Regional instability may undermine neighbors irrespective of the relative success or failure of their own reform efforts. The IIF estimates that Syrian instability has already shaved 2 percent from Lebanon's fragile post-reconstruction GDP.[18] Jordan has experienced an array of aftershocks from the unrest surrounding it: higher oil prices are debilitating, Syrian violence has dampened trade, and sabotage of the Egyptian gas pipeline has cost the government millions of dollars and prompted painful energy rationing.[19] At the same time, anxious North African states have embarked on costly social spending to placate popular dissatisfaction. The Moroccan government hiked minimum wages and pensions to the tune of $5 billion over three years, amid strikes and labor actions, while Algerian president Abdelaziz Bouteflika put forward a plan to expand state spending by 25 percent.[20]

Despite its advantages, particularly the boost that oil prices have received as a result of the Arab Spring, the Gulf is not immune to the economic fallout. The massive payouts initiated by Saudi Arabia and mirrored by other Gulf states represent a real step backward in terms of insulating economies from oil price volatility. The Saudi commitment to new spending on the order of 30 percent of GDP leaves the kingdom once again dependent on high oil prices to balance its budget and further undermines efforts to promote competitiveness and market economies. It remains to be seen whether the Gulf can ride out the tensions on its doorstep—indeed directly within its midst, in the case of Bahrain—without losing any of its luster.

There are many indirect costs as well. The pervasive uncertainty will almost surely intensify corruption in many states, as nervous bureaucrats are often more susceptible to bribery and more prone to efforts to buy off opposition. Wealthy Arabs will seek alternative destinations for their own investments and savings as a hedge against the unknown; according to one regional newspaper, capital flight is well under way, with $30 billion having left Egypt during the early months of the Arab Spring.[21]

Equally disturbing is the likelihood that social unrest will jeopardize the nascent embrace of economic liberalization and prudence that has only just begun to take hold in the region. Among both the haves and the have-nots, the instinctive response has been to support the primacy of the state, through the introduction of and increases in consumer subsidies, as well as the rollback of some economic reforms. In several Arab states, the reversal of tentative steps toward a more market economy has been accompanied by attempts to scapegoat advocates of economic liberalization, including the former Egyptian prime minister and finance minister.[22] More generous subsidies and new taxes on upper-level income and capital gains may play well to the passions unleashed by revolutionary change, but they will only further undermine the prospects for durable growth.

The transition from authoritarian to representative rule can be more favorable to demagogues than to technocrats. Skyrocketing expectations and the eruption of long-repressed fury over perceived inequities create manifold incentives for leaders to pander to popular outrage. As a result of this environment, and together with legal frameworks that were deliberately accommodating of human rights abuses, transitional authorities have used fraud and corruption charges as all-purpose tools for punishing ancien regime officials. Even more disturbing, economic policy already appears to be subject to an ideological litmus test in some countries. The former Egyptian energy minister has been charged with a variety of crimes in association with the gas trade he initiated with Israel.

For current and prospective investors, there are risks and complications that transcend the immediate bottom line. The initial postponement and subsequent cancellation of the February 2011 Formula 1 race that was set to take place in Bahrain highlights the sensitivity of international firms to the reputational consequences of conducting business as usual in the midst of a well-publicized crackdown on protesters.[23] Global telecommunications firms such as Vodafone have struggled to adhere to local legal frameworks while trying to avoid the appearance of complicity in regime repression of free speech and protesters' ability to organize and coordinate via social media. The backlash has even hit Toyota, whose U.S.-made Tundra trucks have drawn considerable unwanted attention as the preferred vehicle of Qadhafi's mercenary militias, despite the fact that the company has had no direct sales to Libya.[24] Moreover, investors have considerable reasons for caution. The good news of democratic empowerment across the Middle East is ultimately problematic news for companies interested in short-term stability. While some surveys suggest that the upheaval will not deter investment, many would-be investors are hedging their bets as long as authority remains unclear and the rule of law is increasingly contested.[25] And there is likely to be continuing upheaval, as the ripple effects of change rebound even in those corners of the Arab world that historically have been particularly resistant to the siren song of representative rule.

The ouster of the Tunisian and Egyptian presidents has validated the logic of protest for many Arabs, and this newfound sense of empowerment and entitlement has continued to incite street protests. As a reinforcement of newly realized freedoms, the persistence of popular mobilization is a positive phenomenon; for the economy, however, continuing demonstrations may exacerbate the very problems that they are bemoaning. A vicious cycle has been established as ordinary Arab citizens demanding better governance and, in particular, the anticipated dividends of democracy take to the streets when jobs do not materialize or other expectations are not met. Instability or even mere uncertainty inhibits investment, which in turn exacerbates financial pressures, which ultimately fuel popular resentment of ruling regimes in some countries or frustration with the process of democratic transition under way in others. As Arabs continue to find their aspirations for better living standards frustrated, their discontent poses a threat beyond the stability and longevity of their own regimes. According to a recent Pew poll, respondents in Egypt, Lebanon, and Jordan attribute their stagnant economies somewhat evenly to domestic factors such as corruption and the lack of democracy and to the policies of the United States and the West.[26]

Advancing an Economic Awakening

The economic prognosis for the Middle East need not be dire. The Arab Spring can serve as an accelerant to various nascent positive trends from the decade that preceded it. Building upon strong oil revenues, renewed incentives for increasing Gulf intraregional investment, and a young, energized population, the Middle East can emerge from this crisis poised for historic growth and development. However, good economic policy will not come on the cheap, and the states that will need the most help tend (naturally) to be those with the fewest resources. Tunisian officials estimate that the government's plans for job creation and economic and social reforms will cost $25 billion over the next five years.[27]

How can transforming governments such as Egypt's and Tunisia's get the economic dimension of the challenge "right"? Perhaps most important for a successful new approach are measures that transcend the specifics of the economy itself and create robust institutions for political participation and a solid framework for institutionalizing accountability and good governance. These are essential components of a well-functioning economy that can attract and employ foreign investment and create new enterprises and opportunities. As the discussion on corruption in chapter 3 suggests, a multifaceted approach to corruption, including investments in civil society and media, has proved more effective than only regulation and enforcement in countries that have transitioned toward democracy. One modest but crucial issue in this regard would be the development and enforcement of norms surrounding clear and enforceable barriers to foreign financing of the political process. This would blunt the capacity of external actors—including Iran and Saudi Arabia—for subverting emergent democratic processes by buying off political parties.

Beyond strengthening state foundations, Arab governments will be confronting an array of painful policy choices exacerbated by regional upheaval. The exigencies are obvious, the remedies are difficult but not particularly contested: investment in education, development of capital markets, prioritization of labor-intensive exports, greater transparency, curbs on corruption and cronyism, and the elimination of costly state interventions in the market through subsidies and overregulation. Still, in the absence of support, advice, and urgency, the impulse for many governments will be to indulge in populist pandering, overspend, and continue to evade necessary reforms. "The economic situation, the financial situation, the foreign debt are tremendous," Taher al-Masri, Jordan's Senate speaker, told an interviewer. "The level of subsidies is unbearable. And yet you're damned if you do and damned if you don't."[28]

For this reason, the role of Washington and the international financial community will be essential. The international community, both through bilateral state mechanisms and multilateral institutions, such as the International Monetary Fund and the African Development Bank, has already begun to step up to the plate with short-term assistance. Washington should seek to ensure robust technical advice and ongoing coordination among donors on implementation and longer-term priorities. An important part of this effort will be to draw in the more reluctant stakeholders, such as China and Russia, which retain significant trade and investment in the region, as well as the Saudis and other regional states that are heavily engaged both in investment and in assistance.

Dedicated mechanisms will likely be needed to address long-term reconstruction in Libya and Yemen; to avoid donor fatigue and amplify the impact, however, country-specific cooperation could be tied into a broader institution, such as the dialogue on economic reform between the Organization for Economic Cooperation and Development and the countries of the Middle East and North Africa. As in Iraq, Washington and international financial institutions should actively seek to engage private sector leaders in the process.

The Obama administration has already been encouraging assistance to Arab reformers and transitional states, marshaling the traditional tools of U.S. economic policy to this end. So far, the options advanced by Washington sound suspiciously reminiscent of prior policies—trade agreements, debt relief, and investment support. This is a laudable start, but without greater firepower, these measures alone will have difficulty reorienting Arab economies in a more competitive direction. If greater access to American markets represented the crux of the region's economic dilemmas, then Bahrain—which was only the second recipient of a free trade agreement with Washington in the Arab world—would not be in turmoil. If economic liberalization were sufficient to ensure democratization and stability, Egypt and Tunisia would not have been the first Arab dictatorships to fall.

9

Terrorism

Al-Qaeda and the Arab Spring

Daniel L. Byman

Looking out from al-Qaeda's hideouts in Pakistan, the Arab world probably appears as uncertain to the terrorist group's new leader, Ayman al-Zawahiri, as it does to many Americans. It certainly has not helped him or his far-flung minions to think about the fact that for two decades and more, separately and together, they attempted to overthrow Arab governments without a single success. Then, suddenly, crowds of peaceful (and often secularly motivated) Arabs rose up spontaneously, took to the streets, and toppled the monolithic dictatorships of Egypt, Tunisia, and Libya—and may yet do the same in Syria and Yemen. This not only caught Zawahiri and al-Qaeda flat-footed; it undermined their message that violent jihad is the only way to bring about regime change. Osama bin Laden's death, coming amid these revolutions, has only further weakened the organization's appeal and ability to operate.

Nevertheless, al-Qaeda and its allies no doubt see in the Arab Spring advantages. For now, the groups have greater operational freedom of action, and Zawahiri and his allies will seek to exploit any further unrest in the months and years to come. They know that revolutions are ripe for hijacking by extremists. They know that democratic transitions often fail. They doubtless believe that if they play their cards well, the revolutions, unrest, and turmoil of the Arab Spring could ultimately turn very much in their favor.[1]

Off Message

The collapse of Zine al-Abidine Ben Ali's regime in Tunisia, followed by the even more stunning fall of Mubarak's regime in Egypt, electrified the Middle East and the world, prompting an outpouring of statements from leaders across the globe. Yet, al-Qaeda's leaders—rarely at a loss for words—were largely silent. Only in mid-February did Zawahiri, then bin Laden's deputy, offer al-Qaeda's spin on recent events. But he did not directly address the revolutions or explain how jihadists should respond. Instead, he claimed that the Tunisian revolution occurred "against the agent of America and France," gamely trying to transform Tunisians' fight against corruption and repression into a victory for anti-Western jihadists. On Egypt, Zawahiri offered a rambling history lesson going back to Napoleon and earlier, and ending with a perfunctory criticism of the tyranny of the Mubarak government. Zawahiri released his statement about Egypt on February 18, a week *after* Mubarak resigned. In the months that followed, however, al-Qaeda developed a more consistent message. It lavishly praised those who demonstrated against Mubarak and Ben Ali, and those who took up arms against Qadhafi, while carping about U.S. hypocrisy in supporting these dictatorships for decades and only changing its position when forced to do so. The true spark, Zawahiri contended, was "the blessed battles in New York and Washington and Pennsylvania"—the 9/11 attacks.[2]

The revolutions in Egypt and Tunisia, according to Zawahiri's statements and the statements of important affiliate groups like al-Qaeda of the Arabian Peninsula (AQAP), were about the publics' hatred of the brutal and corrupt governments they faced and the rulers' pro-Israeli, pro-U.S., and anti-Islamic policies. Al-Qaeda missives went on to declare that the revolutions were not done, however. Other Arab tyrannies must fall, and in all the countries a true Islamic state must replace them, something the jihadists believe the United States will oppose while seeking to reinstall tyrannical, pro-Israel, pro-U.S., and anti-Islamic regimes.[3]

Whether al-Qaeda finds success in its propaganda matters tremendously to the United States and its allies as they continue to combat global terrorism. Al-Qaeda is dangerous not only because it has hundreds of skilled fighters, but also because tens of thousands of Muslims have found its calls for violent change appealing. When dictators reigned supreme in Arab lands, al-Qaeda could score points by emphasizing the struggle against despotism—Zawahiri even wrote a book denouncing the crimes of Mubarak. When dictators such as Mubarak fall, however, al-Qaeda loses one of its best recruiting pitches: the repression Arab governments inflict on their citizens.

Genuine democracy would be a particular blow to bin Laden's acolytes. "If you have freedom, al-Qaeda will go away," claims Osama Rushdi, a former spokesman of the Islamic Group, Egypt's most important jihadist body. Rushdi may be too optimistic. Nevertheless, movement toward a free press, free elections, and civil liberties throughout the Middle East will highlight the least appealing part of al-Qaeda's dogma: its hostility toward democracy and desire to build a theocratic caliphate that is deeply unappealing to the vast majority of Arabs and Muslims, even those who may publicly or privately cheer al-Qaeda's willingness to "fight the power."

As Shibley Telhami discusses in chapter 2, democracy is a popular concept in the Arab world. In contrast, al-Qaeda believes that democracy is blasphemous, arguing that it places man's word above God's. So if Tunisia's emerging democratic movement does not soon hand over power to clerics to build an Islamic state, then—according to a statement by al-Qaeda in the Islamic Maghreb (AQIM)—"the duty upon Muslims in Tunisia is to be ready and not lay down their weapons."[4] Al-Qaeda's message is clear: it will fight democracy as hard as it has fought dictatorship. That is not a message likely to resonate with most of those turning the Arab world on its metaphorical head.

Even more ominous for al-Qaeda is the way in which Ben Ali and Mubarak fell. These momentous changes occurred without an initial blow being struck against the United States. Al-Qaeda has long insisted that Muslims must first destroy the region's supposed puppet-master in Washington (or Jerusalem) before change could come to Cairo, Tunis, or Tripoli. Moreover, al-Qaeda leaders also have long insisted that violence carried out in the name of God is the only way to force change. Zawahiri once demanded that Egypt's youth either take up arms against the Mubarak government or, if that proved impossible, "go forth to the open arenas of Jihad like Somalia, Iraq, Algeria and Afghanistan."[5] The youth of Egypt and Tunisia did not heed his call, of course; the protesters were peaceful and largely secular in their demands.

As a further blow, a number of prominent jihadist scholars praised the protesters' courage and endorsed the revolutions despite their largely secular demands. In danger of becoming virtually irrelevant by the Arab Spring, al-Qaeda has modified some of its fundamental tenets, declaring that peaceful protest is fine when it works, but that "people need to prepare themselves militarily" because nonviolence often fails and because the United States will back a counterrevolution.[6]

Furthermore, the very fact that young people are leading the revolution is bad news for al-Qaeda. Young people, especially young men, are al-Qaeda's target audience—the ones its propagandists expect to take up arms. For over a decade, al-Qaeda portrayed its young fighters as the most audacious and honorable defenders of Muslim lands in the face of Western aggression. Now, youth in the Arab world are afire with very different ideas of freedom and nonviolent action. Recent events have shown idealistic young Arabs who dream of a new political order under which they need not travel to Afghanistan or Iraq to engage in jihad but can accomplish more by remaining in their own countries and marching peacefully against their authoritarian rulers. Al-Qaeda recruitment is likely to suffer as a result.

THE CHAINS COME OFF

U.S. counterterrorism officials have long praised countries such as Egypt and Tunisia for their aggressive efforts against terrorism and their cooperation with the United States. The United States has also tried to work with Algeria, Mali, Mauritania, and Morocco to improve counterterrorism cooperation against AQIM. Until recently, even Muammar Qadhafi—long derided as the "mad dog of the Middle East"—was valued as a partner against al-Qaeda.

From a strictly counterterrorism perspective, Arab tyranny often served U.S. purposes. American counterterrorism officials preferred to work with authoritarian leaders because their regimes generally had a low bar for imprisonment and detention. The United States could send a suspect captured in Europe to Egypt and be assured that he would be kept in jail. Of course, this low bar also meant that many minor players and innocent individuals were swept up in security service roundups. The Egyptian regime was even willing to threaten the families of jihadists, putting tremendous pressure on militants to inform, surrender, or otherwise abandon the fight. Assuming that a truly democratic government comes to Egypt, such easy incarceration and ruthless threats against militants and their families will undoubtedly disappear, and that is an advantage for al-Qaeda and its ilk.

Indeed, one measure of how much progress the Arab regimes are making toward democracy will be how much their security services are purged. The same security services that have fought al-Qaeda and its affiliates have also imprisoned peaceful bloggers, beaten up Islamist organizers, and censored pro-democracy newspapers. Those who replace the current security forces will not necessarily be friendly to Washington, and the governments they report to may also be more standoffish with the United States than their predecessors. If new governments take popular opinion into account, as democratic leaders typically do, cooperation will not be as close as it once was. Many of the new political players, particularly the Islamists, see the United States as a repressive power that aids Israel and other enemies. It is hard to imagine an Egyptian government that includes the Muslim Brotherhood instructing the Egyptian security services to work as closely with the CIA as they did under Mubarak.

If the United States sides in the current turmoil against authoritarian regimes, be they old friends like Saudi Arabia or on-again, off-again adversaries like Syria, cooperation will suffer if these regimes survive. Although these countries and the United States share an interest in fighting al-Qaeda, the autocratic regimes have, at times, also used intelligence and other forms of cooperation as a way to build goodwill in Washington. Anger they feel at a U.S. "betrayal" may show up in a cooler attitude regarding counterterrorism collaboration.

Regional cooperation—vital because al-Qaeda and its affiliates cross state boundaries—was fitful at best before the recent unrest. Arab regimes often distrusted each other owing to regional rivalries, territorial disputes, and personal conflicts. Now it may become even harder, as old regimes and new leaders greet one another with suspicion.

AL-QAEDA'S POSSIBLE RETURN

Despite the challenge secular revolutions have posed to al-Qaeda's narrative, there is a chance that the organization could rebound and become even stronger operationally. The Arab Spring left security services and institutions in turmoil. During the recent unrest, some jails in Libya and Egypt emptied, putting experienced jihadists back on the street. In both countries, many of the jailed jihadists had actually turned away from violence in the last decade, arguing—quite publicly—that their struggle had failed, reflected a misunderstanding of Islam, and led to the death of innocent people. This renunciation of jihad produced bitter polemics against al-Qaeda (which were met by an even more vitriolic al-Qaeda response). Nevertheless, among those released there are some unrepentant extremists, who are willing to wreak havoc upon their enemies, and who threaten U.S. interests at a time when Arab governments are least willing and able to monitor and constrain them. In countries where autocrats still cling to power, the security services may become even less effective against jihadists. The services of Algeria, Bahrain, and Morocco are now likely to make democratic dissenters their top priority, rather than suspected terrorists.

New governments may also be unlikely to go after the recruiters, fundraisers, propagandists, and other less visible elements of the jihadist movement. Freedom of speech may protect some activities. Moreover, many Arabs consider jihadist fights in Iraq, Afghanistan, and elsewhere to be legitimate. For their part, jihadists are media savvy and will try to exploit any new freedoms in these countries to expand their propaganda efforts. These individuals are often far more important to the movement's overall health than the actual bombers and assassins, and their activities can more easily be cloaked as legitimate political action.

A particularly tricky issue is the role of Islamist parties such as Egypt's Muslim Brotherhood. From a counterterrorism point of view, a greater political role for Islamists may be good news. Although Brotherhood theologians such as Sayyid Qutb helped inspire the modern jihadist movement, and many important al-Qaeda operatives were Brotherhood members before joining bin Laden, there is bad blood between the two organizations. In his book, *The Bitter Harvest,* Zawahiri bitterly criticized Brotherhood leaders because they rejected violence and participated in politics. Hamas, a Brotherhood spinoff, has frequently lashed out at al-Qaeda. In turn, Zawahiri has blasted Hamas for adhering to cease-fires with Israel, not immediately implementing Islamic law in Gaza, and otherwise deviating from the pure faith of jihadism. To prevent these ideas from eroding its support, Hamas has harshly repressed al-Qaeda–inspired jihadists in the Gaza Strip. If the Brotherhood gains influence in a new Egyptian government, as seems likely, the group will carry its feud with al-Qaeda into power. And because many jihadists grew out of the Brotherhood's ranks, it knows this community well and can effectively weed out the most dangerous figures.

From the U.S. perspective, ignoring the Muslim Brotherhood and other Islamist movements seemed prudent when they had little chance of gaining power. Now, the tables have turned, and the United States needs to catch up. In particular, it should make it clear that it does not want these movements excluded from a democratic system of government. Inevitably, this will lead to tension as Islamist groups seek policies that do not jibe with U.S. preferences.

But excluding the Brotherhood from power would be worse, for it would endanger the U.S. campaign against al-Qaeda. In 1992 the Algerian government nullified elections that Islamists won, provoking a bloody civil war. This war, in turn, radicalized the country's Islamist movement and dragged Algeria into a frenzy of violence that alienated bin Laden as well as ordinary Algerians with its horrific attacks on fellow Muslims. Bin Laden worked with a faction of Algerian jihadists to establish a like-minded group there, which later became the core of AQIM. Although such an extreme scenario seems unlikely in Egypt and Tunisia, preventing the Brotherhood from participating in government would alienate younger, less patient Islamists. They, in turn, might find al-Qaeda's message attractive, believing that the new government is inherently anti-Islamic.

Here, perhaps, counterterrorism clashes with other U.S. interests. Although the Brotherhood is mouthing all the right slogans, its commitment to true democracy is uncertain. In any event, it will likely seek to restrict the rights of women and minorities in Egypt's political life. Islamist organizations in general are highly critical of U.S. military intervention in the Middle East, skeptical of cooperation with the CIA, and strongly opposed to anything that smacks of cooperation with Israel. The catch, then, is that supporting a strong Islamist role in government risks creating a regime less friendly to the United States; but, excluding the Islamists risks radicalizing the movement and reinvigorating al-Qaeda.

Opportunities for al-Qaeda will also arise if unrest turns to civil war, as in Libya. Civil wars erupted in Afghanistan, Chechnya, Iraq, Somalia, and Yemen largely for local reasons, with little jihadist involvement, but over time al-Qaeda and like-minded groups moved in. First they posed as supporters of the opposition. Afterward, they spread their vitriol using their superior resources to attract new recruits, while the surrounding violence helped radicalize parts of the population. The tactic has been successful, as al-Qaeda now has a strong presence in all these countries.

Counterterrorism after the Revolution

The Obama administration must prevent al-Qaeda from exploiting the increased freedom of movement it has in the post–Arab Spring Middle East, and at the same time take advantage of the fact that the group's message has been discredited. U.S. public diplomacy efforts should highlight al-Qaeda's criticisms of democracy and emphasize the now-credible idea that reform can come through peaceful means. The message should be spread by television and radio, as always, but particular attention should be paid to the Internet, given the importance of reaching young people.

The United States must also continue to put pressure on al-Qaeda's senior leadership in Pakistan, even though these operations at times cost Americans the support of Pakistanis. Part of the reason al-Qaeda has been slow to respond to the events of the Arab Spring is that formulating a response to such momentous change requires extensive consultations among the group's leaders. Yet because of aggressive U.S. efforts in Pakistan, holding an open meeting is highly dangerous—doing so could invite a deluge of Hellfire missiles from U.S. drones. American operations in Pakistan are therefore vital to limiting al-Qaeda's ability to coordinate its message and strategy, and influence events in the region.

As mentioned, one of the greatest risks to the United States lies in the civil wars that have broken out across the region as autocrats resist democratization. The danger is that al-Qaeda will exploit such conflicts, even trying to partner with rebels, so the United States must make clear to opposition figures early on that it will consider aid, recognition, and other assistance, but only if the jihadists are kept out of the rebels' ranks. When jihadists set up shop in the Balkans in the 1990s, U.S. pressure helped persuade Bosnia's mainstream Muslim leadership to purge them. The United States has a major advantage because al-Qaeda cannot compete when it comes to resources or bestowing international legitimacy on the rebels. For the rebels, then, the choice should be easy.

Al-Qaeda will, of course, try to have it both ways. Should the United States not intervene in areas of conflict, the group will blast (and has blasted) the United States as being a friend of tyranny. And should the United States intervene, as it did in Libya, al-Qaeda will try to drum up anti-U.S. sentiment among the locals, while portraying any U.S. intervention as part of a U.S. master plan to conquer the Middle East. In Libya, for example, Zawahiri declared that the American intervention will allow the United States to "occupy it and control its affairs."[7]

In the long term, and more quietly, the United States should renew efforts to train the intelligence and security forces of new regimes. The first step will be simply to gain their trust, as new leaders are likely to see their U.S. counterparts as bulwarks of the old order and a possible source of counterrevolution. Many of the new security service leaders will be inexperienced in countering terrorism. Even more important, they will be unaccustomed to the difficult task of balancing civil liberties and aggressive efforts against terrorism. Here the FBI and Western domestic intelligence services have much to offer. Restoring such cooperation will take time and patience, but the United States should make this a priority.

For now, there is reason to hope that revolutions in the Arab world will benefit U.S. counterterrorism efforts. But hope should be balanced with the recognition that in the short term al-Qaeda will gain operational freedom and that the United States and its allies need to recast their messaging, maintain pressure on the al-Qaeda core, prepare to counter al-Qaeda attempts to exploit civil wars, and renew intelligence cooperation if they are to prevent the organization from reaping long-term benefits from the upheavals.

PART II

COUNTRIES IN TRANSITION

10

DEMOCRATIZERS?

The Pursuit of Pluralism

KENNETH M. POLLACK

If the people of the Middle East could have their way, all of the states there would morph into democracies overnight. As Shibley Telhami makes clear in chapter 2, the Arab publics (as well as the Iranian people) have an overwhelming desire to adopt democratic forms of government.[1] They see this as both an end in itself and a means to stop the economic, social, and political stagnation of their countries. It is for this reason that, across the region, democracy has been the rallying cry for the rebellions that have rocked the lands from Marrakesh to Mashhad.

But the road to democracy is a hard one. Many nations have started down that path only to find themselves lost or waylaid. They may end up as what Fareed Zakaria has called "illiberal democracies," pseudopluralist states in which a group or individual employs the trappings of democracy to legitimize an otherwise autocratic system.[2] In other instances, loosening the structures that hold together internal cleavages may cause the state to collapse altogether, producing intercommunal violence, civil wars, and failed states instead.[3] Likewise, uncorking the djinn of public opinion, with its passions and prejudices, can push an immature democracy into wars and other foreign misadventures that can, in turn, divert the would-be democracy toward a wide range of unintended and undesirable consequences.[4] In short, there is no guarantee that states setting out on the road to democracy will get there, or that they will even get to someplace good.

Nevertheless, and whether the United States likes it or not, a number of Arab states have started down the hard road of democratization. Iraq was the first, although it achieved that distinction by an external (American) intervention that few Arabs outside of Iraq see as having been legitimate. So far, Iraq's democratization has been herky-jerky, with progress in some areas threatened by serious deficiencies in others. Palestine, too, began moving in that direction with its first elections in 1996, but in the interval it has not even come as far as Iraq. Moreover, elections in 2006 produced a Hamas victory that in effect has left democratization dead in the water, even as Prime Minister Salam Fayyad has forged ahead in creating a high degree of good governance. Initial efforts to bring about a democratic transformation have also been under way in Tunisia and Egypt since they overthrew their dictators. Libya too, has now joined this list, although its path—via both popular revolution and civil war—combines many of the challenges facing Egypt and Tunisia with those of Iraq, making for a particularly tricky road to democracy.

In each of these states, an autocrat has been eliminated, and the leadership that has now emerged seems desirous of building a democracy. In each of these countries, however, democratization remains in its infancy. Moreover, all have a contingent of powerful political and military actors who are either ambivalent or outright hostile to democracy, and their wishes may ultimately win out. Thus the movement toward democratization could easily come off the rails in any one of them. Iraq, Palestine, Tunisia, Egypt, and Libya remain works in progress, with civil war, failed states, military dictatorships, Islamist autocracies, and a variety of other calamities lurking just around the corner. It is going to take a great deal of effort on the part of the people of these countries—along with more than a little luck—to bring their nations to stable pluralism.

If they are able to do so, of course, it will be a tremendous step forward not only for their own people, but also for the region as a whole. Stephen Grand points out in chapter 3 that successful democracies have a demonstration effect. Indeed, one reason that democratization in the Middle East will be hard is that neither the Arab states nor Iran have ever known true democracy, certainly not liberal democracy. Lebanon from 1943 until the outbreak of civil war in 1975 was the closest the region came, and while scholars now believe that it was a more durable state than once believed, it was never more than a quasi-democracy with a variety of critical nondemocratic features.[5] A variety of other Arab states and Iran have all enjoyed proto-democratic or semi-democratic periods, although all of them ended suddenly and after too little time for democratic norms and institutions to have taken root.

The absence of such democratic models for the Arab world is part of the challenge facing Iraq, Palestine, Egypt, Libya, and Tunisia; but if they are able to overcome this and the other challenges of democratization, in the decades ahead their success will likely pave the way for similar transformations elsewhere across the Middle East. By the same token, if they fail, their failure might well stymie the aspirations of other would-be democrats across the region, who will find their countrymen less willing to embark on a path that elsewhere produced disaster.

FINDING THE RIGHT PATH

Part of the challenge of democratization is that every nation that has already made the journey seems to have followed a somewhat different path, and there is no set process for building a democracy. Every country finds its own way there, and many that have failed did so even though they tried to follow the examples of ones that succeeded. That said, a number of factors do appear consistently in most successful democratizations. Similarly, in every case of failed democratization, at least one of these elements (if not several) has been notably absent.[6]

One critical factor is the creation of new institutions with the strength to stand up to one another.[7] After all, a core aspect of democracy is the notion of checks to government power and balances to any entity within the government. Such a system needs strong institutions outside of the government (typically called civil society groups) that are able to push back on any inappropriate expansion of its authority. A variety of strong institutions must also reside within the government (such as an apolitical military, an independent judiciary, and respected oversight bodies) so that no one entity is able to have its way all the time on all matters, not even the president or prime minister.

But the concept of "strong" is more difficult to define. Strength certainly derives from an institution's legitimacy, because without legitimacy, no institution can both push back on other institutions *and* do so within the law. Beyond that, strength can derive from a variety of factors that elicit society's respect for an entity's actions, such as the power of the purse, the power to employ (state-sanctioned) violence, popularity, tradition, or a norm of noninterference.

The creation of a democratic political culture is another critical aspect of democratization.[8] Indeed, the culture of democracy is intimately bound up with the strength of institutions, and to a considerable extent each builds upon, and is strengthened by, the other. By way of example, the reason the U.S. military has never overthrown the government has nothing to do with the strength of other institutions. If the U.S. military wanted to, it could deploy the 82nd Airborne Division to Washington in about twelve hours, and its troops could take control of the city in about another twelve hours. Nothing—not the Constitution, not the Supreme Court, and certainly not the Washington, D.C., police force—would be in a position to stop them. What prevents this scenario from occurring is not any checks and balances, but rather the fact that members of the U.S. military have been fully inculcated into a political culture of democracy in which it is impossible for them to even imagine mounting a coup. Ultimately, political culture, more than anything else, is the source of the strength and stability of mature democracies.

Another important aspect of democracy (related to the previous two aspects) is the rule of law. This means that all disputes—whether between individuals, groups, or government agencies, or between the government and any other entity—are handled by a defined and transparent legal system overseen by an independent judiciary able to render judgment and have those judgments respected and implemented *by all parties*. Consequently, the rule of law is bound up with strong institutions, because it takes strong institutions ("strong" in the sense of legitimate, respected, and able to enforce their decisions) to remain independent of corruption and political pressure and able to see their decisions implemented. But it also requires the development of a democratic political culture because often these institutions lack the *physical* power to enforce their decisions without the consent of the parties themselves, the larger populace, security organizations, or all of these entities. And that consent flows from a democratic culture that inclines the individuals who make all of those organizations do what is right, what is in keeping with the laws of the country.

Yet another key ingredient of democratization is patience. Democracies are not built overnight. English democracy took centuries. American democracy took decades, as did Japanese democracy, and that of virtually every other country. It takes a great deal of time to build institutions, develop a new political culture, and establish the rule of law, in large measure because so much of the process is about changing how people think and act, and in some cases it requires a new generation (or more than one) to effect such changes.

Nowhere in the Middle East are there strong institutions *and* a political culture of democracy *and* the rule of law.[9] Indeed, in Egypt, Iraq, Tunisia, Libya, and Palestine, a few strong institutions are the only partial building block of democracy that currently exists. The Egyptian military, Iraq's Shi'i Marja'iyeh (the Shi'i religious leadership in Najaf), and the Palestinian Fatah and Hamas parties are all powerful organizations for different reasons. But each has important limits on its legitimacy as a political actor, none is properly balanced by other governmental or civil society organizations, and none is restrained by a pervasive democratic political culture. And without those constraints, instead of creating the foundations for democracy, they could all wreak havoc on the nascent efforts at democratization.

THE DANGERS OF DEMOCRATIZATION

Since Pericles walked the streets of Athens, democracies have been threatened by a variety of dangers, and new democracies far more so than mature, established ones. It is neither possible nor necessary to catalogue all of the different problems that the Arab states might face. Rather, it is far more useful to point out the most likely threats that they will have to overcome.

The first, and most obvious, threat to new Arab democracies is that they will be hijacked by individuals or groups looking to take power, hold on to it, and rule autocratically, all with the help of the veneer of legitimacy conferred by elections. The problem of illiberal democracy has become widespread in the twenty-first century. Indeed, many of the Arab autocracies have regularly held sham elections to try to legitimize their rule—and as Steven Heydemann of Georgetown

University has pointed out, they are now even willing to rig elections so that they only win 77 percent of the vote, rather than their traditional insistence on outcomes that showed them winning 99 percent. In Heydemann's words, "77 is the new 99."[10]

Unfortunately, there are numerous candidates who might want to play the role of illiberal democrat. Most worrisome to Westerners are Islamist parties. As Shadi Hamid discusses in chapter 4, Islamist intentions across the region have become the subject of considerable debate.[11] Preliminary evidence suggests that at least some of the leading Islamist parties may have moderated their views and no longer seek to transform their societies in ways that clearly would be inconsistent with democracy. Ultimately, however, the jury is out, and as in many other cases in history, how the Islamists behave when they take power will depend on the circumstances in which they take it: If they take power in functioning democracies with relatively strong institutions, strong rule of law, and a burgeoning democratic culture to underpin all of it, then Islamist groups might prove to be nothing more than pious, Islamically inclined politicians no more dangerous to the state than Christian Democrats in Europe. On the other hand, if they take power when institutions, rule of law, and democratic culture are weak or nonexistent, they might move in a very different direction—either because the most radical elements in the group maybe able to prevail or because the intention of the bulk of the members was always to use the guise of elections to take hold and dismantle whatever democratic progress had taken place. At this point, there is not enough evidence to be certain either way, and it is plausible that the region may see some Islamists behaving in a responsible, democratic fashion while others try to seize power, oppress minorities, and otherwise subvert the values of democracy.

Arab militaries are an equally important danger to nascent democracies. At one time, the Middle East was the most coup-prone region of the world, and even now the militaries of the Arab world and Iran remain highly politicized. Yet many Arabs, Americans, and people throughout the world are looking to the Egyptian and Tunisian militaries to play the role of "guardians" of the political transition—preventing anyone from subverting the democratic system while it slowly takes root. However, if they fear that a new civilian leadership might deprive them of their various perks (including their massive economic enterprises and widespread graft), they might decide to take over the political system—perhaps installing a docile civilian to serve as a figurehead leader.[12]

Of course, all democracies are dangerously prone to following demagogues, but new democracies especially so because the naiveté of the electorate in immature democracies makes it easier for demagogues to seduce voters and shout down opponents. In Iraq, Muqtada as-Sadr would like very much to play this role, but is not helped by the fact that he is a miserable speaker, possesses zero charisma, and has even fewer leadership skills. At some point, however, someone else may come along with a silver tongue, and the masses might follow him down a path of ruin, as so many others have in the past.

Still another challenge for new democracies lies in preventing the "tyranny of the majority." In the basest forms of democracy, the group with the most votes can do whatever it wants. Successful democracies usually try to establish voting rules and other procedures that encourage alliances across social groups. So an individual may be in the minority on one issue (say, the level of taxation) but in the majority on another (say, the level of spending on education). Politicians are encouraged to reach across groups to gain office. In such a system, group identities do not translate into political cleavages.

To further guard against the tyranny of the majority, successful democracies include provisions to protect the rights of minorities—ethnic, religious, geographic, tribal, *and* political—and enforcing those rights is one of the most critical elements of the rule of law. The failure of the Iraqi government to protect its Christian minority may not doom the polity, but it is an ominous sign for the future. Moreover, Iraq's Kurds and Sunnis are deeply fearful that the country's Shi'i majority will employ the machinery of the state to oppress, or even attack, them. Not only must this problem be eradicated, but even the circumstances in which the fear of such tyranny persists is deeply harmful to democratization because it erodes the trust that is the foundation of a democratic culture.

Meanwhile, the corollary to the principle that democracies take time to build is that speed kills. It is not that moving too quickly is the sin itself—especially early on, it is important to take advantage of the momentum for democracy. Rather, moving too fast opens the door to all of the problems discussed in this chapter and a host of others. As the disastrous elections in Iraq in 2004 and 2005 and in the Palestinian territories in 2006 demonstrated, moving to elections prematurely simply plays into the hands of those willing to do anything to get votes, those willing to undermine the system, and those best organized before the old regime fell—typically the Islamists. In Iraq, the Balkans, and elsewhere, it has been a recipe for warlords, militia leaders, criminals, demagogues, and a rogue's gallery of others to secure political power. And once they have gained it, they have usually used their positions in government to hang on to power by any means possible, legal and illegal.

In addition, there is some evidence to suggest that new democracies tend to get into wars fairly frequently, and often for the worst reasons. Again, demagogic leaders may try to build popular support by blaming the troubles of the new state on foreign malfeasance, or they may simply use long-standing grievances with a neighbor to divert popular attention from intractable problems at home. Middle Eastern autocracies have certainly not been immune to these tendencies. New democracies in which conspiratorial and, in some ways, deeply spiteful populaces suddenly have a voice in policy should not necessarily be expected to be immune, especially if the legitimacy of key leaders is challenged at a time when neither the states' institutions nor their political cultures are strong enough to check their behavior.

These are the challenges that the newly democratizing states of the Middle East have chosen to try to overcome. They are not insurmountable—scores of other states have beaten them—but neither are they paper tigers. They are very real dangers, and how the new Arab democracies do in confronting them will tell us a great deal about their own future and that of the entire region.

11

Iraq

The Roller-Coaster of Democracy

Kenneth M. Pollack

Iraq was arguably the first of the Arab states to begin the transition to democracy and is arguably the first modern democracy in the Arab world. At the very least, it is the Arab state that is farthest along in a transition to full-fledged pluralism. For that reason, the Obama administration has begun to hail Iraq as a model to be emulated by other nations of the region.[1] Such claims need to be taken with more than a grain of salt. Because Iraq's transition to democracy was the result of an American military invasion that much of the Arab world saw as illegitimate, and was then followed by a precipitous descent into intercommunal civil war that terrified the region, Arabs tend to disparage the Iraqi experiment as irrelevant and unrepresentative of their aspirations or, indeed, as proof of why democracy is bad. While this perspective is unfair to Iraqis and naïve regarding the actual similarities, it is a reality that will likely temper Arab willingness to look to Iraq as an example.

Nevertheless, Iraq does have a number of important lessons to teach other would-be Arab democracies. Unfortunately, most of these lessons are negative, falling into the category of "things to avoid when democratizing," if not the inevitable problems attendant upon democratization.

Beyond its value as a lesson, however, Iraq's future will be significant to the legacy of the Arab Spring and the transformation of the region. If Iraq succeeds in blazing a path toward democracy, it will encourage others to follow suit. If Iraq fails, however, it will discourage others and will allow the extant regimes to use the Iraqi example to justify rejecting reform (let alone revolution) as they have been doing since 2003. Moreover, because Iraq is a fragile state emerging from an intercommunal civil war, the failure of its democratic experiment would most likely mean a recurrence of hostilities, which could have a profound impact on all of the neighboring states. Thus Iraq's successful transition to a stable democracy is of much more than just illustrative value to the rest of the region.

THE RISE OF IRAQI DEMOCRACY

Iraq's problems began in 2003 when the United States invaded the country, toppled the totalitarian dictatorship of Saddam Hussein, and put nothing in its place. As a result, the United States created a failed state and a security vacuum, which in turn spawned a severe terrorism problem; an insurgency among the Sunni tribes of western Iraq, who felt threatened by the belated and ham-fisted American efforts to create a Shi'i-Kurd–dominated government; and eventually an intercommunal civil war in 2005–06.[2]

Indeed, the creation of a power vacuum in Iraq did what it also did in places like the former Yugoslavia, Congo, Lebanon, and Afghanistan: it enabled various criminals and demagogues to lash out at their rivals and use preexisting (even long-dormant) differences as causes to mobilize support and employ violence, which in turn prompted other groups to take up arms to defend themselves, setting off a fear-based spiral of attacks and reprisals that pushed the country into all-out civil war.[3]

In 2006–07 the United States recognized its principal mistake and sought to remedy it. Washington deployed 30,000 additional troops to Iraq and, of far greater importance, adopted a counterinsurgency strategy (more properly, a low-intensity conflict strategy, since the problems of Iraq were much more those of a civil war than an insurgency) emphasizing the protection of the populace, the disarming of militias, and the enforcement of cease-fires among the various warring groups. In effect, this approach, often referred to by the nickname "the Surge," filled Iraq's security vacuum, reversing all of the pernicious trends that had pushed the country into civil war in the first place.

The Surge also reversed the relationship between Iraq's political leadership and the Iraqi people. While the security vacuum prevailed, average Iraqis became dependent on the warlords, insurgent leaders, organized crime bosses, and militia leaders who dominated Iraqi politics, because only they could provide security and access to basic necessities like food, water, electricity, medical supplies, and the like. As a result, the warlords could do as they liked, confident that the people would be forced to vote for them in elections and do their bidding at all other times. Once the United States shifted to a counterinsurgency/low-intensity conflict (COIN/LIC) strategy, however, it was able to break the power of the militias and insurgents because they could no longer control the people, and the people did not have to rely on them for protection. Instead, the people could rely on the Americans and Iraq's rebuilt security forces.[4]

The impact of this change was both dramatic and profound, resulting in the rapid suppression of the civil war and the equally sudden emergence of real democratic politics in late 2008 and 2009. Now that the people of Iraq were not dependent on the warlords, they were able to vote on the basis of their hopes, not their fears. As a result, the provincial elections in 2009 crippled the militia-based parties and rewarded nationalists, technocrats, and secularists. Indeed, the principal beneficiary was Prime Minister Nouri al-Maliki, who was then seen by most Iraqis as a truly national figure who had smashed the worst of the militias, particularly in April 2008 when he ordered operation Charge of the Knights, which drove the Sadrist Jaysh al-Mahdi militia from Basra. Across the board, the powers that be were routed, disgraced, and marginalized. Once the people demonstrated that, without the fear of violence, they could redistribute power through elections, Iraq's political leadership was forced to scramble to learn democratic politics. Therefore the militias had to become political parties and, for the first time ever, had to figure out how to deliver goods, services, and policies to the people—their constituents—rather than simply take as much as they could by force or graft.

This trend culminated in Iraq's March 2010 national elections. Iraqis voted overwhelmingly for the two coalition parties that they saw as being most nationalist and secular, and the least sectarian and beholden to the old militias: Ayad Allawi's Iraqiyyah and Maliki's State of Law. Although Iraqiyyah was largely made up of Sunni members and State of Law largely Shi'i, to average Iraqis they represented progressive secular politics focused on rebuilding Iraq's government and economy and appeared free of the taint of the militias and the civil war. Between them, they captured 180 of the 325 seats in the Iraqi parliament, reflecting a tremendous victory for democracy in Iraq.

The Revolution in Danger

Today, the remarkable flowering of democratic politics that took place as a result of the Surge is under threat. Since the 2010 elections, the pattern of progress has started to unravel. In part the problems date back to 2004, when the United States foolishly handed back sovereignty to Iraq long before the country had a leadership ready to wield it responsibly, and then compounded the problem in 2008 by agreeing to a three-year Security Agreement that allowed American troops to remain in Iraq, but at the price of further restricting their ability to act independently to ensure that the government continued to abide by its own democratic rules. The trend continued after the Obama administration took office in 2009, when the United States began to disengage from Iraq more broadly, withdrawing troops, redirecting resources, diminishing the political capital Washington was willing to expended on the country, and allowing the Iraqi leadership a much freer hand to act as they pleased. The overall result has been that the external incentive structure that forced Iraq's political leaders to do the right thing in 2008–10 is being removed before Iraq has the strong indigenous institutions or political culture that would preserve those incentives. Not surprisingly, Iraq's many bad leaders are going right back to acting badly.

With Iraq's political leaders now dangerously unwilling to make meaningful compromises, the country is beset by political paralysis. There is no movement toward overall reconciliation, and there is equally little movement on addressing day-to-day governance or even pressing policy needs. All of the parties are hewing to the terrible Middle Eastern dictum "When I am weak, how can I negotiate; and when I am strong, why should I?" Those with leverage see it as allowing them to dictate to their rivals, and those without are doggedly clinging to their positions in the hope that something will reverse the situation.

Of greatest concern is the fact that this breakdown in Iraq's democratic political process has begun to reengage the dynamics that drove the country to civil war in 2005–06. All of the mistrust, fear, and desires for revenge that fueled the civil war never disappeared; they merely abated when the emergence of democratic politics in 2009–10 suggested that the country might be able to reach compromises to address the underlying grievances and allow for economic, political, and social progress across the board. Yet now various extremist groups have begun to resort to violence to try to break the political logjam in their favor, causing other groups to worry that this is the wave of the future and to consider rearming as well. It is a very dangerous pattern, which if allowed to fester could drive Iraq right back into civil war.

IRAQ AND THE ARAB SPRING

Iraq has not been immune to the effects of the Arab Spring, although it has affected Iraq differently from other Arab countries. On February 25, 2011, Iraqis organized their own "Day of Rage" in Baghdad, mobilizing thousands to come out in protest of the government. What was striking about Iraq's unrest was that the protesters called on the government to get its act together, rather than demanding the overthrow of the government. Iraqis were angry at the inability and/or unwillingness of their government to address the persistent lack of basic services—particularly, but not limited to, electricity—and the high level of unemployment. Certainly, there were those who wanted to see the prime minister replaced, but there was no demand for Iraq's political system to be replaced. The Day of Rage demonstrated that Iraqis remain committed to democracy, even if they are frustrated by its inability to address the problems they face.

The mass demonstrations in Baghdad panicked the political leadership there, just as it did elsewhere around the region. But again, where Iraq differed was that the leadership did not have to ask whether they needed to reform the system, but whether they needed to compromise with their political rivals to hammer out the kind of deals that could break the political logjam hamstringing Iraqi governance. Although this should have been a positive moment of truth for Iraq's leaders, the ultimate outcome has not been so good.

Briefly, Iraq's leadership attempted to do the right thing. Prime Minister Maliki announced that within 100 days, every ministry would have to demonstrate tangible progress or else face the consequences. But then he did nothing to energize his ministries, and when the 100-day deadline came and went there were no consequences—for him or any of his ministers. The moment passed. No one was held accountable. No one suffered for failure or even inaction. And so, while the Arab Spring at first seemed like it might get the Iraqi political leadership moving in the right direction again, instead, it simply reinforced the leadership's sense that it could ignore the desires of the electorate with no consequences. This repeated the outcome of the 2010 parliamentary elections, in which the Iraqi political leadership effectively ignored the desire for change expressed by the electorate through their vote, and therefore reinforced the lesson that the political process or peaceful protests do not effect change.

Thus the Arab Spring had a different impact on Iraq than elsewhere in the region because Iraq is—at least for now—a proto-democracy. But that impact has not necessarily been positive. Indeed, if the Arab Spring reassured Iraqi politicians that they need not fear the retribution of their constituents, it may actually have undermined Iraq's fragile democratic progress.

Where the impact in Iraq was similar to that in the rest of the region was in Kurdistan. Many young Kurds took to the streets on February 25 to express their anger and frustration with the autocratic behavior of the Kurdistan Regional Government (KRG). They focused particular ire on the Patriotic Union of Kurdistan (PUK), which holds the southeastern half of the Kurdish region. There the Gorran (Change) Party mobilized thousands to demand an end to PUK/KRG control in a deliberate echo of the revolts in Tunisia, Egypt, and elsewhere around the region.

There too, the leadership took notice, but not always in constructive ways. On the positive side of the ledger, PUK leader (and Iraqi president) Jalal Talabani seems to have given greater political leeway to KRG prime minister Barham Saleh to pursue a reform agenda—something he has argued in favor of for many years. It is not clear how much room Saleh will have, or how much support he will get, but Saleh has championed the idea that it is critical for the KRG (and particularly the PUK) to reform if it is not to suffer the same fate as Mubarak's regime. On the negative side of the ledger, the Kurdish leadership chose to move two brigades of its Peshmerga military forces south of the disputed city of Kirkuk, which triggered a crisis that was only resolved by immediate, high-level American intervention. By all accounts, the Kurdish leaders hoped to divert popular anger away from themselves by picking a fight with the Arab leadership in Baghdad—an extremely dangerous precedent for Iraq's future.

THE FUTURE AMERICAN ROLE

Iraq is a special case in large part because of America's unique role, for better and worse.[5] Given the unlikelihood that the United States will invade another country in the Middle East any time soon, it is difficult to generalize from Iraq's experience. Similarly, the United States made a long series of egregious and gratuitous mistakes during the first few years after Saddam's fall that plunged Iraq into civil war. As Dan Byman points out in chapter 24, civil wars create a set of powerful dynamics that are extremely difficult for any state to overcome and put behind it, and this, too, makes Iraq's transition to democracy unusual among the other states of the region. On the positive side, however, the American invasion and reconstruction of Iraq have given the country an external supporter that no other state in the region is likely to have. Although America's role and interest in Iraq have unquestionably diminished and will decline further, as of this writing, the United States still has a large ground force in the country and a commitment to Iraq's success that give Iraq a unique advantage. Indeed, Washington retains considerable sway, and this could be preserved (and perhaps even bolstered) by the savvy employment of America's long-term aid relationship with Iraq.

This is important because Iraq has no strong institutions that could serve as the guarantors of its political system—no monarch or disinterested military that can enforce the rules of the game and prevent any of the players from subverting the system. Many Iraqi military officers would probably relish the role of acting as the ideal type of the "Turkish" military that stands above politics and merely ensures that everyone else works within the parameters of the system. Because the Iraqi military had a long history of mounting coups in the pre-Saddam era, however, the new Iraqi government has been working fervently to politicize it in commissarist fashion (as Saddam did) and ensure its loyalty to the prime minister.[6] Thus America still has a critical role to play in Iraq's future.

Iraq remains devastated by thirty years of Saddam Hussein's misrule, three foreign wars, a dozen years of comprehensive international sanctions, and an intercommunal war. As a result, Iraq needs all the help it can get. Its armed forces continue to rely on the U.S. military for combat and logistical support, and Baghdad has an ongoing desire to purchase large amounts of American weaponry and to retain U.S. training for its still-nascent armed forces and internal security services. The Iraqi economy remains a basket case, and Iraqis from across the country and across the political spectrum recognize a need for American assistance in rebuilding the country's bureaucracy, infrastructure, agricultural sector, education system, and industrial base. Iraq must also be helped to reintegrate into the global economy, overcome a series of lingering diplomatic problems, and avoid excessive intervention by any of its neighbors. Many Iraqis even recognize that their fragile democracy would benefit from a continued American military presence in the country—if only to restrain predatory indigenous politicians and neighboring states alike.

All of these Iraqi needs and desires create leverage for the United States. Anything the Iraqis want from the United States can and should be provided, but only if Iraq's political leaders continue to behave in a manner consistent with the country's long-term best interest in building a strong democracy—which also just happens to be America's principal interest as well. Thus the most important source of American influence moving forward is conditionality. Virtually all American assistance needs to be conditioned on the Iraqi political leadership guiding its country toward greater stability, inclusivity, and effective governance. The Strategic Framework Agreement (SFA), a partnership document between Iraq and the United States that was initiated by the Iraqi government, provides a foundation for this type of assistance. If the United States wants to maintain leverage in Iraq, the SFA must ultimately deliver outcomes that Iraqis value.

Because Iraq's domestic politics is the key to the future stability of the country, and because it remains so fragile, it must be the primary American focus. Iraq's political leaders have a less than stellar record of obeying the rules of the new political game, and the United States continues to provide the ultimate insurance that no group will be able to completely overturn the system and dominate others. Specifically, this will mean that several important standards must be met: continued progress on democracy, transparency, and the rule of law; continued development of bureaucratic capacity; no outbreak of revolutionary activity, including coups d'état; no emergence of dictators; reconciliation among the various ethno-sectarian groupings, as well as within them; a reasonable delineation of center-periphery relations, including a workable agreement over the nature of federalism; and an equitable management and distribution of Iraq's oil wealth, as well as the overall economic prosperity that must result from such distribution.

On the economic front, U.S. assistance to Iraq should be conditioned upon the Iraqi authorities putting in place oversight and accountability mechanisms aimed at limiting the corrupting effects of Iraq's oil economy. The central challenge in this area will be to reconcile U.S. and Iraqi expectations for future American aid and find creative ways to use the SFA and whatever assistance the American Congress and administration are willing to make available in an era of sharply declining resources. The United States will need to be up front with the Iraqi government and make clear that it cannot expect a Marshall Plan and that Washington will only be making relatively limited additional financial contributions to reconstruction. Fortunately, there are key areas of the Iraqi economy where U.S. diplomatic support, technical assistance, consulting services, and technology and knowledge transfers could deliver substantial benefits at relatively low cost.

Although the United States has vital national interests invested in the future of Iraq, it would be a mistake for Washington to determine that it will remain committed to Iraq under any and all circumstances. As long as Iraq's leaders are moving their country in the right direction, the United States can and should remain willing to help the Iraqis generously. However, the United States must acknowledge that the Iraqis may choose not to move in that direction. Many Iraqi leaders resist the rule of law, constitutional limits, and other constraints when they do not suit their own narrow interests. They may regard America's role in Iraq as a hindrance to their acting as they please. If Iraq's leaders are not willing or able to act in a manner consistent with good governance, the rule of law, and the need for national reconciliation, then the risks to Iraq's future stability are so grave that they should cause the U.S. government to reevaluate its level of commitment to the U.S.-Iraqi partnership and the resources it is willing to invest in it.

12

EGYPT

The Prize

SHADI HAMID

When Omar Suleiman announced Hosni Mubarak was stepping down from power on February 11, 2011, the world gasped. Mubarak was everywhere referred to as "pharaoh" because he ruled like a monarch and his regime seemed as immovable (in all senses of the word) as the pyramids. Until it stagnated in the last decade of his reign, Egypt was considered the Arab world's cultural, political, and military leader. It is also the Arab world's largest state, with more than 80 million people. This means that virtually one of every four Arabs is an Egyptian. And it was, along with Saudi Arabia, one of America's most important allies in the Middle East, a second pillar to replace the shah of Iran after he fell.

Thus what happens in Egypt will have profound consequences for the entire region. If democracy wins out—if Egyptians succeed in building a stable, pluralistic system—then people across the Middle East will believe that they can and should do the same. By the same token, if Egypt's bid for democracy fails—if it ends in chaos or just a new form of autocracy—then many will conclude that democratization is impossible in the Arab world. Therefore, what happens in Cairo will not stay in Cairo. And Arabs will be the richer or poorer for it.

UNDERSTANDING THE REVOLUTION

When a regime's survival is at stake, the key question is whether it will shoot its own people. The Tunisian police did—over 300 civilians were killed—but that apparently was not enough. It was easy to imagine the Egyptian regime being more determined and more ruthless in responding to the unprecedented protests that began on January 25, 2011. But more than this, President Mubarak had other things going for him as well, including a close relationship with the United States and a strong, well-paid military that had long served to protect the regime rather than the people.[1] Moreover, the Mubarak regime appeared to have a broader base of support than did its Tunisian counterpart. Altogether, millions of government bureaucrats, police officers, and other functionaries depended on the government for their livelihood. In addition, a powerful business elite had emerged as a dominant force in Egypt's economic and political life.

As in Tunisia, impressive economic growth—5 to 7 percent annually—went hand in hand with economic inequality. The increased visibility of certain businessmen who would join the ruling party, "win" a parliamentary seat, and acquire immunity only heightened the sense of injustice. While Prime Minister Ahmed Nazif's cabinet was courting business and investment, unrest was growing, with protests in Cairo becoming a routine sight. Outside the capital, the labor movement was mobilizing. According to the Solidarity Center, from 2004 to 2008 more than 1.7 million Egyptian workers participated in over 1,900 labor-related protests, which went largely unnoticed in the West.[2] While not explicitly political, they provided a vivid backdrop for the anger and frustration mounting throughout Egyptian society.

If there was any doubt the status quo was untenable, the November 2010 elections—arguably the most fraudulent in Egyptian history—confirmed what many long suspected: reform through the existing system had become impossible. The main parliamentary opposition, the Muslim Brotherhood, was reduced from 20 percent of the seats in the previous parliament to zero. In the first round of voting, the ruling National Democratic Party (NDP) won 99 percent of the seats. Less than two months later, the revolution began.

THE JANUARY 25 REVOLUTION

Over the course of eighteen days, an estimated 6 million Egyptians took to the streets, according to the Abu Dhabi Gallup Center, making the uprising the largest pro-democracy mobilization in Arab history.[3] The most prominent figures in the revolution were young, educated, and Internet-savvy, usually liberal or leftist in orientation. Islamists also played a critical role in the Tahrir Square protests, though they purposely downplayed their involvement.[4] While some ad hoc committees, such as the Revolutionary Youth Coalition, were formed to coordinate actions in the square, the protests, as in Tunisia, were largely leaderless. This led to difficulties when negotiating with the regime. Established groups, such as the liberal Wafd Party, the so-called Committee of Wise Men, and the Muslim Brotherhood all entered into a "dialogue" with then vice president Omar Suleiman. There was, however, a considerable gap between the protesters in Tahrir—many of whom vocally opposed any negotiations as long as Mubarak was in power—and those claiming to represent them.

From the beginning, protesters seemed to grasp the critical role of the military. They self-consciously tailored their chants—one of the most popular was "the army and the people hand in hand"—to appeal to the troops, many of whom sympathized with the opposition. Perhaps as a result, while the police and security forces received orders to shoot the protesters, and many of them did, the military held its fire, a decision that proved crucial. The army was simply not willing to oversee a bloodbath to protect a president who had clearly lost legitimacy. Ironically, the army had been for decades a key pillar of the Mubarak regime. But when it counted most, it forced Mubarak—a decorated air force veteran—to resign after more than three decades in power.

A MILITARY-GUIDED TRANSITION TO . . . WHAT?

Egypt's revolution, rather than representing a sharp break with the past, may be better understood as a popularly inspired military coup. It was the military that ultimately forced Mubarak from power, although the Supreme Council of the Armed Forces (SCAF) was responding to the demands of the millions of Egyptians who had taken to the streets. In this, the events of February 2011 bear some similarity to those of 1952, when the Free Officers overthrew the unpopular King Farouk and were immediately hailed as liberators by the Egyptian people.[5]

In February, the SCAF was thrust into a new, unprecedented role for which it appears ill-suited—governing. The generals seemed to understand that most Egyptians want to see a democratic transition, and the army is at least observing this on the surface, but it is doing so in an undemocratic fashion. Indeed, since Mubarak's fall, the military has operated in a largely opaque manner, issuing cryptic and at times threatening "communiqués" and failing to consult with civil society on major decisions.

On March 9, 2011, the army's honeymoon with the revolutionaries ended. Troops charged into Tahrir Square, dispersing by force protesters who had been continuing their demonstrations since Mubarak stepped down. The army detained nearly 200 people, taking them to a makeshift prison at the Egyptian Museum where many were tortured. Women were subjected to "virginity tests," a practice that officials later defended.[6] Since then, the SCAF has operated in a legal vacuum with little accountability and virtually no oversight. According to Human Rights Watch, more than 5,000 civilians were tried between February and April 2011. "The military courts," Human Rights Watch has reported, "typically handle groups of between five and thirty defendants at a single trial, with a trial lasting 20 to 40 minutes."[7] Fearing repercussions, the Egyptian media (still principally the state media of the Mubarak era) have been reticent to cover either the torture allegations or the use of military tribunals.

Over the opposition's objections, the military was able to impose its own timetable on the democratic transition. In a victory for the SCAF, Egypt ratified a series of constitutional amendments on March 19 by a wide margin—77 percent to 22 percent. Most liberal activists opposed the changes, whereas the

Muslim Brotherhood and Salafist groups lobbied aggressively for a yes vote. This marked the first major break between Islamists and liberals, who had worked closely together during the revolution. The second major break came on May 27, the day activists billed as Egypt's "second revolution," when they organized protests against the SCAF. For the first time, the Brotherhood vocally opposed holding protests in Tahrir Square, saying that they represented a "revolution against the people."[8] Liberals and leftists accused the Brotherhood of colluding with the military council. The divisions were further solidified when tens of thousands of Islamists turned out in Tahrir Square on July 29. What was originally supposed to be a "Friday of Unity" became one dominated by Islamist sentiment and slogans.

The ideological polarization is exacerbated by real power imbalances. The Muslim Brotherhood is the single most powerful force in Egyptian politics today, while Salafis have made their political presence known for the first time. On the other hand, youth movements, liberals, and leftists have been surprisingly weak and disorganized, given their important role in the revolution. This imbalance has played into fears of Islamist dominance in a post-Mubarak government, fears that are not necessarily unfounded. Ironically, part of the Islamists' success has been due to their flexibility, whereas secular forces have been bogged down by tactical rigidity and paralyzing fragmentation. The Brotherhood, for example, supported Friday protests before opposing them, forged a convenient alliance with the military, appointed a Christian as the vice president of its new political party, and moved to the political center on certain issues while holding out the possibility of an electoral pact with far-right Salafis. Of course, the Brotherhood has the advantage of over eighty years of political experience.[9]

Liberals—whose support base remains limited to Cairo and Alexandria— have had trouble gaining traction. They have been effective at organizing protests in Cairo but less so at longer-term institution and party building. They have focused their attention on ending military tribunals, prosecuting old regime officials, supporting women's and minority rights, and extending the timetable for elections (because early elections would favor Islamists). While liberal and leftist activists have successfully used protests to force important concessions from the military, including a postponement of parliamentary elections, it is unclear to what extent these issues resonate with the broader public. Indeed, some Egyptians have voiced concern over a breakdown in security and a stalling of the economy that they attribute to the impatience of the "kids in the square."

Designing Institutions

The rules under which elections are held are the core of a democracy. Yet in Egypt there was relatively little public debate over what system of government would be most appropriate. Perhaps this is not surprising because as Joel Barkan and his coauthors note, political elites in transitional situations "rarely [consider] the likely outcomes of alternative forms of electoral systems when choosing a system for their countries."[10] Egypt had grown accustomed to the first-past-the-post system used in the United States and Britain, where the candidate with the most votes in any single district wins the seat. With minimal consultation, the SCAF announced in July 2011 a mixed system with one half of the seats to be elected under a winner takes all system and the other half under proportional representation.[11] This despite the fact that most opposition parties had come out in support of a full proportional representation system.

The electoral system will have a disproportionate effect on what follows, likely contributing to a further polarization of opinion. The new parliament is entrusted with forming the 100-member Constitutional Council that will draft a new constitution. Egypt's sequencing is the reverse of Tunisia's, where parliamentary and presidential elections will come only after the drafting of a new constitution. Prominent liberal parties and individuals had suggested emulating Tunisia by adopting a constitution first. After that failed, they, along with the military council and cabinet, moved to establish supra-constitutional principles that would protect the "civil" nature of the state and limit Islamist influence over the constitution-drafting process.

One of the reasons for the different transitional approaches taken in Tunisia and Egypt is the distinctive nature of the latter's long-running autocracy. The authoritarian rule of President Anwar al-Sadat and then Hosni Mubarak was never total, nor did it ever attempt to be. In the early 1980s, Mubarak launched political reforms and promised a national dialogue with the opposition. The opening of political space, and the optimism it helped create, contributed to a perception that Egypt was moving toward democracy. In 1989 Nazih Ayubi wrote: "There are [great] hopes that the President will use his significant constitutional and political powers to advance the democratization process even further, and on a much larger scale."[12] The parliamentary elections of 1984 and 1987 were the freest Egypt had ever seen since the 1940s (although far from free and fair in absolute terms). This would not last.[13] Facing not only a rising Brotherhood but also a low-level insurrection waged by radical Islamists, the regime shifted to all-out repression in the early 1990s. The regime, however, never attempted to eradicate the Islamist opposition, as the Algerian and Tunisian regimes had.

Under Mubarak's increasingly autocratic rule, the Brotherhood still managed to win an unprecedented 20 percent of the seats in the 2005 elections. Even though parliament was weak and subservient to the executive branch, it was still a major venue of contestation for both the minority of opposition deputies and the dominant ruling party. Beginning in 2003, a vibrant independent press flourished, and despite Mubarak's best efforts, the judiciary, one of the country's most respected institutions, fought hard to maintain its independence. Egypt, then, did not need to reinvent the wheel. In many ways, the transition has been led by elements of the same regime, using a variation of the same constitution and vying for seats in the same parliament. The Brotherhood was the largest, most popular group before the revolution. And it remains so after the revolution.

At the same time, the revolution has made major gains. Mubarak, his sons, and a host of senior officials are being investigated and tried for crimes under the old regime. The sight of the former president in the defendants' cage of a Cairo court alongside the reviled former interior minister Habib al-Adli was for many a cathartic testament to the achievements of the revolution. The dreaded state security apparatus has technically been dissolved, the ruling party disbanded, and its headquarters set on fire. The March 19 referendum was the first reasonably free poll in Egypt in more than six decades. The question, then, is whether these ostensibly major changes reflect real transformations in the country's power relations and political structure.

A REVOLUTION IN FOREIGN POLICY?

Revolutions have consequences, but not always where one might expect. In the months after Mubarak stepped down, the SCAF, along with the civilian leadership, made a number of bold foreign policy moves, which, taken together, suggest a change in emphasis in foreign policy with important implications for the United States. With a deteriorating economy and a challenging political environment, the government has tried to appeal to popular sentiment by adopting a more critical stand toward Israel, reaching out to Hamas, brokering Palestinian reconciliation, and welcoming diplomatic ties with Iran. As Ken Pollack observes in chapter 10, there is a fine line in new democracies between public servants attempting to reflect the views of their constituents—especially in foreign policy—and demagogues looking to build their popularity by scapegoating foreign countries. It is not yet clear where Egypt will come out on such matters.

In idealizing the Egyptian revolution, analysts argued that the protests were not about America, Israel, or foreign policy, but about democracy and dignity. The line between domestic and foreign policy, however, can be blurry. Mubarak was illegitimate in the eyes of his people not just because he was a repressive dictator but also because Egyptians felt that he was too close to the United States and Israel. If Egypt continues to move toward democracy, governments will need to be more responsive to public opinion. And public opinion happens to be firmly against U.S. policy in the region. In several Arab countries, including Egypt, U.S. favorability ratings have been lower under President Barack Obama than they were under President George W. Bush.[14] Remarkably, in a Pew poll conducted *after* their revolution, more Egyptians said they approved of both Osama bin Laden and al-Qaeda than they did the United States.[15]

As Egypt's new leaders struggle to deliver on economic and political reform, the temptation to grandstand on foreign policy will only grow, particularly during election season. International relations scholars call this the "diversionary theory of international conflict"—the notion that foreign conflicts are emphasized to divert attention from mounting problems at home.[16] Young democracies, newly confident and eager to distance themselves from their predecessors, are particularly susceptible. The crisis of relations with Israel that followed the August 2011 killing of six Egyptian policemen in Sinai is a sign of what is to come. Under the Mubarak regime, protests outside the Israeli embassy would have been quashed. After the Sinai incident, they were not and eventually turned violent. An Egyptian, now affectionately known as "Flagman," managed to climb the embassy building and take down the Israeli flag to raucous cheers. The various presidential candidates and political parties seem to all agree on few things. One of them, though, is the necessity of distancing Egypt from Israel.

These shifts will be reinforced by greater Islamist representation in parliament. Though the Muslim Brotherhood has offered commitments to respect established treaties with other powers—read Israel—such statements are often followed by a promise to leave such questions to the general public, to be determined democratically.

Whatever the preferences of Islamist parties, Egypt will still be bound by old constraints. The country remains vulnerable during what will likely be a long, difficult phase of transition. It can afford to irritate its Western allies but not antagonize them. The United States and the European Union, as Egypt's most important donors, will play a critical role in supporting the country's economic and political revitalization. One obvious red line is the peace treaty with Israel. Fortunately for Egyptian policymakers, a successful model is already in place, with Turkey, Qatar, and Iraq managing to be U.S. allies while maintaining friendly relations with the other side in the Arab cold war. Such an independent posture will likely infuriate some U.S. officials, who grew accustomed to an Egypt that reliably opposed Iran, Hamas, and Hizballah's growing influence in the region.[17] The simple reality is that—on both domestic and foreign policy—Egypt will never again be what it was under Mubarak.

Looking Ahead

According to the same Pew poll cited earlier, a plurality of Egyptians, nearly 40 percent, say the United States played a negative role during the uprising.[18] In stark contrast with the Washington narrative—that President Obama dealt with events in Egypt relatively well—many Egyptians feel that the United States was behind the curve and sided with the protesters only at the very end.

That said, the situation in Egypt is fluid, as are popular attitudes. Egypt, like Tunisia, finds itself in dire economic straits, with GDP growth falling from around 5 percent to 1 percent.[19] The tourism industry, which provides jobs for one out of seven working Egyptians, took a severe hit, with the number of tourists dropping by 46 percent in the first quarter of 2011.[20] Meanwhile, the SCAF rejected aid from the International Monetary Fund on the grounds that this would allow foreigners to dictate Egyptian economic policy. Interestingly, that has not stopped Egypt from accepting large amounts of money from Saudi Arabia and other Gulf states, despite the fact that those countries almost certainly do hope to influence Egyptian behavior.

Inevitably, Egypt's recovery will be slow and uneven. The United States, along with its European allies, has an opportunity to step in and provide much-needed financial assistance. In his May 19 speech, Obama announced $1 billion in debt relief and $1 billion in loans. Considering the scope of Egypt's economic difficulties, this is a paltry amount, particularly when spread out over the course of several years (as a point of comparison, Saudi Arabia's economic aid package to Bahrain—a country whose population is about 1/150 of the size of Egypt's—was $10 billion over ten years). Unfortunately, the U.S. Congress, searching for ways to slash the foreign aid budget, seems unlikely to appropriate significant additional funding.

The United States already gives $1.5 billion in annual assistance to Egypt, with $1.3 billion going to the military. The Obama administration can use this aid as leverage to hold the SCAF to its democratic commitments. The military has extensive economic interests in Egypt, which will make it a critical player in the country's politics long after it returns to the barracks. The political scientist Joshua Stacher estimates that the military controls at least one-third of the Egyptian economy.[21] Will its stake in the economy lead it to intervene in political life if radical or populist forces threaten its interests? More generally, will the SCAF insist on retaining "reserve powers" similar to those held by the Turkish military during the 1980s and 1990s? That is certainly the direction it seems to be heading in, with various announcements that the supreme commander of the armed forces will not be appointed by the civilian leadership, that the military budget will be determined by the military, and that the military will have the right to intervene in domestic politics if certain red lines are crossed. As suggested in chapter 7, so far it seems that the Egyptian military is following the playbook of the real Turkish military, not its fictional ideal.

The ultimate role of the Egyptian military is an open question—and one that will shape Egypt's democratic transition for both better and worse. For now, the military seems willing to allow a carefully controlled transition toward a more democratic government. But it has shown little tolerance for continued dissent, let alone public disorder. Doubtless, the generals decided to let Mubarak fall to a great extent in the belief that doing so would end the unrest. In addition, the military has shown no inclination to give up its considerable stake in the civilian economy; again, the army probably backed Mubarak's ouster in the belief that doing so would leave it best positioned to retain its coveted position at the graft trough. Thus at least two key questions linger over Egypt's transition to democracy, and they will likely be confronted very soon: What happens when a new civilian leadership tries to assert the rule of law and civilian control over the military? And, what happens if the Egyptian military believes that "democracy" is getting out of hand? Whether Egypt continues on the path to democracy that so many in Tahrir Square fought for may well be decided by the resolution of those critical issues.

Taking a wider perspective, although the transition remains largely regime-led and seems to favor established elements, there is little doubt that Egyptian politics has been fundamentally changed by and since Mubarak's fall. In an increasingly open political space, an array of groups and parties, spanning a wide ideological spectrum, are contending for influence, power, and legitimacy in a new Egypt. This competition can lead to conflict—increasing instances of sectarian clashes are particularly worrying—but it can just as easily lead to coalition-building, a renewed political ethic, and, ultimately, slow but steady movement toward greater democracy.

13

TUNISIA

Birthplace of the Revolution

SHADI HAMID

One of the Middle East's most repressive countries, Tunisia, was an unlikely candidate for revolution. There were pockets of dissent—in the trade unions, for example—but no strong, coordinated opposition. President Zine al-Abidine Ben Ali seized power from the senile Habib Bourguiba, a popular Ataturk-like modernizer, in a bloodless 1987 coup. In what was known as the "Jasmine Revolution," Ben Ali promised greater freedoms and democratic reform. Soon, however, he oversaw an unprecedented crackdown on opposition groups and civil society.[1] Unlike Bourguiba, he did not cement his rule through extensive patron-client networks or by appeasing powerful elites. A relative outsider with no political base of his own, Ben Ali opted instead to concentrate power within a small clique, including his family members, who demanded a share in nearly every sector of the economy.

Ben Ali adopted a paranoid style of leadership, routinely firing ministers who showed too much leadership or gained popular support. He relied instead on apolitical technocrats. While this allowed the president to dominate the cabinet and micromanage daily affairs, it also allowed for relatively competent administration, particularly in the economic sphere.

Tunisia was hailed as an economic success story, with impressive annual GDP growth of around 5 percent, comparatively high standards of living, and a sizable middle class. In 2008 the then managing director of the International Monetary Fund, Dominique Strauss-Kahn, called the Tunisian economy an "example for emerging countries," while the World Bank named it a "top reformer" in regulatory reform.[2] But with economic growth came economic inequality and growing regional discrepancies between coastal cities, such as Tunis, and the poorer interior. The first protests broke out in December 2010 in the south, in the now iconic town of Sidi Bouzid, before spreading throughout the rest of the country.

Toppling a Dictator

Within a month, Ben Ali had fallen, the first time in history that peaceful protests had unseated an Arab autocrat. The uprising was buoyed by both its spontaneity and leaderless nature. Without identifiable figures, the regime found it difficult to demonize or decapitate the protesters. Placing the blame on Islamist groups, long the regime's preferred political weapon, no longer found traction. Tunisia's Islamists were either in prison, dead, or in exile. By destroying its main opposition in the early 1990s, the regime lost one of the last justifications for its own existence.

Unsure of how to respond to the protests, the regime resorted to brute force. According to a report by the UN special rapporteur, an estimated 300 Tunisians were killed, a strikingly high number in a nation of 10 million people.[3] Yet the crackdown did little to quell the protests; they only grew larger. Ultimately, the army, one of the country's few independent institutions, sided with the opposition and forced Ben Ali out. The following week, Army Chief of Staff Rachid Ammar stood before Casbah Square in Tunis, telling the gathered crowds that he would act as "guarantor of the revolution."

Though Ben Ali fled to Saudi Arabia, control still lay in the hands of the president's associates from the ruling Constitutional Democratic Rally (RCD). Mohamed Ghannouchi, Ben Ali's longest-serving prime minister, defied calls for his resignation and stayed on, promising to leave after elections. The presence of Ghannouchi and other ruling party figures galvanized a coalition of leftists, communists, trade unionists, Islamists, and human rights activists, who continued holding protests against successive interim cabinets. Calling themselves the Committee to Defend the Revolution, they forced a series of concessions from Ghannouchi's cabinet, including amnesty for political prisoners and legalization of political parties. The ruling party and state security apparatus were dissolved, and governors appointed under the old regime were forced to step down.

On February 27, 2011, Ghannouchi resigned. On March 31, the new prime minister, eighty-four-year-old Beji Caid al-Sebsi, announced that elections for a constituent assembly would be held in July 2011, meeting the protesters' last core demand (owing to difficulties in organizing the polls and registering voters, the elections were postponed to October 23, 2011). Some analysts have called this Tunisia's second revolution.[4]

A Different Kind of Transition

Plagued by sporadic violence and governed by cabinets widely regarded as illegitimate, Tunisia's democratic experiment initially seemed adrift. The international community, for its part, largely shifted its attention to the violent protests and civil conflict in Libya, Bahrain, Yemen, and Syria. Tunisia ran the risk of becoming not just a forgotten revolution but a failed one to boot.

Unlike many of its neighbors, Tunisia had no independent media or vibrant political life of which to speak. Civil society had been eviscerated by Ben Ali's unrelenting repression. There were some token legal opposition parties, but they were denied any real parliamentary representation. The trade unions, under the Tunisian General Union of Labor (UGTT), enjoyed considerable support among workers but had generally avoided outright confrontation with the regime.

Lacking an autonomous opposition and civil society, Tunisia would have to start from scratch, building new organizations and institutions from the ground up. This sort of sharp break from the past is often destabilizing, at least in the short run. De-Ba'thification in Iraq is the most extreme example of a problem that all post-authoritarian polities face. The Ben Ali–led RCD was a mass organization of as many as 2 million people that served less as a political party than as a vehicle for career advancement. If a Tunisian failed to join the party, the government viewed the person as suspect. Despite this, the Higher Council for the Realization of the Revolutionary Objectives—the powerful commission entrusted with setting the course for the country's transition—imposed a ban on the candidacy of those who had served in the ruling party in positions of "responsibility" in the past decade.[5] This raises a question with no easy answers: At what point does punishing regime officials and preventing their participation become counterproductive? In the coming years, Tunisians will need to find their own balance between the desire for accountability and the need to forgive and rehabilitate those who might otherwise seek to undermine the country's transition to democracy.

At the same time, "starting from scratch" can bring clear benefits. As Joel Barkan, Paul Densham, and Gerard Rushton note, leaders in transitional situations tend to choose electoral systems "on the basis of what is familiar."[6] Most Tunisians have no memory of real electoral competition, so there is less interest in using the old system—primarily a "winner takes all" block voting system—as the basis for discussion.[7] The same can be said for constitutional reform. Where Egypt modified its existing constitution, Tunisians gave high priority to the early election of a constituent assembly, which would then draft an entirely new document. Notably, the debate surrounding the sequencing of the transition—namely, whether to draft a constitution or hold elections first—has been less contentious than in Egypt, where the issue has sharply divided Islamists and liberals.

The unvarnished authoritarianism of the Ben Ali regime appears to have produced a greater sense of unity among the population in general and the opposition in particular. While secular groups still do not fully trust Tunisia's Islamists, both sides have been able to work together effectively in the Committee to Defend the Revolution and other coalitions.[8] This bodes well for Tunisia's fledgling transition. So, too, do Tunisia's relatively small size and its homogenous population. Tunisia does not have the deep tribal, ethnic, and sectarian divisions that most of the other Arab countries facing revolts do. Moreover, the country's professionalized (and relatively underfunded) military has a history of nonintervention in civilian affairs.[9] The danger of a Turkish-style activist military—along with the coups and polarization that can come with it—is something that Tunisia is well-positioned to avoid.

That said, the negative effects of autocracy—especially one as total as Ben Ali's—cannot be undone overnight. Twenty-three years of Ben Ali, and the previous thirty years of Bourguiba, had forged Tunisia's political habits into a potent mixture of repression, rampant corruption, and clientelism. As Tunisia presses ahead, these legacies will shape the country's democratic transition for better and for worse.[10]

INTEGRATING ISLAMISM

Al-Nahda, formerly the Movement of the Islamic Tendency (MTI), has emerged as one of Tunisia's most powerful political forces in the post-revolutionary period.[11] This should not be surprising. The Islamist group was the main challenger to Ben Ali's rule in the late 1980s. Despite widespread rigging in the 1989 parliamentary elections, al-Nahda—which like Egypt's Muslim Brotherhood was denied legal status—won 15 percent of the vote and as much as 30 percent in key cities, including the capital Tunis. This was too much for Ben Ali, who soon launched a brutal crackdown on Islamists, sending as many as 10,000 of the group's members to prison. Al-Nahda's leader, Rachid Ghannouchi (not to be confused with Mohamed Ghannouchi, Ben Ali's prime minister), went into exile in London, where he remained for the next twenty years.[12] When he returned to Tunisia on January 30, 2011, he received a hero's welcome, with over 1,000 of his countrymen greeting him at the airport.[13] After waiting for nearly thirty years, the party finally gained legal recognition on March 1, 2011.

Because of Ben Ali's successful crackdown, Tunisians under the age of thirty—more than half the population—have little memory or firsthand experience with al-Nahda. Still, in a crowded field of more than fifty new political parties, the party has a brand that few others can claim—none suffered more for its opposition to the Ben Ali regime. Not only does the party have unique revolutionary legitimacy, but it also has a natural base upon which to draw as Tunisia's main Islamist group. The human rights activist Ilhem Abdelkifi has noted, "Tunisians are religious. [Al-Nahda] will attract those who do not know where to go."[14]

Al-Nahda has long portrayed itself as a more moderate version of the Egyptian Brotherhood. It puts less emphasis on Islamic law and has pledged to uphold the country's Code of Personal Status, which guarantees equal pay for women, grants them the right to initiate divorce proceedings, and bans polygamy. On democracy, Ghannouchi has said, "We drank the cup of democracy in one gulp back in the 1980s while other Islamists have taken it sip by sip."[15] Since his return to Tunis, Ghannouchi has repeatedly compared al-Nahda to Turkey's Justice and Development Party (AKP), a party that, despite its Islamic origins, reconciled itself to the secular confines of the Turkish state. That said, al-Nahda's rank and file are almost certainly more conservative than its self-consciously moderate leadership. The country's secular middle class, meanwhile, remains wary of the group, recalling that in the 1980s some of its members were implicated in violence against the state.

Yet, with a proliferation of Islamist parties, al-Nahda no longer has a monopoly on the Islamist vote. While Salafis are still less popular in Tunisia than elsewhere in the region, they appear to be gaining strength. Al-Nahda is well aware of this, and Ghannouchi, like his counterparts in Egypt, is counting on their support: "I think most Salafis will either join us or back us in the elections. Or they will face marginalization. The Tunisian milieu is not conductive to extremism. A free Tunisia cannot be a base for extremism."[16]

THE UNITED STATES AND TUNISIA

The United States was slow to respond to the outbreak of protests in Tunisia, in part because Ben Ali was considered an ally (from 1987 until its demise, the Ben Ali regime received $349 million in U.S. military aid, much of it meant ostensibly for counterterrorism efforts). On January 7, 2011, nearly three weeks into the protests, the State Department encouraged "all parties to show restraint as citizens exercise their right of public assembly."[17] Just three days before Ben Ali fled—and with well over 100 people already killed—Secretary of State Hillary Clinton said that the United States was "not taking sides." Remarkably, in an interview on the Al Arabiya satellite channel, Clinton said that she had not spoken to the Tunisian foreign minister since the protests began nearly twenty days earlier.[18] The Obama administration explicitly condemned regime violence only after Ben Ali had already fled on January 14. In a White House statement, President Obama applauded "the courage and dignity of the Tunisian people" and called on the Tunisian government to "hold free and fair elections in the near future."[19]

A financial response was also lacking. In the Obama administration's proposed foreign assistance budget for fiscal 2012—submitted in February 2011, after the Tunisian revolution—the amount of democracy assistance to Tunisia was actually zeroed out (from $500,000 in fiscal 2011).[20] In March 2011, the State Department's Middle East Partnership Initiative (MEPI) stepped in, announcing $20 million in funds to assist Tunisia's transition. Another $12 million from various accounts of the U.S. Agency for International Development was also quickly allocated, addressing immediate economic, democracy, and governance needs.[21] Beyond this initial $32 million, the United States has not pledged any additional funding but is offering loans and investment support through the G8's $20 billion Deauville Partnership.[22]

The lack of explicit commitments to Tunisia is disconcerting, given its precarious economic situation. After experiencing an average of nearly 5 percent annual GDP growth for seven years, the International Monetary Fund forecast a drop to 1.3 percent for 2011.[23] According to Tunisia's National Institute of Statistics, around 300,000 of the country's university graduates are unemployed. The government has warned that (official) unemployment could jump to 20 percent, up from the current 13 percent.[24] Taking all of this into account, the Tunisian government says it needs a total of $125 billion over five years to boost employment and revive the economy.[25] The U.S. and EU unwillingness, or inability, to further prioritize the country's transitional needs suggests that Tunisia will need to diversify its sources of financial support.

A PROMISING FUTURE FOR TUNISIA?

Of all of the Arab countries, Tunisia is probably the best positioned to transition to a functioning democracy, however flawed it may be. Its social, educational, and economic indicators are all above average for the region. Empirical studies have long shown that wealthier democracies are better able to sustain themselves.[26] Of course, the causal arrows in the relationship between economic and political success have never been entirely clear.[27] That said, the consensus that better economic indicators increase in some measure the probability that democracy will survive seems sound. This puts Tunisia in good stead, compared with many of the Asian, sub-Saharan African, and Eastern European countries that have undergone transitions in recent decades.

Indeed, Tunisia, at this early stage, seems to have evaded many of the problems—sectarian conflict, military intervention, and crippling ideological polarization—that have hobbled other Arab countries. For a country that seemed on the brink of civil war between Islamists and secularists in the late 1980s, this is a remarkable turn of events. Even in the best of circumstances, however, democratic transitions are messy and uncertain, as will no doubt be the case in Tunisia. Still, it would be only fitting if the country that sparked the Arab Spring became its first real success.

14

LIBYA

From Revolt to State-Building

AKRAM AL-TURK

Four days after the fall of Egypt's Hosni Mubarak, Libyans began their own struggle to topple a long-standing dictator. But whereas the authoritarian regimes in Egypt and Tunisia fell quickly, Libya's regime did not. Muammar Qadhafi refused to step down. Instead, he rallied key supporters and defiantly launched a repressive campaign to try to quell the uprising. Within weeks, a disparate group of anti-Qadhafi revolutionaries managed to win control of most of the eastern part of the country and was making advances in the west. Qadhafi's forces rallied, recapturing a number of opposition-controlled cities and would have likely defeated the revolutionaries had it not been for NATO's eleventh-hour intervention that turned back government troops from the gates of Libya's second-largest city, Benghazi. Six months after the initial protests, in late August 2011, opposition forces, buttressed by aerial attacks and on-the-ground intelligence support from NATO allies, overran Tripoli and claimed control of most of the country.

The fall of the Qadhafi regime, however, was the easy part. The challenges now facing Libya will be difficult to address, and different from those encountered in neighboring countries undergoing transition. The effects of the six-month civil war, which caused the deaths and displacement (both internal and external) of thousands of Libyans and migrant workers, will pose many long-term challenges for the country and, potentially, for the region. As Dan Byman explains in chapter 24, civil wars can have detrimental long-term effects, including, but not limited to, an exacerbation of preexisting societal divisions and the potential radicalization and militarization of some segments of society. In the case of Libya, the consequences of the conflict could harden the historic geographic division (between the eastern and western parts of the country), cause tensions between Libya's many tribes, and, of course, pit remnants of Qadhafi's regime against the forces of the new government. Although Libya does not have the sectarian divisions found in Iraq or Lebanon, it does have an Amazigh (Berber) population that makes up 10 percent of Libya's citizenry and that was discriminated against under Qadhafi. The war has also created new cleavages, with young men often identifying more with the anti-regime brigades with which they fought than with the overall opposition leadership that claims to command them.

In addition, Libya will have to deal with the aftereffects of Qadhafi's four decades of totalitarian rule. During his reign, Qadhafi not only consolidated power but also imposed his own bizarre ideology on Libyans, restricting political and civil society activity in ways that hindered any semblance of political or democratic development in the country. Consequently, many of the challenges in building credible, rule-bound institutions, developing a vibrant civil society and independent media environment, reforming the economy, and ensuring political representation—let alone instilling a democratic political culture—in a post-Qadhafi Libya will prove daunting.

Anti-Qadhafi forces are notionally led by the National Transitional Council (NTC), a political body formed in Benghazi soon after the uprisings began. The body, composed of an executive board and members who represent city councils throughout the country, has been recognized as the legitimate authority of Libya by more than eighty countries and regional and international organizations, including the Arab League and the United Nations. Although the NTC, led by former government officials Mustafa Abdel Jalil and Mahmoud Jibril, has become the face of the anti-Qadhafi opposition and is now tasked with leading the transition, it is still unclear how much command it has over all of the opposition fighters and how legitimate it is in the eyes of all Libyans. How well it leads the transition and begins to address the challenges facing the country will, in all likelihood, determine the fate of post-Qadhafi Libya.

FOUR DECADES OF TOTALITARIAN RULE

Beginning with the 1969 coup that brought him and his Free Officers' Movement to power, Muammar Qadhafi ruled Libya with an iron fist. Qadhafi viewed his takeover as not merely a military coup d'état, but the beginning of a complete transformation of the social, economic, and political fabrics of the country. The core of that transformation consisted of Qadhafi's ideology, which could be generously described as a hodgepodge of Arab nationalism, Islamic socialism, cult of personality, and a hierarchical political system that he claimed would allow Libyans to directly manage their own lives. In reality, however, Qadhafi—and the network of regime loyalists he built over time—was the decisionmaker in the *Jamahiriya* (a word he coined to mean "state of the masses").

Qadhafi's network extended far beyond his family, tribe, and members of the 1969 revolution. Qadhafi relied heavily on revolutionary committees both to spread the ideals of his revolution and to root out any opposition. The regime restricted political dissent and three years after taking power formally abolished any political activity contrary to the ideals of the revolution.[1] Qadhafi initially thought to go further and diminish the influence of the country's tribal leaders, but realized that he needed to maintain ties with some of the most powerful tribes (usually by buying them off) to hold on to power.

Qadhafi also sought to curb the influence of the military and began to rely much more on paramilitary brigades, some of which were eventually led by his sons. His distrust of the armed forces stemmed from numerous botched coup attempts launched by the military beginning in the 1970s, including one in 1993 by generals from the Warfalla tribe, Libya's largest. Under Qadhafi, Libya's military became corrupt and ineffective, performing miserably on battlefields in Uganda in the 1970s and Chad in the 1980s.[2] These incompetent campaigns, especially the decade-long struggle in Chad, undermined military morale, created enormous opportunities for graft, and deepened the rift between Qadhafi and his armed forces that had already developed as a result of the many coup attempts of the 1970s. Qadhafi heavily politicized his armed forces to keep them firmly under his control—and to leave them weak in case that failed. For these reasons, the Libyan military is neither a credible nor disinterested party that could lead a post-Qadhafi transition.

During his four decades in power, Qadhafi was similarly ruthless when it came to any Islamist threat to his rule. Soon after the 1969 revolution, he stripped the religious establishment of much of its authority, restricting the role of the *ulama*— the clergy—and elevating his own role as *the* authority on religious life. He was also successful in quashing the two most prominent Islamist factions in the country, the Libyan Islamic Group (the Libyan branch of the Muslim Brotherhood) and the Libyan Islamic Fighting Group (LIFG). The latter was formed in the early 1990s by Libyan jihadists who had fought in Afghanistan against the Soviet Union. In the mid-1990s, the regime launched ground and air attacks against LIFG bases and arrested suspected sympathizers, quickly disrupting the group's cohesiveness and capabilities.[3] In 1996, in Abu Salim, Tripoli's main political prison, guards killed 1,270 prisoners, many of them Islamists.[4] This incident, more than any other during Qadhafi's rule, would become one of the main rallying cries for the opposition movement that would eventually bring down the regime.

The mixture of repression and personalistic rule created a political system that revolved entirely around Qadhafi and his cronies. As a result, by early 2011 there were effectively no strong institutions, civil society, or independent media in Libya, and wealth was concentrated in the hands of a few. Only the tribes retained some degree of independent strength and freedom of action, but they were inadequate (and in some cases uninterested) either in deposing Qadhafi or holding the state together. As a result, when the Arab Spring swept across Libya, pulling thousands of frustrated people into the streets, including key tribal leaders and defectors from the regime, the revolution was strong enough to cause the collapse of the weak Libyan state, but not enough to immediately oust Qadhafi and his loyalists altogether.

Benghazi Rises Up

The uprising against Qadhafi began on February 15, 2011, in Benghazi, the latest in a number of attempts to overthrow his totalitarian regime. But whereas earlier attempts had been either carried out by a single group (such as army generals or Islamists) or had not had the critical mass needed to place substantial pressure on the regime, the February 2011 protests had a broader base of support and attracted larger numbers of people, and did so for a sustained period of time. Inspired by the stunning developments in Tunisia and Egypt, Libyans from all walks of life decided to seize their chance to get rid of their own dictator.

Initially, the protests were planned for February 17, to coincide with the fifth anniversary of a demonstration in Benghazi that had begun as a protest against the infamous Danish cartoons of the prophet Mohammed but quickly turned against the regime. However, the 2011 protests started two days earlier than planned, when lawyers and judges reacted to the arrest of Fathi Turbil, a human rights lawyer who represented the families of the 1996 Abu Salim prison massacre, by staging demonstrations. The regime initially tried to preempt the planned protests in a number of ways (including the release of political prisoners),[5] but when protesters rejected what were viewed as empty promises, Qadhafi did not hold back. Within a week, his forces had killed more than 200 people in Benghazi. Within a month, the UN estimated that thousands more had been killed in widespread clashes.[6] What began as a demonstration quickly turned into a violent confrontation between anti-Qadhafi revolutionaries and the regime.

For its part, the Libyan army splintered, with some soldiers and even some whole units (manned largely by personnel from tribes that had chosen to side with the opposition) taking up the anti-Qadhafi cause. Other units, particularly those with a high percentage of men from tribes who remained loyal to the regime, rallied behind it. It took several weeks for all of this to sort itself out, and for Qadhafi's top lieutenants to regroup his remaining military strength, during which time the opposition was able to steal a march on the regime. As a result, within weeks the opposition controlled the eastern half of the country, Cyrenaica.

The uprising found its most fertile ground in Cyrenaica because opposition to Qadhafi has always been strongest there. Qadhafi is from Tripolitania (western Libya) and many of his loyalists are also from Tripolitanian tribes (and, to a lesser degree, from central and southern tribes). Moreover, Qadhafi's 1969 coup had unseated the government of King Idris, who was himself a Cyrenaican tribal chief who had been installed by the British and who had relied on loyal Cyrenaicans as the basis of his hold on power.

In early March, when Qadhafi's forces were pushing toward Benghazi—the main city of Cyrenaica and the opposition's de facto capital—the United States, the European Union, and the United Nations imposed sanctions on the regime and froze its assets. But it was not apparent whether the West would intervene militarily, especially since it was unclear what intervention would entail, who would take the lead, and what the parameters of a UN mandate would look like. The opposition leaders were initially against external military intervention because they felt it would diminish their credibility, but when Qadhafi appeared close to retaking Benghazi and likely reestablishing control, the NTC began pleading for help. Despite considerable hesitation among some countries (notably Germany and Turkey) and an unclear endgame, in mid-March U.S., British, and French forces, under UN Security Council Resolution 1973, began implementing a no-fly zone and striking Qadhafi's fighters, stopping them just outside Benghazi.

Although Resolution 1973 was, on paper, a mandate to protect civilians, it became clear early on that NATO's mission was to help the opposition oust Qadhafi from power. NATO took over command of the no-fly zone a week after the initial airstrikes. NATO's airstrikes did begin to tip the scales toward the opposition, but many Western policymakers and analysts feared that NATO help was merely prolonging a civil war that the opposition could not win. Further, in late July, Abdel Fattah Younis, Qadhafi's former interior minister turned military commander of the NTC, was killed, most likely by a faction within the opposition, raising additional doubts about the NTC's ability to command all opposition forces under its umbrella and defeat the regime.

All of this changed suddenly in August 2011, when opposition forces seized Zawiya, a strategic town just to the west of Tripoli, and several more high-level regime officials defected. This seemed to break the stalemate wide open. Within days of Zawiya's capture, opposition forces from outside Tripoli, including those from the Nafusa Mountains and Misurata, along with anti-Qadhafi forces inside Tripoli, were in control of most of the city and of Qadhafi's compound, Bab Al-Aziziyya.[7] That Tripoli was overtaken with such relative ease and by various opposition forces, including those from the western part of the country, seemed to suggest both that the regime was weaker than many had feared and that the conflict was not one between the eastern and western parts of the country.

Challenges Ahead

As has become obvious in other post-conflict situations, including in Afghanistan and Iraq, the fall of the old regime is only the first step in a political transition. With the effects of the civil war and the legacy of Qadhafi's misrule likely to persist in myriad ways for many years, Libyans will have to build a new, functional, and preferably (from their perspective and America's) democratic state. This will mean establishing both safety and security, strengthening the rule of law, delivering basic goods and services, and building the strong political institutions that can, in turn, enable Libyans to live more dignified and prosperous lives.

Establishing Security

As of this writing in the early fall of 2011, Qadhafi loyalists continue to hold out in various pockets of the country. Even assuming that the opposition military forces will be able to reduce their last strongholds and defeat the rest of Qadhafi's remaining military formations, the situation will remain precarious. At the very least, regime loyalists may attempt to fight an insurgency. If the NTC experiences real problems consolidating its political power early on, these remnants might even attempt to retake parts of the country or, short of that, mount attacks to create instability in a bid to undermine the new leadership. Some of this will hinge on how long Qadhafi and his sons are able to avoid capture—as long as they are on the loose, their ability to rally support, even if it is merely symbolic, could hinder the efforts of the NTC to build a new government able to rule the country.

Even beyond the question of the activities of Qadhafi loyalists, it remains unclear whether the NTC will be able to control the various military councils and brigades that brought down the regime and either demobilize them or integrate them into a new, loyal Libyan military. One of the successes of the NTC during the fighting was its ability to preside over, albeit loosely, geographically and ideologically diverse groups of fighters and political representatives. This coalition, however, could easily break up into rival factions, especially since members of the opposition will have competing visions for Libya's future. In fact, soon after the fall of Tripoli, different brigades—usually distinguished by their geographic affiliations—were vocal about their role in the military victory and made clear that it was independent of any assistance from the NTC.

In addition, although most Islamists, including former members of the LIFG, have thus far been supportive of the NTC, Islamist factions, both moderate and militant, will seek to capitalize on the tenuous political and security situation in the country. Moderate Islamists will want to be part of the political process, but more radical elements may be as unhappy with a transitional government as they were with Qadhafi. A further challenge may arise from the hundreds of Islamists released over the past few years as part of a "rehabilitation" program, not to mention the many more released in the days leading up to the revolt. Although not all of these freed prisoners will pose a threat in the future, some may, especially if a post-Qadhafi government does not meet their demands or if it allies itself closely with the West.[8]

If the NTC or the government that leads Libya after the transition period is unable to establish control, provide security, and prove its legitimacy as the governing body of the country, Libya risks becoming a failed or fractured state. Renewed violence would not only affect the security of Libyans, but could also spill over and affect the security of Libya's Arab neighbors and countries on its southern border.[9] A power vacuum would also leave Libya vulnerable to groups like al-Qaeda in the Islamic Maghreb, who would try to gain a foothold on the country and exploit the unrest.

Strengthening the Rule of Law and Delivering Basic Services

Preventing the recurrence of violence in Libya will depend in large part on whether the new leadership can strengthen the rule of law in a country that has never had rule-bound state and political institutions at any time in its modern history. The NTC has so far said and done the right things: it has asked anti-regime forces not to engage in revenge killing and expressed interest in a fair system of transitional justice; it has not shown interest in purging former mid-level government officials, police officers, and military personnel; and it has come out with a draft constitution and talked about the need for building state institutions. These are all positive signs, but the success of these goals will depend on whether the NTC is seen as the legitimate transitional governing body by all factions of Libyan society.

Attaining that legitimacy will require the NTC to do more than establish security and strengthen the rule of law; it will require the NTC to provide immediate humanitarian assistance and basic public goods and services.[10] A fundamental component of successful post-conflict transition is whether the new leadership is able to quickly restore some semblance of normality in the country. The government must not only ensure citizens' basic needs are met, but also oversee an economic recovery. In the case of Libya, the latter will depend largely on how quickly oil production gets back to pre-revolution levels. But, in the long run, a post-Qadhafi government's legitimacy will hinge on much more than service delivery and oil outputs; Libyans will demand better job opportunities and an economy that is free of corruption and inefficiencies, and is more equitable. These are daunting tasks for any government, but in a country that has just experienced months of war, the stakes are higher, since falling short can reignite conflict.

Building Accountable, Inclusive, and Corrupt-free Political Institutions

Over the long term, a post-Qadhafi government will need to build economic and political institutions that address corruption and accountability. More than this, Libya must create a better overall governance structure, one that opens up the political process. Especially in a country now awash in weapons and where the ideological, tribal, and geographic cleavages of the past will likely remain important disruptive forces, there will be a temptation to use violence to secure political and economic gain, particularly if the system in place is seen as unfair or illegitimate. Therefore, how well a new government does in convincing different factions (including Islamists, former regime loyalists, and tribal leaders) that the political process is not just fair, but that being part of it is more beneficial than reengaging in violence, will be a major determinant of Libya's future stability.

Ultimately, all of this must lay the foundation for a more fundamental transformation of Libyan society. Qadhafi's totalitarian rule hindered the cultivation of a political culture that values nonviolent negotiation as the means of resolving political and societal differences. Nor did the regime build independent and effective state institutions intended to manage social disagreement and maintain order.[11] Thus, the new government must take care that its early actions do not exacerbate Libya's problems over the long term. Suddenly repealing various laws and regulations to liberalize the economy or rushing to elections could do tremendous damage to Libya's prospects of building a stable democracy. As in Egypt and Tunisia, however, the new government will be under tremendous pressure to make dramatic changes as fast as possible, even though such measures could destroy the necessary effort to instill a political culture and build the state institutions that will provide the foundations for long-term peace and democracy.

The Role of International Actors and the United States

International intervention played an instrumental role in helping opposition forces bring down the Qadhafi regime, but it was clear from the outset that key international actors differed on how much they were willing to commit to the war effort. France and Great Britain were the most vocal and active supporters of the opposition, providing both arms and on-the-ground intelligence. Even then, after months of stalemate, public support for the intervention, especially in the United States, began to wane.[12] The Arab League supported the initial no-fly zone, but then struck a more reticent tone.[13] The African Union did not aid the effort to oust Qadhafi, and much of the rhetoric of its members suggested a desire to see him stay. The Western powers watered down UN Security Council Resolution 1973's mandate to a humanitarian intervention to bring on board Russia and China, who nevertheless began to criticize NATO almost immediately for overstepping its bounds. Still, the NTC was able to garner significant diplomatic support. Even before Qadhafi fell in late August, more than thirty countries, including major Western powers, Turkey, and four Arab states recognized the NTC as the legitimate government of Libya.

For its part, the Obama administration acknowledged that the Libyan crisis was not a core American interest but argued that military intervention was necessary to prevent regional instability, signal to other dictators in the region that they cannot use force against innocent civilians indiscriminately, and ensure the credibility of the UN Security Council.[14] Nonetheless, the administration was roundly criticized for how it handled its involvement in the NATO campaign, including its failure to seek congressional authorization, develop a long-term plan to bring the Libyan mission to a sustainable end-state, and articulate a clear message about the mission's goals.

Three Areas for Assistance

Libya's new leadership still has much to do and will need further external assistance. So far, several countries have agreed to release billions of dollars of frozen Libyan assets to help pay for immediate humanitarian assistance and basic social services, and have pledged to assist further. Given past post-conflict peace-building experiences, there are three key areas in which international actors can and should play important roles moving forward:

—*Security.* Security is a prerequisite of the state-building process.[15] NATO has agreed that its mission will continue as long as Qadhafi and his loyalists are a threat, but establishing internal security will require much more. For example, the United Nations, with support from the United States and European and Arab allies, could begin to train a professional police force, help the NTC in disarming and demobilizing former fighters, and support the reintegration of remnants of the military and revolutionaries into a professional army. The European Union could deploy a border assistance mission to help with border control and surveillance. Providing security will also require that the NTC work with the UN and international organizations, such as the International Organization for Migration, in resettling refugees and internally displaced persons (including migrant workers), ensuring that they are provided short-term assistance, such as food and shelter, but also long-term opportunities to be integrated back into Libyan society.

—*Institution-Building.* Forging effective new state institutions—constitutional courts, a viable police force, a mechanism for transitional justice, and a legal framework capable of regulating the economy and the political process—takes time. This will be especially true in Libya, where the country will have to start from scratch. The NTC has outlined these institution-building needs, and the UN has already devised a plan to address them. On the political front, the NTC has set a timeline for legislative and presidential elections. While this is a good sign that the NTC is committed to holding elections, history has shown that rushing to hold elections (and for that matter, enact economic reforms) without effective state institutions in place risks sparking conflict or undermining the new institutions.[16] Building the institutions and devising an electoral system that Libyans trust and respect will, in the long run, be more important than simply allowing them to cast ballots. UN agencies, the U.S. Agency for International Development, the U.S. Department of Justice, and international nongovernmental organizations can lend technical support as the new Libyan government begins to build the state's institutions. Similarly, because Libya's opposition has traditionally been divided by locality, working on improving local and municipal governance would go a long way in easing potential tensions between these localities and the nascent national government.

—*Civil Society*. A vibrant civil society will be critical to the long-term socioeconomic and political health of Libya.[17] It can guard against the potential excesses of new government institutions and the emergence of a new autocracy, and it can help instill and strengthen a democratic political culture in Libyan society. Nongovernmental organizations and new media outlets emerged soon after the February protests began, and the revolution has ignited a sense of volunteerism and civic duty among Libyans. International organizations and development agencies can work with local activists to channel that civic duty into building civil society organizations and, potentially, into political parties. For example, USAID's Office of Transition Initiatives (OTI) has recently begun a program in Tunisia aimed at improving governance and increasing political participation by providing support to civil society organizations and local institutions.[18] In Libya, OTI could implement a similar program that would focus on civic education and participation in the democratic process.

The international community must use a deft touch in assisting Libya. The success of post-Qadhafi Libya will ultimately depend on Libyans, but the manner in which international actors lend support can either help or make things worse. For this reason, those involved in the rebuilding of Libya must be cognizant of the dilemmas involved in post-conflict state-building.[19] An overly strong or overly long international presence risks alienating the local population or creating a government dependent on international involvement. On the other hand, minimal involvement may not address urgent security and humanitarian issues. Further, international actors will view local elites as the leaders of the transition and the spokespersons of the country, but must be careful not to prop them up, turn them into another strongman, and alienate the general population. Getting this balance right will be critical. A core guiding principle should be to assist the Libyan leadership in the transition, and not take ownership of the process. Just the perception that outsiders are dictating the way forward can derail any hopes of success in Libya.

Even behind the scenes, the United States played an instrumental role in NATO's military operations during the conflict. After the fall of Qadhafi, the United States has continued to play an active role, initially releasing $1.5 billion in frozen Libyan assets and meeting with top NTC officials. But aside from the immediate short-term financial assistance and diplomatic support, the Obama administration has not indicated that it will take much of a leadership role in the state-building effort. This is not surprising. Given Washington's domestic economic concerns, its overextended commitments abroad, and the potential backlash in taking the lead in another Muslim-majority country, it makes sense that the Obama administration would rather play a supporting role in a much larger effort. Libya will face a number of challenges in the coming years, and as the NATO intervention has shown, the United States does not have to take the lead, at least visibly, to effect positive change. But, as outlined above, the United States can assist in a number of very important ways in Libya's postwar efforts.

15

THE PALESTINIANS

*Between National Liberation
and Political Legitimacy*

KHALED ELGINDY

There is a widespread perception that the Arab Spring has bypassed the Palestinians. This is only partly true. While events in the region have sparked a growing Palestinian protest movement, both inside and outside of Palestine, they have not reached anything close to the mass popular mobilizations witnessed in Tunisia and Egypt, or the sustained unrest seen in Yemen and Syria. Moreover, the few protests that did occur were not aimed at toppling or replacing the current Palestinian leadership. Nevertheless, it would be wrong to conclude that regional events have left Palestinians completely untouched, and even more so to view the absence of large-scale or sustained protests as a sign that Palestinians are content with the current condition.

The Arab Spring *has* reached Palestine, though the manner in which it has manifested itself is quite different from what neighboring countries have experienced. What sets Palestine apart from others is the uniqueness of Palestinians' social and political circumstances. Like other democratizing or transitional societies, the Palestinians face challenges of legitimacy, a fragile rule of law, lack of a robust civil society, and a weak democratic culture—all of which have been exposed, and in some cases exacerbated, by the Arab Spring. However, these are subsumed under a wider array of circumstances that other Arab states do not face and that further complicate Palestinian democratization.

UNIQUE CIRCUMSTANCES

Neither the Palestine Liberation Organization (PLO) nor the Palestinian Authority (PA) has ever exercised true sovereignty over any part of Palestinian territory; nor does either of these main leadership institutions enjoy genuine freedom of action in the political, governance, or security realms. The PA in particular, which is a product of the 1993 Oslo Accords between Israel and the PLO, faces major restrictions imposed by the Israeli occupation.[1] Israel retains control over most of the West Bank's land, natural resources, border crossings, airspace, territorial waters, customs, taxation, population and land registries, immigration policies, and other governmental functions normally performed by sovereign states. The PA is further limited by its dependence on international donor aid—a fact highlighted by congressional threats to cut off aid following PA president Mahmoud Abbas's announcement that the Palestinians would seek full UN membership in September 2011—while the PLO is equally reliant on Arab largesse and the political and diplomatic support of other third parties.[2]

The lines between the PLO and the PA have become increasingly blurred over the years, which has led to a kind of political and institutional "schizophrenia."[3] In theory, the PLO remains the highest Palestinian political body representing all Palestinians, whether inside the occupied territories or in the diaspora. As the "sole, legitimate representative of the Palestinian people," the PLO is the official legal and political address of the Palestinians. For its part, the PA, which derives legitimacy from the PLO (via Oslo), is a temporary body with no political authority, but is (notionally) responsible for managing the day-to-day affairs of West Bank and Gaza residents. Despite their apparent complementarity, the relationship between the PLO and the PA is far more muddled and thus has eroded the effectiveness of both institutions.

There is also the equally unique challenge of governing and representing a geographically dispersed constituency, which highlights some of the traditional cleavages in Palestinian society between those "inside" and "outside" the occupied territories and, more recently, between the West Bank and the Gaza Strip. A little less than 40 percent of all Palestinians, approximately 4 million, live in the West Bank and Gaza, while a little over 50 percent live in the diaspora (mostly refugees and their descendants).[4] Meanwhile, the June 2007 civil war between forces loyal to Abbas's Fatah faction and Hamas, and the subsequent political split between the West Bank and Gaza, has underscored the difficulty in governing two geographically distinct territories.

Democracy Deficit

Over the past several decades, Palestinian political life and political institutions, both inside and outside the occupied territories, have steadily declined. Before the formation of the PA in 1994, the PLO had been the preeminent Palestinian political institution for three decades. As a product of the Palestinian diaspora, the PLO's leadership and rank and file were drawn mainly from the refugee camps in the Arab states that border Israel.[5] The PLO's preeminence continued until the late 1980s, when its legitimacy was challenged by three concurrent developments: the 1987 Palestinian uprising—the Intifada—in the occupied territories, which shifted the internal balance of power from the diaspora back to the "inside"; the rise a year later of the Islamic Resistance Movement (Hamas), a potent political-military force and a potential alternative to the PLO; and the 1990–91 Gulf War, in which Yasir Arafat's support for Saddam Hussein after his invasion of Kuwait cost the PLO crucial political and financial support from Arab Gulf states.

Although the process was already well under way, the 1993 Oslo agreement, which led to the creation of the PA a year later, accelerated the PLO's decline. The PLO's "political infrastructure" was transferred from the diaspora to the newly created authority in the occupied territories, leaving the organization essentially hollowed out from within. Yet the PLO remained the legal and political address of the Palestinian cause. All this had a deleterious effect on the PA as well.[6] Meanwhile, the influx of the PLO's bureaucratic and paramilitary cadres previously based in Tunis, arriving to fill the ranks of the newly created PA, further marginalized the local population, which was already excluded by the PLO's leadership organs, and exposed them to its rather undemocratic political culture.

Like other Arab regimes, the PLO maintained a veneer of democratic institutions that masked a more authoritarian structure. It lacked transparency or genuinely participatory mechanisms and had a reputation for endemic corruption and nepotism. Despite allowances for directly electing members to the Palestine National Council (PNC), its ostensible "parliament in exile" and highest decisionmaking body, no such elections ever took place. Rather, the PNC's members, like those of other leadership bodies, were appointed according to a highly secretive quota system.[7] By the early 1990s, the PNC's proceedings had become, according to the Palestinian analyst Jamil Hilal, "largely formalistic and ceremonial [in] nature," convening only periodically to rubber-stamp decisions of its Fatah-dominated leadership.[8] The eighteen members of the PLO executive committee (EC)—equivalent to a council of ministers—are selected by the PNC, which institutionalized Fatah's dominance. Despite this structure, the actual decisionmaking powers remained firmly in the hands of the PLO's chief executive, the EC chairman, and his inner circle.

The PLO's authoritarian and elitist tendencies were at odds with the more grassroots and independent civic and political life of the West Bank and Gaza.[9] Indeed, according to Hilal, "Despite restrictions and repression, Palestinian civil society existed and developed. It is even possible that certain aspects of civil society were strengthened and enhanced through the population's collective response to the challenge of occupation."[10]

Elections for PA president and the Palestinian Legislative Council (PLC), first held in 1996, helped mitigate the PLO's democracy deficit but could not overcome it. Although the 1996 and subsequent elections were widely considered free and fair, the holding of elections did not fundamentally alter the PA's relationship with those whom it governed. Under Arafat, PA rule was characterized by heavy-handed security measures against political dissidents, namely members of Hamas or other Islamist groups, financial nontransparency, active press censorship, and other systematic restrictions on civil society.[11] The disintegration of the PA and its institutions accelerated dramatically after the eruption of the Second Intifada in late 2000. Israel's response to the Palestinian uprising virtually decimated the PA, leaving its security and civilian governance institutions in tatters. Moreover, some have argued that the influx of Western donor assistance over the years may have actually hurt democratization efforts.[12]

The ability of PA elections to forestall the widening democracy deficit could last only as long as the PLO and PA leadership remained one and the same, which ceased to be the case after 2006. Hamas's surprise electoral victory that year exposed the many contradictions posed by the PA's fusion with the PLO. For the first time in its short history, the PA leadership, with the exception of the presidency, was controlled by a party other than the one controlling the PLO.

The election of Hamas resulted in an international boycott of the PA, undermining the internationally backed "state-building" project. This paved the way for a brief Palestinian civil war in which Hamas forcibly took control of Gaza in 2007, leading to a complete break between it and Fatah. Since then, the PA's democracy deficit has turned into a full-scale process of *de-democratization*. Even Salam Fayyad's much-vaunted state-building program, while making noteworthy progress in security and financial transparency, could not lessen the structural harm caused to the statehood project by the division of governmental institutions, the absence of a functioning legislature, and growing suppression of citizens' rights.[13] Thus, notwithstanding the 1996 precedent, elections have not resulted in a peaceful transfer of power, which continues to be concentrated in the hands of an unelected few. Ironically, the precariousness of the Ramallah government, coupled with U.S. and Israeli threats to defund the PA following Abbas's UN bid, could unwittingly trigger a revival of the PLO and its institutions, particular in the event of the PA's demise.

For their part, Gaza's Hamas rulers may be even more democratically challenged than their West Bank counterparts. Like other mainstream Islamist movements (including its parent organization, the Muslim Brotherhood), Hamas maintains a rhetorical commitment to democratic principles such as equality before the law, peaceful alternation of power, and basic freedoms like speech and assembly.[14] Nonetheless, this commitment is undercut to some extent by its ultimate goal of a state that is more or less in conformity with Islamic jurisprudence (Shari'a). Moreover, Hamas's record on the ground during its four years of governing Gaza has been anything but democratic. As former Palestinian negotiator Yezid Sayegh has explained, Hamas's "assault on public freedoms has also intensified in Gaza since January 2010. The Hamas-led security sector represses

not only Fatah but its own allies whenever they have objected to particular policies or measures."[15]

CRISIS OF LEGITIMACY

Although the PLO had never been a democratic institution, as an umbrella of
diverse political, paramilitary, and ideological groups, it was broadly seen as
representative, and thus legitimate, in the eyes of most Palestinians. Despite the
inherently undemocratic nature of the quota system, factional representation, as
an expression of Palestinian political pluralism, has always been central to the
PLO's legitimacy.[16]

The PLO's "representational pluralism" might have continued indefinitely
but for two crucial deficiencies: the growing crisis of genuine representation (as
opposed to the fiction of the quota system) and the absence of mechanisms of
accountability for its leadership, both of which have severely eroded its (and by
extension the PA's) standing. The exclusion of Hamas (along with several smaller
factions) from the PLO, as well as the ongoing factional division within the PA,
has challenged the leadership's claim to represent all Palestinians.[17] In 2005 President Abbas tried to bring Hamas into the fold through the interfactional Cairo
Declaration, if only to foreclose the possibility of Hamas replacing the PLO altogether. Unlike other aspects of the agreement, however, those related to restructuring and reforming the PLO and its constituent bodies, including expanding
its membership, were never implemented.

Meanwhile, the growing sense of alienation among diaspora Palestinians, who
are not affected by developments in the occupied territories and have no direct
stake in the PA, poses an even greater challenge to the PLO's claim to represent
all Palestinians. While the Palestinian leadership has made some attempt to deal
with the question of political representation, it has yet to reengage with the diaspora in a serious way. The refugee communities, which had once formed the
PLO's political base, have increasingly felt that the PLO has abandoned their
cause.[18] The importance of the refugee issue lies not only in the fact that it is one
of the core issues to be decided in negotiations with Israel, but also in the reality
that any Israeli-Palestinian agreement will require the refugees' political buy-in
to achieve both an end of claims and an end of conflict.

Over the years, the gap between the PLO's political constituency and its base
of support has narrowed substantially. Whereas the PLO once was a diaspora-
dominated institution that nonetheless commanded the loyalty of a majority
of Palestinians, after the Oslo Accords it has been seen as representing only
the interests of those inside the West Bank and Gaza—and increasingly today,
only the West Bank. What is more, recent protests suggest that representative-
ness may be more crucial to the PLO's legitimacy than governance issues or

adherence to strict democracy.[19] Yet as the PLO's support base has narrowed in recent years, so too has the circle of decisionmaking within its leadership. Notwithstanding whatever formal institutions may exist, even today, actual decisionmaking powers remain firmly in the hands of a small clique consisting of Mahmoud Abbas and a handful of his closest advisers.

The PLO's waning legitimacy has also diminished its negotiating capacity and flexibility, if not its mandate to carry out this function.[20] Repeated failures at the negotiating table have further depleted the PLO and PA leadership's credibility with its people. Unlike Hamas, whose street credibility is based on "resistance," President Abbas and his Fatah Party derive their legitimacy through negotiations, which they see as their only means for bringing about change. Thus, although only a Fatah-dominated PLO could deliver a peace deal with Israel, its willingness to engage in seemingly endless negotiations while deriving no tangible gains has severely undercut its moral and political legitimacy in the eyes of ordinary Palestinians.

To be sure, Hamas has serious legitimacy problems of its own. Notwithstanding its rhetoric over the years, Hamas understands the limit of its appeal and sees that it is in no position to replace the PLO. This was evident in the movement's reluctance to rule on its own following its decisive 2006 election victory. Moreover, Hamas's popularity has steadily declined among Palestinians since the 2009 Gaza War (Israel's Operation Cast Lead), which may explain its reluctance to go to elections in the period before the recent reconciliation deal. Despite Hamas's relative success in providing basic law and order in Gaza, the impoverished enclave remains isolated and besieged, while its 1.5 million people have grown weary of Hamas's increasing repression and its lack of a long-term plan for ending their plight. Interestingly, despite its satisfaction with Mubarak's fall, Hamas took a more heavy-handed approach toward pro-Egyptian, and later pro-reconciliation, demonstrations by Gaza's youth than Fatah-led authorities did in the West Bank—largely out of a fear that such public protests could morph into more generalized displays of anger against Hamas rule.

A "Palestinian Spring"

It is in this context of an increasingly weak and undemocratic Palestinian leadership, along with a deeply entrenched Israeli occupation and a discredited U.S.-led peace process, that the Arab Spring has left its mark on Palestinians. The Arab uprisings exposed the internal and external political vulnerabilities of the PLO and PA leadership on all of these issues, beginning with the ongoing split between Fatah and Hamas. Inspired by events in Tunisia and particularly Egypt, Palestinians began to mobilize their own demonstrations. Initially, the protests were directed at their own leadership, as thousands of young Palestinians in the

West Bank and Gaza Strip took to the streets on March 15, 2011. The protesters demaded an end to the division between their two largest factions as a prerequisite to ending the occupation, rallying with the chant of "The people demand an end to the division!" The PLO and PA leadership acknowledged popular calls for national unity and renewed efforts to bring Hamas into the fold.[21]

In the end, it was the shift in the regional balance of power caused by events in Egypt and Syria, which left both Fatah and Hamas weakened and politically exposed, that persuaded them to reconcile (at least on paper) on May 4, 2011, under the auspices of Egypt's new transitional government.[22] For the PA, the loss of its most powerful ally and chief political patron, Hosni Mubarak, capped a series of political setbacks in the preceding months, including the collapse of direct negotiations with Israel in the fall of 2010 and the embarrassment over the leaked "Palestine Papers" in early 2011. For Hamas, suffering its own legitimacy problems, the impact of the Arab Spring in Syria was as important to it as the events in Egypt were to Fatah. Although initially buoyed by Mubarak's departure, Hamas saw the delegitimization of the Syrian regime—Hamas's principal ally—and its potential demise as major blows to its own position. Once their external backers were removed or weakened, both Fatah and Hamas felt that they lacked the strength to remain independent.

Less noticed, and largely ignored by their leaders, were the March 15 protesters' other demands, namely the call for new elections, not only for the PA but also for the PLO's defunct "parliament in exile"—the PNC.[23] Nonetheless, since the signing of the Egyptian-brokered reconciliation agreement in May 2011, the protest movement has shifted its focus to Israel and the occupation. Building on tactics employed for many years by Palestinian and international activists who protested Israel's "separation barrier," Palestinians began to organize more serious nonviolent mass demonstrations directed at other symbols of the occupation. Large protests like the June 5 "march on Jerusalem," held near the Qalandia checkpoint north of Jerusalem on the forty-fourth anniversary of Israel's occupation, were predictable outgrowths of the general mood in the region and the Palestinians' loss of faith in the peace process.

A more surprising manifestation of what may be a budding "Palestinian Spring" was the mobilization of the Palestinian diaspora, particularly refugees in neighboring Arab states. On May 15, Israeli Independence Day—what Palestinians refer to as the *Nakba* (the "day of catastrophe," which commemorates the dispossession of Palestinians as a result of Israel's creation)—thousands of Palestinian refugees and other Arabs in Lebanon, Syria, Jordan, and elsewhere attempted to march on Israel's borders in a symbolic gesture of "return."[24] Although ten protesters were killed under disputed circumstances, the violence did little to dissuade these communities from mounting a second protest, this time in parallel with June 5 *Naksa* protests (commemorating the 1967 "setback" when Israel occupied the West Bank and Gaza) inside the occupied territories. These protests proved even deadlier, with some twenty protesters killed.[25]

The mobilization of Palestinian refugees, a group largely neglected by the peace process and their own political leaders, put the refugee issue back on the political agenda. Where Israelis see any assertion of the refugee issue as an existential threat to the Jewish character of the state, Palestinians consider it a central component of their national narrative and believe its resolution is an essential requirement for peace. One of the June 4 protesters' main chants was "*awda, hurriya, wihda wataniya*" ("return, freedom, national unity")—representing the three main sources of Palestinian frustration: neglect of the refugees, the continued Israeli occupation, and the division between Hamas and Fatah.

Changes in the regional balance of power and mounting domestic pressures have also affected Abbas's thinking at the diplomatic level, narrowing his political options even further. Although the PLO and PA leadership had already despaired of U.S.-led negotiations after the collapse of direct talks and Washington's failure to secure a settlement freeze in the fall of 2010, the Arab Spring confirmed that the "current peace process as it has been conducted so far is over," as PA foreign minister Riad al-Malki put it.[26] Abbas could no longer afford to engage in a process that in the view of most Palestinians had not only failed to produce benefits but in fact had yielded mostly losses.[27] Like other Arab leaders, Abbas was forced to pay far greater attention to public opinion in the wake of the Arab Spring.

In September 2011, despite intense U.S. and international pressure to abandon his UN bid, Abbas made good on his promise to submit a formal application to the Security Council requesting that a Palestinian state along the 1967 borders be admitted to the UN as a full member.[28] The move was a sign of Palestinian displeasure with the United States' stewardship of the peace process. In going to the UN, Abbas hoped to regain some badly needed political leverage vis-à-vis Israel and the United States in any future negotiations, while at the same time shoring up his domestic political standing. Although the United States and Israel staunchly opposed the measure, and most Palestinians did not expect it to succeed, it has been extremely popular among Palestinians.[29]

The Obama administration has vowed to veto the measure (assuming it comes to a vote in the Security Council), all but ensuring its failure. If this were to happen, Abbas has said he would seek a General Assembly resolution recognizing Palestine as a "nonmember state," similar to the status of the Vatican. Meanwhile, both the U.S. Congress and the Israeli government have threatened major punitive action in response to the UN bid. But, as noted in chapter 6, these actions will likely harm not just Palestinian interests but American and Israeli interests as well, and could derail chances for a two-state solution. For instance, congressional threats to cut off aid to the PA may be self-defeating, particularly because the funding is vital to building a well-functioning Palestinian security apparatus—something of vital importance to Israel.

On the other hand, if Abbas were to withdraw his UN bid under pressure he risks incurring the wrath of his own people and perhaps dealing a fatal blow to his already battered credibility. Moreover, with negotiations already at a dead end, this could lead many ordinary Palestinians to conclude that all peaceful options have been closed. Palestinian frustration might be channeled into large-scale mass mobilizations like those seen in neighboring countries, or such protests could become more militarized as was the case during the Second Intifada.

Whether further instances of Palestinian unrest would target their own leadership or Israel depends on two things: the extent to which Palestinians, inside and outside the occupied territories, deem their leaders to be broadly representative and accountable; and the degree to which Palestinians see their leaders as acting on behalf of Palestinian national interests rather than U.S., Israeli, or broader Western wishes. If and when such mass protests occur, the likelihood that they will remain peaceful will depend on how Israel and the United States respond, particularly in the face of nonviolent protests. Should Israel continue or intensify its use of force against unarmed protesters, the likelihood that Palestinian protests might eventually turn violent would increase accordingly. Meanwhile, the fact that most of the core demands of the Palestinians require Israeli approval (or at least acquiescence) means that Palestinian democracy and legitimacy, to a large extent, are dependent on a conflict-ending agreement with Israel, which seems more or less likely at any given moment.

AMERICA AND THE PALESTINIAN SPRING

Events in the Palestinian territories highlight the need for Washington to understand the direct, if not organic, connection between Palestinian reform and the quest for Israeli-Palestinian peace. The absence of a credible peace process increases the likelihood of a resurgence in violence and the likelihood that the PA and PLO will be discredited.

With this in mind, Washington should acknowledge that piecemeal and partial approaches to peacemaking will simply no longer be adequate. Instead of continuing to treat Gaza, Palestinian reconciliation, and the broader regional context as though they are separate and distinct from the "peace process," the Obama administration should seek to deal with all these problems in a more integrated and comprehensive way. As chapter 6 on the peace process argues, the surest way to reduce the potential for a resurgence in Israeli-Palestinian violence is for the United States and its international partners to put forth a credible peace process.

Furthermore, the United States should acknowledge that along with governance issues like institution-building and security, the notion of representation (whether factional or in terms of the refugees) is critical to the PLO's legitimacy. In the absence of such legitimacy, no Palestinian leadership will have the requisite mandate to negotiate an agreement with Israel, much less the credibility to implement one. As such, the United States and the international community should find creative ways to allow (or at least not impede) Palestinian reconciliation efforts. This is a critical component of addressing the Palestinian leadership's growing democracy deficit.

PART III

THE IMPERATIVE
OF REFORM

16

REFORM

Convincing Reluctant Regimes to Change

KENNETH M. POLLACK

Only a handful of regimes in the Middle East have so far fallen to the wave of popular unrest that has swept the region. Many states have found that employing massive repression can succeed in preventing revolutions from succeeding, at least in the short run. Thus, when the Arab Spring eventually ends, a number of the old regimes will likely remain.

But it is not the case that we should necessarily wish for revolutions everywhere. Revolutions are dangerous and unpredictable events. As Americans, we tend to romanticize them because of our own history. But our revolution was something of an anomaly in that it turned out exactly as its makers had intended when they first threw tea into Boston Harbor, manned the defenses at Bunker Hill, and affixed their names to the Declaration of Independence. Many other revolutions ended badly, and not at all as their authors had imagined. None of the Frenchmen who stormed the Bastille envisioned the Terror. None of the Russians who stormed the Winter Palace could have foreseen the horrors of collectivization and the Gulag; few of them wanted communism at all. Even "nonviolent" revolutions typically result in considerable bloodshed. In Egypt, more than 800 people died and thousands of others were injured in what has been a relatively peaceful revolution so far.[1]

In addition, even if the United States decided it wanted immediate regime change in country after country in the Middle East, Washington's ability to foment revolutions, let alone guide them to the best outcomes, is extremely limited. We can push. We can plead. We can prod. We can use our economic clout to make the lives of some Middle Eastern governments harder. But unless we are going to invade these countries and topple their governments as we did those of Afghanistan in 2001 and Iraq in 2003, we cannot bring about revolutionary change. At this point there are few (if any) Americans with any interest in another round of massive military interventions for regime change. Thus, even if Americans would prefer to see more revolutions in the Middle East, there is no practical way for us to bring it about.

Nevertheless, if the events since January 2011 have proven anything at all, it is that *change is coming to the Middle East whether the United States or the current leaders of the region like it or not.* People in the Middle East are desperately unhappy, and across the region they have demonstrated a willingness to take great risks to bring about change. The regimes can no longer ignore their own problems and their people's demands for such change. Syria, Iran, and Bahrain have proven that the regimes can still use massive, violent repression to thwart revolution in the short term, but as Egypt, Libya, and Tunisia have reaffirmed, repression cannot indefinitely keep down an aggrieved people. If the response of the regimes is limited to repression, the regimes' end, when it comes, will be swift and terrible.

For all of these reasons, the next stage of the great Arab Awakening—and U.S. policy toward the region—then, may well be more about reform than revolution. Where there has not been revolutionary change, there will have to be evolutionary change to transform the political system more slowly in the years to come. Thankfully, the United States has more tools available to it to support reform than to spark revolution, and many of the states in need of reform are American allies.

The Nature of Reform

It is worth starting with at least an outline of the needed reforms before wading into the more pressing topic of how to see reform implemented.[2] In the political realm, Middle Eastern states need to move toward a system that guarantees basic individual rights, such as freedom of speech, freedom of assembly, freedom of religion, and freedom from arbitrary arrest and torture. They will need to embrace protections for minorities so that the state or the majority cannot oppress unpopular groups and to ensure that every person and every group is assured full equality. Government will have to be transparent, be accountable to its people, and derive legitimacy by representing the will of the people. There will need to be political and structural checks on the power of the different institutions of governance, and the government must be served by an apolitical and meritocratic bureaucracy. The wealth of the nation will have to be viewed and treated as the wealth of the people, not of those governing, and that wealth must be employed for the common good.

These political reforms will have to be built upon a foundation of legal reforms that establish the rule of law. Legal codes must be clear, well articulated, accessible to all, and the product of a meritocratic process of jurisprudence. All citizens must receive the same fair and impartial treatment, and none can be above the law. As part of establishing the rule of law, all of these countries will need to develop an independent judiciary that will be largely (ideally, completely) free of contamination by financial inducement, political pressure, or fear of violence, and served by a principled legal process and a humane penal system. They will also require proper anticorruption guidelines, complete with all of the institutions (including an independent press) needed to enforce them.

Educational reforms are equally important. In particular, schools need to introduce modern instructional practices that emphasize active learning, facilitate teacher-student and student-student interaction, and push students to learn through doing and discovery. In addition, education should focus not just on the acquisition of knowledge, but also on the creation of new knowledge.

In the realm of economics, the dismal science offers a less clear path. Although many in the West continue to believe that the "Washington consensus" regarding economic reform is the only path of economic reform that has been proven to work in practice, others have suggested that different strategies are possible.[3] At the very least, economic reform must encompass the eradication of the corruption endemic to the region. It must include programs to increase worker productivity (where educational reform is one of the keys), encourage foreign investment, and rationalize policies on both subsidies and privatization of industry. It must eliminate the crippling monopolies of the Middle East and create incentives for trade and direct foreign investment. And it must improve the efficiency of markets and the ease of transactions, as well as the efficiency of governmental regulation, by modernizing, streamlining, and reforming political and financial bureaucracies (including the banking sector), and by eliminating patronage networks that subvert good economic practices and the efficient functioning of markets.[4]

THE CHALLENGES OF REFORM

If convincing the Arab regimes to reform were easy, it would have happened a long time ago. But the regimes continue to resist reform, while outside powers remain ambivalent about whether to push for reform, let alone how best to aid it from the outside or even structure it from the inside. As a result, reform has often faced an uphill struggle.

The first, and most obvious, challenge to reform as a credible alternative to revolution or repression is that the regimes have repeatedly promised reforms and just as consistently failed to deliver. The Arab autocrats understand the psychological power of promising change and how this promise alone can disarm militant oppositionists seeking a more radical solution. As a result, reform has gotten a bad name in the Middle East, where it is often seen as code for "doing nothing." Indeed, this problem is so important to the Middle East and the outcome of the Arab Spring that chapter 17 is devoted entirely to the question of how to make reform credible.

Arab regimes have consistently failed to make good on their promises of reform for two reasons: first, they are simply loath to share power, and second, they are afraid that once they start down the path of change they will get swept off their feet. The problem is that reform can get out of hand. Loosening political controls can bring disruptive, or even dangerous, elements into government, from which position they might try to undermine the regime or even seize power. After the 1991 Persian Gulf War, the Kuwaiti royal family reconstituted a parliament that had been suspended in 1986 and allowed reasonably fair and free elections: for doing so, they were rewarded with a parliament that has been dominated by Islamists, conservatives, and other vehement oppositionists who have caused the government fits and endlessly hamstrung Kuwaiti policymaking. Persuading the Arab regimes to embrace real reform—not the sham measures they have adopted in the past—is going to mean convincing them that these risks are far less dangerous than the risks of doing nothing.

Perversely, history has demonstrated that a government that embraces reform half-heartedly often runs similar risks. Reforms have a psychological impact that often far exceeds their actual transformative value. In some ways, this is positive because even starting down the path of reform can quickly take the wind out of the sails of would-be revolutionaries. Since most people would prefer gradual, peaceful reform to sudden, unpredictable revolution, merely inaugurating a process of reform can lance the boil of popular anger that leads to revolution. However, reforms also raise popular expectations, and what produces popular unrest (and eventual revolutions) in the first place is a large gap between those expectations and reality. In particular, if the regime suddenly eliminates or reneges on its promise of reform, the hopes of the populace will be dashed, creating the perfect psychological conditions for large-scale revolt.[5] That is why, once a country embarks on reform, it is critical that it keep moving, even if slowly.

Autocratic regimes are always hesitant to give up their control of the economy, but they will often sacrifice that in order to hold on to political control. China is the best example of this phenomenon: In the 1980s, Beijing realized (in part from the shock of the Tiananmen Square revolt) that its people were extremely unhappy, so the regime decided to hasten the process of reforming the economy. The hope was that prosperity would satisfy the Chinese people and undermine their demands for political reform. To a certain extent, this strategy seems to have worked. Consequently, there is a debate in the West over whether to foster or oppose the same approach in the Middle East. Some argue that economic reform should be allowed to proceed without political reform (or outpace it), in part because economic reform will eventually create political reform. Others believe that the United States cannot afford to allow the regimes to neglect political reform both because political reform is necessary to bring economic reform to full fruition and because decoupling them could allow the regimes to ignore political reform altogether.[6]

Another major question mark hangs over the nature and extent of American and other international assistance for reform in the Middle East. The Middle East has a love-hate relationship with the United States. On the one hand, since the Arab Spring began in January 2011, oppositionists throughout the Arab world have consistently sought American support and have been angered when they did not receive it—and have not much cared about whether any other states supported them. On the other hand, public opinion polls continue to demonstrate high levels of anti-Americanism across the region.[7] For decades, Arab reformists have often been pilloried and discredited by both the regimes and the Islamists as being "puppets" of the United States.[8] Consequently, it is just not clear how much help Arab (and Iranian) reformists will actually want from the United States. In some cases, it may be necessary to work through the auspices of other countries, or international organizations, to make American encouragement, pressure, and assistance palatable to the states it is seeking to help.

Moreover, it is equally uncertain how much help the United States can provide. Given America's current economic and financial problems, the U.S. Congress and the American taxpayer are not exactly in the giving vein. Consequently, much U.S. support will have to come in other forms: providing access to American markets, encouraging investment in Middle Eastern economies, organizing the aid efforts of other countries, furnishing expertise and advisers to help rebuild existing institutions or build new ones, and using America's military might to prevent external aggression—thereby eliminating external security as a distraction from internal reform. In any case, financial aid can often prove counterproductive to reform, as it can strengthen a regime at the expense of the people, allowing it to put off structural change and even deepening corruption.[9] The challenge for the United States, then, is to find different ways to help countries strive for meaningful reform.

THE SAUDI WILD CARD

There is yet another potentially important obstacle to reform in the Arab world: Saudi Arabia. As Bruce Riedel explains in chapter 18, the Saudis were terrified by the fall of Mubarak and Ben Ali, the unrest that broke out in countries throughout the region, and Washington's seemingly casual abandonment of those regimes in favor of nascent democracy movements. The Saudis have so far reacted to events across the region by largely opposing them as best they can. In Bahrain, this meant armed intervention. In Egypt, it meant offering to replace lost American aid with Saudi aid if Mubarak would hang on. In Syria and elsewhere, it has meant providing the autocrats with money and other support to tough it out and resist calls for reform, let alone revolution.

In other words, American efforts to promote reform (even as an alternative to revolution) may be met with a Saudi determination to promote repression instead. To some extent, the United States may be "playing" not against its usual foes, like Iran, but against its oldest ally in the region. The respect that the kingdom commands because of its wealth and its custodianship of the holy sites of Mecca and Medina would make it a very formidable foe if this conflict persists.

For this reason, the United States, as well as would-be reformers in the region, must try to convince the Saudis that reform is not a threat to their interests. As Riedel also explains, King Abdullah of Saudi Arabia has himself been willing to push for gradual change within the kingdom even as Riyadh refuses to tolerate it beyond Saudi borders. This creates a critical opening that all who favor reform as the best alternative to revolution or repression must try to use to mollify Saudi fears and perhaps even convince the Al Sa'ud that reform is actually in their best interests too.

ENABLING REFORM

There is no magic formula for overcoming the resistance of regimes that are reluctant to embrace economic and social, let alone political, reform. The United States and its allies will have to be flexible, creative, and adaptive in trying various tactics and tailoring them to meet the specific circumstances of different countries at different periods of time (again, see chapter 17 for a set of creative approaches).

Above all, it is essential to recognize that the regimes themselves will need to be part of the reform process. In other words, if the United States hopes to foster reform, it needs to find ways to partner with the regimes, rather than treating them as adversaries. *This does not mean that reform should be a wholly top-down process, completely controlled by the regimes.* That approach has repeatedly led nowhere in the Arab world. Rather, Washington will have to work with the regimes to make them feel comfortable with reform and with allowing other actors—councils of wise men, civil society groups, international organizations—to participate in determining both the nature of reform and its execution.

To encourage the Arab monarchies and remaining dictatorships along this path, the United States should provide incentives to these states to allow reform, remove their incentives (and excuses) to resist reform, and help the rulers feel comfortable about making an effort to change. If the United States starts from an adversarial position, it is bound to fail. Instead, Washington will have to persuade the Arab regimes that change is coming, one way or another, and that the choice they face is either to allow for controlled, gradual transition or to prepare for another wave of revolts—one they might not escape next time. In other words, they need to recognize that their survival, albeit in modified form, is only possible if they are willing to adapt to the new realities of the world and the region. In this regard, the United States should not be averse to the idea that the leadership will retain a role in governance well into the future.

This is both especially true and especially easy with the monarchies of the region, which tend to enjoy greater popular legitimacy and so can imagine ceding some power to democratic institutions while still retaining an important role in governance, one way or another. The greater ability of the monarchies to allow real reform is another potentially important development of the Arab Spring, one slowly dawning on both the people and the regimes of the region.[10] It is why the far-reaching reforms promised by King Mohammed VI of Morocco in March 2011, and discussed by Sarah Yerkes in chapter 22, are so important. The king has sketched out a vision of reform in which economic policy and domestic politics are effectively turned over to a new, freely elected parliament, while he retains control over defense and foreign policy. If King Mohammed makes good on these pledges and his reforms are seen as positive and constructive by his people, they could furnish a model of reform in the near term, and a vision of a new Arab state, one that may be far more acceptable to other people of the Middle East than what they have had in the past.

17

MAKING REFORM CREDIBLE

The Critical Piece of the Puzzle

STEPHEN R. GRAND, SHADI HAMID,
KENNETH M. POLLACK, AND SARAH E. YERKES

There should be little question that reform is both more likely than and preferable to revolution as a means of bringing about necessary (and inevitable) change in the Arab world. Revolutions are violent, unpredictable, and often end very badly. Reform is gradual, mostly peaceful, and deliberate, and can correct for mistakes. Although the regimes of the region will resist addressing the problems that give rise to revolution tooth and nail, they will sometimes embrace reform readily (at least rhetorically) and perhaps can be brought around to accepting it in substance as well.

However, as Ken Pollack notes in chapter 16, it is all too easy to announce sweeping reform programs, use those announcements to defuse popular unrest, and then over time simply fail to implement the promised policies. The Arab world has seen this movie time and again. The regimes in Jordan, Syria, Bahrain, Yemen, Egypt, Tunisia, and even Morocco have frequently promised far-reaching changes only to renege on them when they became inconvenient or authorities became frightened of losing control.

The predicament that Arab political leaders now find themselves in is that their citizens are much less likely to believe them this time around. Even if a leader became wholly committed to wide-ranging, fundamental reforms—which in almost every country remains a big "if"—he would still face a major credibility problem. Citizens have heard promises of reform so many times before that they would be deeply skeptical, if not outright cynical. A leader who declares major reforms at this point, rather than winning the gratitude of his citizens, may only invite scorn, risk being seen as weak, and leave himself open to even greater demands from his citizens.

As a result, one of the greatest challenges for the Arab world, and for outside powers like the United States that favor change through deliberate reform rather than sudden revolution, is to see that promised reforms are actually implemented. This is a very tall order, but in some respects it could be the most important legacy of the Arab Spring. If it succeeds, and programs of reform become tangible across the Middle East, then the likelihood of another round of wrenching revolutions will dwindle if not evaporate altogether. On the other hand, if the reform agendas promulgated again prove to be meaningless, then additional revolts, regime changes, failed states, civil wars, insurgencies, and terrorist campaigns are probably inevitable.

PROMOTING REFORM FROM THE OUTSIDE

It is not just the regimes that have failed to live up to their commitments when it comes to promoting reform. The United States has talked about the need for reform in the Arab world for nearly two decades, but successive American administrations have done little to actually back up those words.[1]

Not surprisingly, the result has been that promises of reform and U.S. rhetoric in support of it have become badly discredited in the Middle East. Indeed, if it wants to be believed, Washington may need to find a new term to describe the process—"transformation" perhaps. But the bottom line is that reform cannot become an excuse for inaction.

The task of encouraging reform is going to be difficult in part because sometime soon, if the counterrevolutionary repression succeeds in precluding any further revolutions, the regimes may think that they have successfully weathered the storm and no longer have anything to fear. Rather than realizing that they have merely dodged a bullet (or that another one may be coming soon), they might assume that they now know how to deal with even large-scale popular uprisings and therefore have no need to undertake meaningful reforms. That kind of thinking is exactly how they found themselves—and the United States found itself—in the current predicament. Many of the regimes believed that merely by promising reforms and making minor gestures in that direction (coupled with the threat of violence if the people objected) they could head off large-scale insurrection.

As the events of 2011 have demonstrated, this idea is disastrously mistaken. Yet most regimes continue to resist making real changes and ceding real authority, which suggests they are slipping right back into the same old bad habits.

That is where the United States and other like-minded nations must come back into the picture. One of America's roles in moving forward must be to convince the regimes that they really do have to reform, that the reforms must be meaningful and must set in motion an inexorable process of economic, social, and political transformation. They must accept that the eventual result will be pluralist societies, although ones that need not exclude the current ruling elites entirely.

New Approaches

In short, one of the greatest challenges for the United States and its allies in the aftermath of the Arab Spring is *how to ensure that the Arab regimes make good on their pledges to change so that reform can become the preferred alternative to repression and revolution.* It is impossible to know for certain what strategy is best to achieve this, especially given how many times we have tried and failed in the past. The following are a half-dozen courses of action informed by past American experiences that could succeed where others have failed.

Positive Conditionality

The most obvious strategy for encouraging those Arab leaders who have already promised reforms to implement the measures is to condition U.S. and other international aid on their living up to these commitments.[2] Even in an era of harsh budget cuts, the United States can be expected to provide not insignificant amounts of economic and military assistance to Egypt, Iraq, Jordan, Lebanon, Morocco, the Palestinians, Tunisia, perhaps Yemen, and someday Libya. It may more often be measured in the hundreds of millions of dollars, rather than billions as before, but it is not nothing. Indeed, such aid has proven to be quite important to many of these regimes.[3] In addition, American diplomatic support is critical for loans and grants from, and membership into, international financial and trade organizations. Moreover, American allies in Europe, East Asia, and the oil-producing states of the Arab world itself should provide aid to these countries, and the United States can often influence their decisions as well.

In dealing with Middle Eastern governments, Washington has tended to view aid principally as a stick with which to threaten, or talk about threatening, to cut or withhold aid if governments did not adopt significant reforms. Under the right circumstances, this type of threat can have some impact. As an extreme example, the loss of external economic support (from the Soviet Union) led to the collapse of the Eastern European communist dictatorships. Similarly, America's unwillingness to fund Latin American dictatorships in the 1990s crippled many of those regimes, forcing them to start down the same path of reform that it would like to see the Arab states take.[4]

However, sticks, like withholding aid, should only be part of the approach, and probably only a small part. While significant, the loss of American aid is not likely to break the finances of any of the region's governments. The oil-producing states do not need direct American funding (although they do benefit from American support with international organizations), and even the non–oil producing states often receive grants from the wealthy Arab Gulf states that at times match or exceed American funding.[5]

Moreover, if the states that constitute the Gulf Cooperation Council (GCC), led by Saudi Arabia, come to see American efforts to promote reform elsewhere in the region as inimical to their own futures, they could easily replace whatever sums the United States and other Western powers threatened to withhold—as they reportedly offered to Mubarak. In addition, all of the Middle Eastern states, particularly the most important (such as Egypt and Saudi Arabia), are fiercely nationalistic and bristle when the United States tries to bend them to its will, especially when the regime's leadership believes that doing so will threaten its grip on power.[6]

Thus, the United States must think about its aid to the Arab world in terms of carrots as well as sticks. Rather than just threaten to cut aid if the regimes of the region fail to embrace reform, Washington should make a much greater effort to entice and reward them for pursuing it. Such aid should be seen as more than just a bribe; it should be seen as providing necessary economic resources to help the states of the region make these transitions and deal with the inevitable problems and dislocations that large-scale reform would cause. After all, Washington will be trying to persuade Middle Eastern governments to fundamentally restructure their societies by rewriting their legal codes, reorganizing their judiciaries, revising their curricula, retraining their teachers, privatizing their industries, breaking down monopolies, lifting trade barriers, limiting state controls, and allowing greater political freedoms. All of this is going to cost money. In some cases, a lot of money. And the United States and its allies should provide the poorer states of the region with generous assistance to make these changes possible without further impoverishing the people or alienating key constituencies.

Egypt has already voiced its interest in increased economic assistance. The United States could offer a large package, between $500 million and $1 billion in additional annual aid (enough to give it leverage but still be fiscally reasonable), conditioned on meeting a series of explicit, measurable benchmarks on democratization. These benchmarks should be the product of extensive bilateral negotiations. If Egypt failed to meet them, the aid would be withheld and carried over to a reform "escrow" for the next fiscal year, meaning that the more Egypt ignored the requirements in the present, the greater the incentive would be to meet them in the future.

Of course, Arab governments might opt to forgo the additional aid. But if the United States, in a major policy rollout, announced a coupling of economic assistance *and* political reform, it would be risky for governments to make a public show of refusal. Even if they did, an important purpose will still have been served: demonstrating America's newfound seriousness on democracy, something that has long been doubted by the region's citizens.

Still, there is the danger of being outbid. Saudi Arabia is throwing around considerable economic resources itself, and largely to those who will oppose change.

Consequently, $1 billion on its own may not be enough to have a significant impact. That is why, as Ken Pollack and Bruce Riedel both argue in chapters 16 and 18, respectively, the United States has to make a major effort to reassure Riyadh about America's goals for reform in the region. It is also why any conditionality schemes must be coordinated with the European Union, individual European countries, Canada, Japan, Norway, Turkey, and other significant international donors. Here there is considerable good news: In recent months the European Union has explicitly endorsed positive conditionality by calling for a "more-for-more" approach to assistance. The Millennium Challenge Corporation (MCC) also has a more-for-more model, but it has been oriented to economic development rather than political reform. Instead, the MCC's mandate might be expanded to have a more explicit emphasis on the goal of democratization.

Concrete Benchmarks

There is a sense among many Arabs that the United States is easily satisfied by cosmetic reforms or substantive reforms that do not affect entrenched power structures. The feeling is that Washington is willing to see partial economic reforms, and things like improved women's rights and religious tolerance, as "checking the box" of reform. The United States should therefore clarify that the ultimate goal is a revamped political system in which the king or dictator relinquishes significant power. The United States should judge, and make clear that it will judge, reform by that standard.

This points to the need for the United States to devise new, concrete benchmarks for reform in conjunction with reformists from the region. For democratizing states like Egypt and Tunisia, benchmarks could include things like certifiably free and fair elections (requiring international monitors) and military nonintervention in civilian affairs. For liberalizing autocracies with some semblance of electoral competition, such as Jordan and Morocco, benchmarks should focus on expanded political space for opposition groups and fair (rather than merely "free") elections. Opposition groups should have the right to criticize the regime (including the monarchy's prerogatives), to organize and operate without government interference, and to freely campaign and gain access to national media.

Holding free elections is positive, but much less so if they have little meaning as a product of gerrymandering and manipulative electoral laws that limit opposition representation.[7] Perhaps more important—and this applies to all the monarchies of the region—is the devolution of executive power, with the understanding that some (like Morocco) may proceed more quickly than others (like Saudi Arabia). No matter how free and fair elections are, their effects will be limited as long as elected parliaments wield little power relative to absolute monarchies that continue to enjoy veto power over all major decisions.

Aid Coordination

Another important step that the United States should press for is the coordination of international aid that goes to the region, which would promote and enable both reform and democratic transitions in all of their complex dimensions. First, this would address the tremendous replication of aid efforts across the Western world, which is making Western assistance much less than the sum of its parts. Second, because persistent anti-Americanism often makes it difficult for various Middle Eastern groups to accept aid from the United States itself, collective, multilateral aid efforts are more likely to have a positive impact. Third, the positive conditionality proposed above will not work if only one country pursues it, because the target states could simply turn to other donors who have not conditioned their aid. The Deauville Partnership of the G8, announced in May 2011, could be a good starting point.

As part of a broader effort to coordinate the provision of aid, the United States could actively explore the notion of a "reform endowment." This would be a new international institution funded by a range of Western, Asian, and oil-producing Arab states. Ideally, it would have an international board to apportion loans and grants, or both, to states or sub-state actors seeking to bring about real reform. The European Neighborhood Policy/Euro-Mediterranean Partnership represent, in theory, more integrated approaches to aid that can serve as useful models.

International Institutions

It is important for the international community to find ways to make leaders' pledges to reform more credible. In particular, these commitments need to be accompanied by real consequences if leaders violate them. Again, "negatively" conditioned aid can play a role, but probably only a limited one. For that reason, external actors like the United States and its allies should consider devising new international institutions that may be able to help in this regard.

By way of example, the Helsinki process played a useful role in helping to lock in political reforms in Eastern Europe and the former Soviet Union. The Helsinki Final Act negotiated in 1975 traded American agreement that European borders could only be changed peacefully for Soviet agreement to respect certain basic social and political rights. The Soviet negotiators agreed to the latter because they were convinced such a commitment could never be enforced. But dissidents in Eastern Europe and governments and advocacy groups in the West used the agreement as the basis for criticizing human rights practices in the Eastern Bloc. Since the fall of the Soviet Union, the Organization for Security and Cooperation in Europe (OSCE, the successor to the original Conference on Security and Cooperation in Europe that initiated the Helsinki process) has provided a mechanism for member countries to observe each other's elections and evaluate each other's performance in protecting basic political and social rights, including minority rights. The OSCE helps countries live up to their reform commitments by subjecting them to a sort of peer review by their neighbors. Countries that do not match up find themselves "named and shamed" in the OSCE's reports and press releases.[8]

Regional organizations elsewhere in the world have come to play similar roles over time in their particular regions. For instance, the Organization of American States has become a kind of club of democracies, shunning leaders who stray from the democratic path. The international community should consider a similar regional organization for the Middle East in which member countries could monitor, and if necessary criticize, the progress of fellow members as a way of providing additional incentives for leaders to make good on their promises of reform.

Making the Press a Reform Watchdog

Another path for the United States and its allies to pursue in trying to ensure that promises of reform are fulfilled in the Arab world would be to strengthen institutions that traditionally push for reform and that regimes must respect. The media are one such entity. The media have the ability to embarrass governments and help ensure that if they do not follow through on their commitments, international organizations and international aid will know about it.

In 2009, in response to the birth of the Green Movement in Iran, Washington began to try to find ways to protect and distribute social networking technology around the world. This is an idea that should be expanded to empower journalists and others who are interested in building, or strengthening, a free press. Beyond this, the more that the United States can play its role of guardian of the freedom of the press in the Arab world (even when the Arab press criticizes the United States), the more that a local, independent press—with far more legitimacy than any outside power—will be able to hold the regimes to account and call them out when they renege on their promises. Although few Americans like Al Jazeera, over the past decade, the network and its peers played an indisputably important role in fomenting the Arab Spring by relentlessly contrasting the autocratic reality of the Arab regimes to their sham democratic rhetoric.[9]

Bottom-Up Reform

One of the primary explanations for the failure of American efforts to promote democracy in the region up to now has been that they have relied too much on top-down, rather than bottom-up, methods.[10] Gently pushing, or even harshly prodding, Arab leaders to enact democratic reforms resulted not in an opening of the political space or increased citizen participation throughout the region, as was intended, but rather in a series of superficial measures by adept Arab leaders. For instance, autocrats held "elections" in which incumbents won

90 to 99 percent of the vote, allowing the regime not only to stay in power but also to deflect pressure for reform. In the context of the Arab Spring, in which the relationship between societies and their governments has shifted dramatically, it is essential that U.S. efforts to push for democratic change reflect that shift and engage society as well as the state. During the past decade there was a clear backlash against the idea of promoting civil society as a force for democratization in the Middle East, with scholars arguing that civil society, particularly in the Arab world, was too weak, fragmented, and co-opted by Arab regimes to bring about any real change. It was therefore not worth spending U.S. aid dollars on civil society groups in the region.[11] However, political scientists writing on democratic transitions in Latin America, Eastern Europe, and Southeast Asia have shown that while elites are most likely to determine whether a democratic transition will occur and how, an engaged citizenry and a vibrant civil society are essential to ensure that the transition stays on track.[12]

Developing civil society is, therefore, a necessary but insufficient condition for democratic consolidation as it is civil society, not the elites, that generates the impetus for reform beyond the initial transition period.[13] By slowly building grassroots networks, and bringing together individuals, civil society can enable citizens to make demands of the state that they might not otherwise be ready, or able, to make on their own. Civil society can also play the role of educator, introducing people to rights and liberties that citizens in other countries possess but that they do not, thereby sparking a desire for greater democratic changes. Civil society organizations can help move a competitive authoritarian regime, in which the state uses coercive means to secure repeated electoral victories, to a true democracy in which elections are free and fair.[14]

Thus, it is imperative that U.S. efforts to promote democracy adjust to provide more sustainable and practical support for civil society organizations and citizen networks. First, the U.S. Agency for International Development (USAID) and the State Department's Middle East Partnership Initiative (MEPI) must be willing to provide grants to new organizations. USAID, in particular, has a tendency to provide grants repeatedly to the same organizations, thereby disadvantaging the new, informal citizen networks that have emerged in the wake of the Arab Spring and are often employing more creative means to push for reform.[15]

Second, across the region, coalitions of civil society groups are forming for the first time, defying the previous characterization of Arab groups as competitive with each other and unwilling to work together. There is an opportunity here for USAID and MEPI to help those coalitions build capacity and identify the stronger organizations to serve as coalition leaders. In addition, U.S. democracy promoters can work to create strong cross-country or regional coalitions of civil society groups so that they can develop stronger personal networks and learn best practices. Reform movements in Morocco or Jordan, for example, have lessons to learn from nascent political parties and civil society groups in Egypt and Tunisia.

Third, a bottom-up focus means supporting development organizations.[16] Democracy will not take root without citizen investment, but it is very difficult, if not impossible, to create a vibrant, politically active citizenry when large swaths of the population live in poverty.[17] Economic conditions were instrumental in fueling the revolutionary fires in both Egypt and Tunisia. Thus, in the Arab monarchies, particularly Jordan and Morocco, where it is in the U.S. interest to avoid revolution, it is imperative that USAID and MEPI fund development organizations.

However, bottom-up reform alone is not likely to succeed. As the previous decade has shown, civil society under authoritarianism is extremely limited in its ability to act owing to strict association laws, government intervention, and a lack of basic political freedoms and civil liberties. Arab civil society organizations and individual citizens are able to scream loudly for reform, as they have done across the region, but the decision to initiate a democratic transition still lies in the hands of the authoritarian regime. The reason Tunisia and Egypt are currently transitioning while Syria, Yemen, and until recently Libya have been wracked by violent conflict is that Zine al-Abidine Ben Ali and Hosni Mubarak *chose* to step down whereas Bashar al-Asad, Ali Saleh, and Muammar Qadhafi refused. Thus, it is essential for the U.S. government to both support the bottom-up reform efforts described in this chapter and simultaneously continue to pressure the Arab autocrats, both kings and presidents, to allow some measure of reform.

Putting the Military Relationships on the Table

We propose this last approach warily. It is an idea worth considering, but it could also backfire—easily and badly. This is the hitherto unimaginable idea of treating America's military-to-military relationships as part of the conditionality meant to encourage U.S. allies to reform. It could mean cutting U.S. military assistance to long-standing allies. It could mean withdrawing U.S. bases from countries that refuse to reform and shifting them to countries that really take up the cause—assuming that they want U.S. bases.

As Ken Pollack warns in chapter 7, if the United States is not seen as pushing for reform in a country with military ties to the United States, a great many people will assume that behind the scenes it is providing that country with military support to help the leadership *resist* calls for reform. Whether the United States likes it or not, that is the reality of the region. Thus, continuing to provide military aid and maintaining American military bases in a country where the regime refuses to address the legitimate grievances of its citizens has a cost for the United States.

Moreover, because cutting military relationships would be both so drastic and such a novelty, it would likely have a real impact on the regimes themselves. Across the region, the curtailment of American military aid, let alone the withdrawal of an American base, would be considered a withdrawal of American backing for the government. It might embolden the internal opposition—many of whom may have pulled their punches in the belief that the United States ultimately supported the regime and would come to its aid. In some cases, it might call into question the legitimacy of the regime.

However, such a move would not be without serious risks. First, cutting back military aid, let alone severing a military-to-military relationship, could deprive the United States of a critical source of leverage over the behavior of a regional military in a crisis. As Ken Pollack discusses in chapter 7 and Shadi Hamid in chapter 12, the American military's relationship with the Egyptian armed forces appears to have had an important role in moderating the behavior of the Egyptian high command and persuading them to force Mubarak out. Cutting military ties with other Arab regimes could mean forfeiting that trump card in future such situations.

Second, only a dramatic reduction or cutoff of American military aid would be enough to have any kind of impact on any of the governments of the region, and doing so might drive them in a very dangerous direction. Some governments might choose to realign with rejectionists like Iran and Syria. Others might go looking for other (rising) great power backers with fewer scruples about their internal or external behavior. Still others might try to go it alone, which in itself could be dangerous given all of the problems that every Arab state currently confronts. Pakistan is an ominous example, where the cutoff of American military aid after the Pakistani nuclear tests in 1998 drove the country into anti-Americanism, a deeper relationship with terrorist groups like al-Qaeda, and a more dangerous policy toward India, while reducing Washington's ability to help Islamabad deal with its worsening internal problems.

Third, the United States might lose a base in a vital part of the world because no other country there might be willing to replace it. For instance, it would not significantly discomfit the U.S. strategically to withdraw the Fifth Fleet headquarters from Bahrain—in truth, that capability could be performed afloat by U.S. naval assets in the region, if absolutely necessary.[18] However, Camp Arifjan in Kuwait or al-Udayd airbase in Qatar would be much harder to replace. Indeed, it could be very problematic if the United Arab Emirates, Oman, or Saudi Arabia were not willing to step up and take their place—and that might be impossible if those states were not reforming as well under this scenario.

The United States might be forced to relocate its military forces from the region altogether, perhaps relying more on the facilities at Diego Garcia, but this would constitute a very significant degradation of American military responsiveness that could significantly affect its ability to deter aggression in the region. Studies of extended deterrence have demonstrated that success rests heavily on the aggressor's perception of the local balance of power—not the global balance. Aggressors typically calculate that they can act quickly and create a fait accompli, at which point the deterring state will not be willing to bring all of its strength to bear to reverse that development. Saddam Hussein's invasion of Kuwait was a perfect example of this phenomenon. Thus, removing American military forces from the region could seriously affect their deterrent value.[19]

A FLEXIBLE RESPONSE

If the remaining old regimes of the Middle East come to see any movement toward reform as a threat to their interests, let alone their existence, reform is likely to come slowly to the region. To some extent, that is not bad because it is the nature of reform to be somewhat slow—certainly slower than the breakneck pace of uncontrollable revolution. But the people of the region will not be denied forever, and the pace cannot be allowed to slow to a standstill.

Nevertheless, change is likely to come faster in some countries than in others depending largely on the willingness (and foresight) of their leaders to countenance real steps toward reform. Because American power and wealth—and that of America's allies—is ultimately limited, that reality must be factored into Washington's thinking. It means that the United States, and those countries willing to partner in this effort, need to take advantage of opportunities wherever they manifest themselves and show greater patience when they meet strong resistance. It means prioritizing efforts to foster reform by concentrating on those states most willing to start briskly down the path—like Morocco, Oman, and perhaps Jordan. Indeed, to return to the idea of positive conditionality, it will mean demonstrating tangible, sizable rewards to those countries willing to embrace reform in order to show others that it is worth doing. In decades past, the United States talked about helping countries to take risks for peace. In the years ahead, it must learn to help countries take risks for change.

18

SAUDI ARABIA

The Elephant in the Living Room

BRUCE O. RIEDEL

The Kingdom of Saudi Arabia, one of the last absolute monarchies in the world, was caught off guard by the unrest that began in Tunisia and then spread like a tsunami to the rest of the Arab world. To add to Saudi angst, both the king and crown prince are in poor health, and succession is a complex political process. King Abdullah returned earlier than expected from surgery and recuperation in New York and Morocco to deal with the emerging crisis.

Since then, the kingdom has become the de facto leader of the counter-revolution in the Arab world. The Saudis quickly gave refuge to Tunisia's president Zine al-Abidine Ben Ali and were shocked when Egypt's Hosni Mubarak fell from power. In an unprecedented move, Saudi troops deployed across the King Fahd Causeway in early March 2011 to support a brutal crackdown on mostly Shi'i protesters in Bahrain. Led by Saudi Arabia, the monarchs of the Gulf Cooperation Council have agreed to jointly quell any revolutionary movement in the six Arabian Peninsula monarchies. Riyadh has made it clear it also will stand behind the Hashemite monarchy in Jordan, in effect creating a club of monarchies under Saudi protection. In reality its capacity to shepherd this group is doubtful, given the historic rivalries among the seven monarchs.

The new dynamics in the Arab world have also disrupted Saudi Arabia's traditional alliance with the United States. The Saudis believe Washington was too quick to abandon Mubarak and naïve about the unrest in Manama. To create a counterweight to its long-standing relationship with Washington, Riyadh is reaffirming old alliances with Pakistan and China. Even so, Washington remains Saudi Arabia's closest security partner, and despite the frictions in the alliance, the United States is still supporting the kingdom's survival as an absolute monarchy.

Ironically, King Abdullah is a reformer by Saudi standards, and his modest steps toward political change may endure. But bold, systemic change is unlikely anytime soon, and for now the kingdom will fight to resist the onrushing tide. The king's hard-line half-brother, Prince Nayif, already is the animating spirit of the kingdom, if not yet the king. But the country is not immune to the winds of change, and the House of Sa'ud is entering uncharted waters with its own people.

UNREST INSIDE AND OUT

So far, the Arab Spring has inspired only limited unrest inside Saudi Arabia. Saudi reformists tried copying the Tahrir Square model and used Facebook to call for a "Day of Rage" for March 11, 2011. The Saudi government responded with a massive show of police and security force across the country to preempt any demonstrations. For its part, the Wahhabi clerical establishment preached in mosques against reform and protests to further intimidate potential demonstrators.[1] It worked, and the Day of Rage passed with little rage.

The few demonstrations that have occurred have been in the traditionally restive Shi'i minority communities of the Eastern Province, home to most of Saudi Arabia's oil reserves. This is no surprise since the Shi'ah have often expressed anger at their status as second-class citizens. The Shi'ah's place in Saudi society stems from the alliance between the Saudi royal family and the extreme Sunni Wahhabi clerical establishment, which dates to 1744. Saudi and Wahhabi animosity toward the Shi'ah goes back to the early 1800s when Saudi warriors pillaged Shi'i holy cities in Iraq during the first great Saudi expansion out of their base in the center of the peninsula in the Najd.[2]

King Abdullah has tried to accommodate Shi'i demands for greater autonomy over the years, but the unrest throughout 2011 shows that tensions remain high. Still, the Shi'ah are far too few to threaten the kingdom's stability. Even if they engage in terror attacks like the bombing of the U.S. air base at al-Khobar in 1996, which U.S. and Saudi officials blamed on Saudi Hizballah, a pro-Iranian, Shi'i terror group that has been by and large dormant since the 1990s, the Saudi Shi'ah are a nuisance, not a threat to the regime.

More potentially serious has been unrest among Saudi women. This turmoil could open up not only gender but also generational and regional fault lines between the Wahhabi heartland in the Najd and the restive, more progressive western province of Hijaz, which the Al Sa'ud only conquered in the 1920s. Saudi women are not allowed to vote in the country's limited elections, or to drive automobiles. In September 2011, the king granted women the right to vote, but not until 2015. The ban on driving has remained, and a few Saudi women in Riyadh and Jeddah challenged the law in 2011 and were arrested. The authorities quickly suppressed efforts to organize social protests on the issue via Facebook and Twitter. The ban constitutes a major economic cost for the kingdom as some 800,000 foreign taxi drivers, usually South Asians, are employed to transport

Saudi women. As a result, the average middle-class family spends $350 a month getting female family members from place to place.[3]

Though the women's protests and other ripples of dissent have been effectively and quickly repressed, the storm outside the kingdom has been harder to suppress. In March 2011, the Saudis feared that the majority Shi'i population in Bahrain was on the verge of forcing the Sunni al-Khalifa dynasty there to accept a transition to constitutional monarchy. For Saudi royals, who do not differentiate between Shi'ah and Iran, it meant an Iranian challenge to Sunni absolutism just across the causeway from their own Shi'i population. Worse still, the United States seemed to be actively encouraging the problem.

To preempt a deal, on March 14, 2011, over a thousand Saudi troops and a contingent of police from the United Arab Emirates publicly and visibly crossed the sixteen-mile causeway in armored vehicles to help the al-Khalifa hard-liners crush the rebellion. The Saudis had practiced this maneuver for years (one of the key reasons the causeway was built was to provide an emergency invasion corridor), but never before had the kingdom actually used its own forces to help crush a popular rebellion in a Gulf Cooperation Council state. Even if, and when, the Saudi troops return to the kingdom, they will be only hours away from coming back if needed. (As a further bond between the two royal families, King Hamad's son is now engaged to King Abdullah's daughter.)

In effect, Saudi Arabia was proclaiming a twenty-first-century equivalent of the old Soviet Brezhnev doctrine for its own backyard: no revolution will be tolerated in a bordering kingdom. The rest of the GCC monarchs saluted. Like Russia in 1848 and again in 1968, Saudi Arabia became the guarantor of counterrevolution. The Saudi press dismissed American and European criticism of the operation, including President Obama's May 19, 2011, speech on the Arab Spring, as "drivel."

The Saudis have also made clear to Jordan that they do not want revolution on their northwest border either. They have encouraged the Hashemites to take a tough line on political reform and invited Jordan (as well as the more distant Morocco) to join the GCC. Jordan probably will take up the offer since it needs GCC money, which will only further Saudi influence there.

Meanwhile, the Saudis are pushing the GCC to expand the size of its expeditionary force based at King Khaled Military City in northeast Saudi Arabia from its current strength on paper of 40,000 to a larger force, the size yet to be determined. Not coincidentally, that base is perfectly placed to block any overland problems coming from what the Saudis see as a Shi'i-dominated Iraq.

However, Saudi Arabia's attempts to forge an alliance among the Middle East monarchs may be easier said than done because these seven monarchies have decades, even centuries, of rivalry. The Hashemites and Saudis have been enemies since the eighteenth century. Similarly, the Qataris chafe at Saudi leadership, and the Omanis look east to South Asia for direction, not west to the kingdom. Even the UAE is more disunited than united. Thus, any cooperation is likely to be tactical, not emotional.

Then there is the Achilles' heel of the Arabian Peninsula, Yemen, which is beyond Saudi control. Riyadh has never been fond of President Ali Abdullah Saleh, who backed Saddam Hussein in 1990 and who Saudi Arabia tried to overthrow in the Yemeni civil war in 1994. As a result, while Riyadh is not sad to see him go, it is worried about what may come next in the poverty-ridden southwestern corner of the peninsula, where more than half the entire peninsula's population resides. Moreover, chaos and anarchy in Yemen will fuel the Saudis' worst enemy—the Salafist terrorists bred by Saudi Arabia's own prodigal son, Osama bin Laden.[4]

AL-QAEDA

What alarms the Saudis most is the Yemen-based al-Qaeda in the Arabian Peninsula (AQAP) terrorist group. The kingdom fought a vicious and violent struggle against al-Qaeda inside its own borders between 2003 and 2006. It was the most sustained and serious internal threat to the Saudi monarchy since the formation of the modern Saudi state in 1932. Gunfights and bombings wracked every major Saudi city as al-Qaeda supporters tried to fulfill the urging of Osama bin Laden to overthrow King Abdullah and his brothers. It was a frightening and defining moment for this elderly generation of royal leaders and for the next generation in waiting.

The man who led the Saudi effort to crush al-Qaeda in the kingdom, Prince Mohammed bin Nayif, son of Prince Nayif, was almost assassinated by an AQAP suicide bomber in 2009. MBN, as he is known, is the epitome of the next generation of Saudi princes: smart, savvy, sophisticated, and determined not to have the family lose control of its birthright. By all accounts, he waged a brilliant campaign that has virtually snuffed out al-Qaeda in the kingdom, at least for now.

The Saudis are right to worry. Al-Qaeda is still a factor in Saudi internal politics. Its extreme views resonate with a constituency in the Wahhabi heartland and in poorer parts of the kingdom like the Asir region, which borders Yemen. If the counterterrorism pressure is loosened by the princes, the risk of a renewed al-Qaeda challenge is significant, especially as the AQAP base in Yemen has grown stronger since central authority has collapsed beyond Sana'a. AQAP has exploited the Yemeni civil war to strengthen its safe havens and sanctuaries in southern and eastern Yemen, allegedly even taking control of small cities like Zinjibar, outside Aden, for a time. To reinforce their ultimate goal, al-Qaeda's leading propagandist in Yemen, the New Mexico–born Anwar Awlaki, has called the Arab Spring a "tsunami" of revolution that is destroying al-Qaeda's enemies like Mubarak and will inevitably lead to revolution in the Arab monarchies.[5]

Looking for Friends

Despite President Obama's efforts to build ties with the Saudis (his first visit to an Arab capital as president was to Riyadh), the royal family has soured on the president. The Saudi monarchy believes he has promised but not delivered on the Israeli-Palestinian peace process and has done too little to counter Iran, especially in Bahrain. Members of the royal family were shocked that Obama did not stand by Mubarak to the bitter end. As a result, while the Saudis know they cannot ignore Washington, they are looking for alternatives to the east.

Pakistan, whose own relations with Washington are deteriorating, is a long-standing Saudi ally that provided thousands of troops to defend the kingdom in the tumultuous 1980s, in the wake of the Iranian Revolution. Pakistan has been the largest recipient of Saudi foreign aid for decades, and Pakistan's 20,000-strong Khaled ibn al-Walid Brigade was deployed in Saudi Arabia as the ultimate Praetorian Guard until Saddam's invasion of Kuwait, when King Fahd found a bigger bodyguard in the U.S. Army. Saudi and Pakistani intelligence connections are very close, and the kingdom provided sanctuary to exiled former prime minister Nawaz Sharif after the Musharraf coup in 1999. The Saudis continue to heavily fund his political party, and Sharif is favored to be the winner of the country's next elections.[6] Abdullah is now looking to Islamabad for contingency support.

Prince Bandar bin Sultan, former ambassador to the United States and now national security adviser, traveled to Islamabad in late March 2011 to raise the idea of bringing the Pakistani Army back to the kingdom. Islamabad was quick to agree. Indeed, long before the Bandar trip a Pakistani battalion was already in Bahrain to back up the al-Khalifas if needed. Other Pakistani advisers or retired officers man much of the armed forces of the UAE and Oman.[7]

Bandar also looked farther east. He traveled to China to offer contracts in return for political support. As Jonathan Pollack explains in chapter 34, Beijing is no fan of the Arab Spring, and it is eager for Saudi oil and investment. Bandar secretly negotiated the first big Saudi-Chinese arms deal for intermediate range ballistic missiles in the 1980s and is the kingdom's premier China expert. Abdullah has long believed that China and India are the future markets for Arabian energy. Not coincidentally, he made his first foreign trip abroad as king to these two emerging powers.

Nevertheless, Saudi foreign policy is always pragmatic and adaptive. Despite their disappointment at Mubarak's fall, the Saudis have reached out to the new power centers in Egypt, offering economic aid and debt relief to the transitional government. And Saudi Arabia's past ties to elements of Egypt's new political forces offer opportunity as well—the kingdom has been a sanctuary for the Muslim Brotherhood for decades, and Abdullah has long-standing connections to Brotherhood leaders from across the Arab world. Riyadh will undoubtedly try to cash in on that connection in the new Egypt. In short, democracy in Egypt will not be enough to sever relations between the two leaders of the Arab world.

SUCCESSION AND REVOLUTION

Perhaps Abdullah's most important reform came in 2006 with the creation of a royal council to choose Saudi Arabia's line of succession. Composed of the thirty-six surviving sons, or grandsons, of the modern kingdom's founder, King 'Abd al-Aziz ibn Al Sa'ud, the Allegiance Council is charged with choosing who will be crown prince once Abdullah dies and his brother Sultan succeeds him. But Sultan, who has been defense minister since 1962, is frail and infirm; he would only be a figurehead if he lives to be king at all. So Deputy Prime Minister and Interior Minister Prince Nayif is likely to be next, and he is the ultimate hard-liner on political reform.

The danger here is that Saudi Arabia suffers from all of the same problems as Egypt, Tunisia, Libya, Syria, and the other large Arab countries—the countries that have experienced the most unrest and revolutions. On paper, Saudi Arabia does not look much different from Egypt, even taking into account Saudi oil wealth. There is considerable debate among Western experts on Saudi Arabia as to how much Saudi immunity from large-scale unrest so far has been the product of the inherent conservatism of the Saudi people, and how much has been a product of King Abdullah's own popularity. Abdullah is personally respected for his piety, integrity, and efforts to fight corruption among his family members. In addition, Saudis have supported his introduction of gradual, Saudi-style reforms that have—in their own way—begun to address their grievances. Abdullah has made important efforts to reform the kingdom's educational system, economy, judiciary, and legal systems, and to curb corruption across the board. He has made small steps on women's rights and the treatment of the Shi'ah, and even some (even smaller) steps on political reform. Taken together, these hardly represent a revolution, but they set the stage for a long-term transformation of the Saudi economy and society in a very positive manner. What has so far been lacking has been commensurate reforms in the political realm, although it is not yet clear that this is a priority for the majority of Saudis, who tend to focus first on their economic situations. Soon after returning from Morocco in early 2011, where he had been convalescing after medical treatment, King Abdullah announced over $30 billion in new bonuses, mosque building, and other payoffs. But he offered nothing on political reform.

The assumption that the kingdom's relative tranquility is principally a product of the popularity of Abdullah and his reform program raises important questions about Saudi stability after Abdullah departs, especially if he is succeeded de facto or de jure by Prince Nayif. Hated by people from all wings of the country—Shi'ah, progressives, and al-Qaeda—Nayif is not likely to usher in any significant reforms. He could well do away with the Allegiance Council once Abdullah is gone, and if not, render it meaningless. Many of Abdullah's reforms have moved forward only due to the efforts of the king and his closest advisers, because most of the Saudi bureaucracy, and many in the kingdom's clergy, dislike the changes. Even if all Nayif does is to not keep pushing these reforms forward, they might quickly wither. And historically, revolutions have most commonly occurred when a nation has faced a long period of growing problems and frustration, followed by a brief period of hope when a reformist began to turn things around, only to have those hopes dashed when the reforms were unexpectedly halted. That might be precisely the scenario the Saudis encounter if Nayif succeeds Abdullah and attempts to supplant his reforms with repression.

Of course, Nayif is no spring chicken either, and his own health is a question mark. Should Nayif become incapacitated, there are still several more surviving sons of King Sa'ud in line—like the Riyadh province governor Prince Salman, or the intelligence chief, Prince Muqrin—before the next generation gets its chance. At the very least, power is likely to remain with the old-timers for the foreseeable future.

SAUDI CHALLENGES

The biggest unknown is how the kingdom's youth will act. Like everyone else, young people in Saudi Arabia have watched the drama in Tahrir Square, Benghazi, Sana'a, and Dara'a on Al Jazeera. The kingdom has the same demographics as those of its Arab neighbors—specifically, a large youth bulge that is chasing too few jobs. Eighty percent of Saudis are under the age of thirty, and 47 percent are under eighteen.[8] While the kingdom has tried to appease many of their demands for jobs and bonuses, their numbers are so great that the measures have often fallen short, and youth unemployment has remained as dangerously high as anywhere else in the Middle East. Unemployment is officially only 10 percent, but the real number is probably around 25 percent (only men are counted since few women seek employment). And even the Saudi government believes that youth unemployment reached 39 percent in 2010, up from 28 percent in 2000.[9] The underemployed young Saudi man may have more money in his pocket than his Egyptian counterpart, but he, too, is frustrated by a system that is closed to non-royals and completely opaque. If the Egyptian experiment in governance looks to be a winner and Cairo produces a more transparent, accountable, and democratic Arab government, it could be very attractive to many Saudis, especially among the more cosmopolitan Hijazis—those living in the cities along the west coast.

Indeed, the Hijazis have never fully accommodated themselves to Saudi and Wahhabi rule. The region has always seen itself as more sophisticated than the Najd, looking across the Red Sea to Egypt and north to Syria rather than to the harsh interior. For centuries it was part of the broader Islamic world, a part of the great Islamic empires of the Umayyads to the Ottomans. The Najd, in contrast, was outside those empires, largely because of its remoteness and barrenness. Moreover, the Hijaz is home to the holy cities of Mecca and Medina, the former visited by Muslims from all corners of the *ummah* (the Islamic world) each year for the *hajj*. Some Hijazis resent Wahhabi rule, many are critical of the ugly remodeling of the holy cities to allow plush apartment blocks and designer stores, and a few even long for the return of the Hashemites.[10] The Arab Spring in other countries has flourished along fault lines similar to the one between the Hijaz and the Najd, most notably in Libya, where the rebellion has revived the differences between Tripolitania and Cyrenaica. The issue of women's rights, discussed earlier, is another area that could exacerbate the geographical divisions of the country. The Saudis must be concerned that what happened in Libya could happen in the kingdom, especially because its current borders are less than a hundred years old.

But one should also be careful not to count the Saudi royal family out. They are among the world's most proven survivors. They have shown themselves to be wise and perspicacious leaders, willing to remove a king who has proven himself unfit, and to pass over would-be monarchs in favor of more suitable candidates. Their first kingdom survived from 1744, when they made their alliance with Mohammed bin Abdul Wahhab, until 1818, when an Ottoman-Egyptian army crushed it. A second kingdom controlled the Najd from 1824 to 1891. The current kingdom began with ibn Al Sa'ud's conquest of Riyadh in 1902 and was consolidated in the 1920s after wresting the Asir from Yemen. The Al Sa'uds are come-back kids.

They also outlasted the Arab revolutions of the 1950s and 1960s. The monarchies in Egypt, Iraq, Libya, and Yemen all collapsed, but the kingdom fought back, ultimately bogging down Gamal Abdel Nasser's Egypt in a bloody insurgency in Yemen. They outlasted Saddam Hussein and the Iraqi threat in the 1990s. The Al Sa'uds are skilled at handling inter-Arab conflict.

And they outfought Osama bin Laden. The Saudi crackdown against al-Qaeda inside the kingdom has been one of the most effective campaigns against al-Qaeda in the Muslim world in the past decade. Bin Laden tried hard to rally Saudis against the royal family and its corruption, hypocrisy, and links to America, but he failed to inspire them enough to rise up to topple the family. Led by the

Nayifs, the family fought back with a sophisticated campaign of detective work, rehabilitation, reconciliation programs, and sheer ruthlessness.[11]

SAUDI ARABIA, THE ARAB SPRING, AND THE UNITED STATES

Change comes to Saudi Arabia very slowly. The United States began raising the issue of slavery in the kingdom shortly after the historic meeting between King 'Abd al-Aziz ibn Al Sa'ud and President Franklin Delano Roosevelt at the Suez Canal in 1945 that inaugurated the American-Saudi alliance. John F. Kennedy finally persuaded the family to abolish slavery in 1963. Aside from jaw-boning, the United States has little leverage with the kingdom. The Saudis are on track to purchase over $60 billion in new arms from America, critical to jobs in many states, and they are the swing producer in the global oil market with the unique power to set oil prices. In short, the United States needs Saudi Arabia not just for strategic reasons but for the health of the U.S. economy at a time when the country is broke.

Despite frictions, the truth is that the United States remains the kingdom's foremost supporter. Over the decades, Washington has provided tens of billions of dollars in arms and critical intelligence support to fight Nasserists, Ba'thists, Iranians, and al-Qaeda. The continued American support in military and intelligence channels is vastly more important to the survival of the House of Sa'ud than occasional mild rebukes from the secretary of state about the law against women driving. Because of this, the United States is the counterrevolution's biggest backer. The $60 billion in U.S. arms sales to the country, for example, is primarily for the National Guard, the kingdom's praetorian force, and for helicopters that the guard will use for internal security. America also needs Saudi counterterrorism help. It was the Saudis who provided the key intelligence that thwarted AQAP's effort to blow up a jet over Chicago in October 2010. The Saudis will also be key to any effort to deal with Yemen.

In his speeches on the Arab Spring and U.S. Middle East policy, President Obama implicitly recognized Saudi Arabia's importance (and America's impotence) by not mentioning the kingdom at all. He was probably right. American public exhortations for reform in the kingdom would serve little purpose. They would only alienate the royals and lead to unrealistic expectations among the public. But in private, Washington needs to talk quietly to the family about the long-term direction of change in Arabia, and how the kingdom plans to adapt to those changes. The key is for Washington to convince Riyadh that, as King Abdullah's reforms have already implicitly acknowledged, change must come to the entire Arab world, even to the kingdom. The question is how the United States and Saudi Arabia can partner to ensure that change comes about in positive and constructive ways. If they can do so, it will become the basis for maintaining the U.S.-Saudi alliance in the twenty-first century.

19

JORDAN

An Imperfect State

SALMAN SHAIKH

Jordan has long been a critical partner for the United States in the Middle East. Its position as a "moderate" pro-Western monarchy has earned it a privileged place among American allies in the region. When Jordan signed a peace treaty with Israel in 1994, it became even more important to U.S. strategic interests in the Middle East. Amman's role as a key source of American intelligence in the region has also grown considerably over the years. Information from Jordanian intelligence agencies was reportedly crucial in aiding the U.S. forces that killed al-Qaeda in Iraq's Abu Musab al-Zarqawi in 2006.[1] At times, Americans have also viewed Jordan as an agent for reform in the region and even held it up as evidence that moderate monarchies in the Middle East can help secure both American democratic values and Washington's vital security concerns.

In turn, Jordan has benefited a great deal from its relationship with the United States. It is currently the second largest per capita recipient of American aid, with total U.S. assistance having increased from $228 million in 2001 to $818 million in 2010.[2] Furthermore, the United States and Jordan signed a free trade agreement in 2000, which granted Jordanian businesses access to American companies. Jordan is one of only five nations in the region that have been accorded such an arrangement.[3]

However, Jordan's situation is more unstable and unsustainable than many of its key allies, particularly the United States, realize or are willing to acknowledge. Domestically, the nation has long faced challenges threatening its stability, which have not been quieted by past "top-down" reform efforts aimed at moving toward a more representative political system. Serious doubts have surfaced regarding King Abdullah II's commitment and vision for a transition to a constitutional monarchy, despite his claim in 2005 that Jordan would "absolutely" become one in the future.[4] Many Jordanians fume that his rhetorical promises are little more than that: cosmetic statements that have no real bearing on reality. The Arab Spring has brought these destabilizing forces to the fore.

King Abdullah has had nine cabinets in his eleven-year reign, with the latest appointed on February 1, 2011, to quell protests that broke out in Jordan after the overthrow of the Ben Ali regime in Tunisia and the start of Egypt's own revolution. Jordan's overall commitment to democratic governance remains shaky. The Economist Intelligence Unit's 2010 democracy index rated Jordan 117th out of 167 nations, placing it firmly among those considered "authoritarian."[5] Nonetheless, the country continues to benefit from a great deal of unconditional U.S. support. In a July 2008 speech, then-candidate Barack Obama praised King Abdullah, proclaiming that "Jordan's leadership is a source of pride for its own people. I have long admired King Abdullah's example of moderation and modernization."[6] On that same visit during his presidential campaign, Obama went so far as to tell the king, "We need to clone you."[7] There has also been surprisingly little mention of Jordan's protests in official U.S. statements on the Arab Spring, though high-level officials like Assistant Secretaries of State William Brownfield and Jeffrey Feltman visited Jordan during the height of the unrest. The U.S. commitment to Jordan remains strong, yet Jordan's commitment to reform is uncertain.

The changes in the region have also increased the potential for instability. Recently, the Gulf Cooperation Council (GCC) sought to shore up Jordan with the prospect of greater economic and energy support while opening up the possibility of more integrated security partnerships with its well-trained military and intelligence services. The possible expansion of the GCC to include Jordan and Morocco represents those Gulf nations' "security-first" approach to containing the uprisings sweeping the region. By expanding an organization of monarchies in the Middle East, the GCC hopes to ride out the wave of reform while maintaining the status quo in their countries.[8] However, the effects on Jordan domestically, especially if it further slows down any meaningful reform efforts, could be disastrous.

In addition, the recent turmoil in the region, particularly the ouster of President Mubarak in Egypt and the uprising in Syria, has led to heightened Israeli concerns about its security. Israel has become more isolated than ever in the region, making Arab-Israeli peace that much more elusive. Because of the unrest, Israel and the United States have placed an even higher emphasis on Jordan's ability to maintain its peace treaty with Israel and its stable relations. Whether Jordan will continue to be able to do so in the absence of a credible peace process is a question that is relevant for the first time since 1994, especially as the Jordanian monarchy faces mounting troubles in the kingdom.

A History of Uneven Reforms

The Arab Spring came early to Jordan. Since mid-January 2011, protests have occurred with surprising regularity, yet they have not reached the same level of intensity as elsewhere in the region. The demonstrations have primarily focused on economic and political inequalities, with the country's main opposition party, the Islamic Action Front (IAF), calling for constitutional and democratic reform.

In essence, these protests have proved what many have known for years: Jordan is unstable politically, economically, and socially. Indeed, it is not surprising that Jordanians took up the cause first introduced by Tunisians and Egyptians so quickly. Despite the apparent stability of the Hashemite Kingdom, there have been frequent demonstrations and widespread discontent with Jordan's state of affairs for many years.

In response to repeated popular demands, Jordanian monarchs have regularly introduced incremental reforms to try to deflect or defuse the opposition. In 1989 King Hussein oversaw the country's first parliamentary election in over thirty years in response to the kingdom's first political protests, which took place in Maan. Shocked by this sudden outpouring, King Hussein was forced to make political liberalization a priority, and in 1990 he appointed a royal commission of sixty people, including members of leftist parties and the Muslim Brotherhood, to draft a National Charter.

The National Charter was not quite a new constitution, but it was meant to open up Jordanian politics and enable the creation of new political parties—ones that would operate within limits set forth by the National Charter. Its impact was decidedly mixed. On the one hand, even after the king approved it in 1991, the pact "remained a document without formal legal standing," according to analyst Glenn Robinson.[9] On the other hand, Jordanians treated it as one of the foundational documents of what was to be a new "democratic" order. Demonstrating the ambiguities, the charter allowed for the establishment of political parties but did not change the laws that restricted their formation. The prime minister and parliament were able to pass a Political Parties Law in 1992, which did legalize political parties. However, the regime, according to the pact, required opposition parties to recognize the legitimacy of the monarch in order to compete in political life. Overall, these ambiguities reflected Jordan's conflicted approach to reform.

Throughout the 1990s and after King Abdullah came to power in 1999, there was little real reform in Jordan. Rather, opposition parties were constricted in an effort to bolster the monarchy and consolidate power in the hands of loyalists. The professional associations crisis of 2005 was evidence of this new approach. In January 2005, Interior Minister Samir Habashneh ordered professional associations to "completely halt" all political activities and promote only the skills of their members.[10] In a further restriction, the government required the groups to receive formal authorization for all political gatherings. Two new and more restrictive laws were also proposed that year—the Professional Associations Law and Political Parties Law—but before they could be enacted, King Abdullah dissolved the government and once again spoke out in favor of reform in response to a new wave of public anger. Perhaps not surprisingly, Jordan's 2007 elections were widely considered tainted and unfair, with many opposition figures and independent watchdogs reporting vote-rigging on the part of the government.

Recent Developments

When King Abdullah saw his people taking to the streets in protest of Jordan's autocratic government, this time as part of the Arab Spring in 2011, he once again quickly announced new programs and new personnel to implement them, all in the name of reform. But as before, the king's gestures are less significant than they may seem. In one instance, the king sacked his cabinet on February 1, 2011, appointing retired general and former prime minister Marouf al-Bakhit as the new prime minister, in an apparent concession to protesters' complaints that the previous prime minister, Samir Rifai, had failed to address Jordan's economic problems.[11] But this was more an affirmation of the king's commitment to the status quo. Al-Bakhit is decidedly a member of the "old guard." The new cabinet similarly seems to have undergone primarily superficial changes, with six key former ministers remaining in the twenty-seven-member body.

A potentially more meaningful development was the king's creation of the National Dialogue Committee in March 2011, chaired by Senate president Taher al-Masri. Although an appointed body, it has been charged with revising the electoral law and the Political Parties Law, and amending the constitution in particular. Moreover, on June 12, in his first televised speech since the outbreak of the protests, King Abdullah pledged that the country's parliament would be reformed. He said that a new electoral law would create "a parliament with active political party representation . . . that allows the formation of governments based on parliamentary majority . . . in the future."[12] He further said the National Dialogue Committee was reviewing the constitution, and promised to fight corruption and promote democracy.

In other words, King Abdullah said exactly what the United States wanted him to say, yet it remains to be seen whether this rhetoric will be converted into action. If enacted, these reforms would transform the character of the country's government. Currently, the parliament's upper house is appointed, with only the lower house elected, thus granting the king the balance of power in government. An elected parliament could allow greater representation for more opposition parties, depending on the electoral law.

However, having been disappointed by the king's promises so many times in the past, opposition parties are proving difficult to satisfy. Their response to King Abdullah's latest pronouncements has been skeptical at best. For instance, Zaki Bani Rsheid, head of the IAF's political office, responded negatively to King Abdullah's latest offers of reform, charging that "there was nothing new in the speech." He also criticized the king for "not giv[ing] specifics, and there were no guarantees."[13] IAF Shura Council president Ali Abul Sukkar was similarly suspicious of the king's commitment to reform, stating, "There is clear intent to dwarf political parties to empower other groups. Political parties have been given 15 seats, equal to the women's quota. I do not see any genuine intention for reform."[14] There remains therefore a pervasive belief that the king is still fine-tuning "the political process game" but not fundamentally changing what is at stake in the country.

This cynicism prompted most opposition groups to reject the June 2011 proposals for elections put forth by the National Dialogue Committee. Its plan created a complicated scheme for filling parliamentary seats, rather than allowing for the straightforward proportional representation system that the opposition parties had demanded.[15] Earlier, in May, the opposition created a pro-reform political coalition, the National Front for Reform (NFR), calling for the "rule of law" in Jordan. The NFR demanded constitutional amendments, government accountability, anticorruption efforts, a guarantee of press freedoms, and improvements in the educational system, as well as economic, judicial, and security reforms.[16] The group has united the IAF—which refused to participate in the king's dialogue—with the Jordanian Communist Party, the Jordanian Democratic Popular Unity Party (Wihda), the country's two Ba'thist groups, the Jordanian People's Democratic Party (Hashed), the National Party, the Social Left Movement, and the Jordanian Women's Union.

The creation of these two bodies—the government-backed National Dialogue Committee and the opposition's NFR—demonstrates the polarization of politics in Jordan, a development that is likely to continue unless and until a genuine and all-inclusive political dialogue begins.

POLITICAL, ECONOMIC, AND SOCIAL CHALLENGES TO REFORM

One of the greatest challenges facing Jordan's political system is the lack of viable opposition parties. This is less a fault of the parties themselves than of the conditions under which the government has allowed them to operate. Aside from the IAF, few parties have the ability to mobilize supporters. Opposition figures often complain that the Political Parties Law makes it difficult for parties to gain official government recognition. Further, Jordan's "one-vote" electoral law is widely criticized for the negative effect it has on opposition parties that are able to form. The 1993 law did away with the previous system in which voters could cast as many votes as there were seats allocated to their district. Because each person is now allowed only one vote, people tend to select candidates with whom they have tribal or family connections, rather than IAF or other opposition candidates to whom they lack personal connection.[17] These two laws have curtailed the formation of a strong opposition movement outside of the IAF.

Economically, Jordan's situation is far less favorable than many realize. The primary complaints of the January 14 protests were rising fuel and food prices, heavy tax burdens, and high unemployment, which reached 11.9 percent in the fourth quarter of 2010.[18] Furthermore, although often hailed as a nation moving toward an open economy, Jordan ranks surprisingly low in terms of "ease of doing business"—111th out of 183 nations listed—in the World Bank's 2011 *Doing Business* report.[19] And despite being praised for reforming its economy, Jordan maintains a complicated bureaucratic system that makes it difficult for Jordanians to make investments and start businesses. Many of the praised economic reforms, such as the establishment of Qualified Industrial Zones (QIZs), have benefited primarily international companies, rather than the local business community. As a whole, economic reforms have been "slow, selective, and uncoordinated," according to the Carnegie Endowment for International Peace's Sufyan Alissa.[20] Incentives to embark on meaningful reform are few, as Jordan receives a substantial amount of unconditional foreign aid.

Jordan also faces demographic and social challenges. An estimated 60 to 65 percent of the population are Palestinians, and there are marked social cleavages. Economic inequality has exacerbated this, as Palestinians tend to occupy the business elite whereas non-Palestinian Jordanians have done less well financially.

Adding to these challenges are Jordan's tribal divisions. Some 40 percent of the country's population is affiliated with one tribe or another, and Jordanian officials have in effect allowed tribal justice to take the place of civil law in intertribal conflicts. The result has often been something closer to anarchy. In early January 2011, tribal spats broke out across the country, and in Salt, tribesmen went on a two-day rampage after a young man was killed by police. Meanwhile, a feud between rival tribes in Maan led to thousands of rioters setting a court building afire.[21]

The tribes have traditionally been loyal to the Hashemite monarchs, but some have echoed protesters' demands—something that has been very disconcerting for the regime. In a joint statement issued on February 5, 2011, thirty-six tribal figures warned that if political reform is not implemented, Jordan will experience protests of the type seen in Tunisia and Egypt. The statement demanded immediate change: "Political reform is now an urgent matter that cannot be delayed, holding the corrupt and thieves accountable and freezing their assets, prohibiting them from traveling are all part and parcel of political reform."[22] The tribal leaders' statement made it less certain that they are reliable supporters of the regime. Whether it can survive without them also remains to be seen. Perhaps most shocking to the regime was that the statement singled out Queen Rania, comparing her to Leila Trabelsi—the wife of the former Tunisian president—who has been accused of large-scale corruption. Such an attack on the queen is unprecedented and signals the seriousness of their call for reforms, particularly in the realm of corruption.

Corruption remains a major issue in Jordan, with some of the largest protests in May having been specifically devoted to this issue. In the words of the IAF's Zaki Bani Rsheid, "The government is corrupt and oppressive. Reform is inevitable, and the rulers have two choices: adopt reforms or quit."[23] The latest corruption scandal concerns powerful businessman Khalid Shahin, who, with three others, including a former minister, was imprisoned for three years for graft payments as part of a multibillion dollar project to upgrade the Jordan Petroleum Refinery Company. Shahin was allowed to leave prison for medical treatment in the United States in February, yet was seen in a London restaurant in April, leading the justice and health ministers to resign and uniting leftist and Islamist opposition forces in the country against the al-Bakhit government.[24]

A New "Jordan First" Deal

The task of reform has become urgent. More than post-Arab monarchies, due to political, social, and economic features, Jordan risks facing the chaos and stability that could spread throughout the region if it does not reform itself. Yet the experience of the past decades and especially the superficial reform efforts of King Abdullah make it difficult to imagine that the Jordanian people—particularly their opposition parties—would trust in purely "top-down" reforms. The king has simply "cried wolf" too many times. Most recently, in August 2011 King Abdullah announced constitutional amendments proposed by the appointed ten-member Royal Committee on Constitutional Review. These changes, approved by cabinet and undergoing review in parliament, represent the most significant changes to the constitution since its drafting in 1952. Nonetheless, they were not made through consultation with the Jordanian public and did not push forward demands for constitutional monarchy; the king retains his power.

Transparent and politically inclusive discussions, which have the confidence and involvement of all political parties and elements of civil society, should lay the foundation for long-term changes in the structure of Jordan's political system and economic arrangements. As it stands today, Jordan's government operates as an absolute monarchy, despite claims to greater democratic practice.[25] Only broadening the process of reform is likely to satisfy most Jordanians and—if the historical record is any indication—produce meaningful change.

It is also time for the United States to recognize that Jordan is not the stable and democratic entity it has long considered the kingdom to be. The United States must use its leverage to place specific demands on the Jordanian monarch. First and foremost, the United States needs to determine—ideally through conversations with a variety of Jordanian political and civil society leaders—what the goal of a reform process ought to be. After so many years of false reform in the Hashemite Kingdom, which Americans nonetheless regularly praise, the U.S. position in this regard is unclear. In advocating reforms, this time the United States must not take no for an answer. The lesson of the past decades is that when the United States accepts its allies' refusal to reform, U.S. values and long-term interests in the region are harmed. This was the case in Egypt and Tunisia, and it may be the case in Jordan in the future if the United States does not signal that it is serious about democratic reforms in Jordan.

Equally important, a viable and serious effort at Arab-Israeli, particularly Israeli-Palestinian, peacemaking would help relieve the Jordanian government's burden in maintaining quiet along its border with Israel. As was the case with Egypt, Jordan's existing "aid for peace with Israel" deal is increasingly in danger of being swept away by a population that does not support it. After Mubarak's ouster, the question is increasingly being asked: How long will this unstable structure last?

20

KUWAIT, QATAR, OMAN, AND THE UAE

The Nervous Bystanders

SUZANNE MALONEY

Situated on the western shores of the Persian Gulf, the smaller Arab sheikhdoms of Kuwait, Qatar, Oman, and the United Arab Emirates have long been accustomed to the contradictions of their geostrategic fate. Distance, deserts, and eventually the discovery of epic oil and gas resources have insulated their societies and their states from encroachment and uncertainty. Yet their location at the chokepoints of the world's foremost energy transit corridor and in the shadow of historically predatory regional and world powers cannot help but cultivate a persistent existential insecurity. Oman shared in at least a portion of the 2011 drama, but for the other three states, the Arab Spring has transpired largely at arm's length, experienced primarily through the comfortable prism of satellite television and social media. Yet the movement's continuing evolution and prospect for spillover effects will undoubtedly have direct and potentially profound implications for their security and governance as well.

The political characteristics of the smaller Gulf sheikhdoms diverge in significant fashion—Oman is a sleepy monarchy, the UAE a cloistered federation of well-heeled city-states, Qatar a dynamic upstart, and Kuwait a constitutional monarchy proud of its pioneering (yet dysfunctional) parliament. Still, the broad similarities that bind these states—in particular, bountiful resources, small indigenous populations, a leadership that places a high premium on domestic and regional stability, and a preference for oblique diplomacy—provide them with an important and illuminating vantage point on the historic developments that have engulfed the broader Middle East since December 2010. What is more, because of their history as valuable American partners, and their uncomfortable proximity to existing and potential sources of instability, their success or failure in navigating the regional upheaval will reverberate well beyond their borders.

THE BACKDROP: KUWAIT

With its miniscule territory and population, massive wealth, and outsized existential threats looming along each border, Kuwait stands in many respects as the poster child for the region's contradictions and complications. It is at once an extremely stable polity—ruled for more than 250 years by the same family—but also the tumultuous home of the Gulf's first real parliament, which routinely indulges in bringing down the government and paralyzing decisionmaking. An aging leadership and cultural conservatism have produced a sense of domestic stagnation, yet in 2005, thanks to an active and boisterous suffrage movement, Kuwait became the third state in the region (after Qatar and Bahrain) to grant women the right to vote. The 1990 Iraqi invasion galvanized a strong sense of Kuwaiti nationalism, but sectarian, tribal, and family identities remain paramount. Kuwait is buffered by its endowment with the world's fifth largest petroleum reserves but feels perpetually insecure because of its neighbors: hostile giants that are practically within eyeshot of the capital.

The 2003 ouster of Saddam Hussein should have had a liberating effect on Kuwait. After twelve years of an almost obsessive focus on its threatening neighbor to the north, Kuwait was suddenly free to devote its political and economic resources to internal needs. Moreover, the past decade has been an extremely lucrative one for Kuwait as a result of the 2003–08 oil price boom and the opportunities to cash in on Iraqi reconstruction. Still, steady population growth has created disproportionate public sector burdens since the vast majority of all Kuwaitis in the labor force are employed by the state. Unfortunately, the infirmity of its senior leadership, the consensual nature of decisionmaking, and the tenacious but petty conflicts between the government and the parliament have meant that decisionmaking remains excruciatingly slow and that major issues tend to be deferred rather than decisively resolved.

Kuwait has real politics as well as real institutions. Political parties are not permitted under Kuwaiti law, but since the 1991 liberation and reconstitution of the parliament, several factions from disparate ends of the ideological spectrum have dominated the debate. These include Islamist groups, which tend to function as a vocal opposition to government positions and vary in their degree of religious orthodoxy, as well as a more secular and liberal faction that also engages in criticism of the government.

THE BACKDROP: THE UAE

Despite the many superficial similarities between the two states, the United Arab Emirates in many ways occupies the opposite end of the spectrum from Kuwait. A confederation of seven politically and economically diverse sheikhdoms, the UAE has managed to fashion a uniquely stable and prosperous political compact in the short forty years of its independent existence. Any previous uncertainties about the smoothness of the inevitable leadership transition and the durability of the federation itself have been almost entirely eliminated. The UAE has an extraordinarily successful track record of balancing the country's conservative social mores and dramatically uneven resource endowments with a strong federal system and an enterprising approach to development and foreign investment.

The UAE has emerged from several significant tests of its durability and vitality in recent years—first, the 2004 death of its widely admired founder Sheikh Zayed bin Sultan al-Nahyan, whose personal charisma and authority had been crucial to maintaining the federal structure. The country's first-ever experience with succession proceeded smoothly, with the ascension of Sheikh Khalifa bin Zayed al-Nahyan as president and a vigorous, but not overly distracting, competition for power among the ambitious second-generation royals of the preeminent emirate, Abu Dhabi, as well as those of Dubai. The UAE also rode out several other challenges to its greatly prized stability, including the regional upheaval that ensued as a result of American military actions in Afghanistan and in Iraq. Most acutely, the federation was tested yet again by the devastating impact of the 2008 global financial meltdown and the ensuing collapse of high-flying Dubai's real estate sector. The subsequent reassertion of Abu Dhabi's traditional primacy is still reshaping the state's priorities and policies.

Unlike some of its neighbors, where ruling families have recently initiated substantial steps toward greater popular political participation, the UAE has made no moves in this direction. Both the populace and the government have shown much less interest in implementing democratic reforms that would open up the current system. The UAE's stability and prosperity have generated relatively few political grievances, at least among the small proportion of its residents who hold UAE citizenship.

The Backdrop: Qatar

For better and for worse, Qatar has established itself as the most energetic actor in the Gulf over the course of the past decade. After ousting his father from power in 1995, Sheikh Hamad bin Khalifa al-Thani seized the reins of this tiny, historically impoverished peninsula and undertook a wholesale transformation of its economy and social life. Although he retains a firm grip on power, the emir has broken new political ground over the past sixteen years, including nationwide elections with full suffrage and a 2005 constitution that includes notable guarantees of political freedoms and separation of powers.

Political competition among the ruling family members and associated elites remains very limited, and the country's government is quite stable. Concerns surrounding the emir's health persist, however, assuaged only somewhat by a 2003 shift in the succession lineup to favor Sheikh Hamad's fourth son, who has been slowly assuming greater responsibilities in his role as crown prince.

Even more dramatic was the emir's acceleration of the development of Qatar's massive natural gas resource, which has brought billions of dollars in foreign investment over the course of the past decade. The pace of development proved so intense that the government declared a moratorium on new projects that will likely last until at least 2013. Neither this hiatus nor the ripple effects of the global economic slowdown have impeded Qatar's boom significantly, and with an indigenous population of only approximately 350,000, per capita income is among the highest in the world.

Qatar's rapid ascent in the international gas business fueled an equally ambitious and fast-paced effort to modernize and remake essential components of the country's social infrastructure, with a particular focus on education that has brought at least eight Western universities directly to Doha and pioneered a model that has been borrowed by its neighbors. Through its deep-pocketed support of the raucous Al Jazeera satellite channel, Qatar has also played a crucial role in eroding the region's long-standing strictures on public debate. Al Jazeera has been a convenient tool of Qatari influence, tweaking Doha's rivals and asserting its ambitions across the Arabic-speaking world. Its reach and impact, however, have often surpassed the government's intentions or control, unleashing public passions on sensitive issues such as Iraq and the peace process and ultimately contributing very directly to the changes that have unfolded across the region over the past year.

While Al Jazeera has been the hallmark of Qatar's regional ambitions, the emirate's efforts to punch above its weight diplomatically have been assiduous and diverse. It has deliberately sought opportunities to promote itself by staging major international sporting events (including the forthcoming 2022 soccer World Cup) and conferences, establishing itself as a maverick on issues such as Israel and Hamas, and being an assertive would-be mediator on disputes from Iran to Sudan.[1] During the 1990s, Doha also agreed to host the forward headquarters of U.S. Central Command and a massive American air base—a decision that represented an investment in the bilateral relationship with Washington that came with real risk and political costs for the Qataris. These efforts have often compounded Doha's historic frictions with its immediate neighbors, particularly Bahrain and Saudi Arabia, as well as with Washington, which has repeatedly clashed with Qatar over both its brash style and provocative policies. Ultimately, Doha's ambitions and preference for stirring the pot remain a contentious factor in a region in flux.

The Backdrop: Oman

Sultan Qaboos bin Said al-Said has ruled Oman as an absolute monarch since coming to power in a bloodless coup in 1970. Internal politics have been almost entirely nonexistent, which has been convenient given the restrictions on organizing and mobilizing. In 1990 an advisory Majlis al-Shura (consultative council) with little if any independent authority was established, and over the decades a system of partial suffrage has taken root. On the whole, political development and democratization have not been parts of the sultan's agenda; rather, he can rely on the loyalty of most Omanis because of their closed tribal structure and the popularity of the economic transformation that he instituted.

In 1996 the sultan promulgated the Basic Law—in effect, Oman's first-ever constitution. But the new legal framework and evolving selection process for the Majlis al-Shura have not been sufficient to address the aspirations of some young Omanis who are frustrated at the lack of power granted the Majlis and at the increasingly difficult employment situation. Oman has experienced low-level political activism persistently over the past decade, albeit not in a fashion that would suggest the emergence of a movement that could pose a real challenge to the political system centered on the sultan. The other main uncertainty is succession; the sultan has no children and is unlikely to produce any. Meanwhile, the Basic Law provides an unusual and untested succession process, and its viability is a subject of deep concern.

As in most Gulf countries, hydrocarbons form the most important sector of the Omani economy, but Oman's oil reserves are comparatively small, and even those will be exhausted in relatively short order at the present rate of extraction. The government has recognized that it must seek a medium-term replacement for its modest oil earnings.

In terms of foreign policy, relations with the United States and United Kingdom form the central plank of Oman's defense and security strategy. Bilateral relations with nearly all Middle Eastern countries are good, and Oman has a particularly close relationship with the UAE. The sultan and his foreign minister have proved valuable intermediaries over the years in brokering accords among adversaries within the region, and the country is one of the few Gulf states to have close ties to Iran.

Popular Response to the Arab Awakening

Thanks in large part to their considerable wealth, high living standards, and tradition of quietism, none of these four countries experienced the full frontal onslaught of unrest and popular mobilization that has engulfed other parts of the Arab world, although Oman certainly had a taste. Nevertheless, all of the countries share some of the same vulnerabilities that have sparked dissatisfaction elsewhere in the region—disproportionately young populations with widespread access to communications technology and, in at least some cases, an increasing sense of discontent with the prevailing social compact primarily as a result of the lack of employment opportunities. Consequently, each of these countries has found itself contending with the embers of revolutionary upheaval in different fashion.

Of the four, Oman saw the most serious and sustained unrest with a wave of protests that began in February 2011 and then resisted a variety of determined government attempts to quell them. Not surprisingly, given its relatively limited oil wealth and correspondingly more modest economy, Oman's unrest was focused on economic grievances at least as much as on political ones. In April 2011, more than 1,000 job-seekers gathered at Muscat's Bait al-Barka roundabout demanding employment, while the Oman Air staff launched a strike for higher salaries.[2] In Salalah, similar numbers marched through the city demanding better wages, more employment opportunities, and an end to corruption. A month later, Omanis seeking employment in Jalan Bani Bu Ali rioted and looted government offices to protest a recruitment event that they considered inadequate. The protests became routinized and spread to smaller cities, typically manifesting after Friday prayers. Activists staging sit-ins outside the Majlis al-Shura premises formed an Omani Association for Reforms and asked for government recognition by applying to the Ministry of Social Development for a formal approval.

Kuwait also experienced a series of sizable public demonstrations, initially involving mainly stateless Arabs (*bidou*), a perennially disempowered minority group in Kuwait that numbers approximately 120,000.[3] The bidou have long been agitating for more meaningful political participation as well as the economic rewards associated with Kuwaiti citizenship, but their activism only exacerbates the suspicion with which they are regarded by the country's elites. Protests forced the resignation of Kuwait's interior minister in early February 2011, and less than two months later led to the mass resignation of the cabinet in response to allegations of poor performance and corruption.[4]

For many Kuwaitis, these developments had a familiar ring. Parliamentary inquiries and subsequent ministerial resignations are relatively commonplace political tactics in contemporary Kuwait, but the latest round transpired in a unique and unpredictable regional environment. As a result, the protests escalated rapidly and began to affect heretofore apolitical groups that are considered vital constituencies for the regime, such as youth. This conjured fears that the combination of elite political wrangling and street violence could imperil the stability of the state itself.

Given the regional context, the most significant development in Kuwait was the emergence of youth groups, including Kafi (Enough, a reference to the

Egyptian group of the same name, known as Kifaya) and al-Soor al-Khames (the Fifth Fence), which emerged in early 2011. These groups called for significant political reforms, demanded the prime minister's resignation, and organized a series of sizable demonstrations beginning in early March 2011.[5] From gatherings of several hundred, the protests swelled to 1,000 and by June to 2,000, making these the largest organized political activities the country had ever experienced. Refrains of "freedom, freedom, we want a popular government" signaled their demand for a prime minister from outside the ruling al-Sabah family.

In May and June 2011, the situation devolved further, both within the parliament and on the streets. Meetings of the National Assembly were suspended for several weeks after an unprecedented fight broke out between members of parliament over the issue of Kuwaitis detained at Guantanamo Bay in mid-May 2011.[6] In June the country's deputy prime minister, a senior member of the ruling family, resigned rather than face questioning by the parliament. Meanwhile, approximately 500 Kuwaitis staged an antigovernment protest, chanting, "The people want the overthrow of the head (of government)" in response to allegations of corruption and inefficiency.[7]

The prime minister also faced opposition within the parliament for meeting with the Iranian foreign minister, who was touring the Gulf in an effort to mitigate rising tensions. Interestingly, the eruption of political opposition that Kuwait experienced in the early months did not seem to engage the country's historically restive Shi'ah, who account for 30 percent of the Kuwaiti population.[8] With the exception of a May 2011 parliamentary brawl over the government's Iran policy, the Shi'ah restricted their opposition to the normal institutional channels. This factor did not appear to mitigate the country's anxieties over Iran, which was perceived to be the beneficiary of the regional turmoil and was accused of smuggling in weapons, dispatching espionage rings, and spewing aggressive rhetoric to destabilize Kuwait.

In June 2011, the Kuwaiti leadership attempted to draw a line in the sand, aimed as much at parliamentary hijinks as at the street protests. Kuwaiti emir Sheikh Sabah al-Ahmad al-Sabah gave a televised address in which he declared that "conditions no longer permit more chaos, lawlessness, and confrontations . . . which threaten the security of our nation and its resources." In what was an unprecedented public move for a leadership accustomed to behind-the-scenes politics, the emir chastised both the parliamentarians and the youth protesters, adding that "enough is enough" and noting that he had instructed the interior minister "to continue to take measures to protect Kuwait's security and stability and to show zero tolerance towards anyone who tries to compromise the security of the country."[9]

Popular unrest in Qatar and the UAE has been substantially more muted, in part because of the small size of their citizen base and a legacy of political quietism that owes much to a generous public dole. Al Jazeera has proved a useful foil in this respect, rallying public interest around dramatic events in North Africa while being relatively more circumspect on developments that strike closer to home, in particular the Shi'i uprising and subsequent Saudi-backed repression in Bahrain.[10] Still, small-scale testing of the limits on dissent by some Emiratis suggests that the ripple effects of the regional changes will permeate the affluence and ease that has long characterized the political environments of the small sheikhdoms. In this respect, the rather modest top-down reforms initiated by Doha over the past decade appear to have been a more successful inoculation against popular pressure than Abu Dhabi's dogged refusal to open space for meaningful political participation or discourse. However, political aspirations and grievances appear to be less salient for some in these countries. In a survey of young Arabs undertaken during the genesis of the Arab Spring, Qataris actually ranked democracy lower among their priorities than any other Arab citizens across the region, and their relative interest in democracy had declined considerably from previous years.[11] Still, the continuing percolations of regional unrest will continue, and the events of the past year have demonstrated the capacity of previously depoliticized populaces to become quickly and vehemently galvanized. Indeed, at least one regional analyst has warned that a second wave of political mobilization and potential unrest is likely to sweep the Gulf states before 2012.[12]

One question that looms on the horizon for these small states is that of citizenship. The debate has historically been most acute in Kuwait, as a result of the "stateless" population, but it is likely to take on new relevance amid a broader regional environment of political empowerment. Unlike Saudi Arabia, where expatriate workers represent an increasingly prohibitive luxury given domestic un- and underemployment, the smaller sheikhdoms cannot sustain their productive economies without importing labor that outnumbers their citizenries. As the Arab Spring begins to redefine the traditional social contract between ruler and ruled, the Gulf states will have to contend with the implications of these changes for their huge expatriate populations.

Regime Response to the Arab Awakening

The initial response of each of the four governments to the Arab Spring was based on the countries' strengths and was meant to take the wind out of any public dissatisfaction. For each of the Gulf states, economic resources provide the traditional bulwark of legitimacy and stability, and these resources were enhanced by the bump in oil revenues that was a convenient consequence of the Arab uprisings. This inspired massive and multiple measures to effectively buy off the opposition with generous handouts. In January the Kuwaiti government announced that every citizen would receive approximately $3,500, as well as free food rations for fourteen months.[13] In February Oman's Sultan Qaboos promised to create 50,000 public sector jobs in response to public agitation over the economy. The sultan followed up in March with a monthly benefit of approximately $400 for registered job-seekers and a hike in the minimum wage for private-sector Omani nationals.[14] A month later, he unveiled a $2.6 billion spending package.[15] Doha expanded zero-interest housing loans and has set aside funds for wage hikes for public employees. Meanwhile, the UAE pledged $1.6 billion to develop infrastructure within its oil-poor northern emirates, raised military pensions by a whopping 70 percent, and introduced bread and rice subsidies.[16] In stopgap measures aimed at the long-standing problems of inflation and indigenous unemployment, the government also intervened with retail merchants to try to hold down prices and announced plans to raise the proportion of citizens that must be hired by businesses.[17] The Gulf Cooperation Council also pledged $20 billion to aid Bahrain and Oman to quell opposition protests. (Both Kuwait and Qatar have contributed hundreds of millions to the Libyan opposition.[18] Doha has sought to capitalize on the opportunities initiated elsewhere as a result of the upheaval, sending a trade delegation to Egypt to discuss $10 billion in potential projects there.)

Academic studies have found, however, that oil wealth is no guarantee against internal unrest, and it is unclear to what extent these payoffs actually calmed or prevented the unrest in these four Gulf states, although that does appear to be what their leaderships believe.[19] In addition to handouts, the Kuwaiti and Omani responses featured elements of compromise, repression, and a skillful use of popular respect for the institutions of the state (including the monarch).

Indeed, the Gulf sheikhdoms have also employed other tactics to stave off threats from within, such as mollifying protesters by meeting some of their demands. Sultan Qaboos in Oman has initiated plans for a new university and bank and has also sought to demonstrate leniency by sporadically pardoning protesters and releasing political prisoners. Like Kuwait, Oman has dismissed a number of cabinet ministers—in early March, the sultan announced a new cabinet that reflected the fact that at least twelve members lost their jobs. However, many protesters deemed this insufficient, demanding the trial of the sacked ministers, who were tied to corruption.[20]

For its part, the UAE unveiled much-hyped plans for the nation's second-ever election, scheduled for September 2011.[21] Critics and dissidents have been pressing the government to expand the voting base and the authority of the Federal National Council—the legislature, such as it is—but its latest moves appear to be relatively modest in scope. Notably, the population eligible to vote remains capped at only 12,000, and the council itself has extremely limited powers and in effect functions as a purely advisory entity.[22]

Where handouts and half-hearted political reforms have not proved suffi-cient, several of the Gulf states have resorted to more forceful responses, espe-cially where protests were beginning to resemble those in Tunisia and Egypt. In Oman, for example, several pro-democracy activists were reportedly kidnapped and beaten, hundreds (at a minimum) have been arrested and detained, and thousands more have been violently dispersed from demonstrations by baton-wielding security forces.[23]

Kuwait has sought a lighter touch. Several demonstrations in February and March 2011 by stateless Arabs demanding equal status and citizenship were dis-persed by security forces reportedly using tear gas and smoke bombs, with at least fifty people being arrested at one protest.[24] Kuwait's interior minister issued an ominous warning that called on the stateless to refrain from continued activism in order to "preserve their safety."[25] The government adopted a more kid-glove approach to the rising tide of activism among Kuwaiti youth, although a dispute in late May 2011 over the location of a planned protest provoked stern warnings and a show of force by hundreds of policemen and elite special forces, who cordoned off the capital's main Safat Square to prevent the students from gathering there.

Notably, the United Arab Emirates, which has experienced almost no serious domestic unrest, has nonetheless reacted forcefully to stamp out even the slightest whispers of dissatisfaction. In April 2011, the government arrested five activists who signed a petition for democratic reform, including two prominent bloggers and a financial analyst-professor, on suspicion of charges including "perpetrat-ing acts that pose a threat to state security."[26] The UAE has quietly cracked down even on seemingly innocuous organizations, evicting the Gulf Research Cen-ter from its foothold in Dubai despite the think tank's wholly noncontroversial activities. An Emirati lawyer who is a long-standing critic of the government's approach to human rights issues declared that the security services "are taking us backwards. They are creating hate between the people and their rulers."[27]

In addition, Abu Dhabi has begun to reinforce its already robust infrastruc-ture for ensuring internal tranquility. Long-standing restrictions on informa-tion, organization, and political speech have been strengthened and expanded in the wake of the Arab Spring, including an attempt to outlaw secure use of the Internet from handheld devices like BlackBerries. The UAE has also reportedly contracted with a notorious U.S. security firm—led by the founders of Black-water—to establish a battalion of foreign mercenaries to serve as a second line of defense against internal and external threats.[28] The reality is that technologi-cal quarantines are illusory weapons against social pressures, as the Mubarak regime found in its failed bid to quash anti-regime protests by shutting down the Internet. Moreover, the intensification of repressive policies will undercut the very qualities—openness and modernity—that made the country an attractive destination for foreign capital and tourists.[29]

The Gulf states have also diverged somewhat in their diplomatic responses to both the regional and international implications of the Arab Spring. Their actions here have been shaped in equal measure by their divergent inclinations toward activism and the degree to which their leaderships are distracted by internal issues. In general, the Gulf nations have preferred to bankroll measures from a distance, except in Bahrain, where the Emiratis have played an unusually direct role in contributing troops to the Saudi-led effort to repress pro-democracy protests by the country's Shi'i majority.

Somewhat predictably, Doha has taken a different tack, jumping into the breach opened by the shifting balance of power in the region. Qatari foreign minister Hamad bin Jassem al-Thani has been actively involved in formulating both the regional and broader international response to the devolution of political order in Yemen and Libya. Even as the rest of the Arab League appeared to get cold feet about its advocacy of intervention in Libya, Doha stepped up to the plate in a public and dramatic fashion. Qatar has contributed fighter jets to the NATO-led effort to enforce a no-fly zone there, brokered oil deals to enable the opposition to market the country's resources, and dispatched trainers to guide the rebel army. One of the Libyan rebel leaders declared that the Qataris "have been more effective than any other nation."[30] In Yemen, Qatar's assertive efforts to craft a transition pact prompted accusations of meddling from the Yemeni president, before he fled the country for medical treatment. In addition, Doha remains actively engaged with the various Palestinian factions and has hosted gatherings of the Syrian opposition as well.

Qatar has clearly used the Arab Spring to advance its long-standing foreign policy agenda and enhance its prominence on the regional stage. One of the Qatari military commanders commented: "Certain countries like Saudi Arabia and Egypt haven't taken leadership for the last three years. So we wanted to step up and express ourselves, and see if others will follow."[31] This will likely create as many problems as it resolves, as Qatar's increasing independence puts it into occasional conflict with U.S. policy as well as with its neighbors, who are less likely than ever to appreciate the hubris that typically accompanies Doha's actions.

AMERICAN ISSUES AND OPTIONS

Consumed with the demands of rapidly proliferating crisis management and the more routine but equally pressing exigencies of supporting an orderly transition in Egypt and elsewhere, Washington has remained relatively disengaged from the low-level clamor emerging in the smaller Gulf states. To the extent that senior U.S. officials have engaged with their counterparts in Kuwait, Oman, Qatar, and the UAE, such as in President Obama's closed-door April 2011 meeting with Abu Dhabi's crown prince Sheikh Mohammad bin Zayed al-Nahyan, the conversations have focused on regional security—a euphemism for Iran.[32] This is hardly surprising, but it is insufficient to ensure that the region is equipped to emerge from the current tumultuous period intact.

Washington must walk a delicate tightrope with these four states in hopes of assuaging their increasing sense of insecurity while bolstering their readiness to confront both internal vulnerabilities and external threats, all the while augmenting their capability to steward a process of meaningful change rather than be subsumed by it. This is much easier said than done; American attention is already strained to the maximum by the demands of dealing with ongoing regional crises and the aftermath of regime change in Egypt and elsewhere. Moreover, there is a dangerously credulous tendency to presume that the sleepy Gulf monarchies can continue to simply buy off dissent. The stakes are sufficiently high and U.S. interests sufficiently vital to justify a real investment in dealing with these small states. As a result, U.S. cooperation with the Gulf states should entail efforts to devise meaningful mechanisms for managing a credible program of political and economic reform and for strengthening multilateral cooperation.

21

Bahrain

Island of Troubles

Michael S. Doran and Salman Shaikh

The crisis that flared up in Bahrain in February 2011 and the government's subsequent crackdown the following month have presented challenges for the United States regarding its interests in the Gulf. For the ruling al-Khalifa family and its supporters in the Gulf Cooperation Council (GCC), particularly Saudi Arabia, the crisis represented the latest attempt by Iran to meddle in the kingdom's internal affairs where the majority of Bahrainis are Shi'i. For the thousands of protesters, it was the culmination of economic, social, and political grievances. Like the people of Tunisia, Egypt, and elsewhere in the Arab world, they took to the streets to demand greater equality, justice, and political representation.

The government's crackdown on the protesters and its imposition of a State of National Safety (in effect, martial law) in mid-March with the help of GCC forces only added fuel to the fire. Thirty-five protesters were confirmed killed—four in police custody—and scores were injured. In addition, more than 600 were arrested, including political leaders, journalists, civil society activists, and nearly fifty medical staff. Special security courts were set up on the eve of the crackdown, which tried dozens of people, handing down death sentences for two protesters alleged to have killed two policemen. The International Labor Organization denounced the mass sackings of an estimated 1,000 workers—300 of them employed by the Bahrain Petroleum Company—for allegedly taking part in the protests. As part of the crackdown, the government also tore down almost thirty Shi'i mosques, claiming that they had been built illegally.

Although riots and demonstrations have not been uncommon since the 1980s, Bahrain has entered a new era of instability fueled by a combination of long-standing local grievances, the competition of regional powers, and transformative aspirations stirred up by the Arab Spring. This instability threatens to have a wide impact on the region, particularly with regard to rising tensions between the GCC and Iran. The crisis has also led to fresh scrutiny of the Obama administration's dealings with two key allies—Bahrain and Saudi Arabia—especially in the face of persistent reports of serious human rights violations during the GCC-assisted Bahraini crackdown.

As a result, the government of Bahrain faces a very difficult but very common choice: King Hamad bin Isa al-Khalifa and his regime can embrace reform and put in place a new process that genuinely delivers far-reaching political, economic, and social change to address the legitimate grievances of the Bahraini people—Sunni, Shi'ah, and non-Muslim alike. Or they can continue to rely on repression to prevent change. The events of the Arab Spring, particularly in Egypt, Libya, and Tunisia, should make clear which of these is the better choice—the choice most likely to result in peace and prosperity for Bahrain and a continued role for the royal family over the long term.

Simply put, the best course of action for the future of Bahrain rests on the ability of the ruling family and the main Shi'i opposition parties to enter into a sustained dialogue, without preconditions, on political, social, and economic reforms. Doing so will prove more difficult than previous attempts in 1999–2000 and mid-March 2011, just before the violent crackdown. The well of mistrust has deepened among ordinary Shi'ah, particularly youth, who will need to be assured that the parties will faithfully represent their views and that the ruling family will deliver on promises of a genuine dialogue and political reform. To make matters more complicated, divisions have widened within both the ruling family and the opposition parties—between hard-liners and pragmatists—as to the best way forward. It has therefore become urgent to support the pragmatists within both camps, so that dialogue, rather than confrontation, emerges, in an effort to instigate far-reaching democratic reforms in the kingdom. The role of the United States as a facilitator could prove to be critical in helping Bahrainis achieve a new deal through serious and sustained talks.

NATIONAL DIALOGUE AND REFORM EFFORTS

King Hamad's lifting of the state of emergency on June 1, 2011, and his call for a national dialogue that is "serious, comprehensive, and without preconditions" was a direct attempt to restart discussions with opposition forces after the upheaval of the previous two and a half months. The king's interest in dialogue was a welcome return to his earlier tone, when he had championed a program of democratic reform shortly after his ascension in March 1999.[1] At that time, he established a committee to create a road map that would take Bahrain from a hereditary emirate to a constitutional monarchy within two years. He also pardoned all political prisoners and abolished the special State Security Court that had granted the government undue ability to detain people.

In February 2001, 90 percent of the public endorsed a National Action Charter in a referendum—the first such vote since the 1970s. The charter led to the establishment of a bicameral parliament with elections for the representative lower house in late 2002. The subsequent 2006 elections were notable in that the main, largely Shi'i opposition political party, al-Wifaq, participated for the first time and won the largest share of the votes. The elections also led to a split in the party and the establishment of al-Haq as a more radical off-shoot. Al-Haq ultimately boycotted the elections because its members objected to the new constitution.

Almost from the outset, however, the public questioned the king's intentions and the sincerity of his reform agenda. Many were troubled by the lack of consultation in drawing up the 2002 constitution, especially given the king's assurances that opposition parties and civil society would be involved. Opposition parties, particularly al-Haq, voiced concerns that the new constitution rescinded the liberties granted by the (suspended) 1973 constitution and that it gave equal legislative authority to the parliament's elected lower chamber and the upper house, which the king appoints.

Over time, the government delayed or even ignored many of its promised reforms and ruled in increasingly autocratic fashion. Inevitably, this provoked greater and greater popular discontent. With the reform project floundering and opposition growing, Bahrain seemed to be backsliding to the 1980s and the 1990s, when widespread unrest led to Iranian-backed coup attempts in 1981 and 1996, and a popular uprising in 1994. The majority Shi'i population, in particular, once again began to demand greater respect for their civil and human rights, economic opportunity, and better social conditions. As part of this, they wanted an end to discrimination that had largely excluded them from the most important bureaucratic, political, economic, and social positions.

It was perhaps no coincidence that the 2011 uprising started on February 14, the tenth anniversary of the referendum vote that had endorsed the National Action Charter. A decade later, the reform effort had failed to reach its stated aim of moving the country to a constitutional monarchy. More strikingly, this outcome emboldened oppositionists who argued that working for reform from within the system had proved to be a dead end and that the Shi'i majority needed to assert itself in a new way to change the country's political system.

The 2011 uprising has made serious and credible political and democratic reforms that much more difficult. The unrest has brought to the fore hard-liners on both sides who have only one thing in common: they all oppose dialogue. In the ruling family, the hard-liners are led by Prime Minister Khalifa bin Salman al-Khalifa—the king's uncle and the prime minister since Bahrain's independence in 1971. Among the opposition, the hard-liners are led by the Bahrain Freedom Movement, which was created in March and includes the Shi'i al-Haq Party.

A clear indication of this increasing polarization came in early February when the ruling family, led by the reformist crown prince, Shaikh Salman bin Hamad al-Khalifa, offered a serious dialogue with the mainstream opposition National

Alliance grouping, which includes al-Wifaq and the liberal Sunni al-Waad Party. On the eve of the March 14 crackdown, and apparently under pressure from within the al-Khalifa family and Saudi Arabia, the crown prince made what became his best offer—a dialogue based on seven principles, which included representative government and a parliament with full powers. With the protests on the streets escalating, the opposition parties hesitated. Mindful of losing their support from the street, they asked the crown prince for further clarifications before entering the talks. It was too late. The next day, the government launched its crackdown with the help of the GCC Peninsula Shield Force. The hard-liners in the regime had won and in so doing had helped empower their counterparts in the opposition, all of which will make future dialogue more difficult. The effort that is most likely to yield a conservative outcome, however, is the Bahrain Independent Committee of Inquiry that was established in July 2011 to report on human rights abuses that took place during the crackdown on the protests (as of this writing, the committee was scheduled to submit its findings to the king on October 30, 2011).

THE SPECTER OF IRAN AND THE GCC RESPONSE

The al-Khalifas' fears of Iranian hegemony and Tehran's ability to galvanize Bahrain's majority Shi'i population stem from a long-standing, and oft-deserved, suspicion of Iran. Ayatollah Khomeini's revolutionary Iran threatened Bahrain's pluralist traditions that grew out of the need for Shi'ah, Sunnis, and members of other minority faiths to coexist peacefully in the kingdom. In particular, Khomeini's regime saw its coreligionists in Bahrain, who were already growing more conscious of their religious identity, as prime targets for the export of the Islamic revolution. The al-Khalifas' fears were realized in 1981 when they squashed a coup attempt by the Islamic Front, a Shi'i organization with ties to Iran's Islamic Revolutionary Guard Corps (IRGC). Today, both al-Haq and another dissident party, al-Wafa, which is led by the hard-line cleric Abd-al-Wahab Husein, are thought to be pro-Iranian and have sympathies for, if not direct ties to, Hizballah. U.S. officials, including President Barack Obama, have stepped up their rhetoric on this issue in recent months, with the president stating that "Iran has tried to take advantage of the turmoil [in Bahrain]."[2]

However, there is little to no evidence that Iran was behind the latest uprising, despite the claims of King Hamad and Bahrain's GCC partners. Then secretary of defense Robert Gates publicly remarked on Iran's efforts to "exploit the situation in Bahrain" but has also indicated that the Pentagon sees little sign of Iranian instigation. Several other American officials have added in private that they don't think Iran is the cause of the current revolt.[3] Moreover, an August 2008 cable from the U.S. Embassy in Manama published by Wikileaks revealed that the United States had not uncovered any evidence of Iranian material support (weapons and money) to the Bahraini opposition since the mid-1990s.[4]

There is also little evidence to suggest that Bahraini Shi'ah have been looking to Iran for guidance, let alone orders. In fact, most Shi'i protesters work hard to make clear that they see themselves as Bahrainis first. A 2009 survey of Bahraini households revealed that the vast majority of Bahraini Shi'ah joined Sunnis in rejecting a system of governance based on or limited to religion. The survey also showed that support for parliamentary democracy was some 15 percent higher among Shi'ah than Sunnis.[5] In addition, Sheikh Ali Salman, the head of al-Wifaq, has repeatedly stressed that "we have national demands that have nothing to do with Iran" and that the party does not "need to take instructions from Iran."

Yet, in the absence of a political solution in Bahrain, we are likely to see a radicalization of its Shi'i community, inflamed sectarian tensions throughout the region, and Iranian involvement in the country. If Shi'i youth do not see a clear path to reform through established legal channels, peaceful protest, and dialogue, there is a danger that they may turn to armed resistance, which Iran and its agents would exploit.

In response to the unrest, the GCC has promised a $10 billion aid package to Bahrain to support its ailing economy and help King Hamad provide generous social welfare packages that include increased salaries and benefits, as well as subsidized housing. This response, however, did little to placate protesters and has only put a greater burden on the Bahraini exchequer, making it even more reliant on its main financial backer, Saudi Arabia. In fact, Saudi Arabia funds up to 75 percent of Bahrain's budget through the countries' shared Abu Saafa oil field.

Because of Saudi Arabia's strong advocacy for the use of GCC forces in Bahrain, many see Riyadh as a counterrevolutionary agent in the Bahraini context and more broadly in the Arab Spring. Reports indicate that Saudi Arabia has even approached other Muslim countries—notably Malaysia, Pakistan, and Indonesia—to seek diplomatic and possible military support to help counter protests in Bahrain. Saudi Arabia's actions will likely further regionalize Bahrain's unrest and could exacerbate its own existential concerns about Bahrain's problems spilling over into Saudi Arabia itself.

The United States as a Facilitator

From its onset, the crisis in Bahrain has presented the Obama administration with a series of challenges. The speed at which events have moved has opened up the administration to criticism from supporters of both the ruling family and the opposition. For the al-Khalifa family and other traditional Gulf partners like Saudi Arabia and the UAE, the United States has become an unreliable ally, as it has sought to voice support for protesters without isolating its allies. The decades-old contract between Gulf rulers and American administrations based on oil and security is being rewritten by the Arab Spring. Future U.S. influence in the region will depend on America's ability to persuade its traditional allies to enact far-reaching political, social, and democratic reforms. Bahrain, as the only GCC state in crisis (at least so far), will be a test case of this approach.

On May 19, 2011, President Obama made his clearest statement on the need for dialogue and political reform in Bahrain, saying, "The only way forward is for the government and opposition to engage in a dialogue, and you can't have a real dialogue when parts of the peaceful opposition are in jail."[6] His speech had been preceded by a series of visits to Bahrain by senior U.S. officials, including Secretary of Defense Robert Gates and Assistant Secretary of State for Near Eastern Affairs Jeffrey Feltman, who had sought to encourage the ruling family to speed up political reforms. Notwithstanding these efforts, the Obama administration has been a reluctant player in the Bahrain crisis, only intervening as events on the ground required it to do so. In part, the administration had hoped that King Hamad would enact reforms without requiring Washington to exert pressure. In many ways, it was a clear divergence from U.S. policy toward Egypt, Tunisia, Libya, and much of the rest of the Arab Spring countries.

This tortured U.S. behavior is best understood as a product of the Saudi factor. The Saudis have made it clear that they regard what happens in Bahrain as vital to their security. Consequently, anything that the United States does to Bahrain it is also, in effect, doing to Saudi Arabia. In private, Obama administration officials have indicated that they recognize how bad their double standard on Bahrain looks, but they feel trapped by their desire not to antagonize Riyadh any more than they already have. Thus, what Bruce Riedel calls Saudi Arabia's Brezhnev doctrine (see chapter 18) is constraining American policy toward Bahrain.

While this may have been an understandable approach, it is reasonable to ask whether it was the right course of action, especially in light of the lessons of the Arab Spring thus far. First, as Riedel also notes, the Saudis have engaged in reforms of their own that could create an opening to discuss how reform could move forward in other GCC states. By determining Riyadh's red lines, it might be possible to secure Saudi agreement to meaningful political change in Bahrain that would head off future unrest and Iranian involvement—both of which the Saudis desperately do not want. And, as Ken Pollack notes in chapter 16, the key is to find ways to work with the regime and not treat it as, or make it into, the enemy of reform.

Second, when it comes to encouraging political dialogue in Bahrain, the United States is not without leverage. The American military has served as the main guarantor of Bahrain's security at least since the two countries signed a Defense Cooperation Agreement in 1991, and arguably well before. Bahrain has served as a base for U.S. naval activity since 1947, and today provides the head-quarters for the U.S. Navy's Fifth Fleet, responsible for defending the Gulf, the Red Sea, the Arabian Sea, and the east coast of Africa. This, as well as U.S. bases in Qatar and the UAE, has given Bahrain a security shield against possible attack. Bahrain's strategic partnership with the United States intensified in 2001 when Washington designated the country a "major non-NATO ally." In addition, the United States can capitalize on its commercial and business ties to the country, having signed a free trade agreement in 2004 with Bahrain.

The Obama administration has been correct in emphasizing that only a politi-cal solution can end the crisis in Bahrain and in highlighting the necessity of dialogue between the government and opposition parties. However, it needs to do much more to press the parties in Bahrain and Saudi Arabia to create the space for a meaningful dialogue process, learning from the mistakes of the past and helping to stabilize Bahrain and the Gulf.

A Bahraini Model for Political and Democratic Reform

A key objective of the al-Khalifa family has been to restore normality to Bahrain after months of upheaval. However, the end of the State of National Safety only brought more protests and instability to the kingdom. The economy, in particu-lar, continues to suffer, with Bahrain's credit rating plummeting to the third low-est investment grade. International banking and insurance companies continue to downsize their operations, with some already relocating to other financial centers in the Gulf like Dubai and Doha.

The only real path to normality is dialogue between the ruling family and all opposition parties, including the youth protesters and imprisoned opposition leaders. What reforms are possible in the kingdom will depend on the willing-ness of all Bahrainis to compromise. However, it has already become clear that a power-sharing formula that redistributes political power and guarantees eco-nomic and social rights for all Bahrainis is the way forward. A number of models exist wherein an absolute monarchy has devolved power to its subjects.[7]

For the al-Khalifa family that has ruled Bahrain for over 200 years, the notion of sharing power with the Shi'i population raises existential fears that will have to be addressed. The opposition will have to recognize that it, too, must compro-mise. In particular, it has to understand that calls for the immediate establish-ment of a republic will meet continued and forceful opposition, not just in Bah-rain but from the entire Gulf. The commitment of Sheikh Ali Salman of al-Wifaq to the resumption of dialogue aimed at achieving "a constitutional monarchy not a republic" should be welcomed and should inspire other opposition leaders to do the same. However, time may be running out for such an outcome if the regime continues to pursue its security-first approach to the crisis. Ultimately,

King Hamad's stated commitment to reforms and a constitutional monarchy needs to be translated into tangible results. In his son, Crown Prince Salman, the king has a ready and capable partner who has shown a sincere desire for a meaningful national dialogue. The United States and its allies must redouble their efforts to support this process. The future stability and prosperity of Bahrain and perhaps the entire Gulf region may very well depend on it.

22

MOROCCO

The Model for Reform?

SARAH E. YERKES

The case of Morocco is frequently cited as a model for reform for the Arab world. This is hardly a surprise. Since he succeeded his father in 1999, King Mohammed VI has seen himself as a reformer, initiating social and political reforms exceptional to the Arab world. Particularly in the areas of economic and human rights, the king has been true to his word, carrying out reforms that have had at least a minimal impact on the lives of Moroccans. Consequently, Morocco is among the most progressive of the Arab states in regard to economic and civil rights, although the competition is relatively weak. Nevertheless, the king's willingness to engage in limited reform has contributed to his popularity both with his own people and the West and has allowed him to weather the Arab Spring better than many of his peers.

However, just as often, the king has fallen short of his promises. Many of his "reforms" have turned out to be modest, marginal, or even superficial. Indeed, throughout the first decade of his reign, King Mohammed was adept at appeasing calls for change from both home and abroad, while still ensuring that real power remained in his hands. Thus observers in the Middle East and the West have been watching Morocco closely during the Arab Spring to see how the nation branded by many as the most modernized and Western-oriented in the region would respond to the upheaval.

Moving forward, what matters is whether the king has finally recognized that the future is now and it is the time for real change. Will the new slate of constitutional reforms presented by King Mohammed result in a real devolution of power to a truly representative government? Will the current round of reforms be a first, giant step on the long road of democratization? Or will they turn out to be just the latest in a decade-long series of mostly cosmetic, top-down political reforms the Moroccan regime has fed to the people in a successful attempt to maintain relative stability and dampen calls for change without yielding any real power?

Morocco before the Arab Spring

Before 2011 Morocco was governed by the 1996 constitution, which gave the king tremendous power, including the authority to appoint all senior government officials, high-ranking military officers, and the prime minister, without consideration of parliamentary electoral results. The king was also given the power to initiate legislation, enabling him to pass some significant reforms, such as the *Mudawwana* (the revised family code that granted more rights to women). He was also able to ensure free and fair elections, foster a multiparty political system, and address the human rights violations committed under his father, King Hassan II. King Mohammed not only allowed Transparency International to open a chapter on Moroccan soil, but also released political prisoners, including the leader of the banned Islamic political party, 'Adl wal Ihsan (Justice and Charity). He even went so far as to acknowledge the government's role in disappearances during Morocco's "years of lead"—the 1960s and 1970s—and abolished torture. Morocco's Truth and Reconciliation Commission, established by the king in 2004, was the first of its kind in the Arab world and allowed hundreds of victims of torture to tell their story.[1]

In part because of these reforms, King Mohammed established a strong relationship with the West. A major non-NATO U.S. ally, Morocco secured a free trade agreement with the United States in 2004 and a $700 million Millennium Challenge Grant in 2007. In addition, Morocco is a darling of the World Bank, which provides about $700 million of aid to the country annually.[2] It is also an important partner of the United States and Europe in counterterrorism, a partnership that Washington should be careful to protect. Al-Qaeda in the Islamic Maghreb (AQIM) has a small but continuing presence in Morocco, using Morocco as a base from which to train and export terrorists. Although AQIM has denied carrying out the April 28, 2011, bombing at Café Argana, a tourist hotspot in Marrakesh, that killed seventeen people and injured twenty-one, AQIM members have been arrested in Morocco in the past and accused of planning domestic attacks.[3] Other smaller Islamic militant groups that may have ties to AQIM have carried out major attacks in Morocco, including the 2003 and 2007 bombings in Casablanca.

Even more than his counterpart in Jordan, King Mohammed has managed to stay above the fray during the Arab Spring and previous bouts of unrest. This is largely a product of his dual position as head of state and religious leader (*emir al-mu'minun,* or commander of the faithful) and his vast network of patronage in the form of the *makhzen* (literally, "storehouse," but meaning the network of elites and regime allies). The king therefore has a unique source of legitimacy. He does not need to resort to fear and coercion the way some of his regional compatriots must. The king's religious role was further entrenched in the latest constitution, where a new article formalized his role as head of the religious establishment. All in all, he has succeeded in separating his image from that of the corrupt political institutions. While public opinion regarding the parliament, judiciary, and other government institutions is very low, with regime opponents and ordinary citizens accusing the government of massive corruption and clientalism, public opinion of the king remains high.[4]

MOROCCO'S ARAB SPRING

Morocco's experience with the Arab Spring began in force on February 20, 2011, when 37,000 protesters, largely made up of youth, human rights groups, and journalists, took to the street in more than fifty cities across the country, demanding, above all else, limits to the king's power and the replacement of the parliament and cabinet with a freely and fairly elected government, accountable to the people. King Mohammed responded to the demonstration more quickly and comprehensively than any other Arab leader, making a public speech on February 21, 2011, and announcing just two and a half weeks later, on March 9, that he would appoint a committee to draft a series of constitutional reforms that would be voted on in a July 1 referendum. The goal of this reform process, according to the king, was to move Morocco from an absolute monarchy to a constitutional monarchy by shifting power from the unelected executive to the elected parliament and ensuring the independence of the judiciary.

However, the king's first moves did not satisfy his critics, and a series of protests followed, calling for more action to limit the power of the monarchy and criticizing the proposed reform itself. The constitutional reform committee was handpicked by the king, and although it was a consultative process involving members of civil society and the political opposition, the process was seen by some in the opposition as another superficial effort by the regime to appease its critics without relinquishing any real power. (The king did invite representatives from the February 20 Movement—the youth-based group that spearheaded the protests—to participate in the constitutional revision process, but they chose not to.)[5] If the protest movement in Morocco has a single target, it is this overextension of the king's power. Nonetheless, the king remains far more popular than his colleagues across the Sahara. Thus, the primary slogan of the protests quickly became "A king who rules but does not govern."

The protest movement gained further momentum on Labor Day (May 1, 2011), when members of the trade unions started marching with members of the February 20 Movement. Earlier, King Mohammed had tried, unsuccessfully, to appease the unions with a promise to raise both public sector salaries and the minimum wage. This move was part of the divide-and-conquer strategy the Moroccan regime had successfully employed for decades. By isolating the demands of individual civil society or political movements, the king ensured that no call for reform ever got too loud or too strong.[6] In the first two months of the protests, the king successfully kept the labor unions from coordinating with the larger February 20 Movement by addressing each group's demands separately. The addition of the trade unions to the larger gatherings not only was a defeat of the king's strategy by lending increased numbers to the protests—it lent symbolic weight, because in Tunisia it was the decision of the labor unions to join the protests that was the key to bringing down Ben Ali's regime.

All the same, Morocco managed to weather the Arab Spring, perhaps because of its history of protest. Labor Day protests are nothing new. In fact, regular, vocal, peaceful protests have been tolerated throughout King Mohammed's reign, within legal limits. On any given day, long before the Arab Spring began, small groups of workers or other activists could be seen protesting outside of the parliament building in Rabat. Thus the regime is practiced in handling peaceful protests; more important, the Moroccan people have, for over a decade, regularly used protest as a release valve, letting off the steam that activists in Egypt, Tunisia, and Libya were forced to keep bottled up. Furthermore, Morocco has already been through one significant period of protest—the "years of lead" —in which those who opposed the regime were harshly punished by the king's father. While the youth who make up the bulk of the February 20 Movement did not experience this period of Moroccan history, their parents did.

Thus Moroccans, even more so than Egyptians or Tunisians, are unwilling to put up with any sort of violent or harsh regime backlash against protesters. This was clear in May 2011 when the Moroccan government used some degree of force against protesters for the first time. Most troubling was that Mohammed Essabbar, head of the Moroccan Human Rights Council, an official government body, defended the harsh actions of the police, who beat protesters supposedly for not following proper legal protocol for public demonstrations.[7] Still, the level of brutality in Morocco has remained exceptionally low. The international community condemned the government response to the May 23 protests, and thereafter regular protests remained relatively peaceful. On June 2, however, Khaled al-Amari, a thirty-year-old member of the February 20 Movement, died during a protest in Safi, allegedly as a result of police violence.[8] The government denies that Amari was beaten, but he has become a martyr for the protesters' cause, his name now synonymous—like Khaled Said in Egypt—with regime violence.

WHAT DOES REFORM LOOK LIKE?

The official constitutional reforms approved by an overwhelming majority of voters in the July 1 referendum provide for many significant changes to the Moroccan political system. Even if implemented, they would not make Morocco a constitutional monarchy, but if they are actually honored in spirit and letter, they might be an important step on a longer path that could take Morocco to that destination. However, no one has suggested that there might be additional reforms.

Under the new constitution the prime minister will become head of the executive branch and will take on further powers, including full responsibility for the government and civil service. The prime minister will be chosen by the king from the political party with a majority in parliament. This is a new stipulation: in the 1996 constitution, the prime minister was appointed by the king and, with one exception, was always a member of the regime's inner circle.[9] The new constitution also gives more power to the parliament and expands the areas in which it can pass legislation. However, the king remains commander of the armed forces and retains the power to select the regional governors who hold a significant amount of political power.

The new constitution promises a variety of other important reforms. The judiciary will have greater authority and freedom. The new constitution removes monarchical control over the Judiciary Supreme Council and puts more teeth into the principle of judicial independence. In addition, the reforms offer significant decentralization, creating directly elected regional councils responsible for overseeing regional issues and resources. The new constitution also addresses the rights of both women and the Amazigh (Berber) population. The Amazigh language will become an official language of Morocco in addition to Arabic, and new mechanisms will be put in place to increase women's representation in parliament and in the regional and local councils. The continuation of a quota system will guarantee a certain number of seats for women in parliament.

Mixed Messages

Despite the far-reaching changes put forth in the new Moroccan constitution, King Mohammed's level of investment in the reform process is not entirely clear. As much as both he and the makhzen have shown signs of taking the protesters' demands seriously, other evidence suggests that the overhaul of the constitution may just be the latest smoke-and-mirrors attempt at superficial "reform" by an adept monarch intent on hoarding power.

Positive Signs

Not surprisingly, given King Mohammed's history of promoting human rights, the Arab Spring has resulted in some significant improvements in human rights in Morocco. During the first weeks of the Arab Spring, the king freed close to 100 political prisoners and invested more power in the National Council for Human Rights. In addition, he appointed the founder of the Moroccan branch of Transparency International, Abdesselam Aboudrar, president of the national anticorruption agency. This is particularly salient given that Aboudrar was one of the left-wing activists who tried to overthrow the king's father in the 1970s. The Moroccan government also announced that it would ratify the Optional Protocols to the UN Convention against Torture as well as the Convention on the Elimination of all Forms of Discrimination against Women (CEDAW), thereby allowing independent and international bodies to monitor human rights abuses in Morocco. These are all serious steps toward furthering Morocco's respect for human rights.

A second positive sign is the level of public participation in the reform process. While 60,000 protesters out of a population of 32 million is hardly a large percentage, it does mark a turning point in civic engagement in Morocco, which has steadily declined over the past decade as citizens became more and more disillusioned with the corrupt and meaningless political system.[10] With the onset of the Arab Spring, Moroccans who had given up on activism renewed their interest, as indicated by the number who visit the website http://reforme.ma, created by the government to allow individuals to comment on articles of the former constitution and propose changes. In its first month alone (March 11–April 16), the website had 85,400 visitors, 74 percent of whom were Moroccans. In response to the reform announcement in March, Moroccans formed the Moroccan Alternatives Forum (FMAS) to encourage citizen participation and unite civil society groups. Among its activities, the FMAS holds citizen debates throughout the country to ensure that a range of citizen opinions is heard. These efforts, if continued over the next few years and formalized into civil society organizations or political movements, would greatly strengthen civil society and bolster citizen participation.

The third positive indicator is that the new constitution takes a major step forward in providing for a balance of powers. Under the previous system, the executive held all power, with the parliament acting more like a rubber stamp than a legislative body. Now the Moroccan parliament will have real authority: not only will the prime minister have expanded powers, but the parliament will also find the threshold much lower for forming an inquiry commission (one-fifth of members of parliament) and presenting a motion to censure or remove the government (one-third of members), compared to the absolute majority required before.

Equally important, many of the king's new reform efforts address social and economic issues. These should not be written off as irrelevant. Democratic change means very little to the people who cannot feed their families. However, social and economic change alone will probably not be enough to address the deep societal cuts brought to the forefront during the Arab Spring.

Negative Signs

One problematic aspect of the Moroccan reform process is the timeline. Parliamentary elections were originally scheduled for September 2012, but in

June they were moved forward to November 25, 2011.[11] This shortened timeline clearly favors incumbents, making it more difficult for newly formed political parties to develop a strong platform and campaign effectively. In its defense, the regime claims this move will bring a representative new legislature to office sooner and thereby demonstrate the sincerity of its reforms. Either or both may ultimately prove true.

Second, the reforms aimed at women and minorities are disturbingly superficial. Making Amazigh one of the national languages is a nice gesture to that traditionally underrepresented and mistreated community, but it is merely a gesture, and nothing more. The Amazigh men and women who face regular discrimination will get little more recognition now that they speak an official language. Regarding women's rights, Morocco's parliament has had a quota system since 2001 (in the current system, 30 out of 325 seats in the Chamber of Representatives, the lower house, are reserved for women), but this has done little to address the underlying societal and cultural impediments to women's empowerment. Morocco's experience with the reform of the family law (the Mudawwana) in 2004 is an example of the inability of even far-reaching reforms to effect real change. On paper, the Mudawwana represented an exceptional improvement to women's rights in Morocco—more impressive than anywhere else in the region. But in practice it has largely proven a failure because it has not been fully implemented, particularly in rural areas, where women are largely uninformed of their rights.

The most troubling sign that the Moroccan government is not taking reform seriously, however, is the continuing crackdown on the media. While Morocco has a relatively free and vibrant press, journalists who cross relatively minor red lines, such as insulting the king or blatantly criticizing certain policies, have been jailed. In a particularly glaring and strange example of the tenuous regime-media relationship, in 2009 the Moroccan magazine *Tel Quel* and the French newspaper *Le Monde* conducted a poll throughout Morocco assessing the king's performance in his first decade of leadership. Although 91 percent of the respondents said they approved of the king's performance, the Moroccan government decided to seize and destroy all copies of the magazine before it could reach the newsstands, sending a message that anything that suggested less than perfect approval of the king was *haram* (forbidden).[12] During the Arab Spring the government has continued to crack down on the media. Most notably, in May 2011 Rachid Nini, the editor of the newspaper *Al Massae* (*The Evening*), was arrested and charged with "denigrating judicial rulings" after he criticized the Moroccan intelligence agency.[13] Nini, a frequent critic of the Moroccan regime, particularly on the terrorism law and corruption, was found guilty in June 2011 and sentenced to a year in jail and fined 100 euros.

Another twist to the Moroccan story with potentially negative implications is the May invitation for Morocco and Jordan to join the Gulf Cooperation Council

(GCC). This ploy by the Gulf states to shore up the Sunni monarchies of the region is unlikely to bear fruit. The Moroccan opposition is against joining the GCC, the Moroccan government has not officially decided to apply for membership, and any ascension process would be lengthy. Furthermore, as Anouar Boukhars argues, "[King Mohammed] does not have the close personal connections that his father had with Gulf leaders, nor has he maintained King Hassan's active involvement in Arab causes."[14] Perhaps of most importance, the GCC may no longer be willing to take into its midst a weakened Moroccan monarch who has put the country on the path toward democratic reform. Yet another sign of problems for the future is that Morocco's opposition, the February 20 Movement, is not yet well organized and does not appear to have a clear agenda. At times, the movement has received support from such disparate groups as the Moroccan Association for Human Rights (AMDH) and the banned Islamic movement 'Adl wal Ihsan. And while a diverse coalition could help strengthen the protest movement's calls for reform, so far the reform experience elsewhere—particularly in Egypt—suggests that groups sitting together for the first time and blissfully calling for unity in the heat of a revolution quickly return to their old, opposing positions when the protests subside. Thus the political movements that are forming and transforming in the midst of the Arab Spring in Morocco should be encouraged to develop clear, coherent platforms with tangible demands.

America's Role

Above all else, the United States must be willing to offer praise where praise is due and speak out when Morocco appears to be veering off the path of reform. Although King Mohammad has initiated and overseen substantial constitutional reforms, for which he should be applauded, he is still the king and he still rules, not just reigns. Under the new constitution, the king is the "Supreme Representative of the State" rather than the "Supreme Representative of the Nation." This indicates that the monarchy still maintains ultimate control over the political system. Therefore it is imperative that the United States, as a close ally and partner of Morocco, use that relationship to gently prod the king should he return to his old ways and fall short of his impressive new promises.

King Mohammed's government has a history of responding cooperatively to incentives for reform. Conditioning aid positively, by offering incentives to reform, as proposed in chapter 17, is one possibility to entice the Moroccan government to stay on the path toward democracy. While not directly correlated, the passage of the Mudawwana came shortly after Morocco's receipt of an MCC grant. Conditioning aid will only work, however, if the United States develops another strategy discussed in chapter 17—a unified donor strategy. If the United States does choose to positively condition aid on serious, sustained reform, Morocco may still choose to turn away. Unlike other states in the region, however, it is unlikely to turn to Saudi Arabia, China, or other major donors. Rather, the Moroccan government and Moroccan people strongly value their connection to the European continent just nine miles across the Strait of Gibraltar. Thus Morocco's preference will be to turn to the Europeans for aid and counterterrorism cooperation should the United States begin issuing stronger demands on Moroccan reform. For this reason, it is important for the United States and Europe to develop a coordinated effort for aid conditionality.

Furthermore, the constitutional changes announced by the king in June 2011 should not be considered the end of the reform game. The constitutional reforms are a much bigger first step than any other Arab incumbent has taken so far in response to the Arab Spring, but they are only the very first step if Morocco is serious about transitioning to a constitutional monarchy. During his twelve-year reign, King Mohammed has become very adept at taking first steps, but he has taken very few long walks.

To ensure that Morocco stays on this path, the United States and Europe should work together to encourage civil society to adopt its rightful role as government watchdog, ensuring that the reform process moves forward, even if that movement is slow. This will require civil society and the political parties to re-jigger themselves and their internal cultures—in other words, transform themselves into transparent and internally democratic bodies that speak with a coherent, clear voice. At the same time, the political spectrum and civil society environment should welcome diverse opinions and backgrounds. While Morocco does not face the same sectarian issues as some other states in the region do, the political sector has not historically done a good job of welcoming marginalized groups such as the Amazigh population and women.

This is an area where international organizations can play a large role. International nongovernmental organizations such as the Ford Foundation, CARE, and Save the Children, along with international bodies such as the United Nations and the World Bank, have a long history of supporting civil society efforts throughout the Middle East. King Mohammed has been open to the presence of these organizations on Moroccan soil and vocally supported them. The United States government, through programs such as the State Department's Middle East Partnership Initiative, can work with international organizations to support civil society groups without duplicating efforts that promote inconsistent policies and values.

King Mohammed is adept at opening up the political space just enough to alleviate pressure at home and abroad without significantly limiting his own power. U.S. policymakers should therefore keep a close eye on Morocco to make sure the reforms are enacted both in letter and in spirit and that they are done so at a pace rapid enough to appease the major opposition forces on the ground, but not so rapid as to prevent new political actors from entering the scene.

Morocco has a strong and strategic relationship with the United States, and an even stronger one with the European Union. Both the United States and Europe thus have a responsibility and an opportunity to ensure that Morocco is a model for the rest of the Arab world. Morocco has the potential to be a guiding light for struggling reformists throughout the region. The way the reform process unfolds over the next year or two will send strong signals to other Arab leaders contemplating reform. Americans should not be afraid to publicly applaud, support, and reward Morocco should it become the first Arab state to truly transition to democracy. Nor should Washington be afraid to criticize Morocco publicly and privately if it fails.

23

ALGERIA

Whistling Past the Graveyard

BRUCE O. RIEDEL

Although the Arab Spring is typically said to have begun in Tunisia with Mohammed Bouazizi's self-immolation in December 2010, it actually struck Algeria first. Even before demonstrations rocked Tunisia next door and toppled President Ben Ali, there were unprecedented protests in the first half of January 2011 all across Algeria. Then, just as quickly as the wave rose, it began to ebb. Fewer and fewer protesters turned out, and the regime regained the upper hand.

The explanation for the sudden evaporation of the unrest is simple: Algeria is a haunted nation. Its people are so afraid of a return to the terror and violence of the 1990s that they put a brake on the Arab Spring even before the winter of 2011 had ended.

Yet Algeria remains acutely vulnerable to the contagion of anti-regime and anti-establishment unrest that has rocked the rest of the Arab world. It has a huge youth bulge, high levels of unemployment and underemployment, and a sclerotic regime that permits virtually no public participation in the decisionmaking process. It is also home to a violent branch of al-Qaeda—al-Qaeda in the Islamic Maghreb (AQIM)—that has a proven track record of seeking regime change. But the memories of the civil war and the "lost decade" of the 1990s are very strong among Algerians, and there is no appetite for another descent into the abyss.

THE SHADOW OF THE PAST

The People's Democratic Republic of Algeria is the largest Arab country (in terms of territory) and the largest country in Africa now that Sudan has split. It achieved independence from France in 1962 after a bitter, decade-long struggle in which a million people died. The socialist government that followed aligned Algeria with the Soviet Union in the cold war, and with the revolutionary states in the inter-Arab struggles of the late twentieth century. Oil and natural gas brought economic growth but not enough to keep pace with population growth.

In the 1980s, a relatively large number of Algerians went to fight the Soviets in Afghanistan and returned determined to bring jihad to their homeland.[1] Other nonviolent Islamist groups began challenging the regime in local and regional elections. The Front Islamique du Salut (FIS) won local elections in 1990. Then it won in the national parliamentary elections in December 1991 and was poised to form a government. The army stepped in instead and the generals took control.[2]

A nightmare followed. The Islamists, led by those who had returned from Afghanistan, took up arms against the regime. The army sought to repress the uprising, and a decade of violence, terror, and civil war ensued. The Groupe Islamique Armé (GIA), the largest rebel group, became increasingly fanatic and extreme. The army infiltrated the terror groups, creating rogue elements that got out of control. The GIA splintered into factions that fought each other as well as the army. By the end of the 1990s, a new group, the Groupe Salafiste pour la Prediction et le Combat (GSPC), emerged and was even more violent and fanatical than those that had come before. Estimates of the dead ran as high as 160,000 or more.

In time, the fury began to wear itself out. The election of President Abdelaziz Bouteflika in 1999 produced a more legitimate government, and Bouteflika began a series of reforms and amnesties to try to undermine the insurgency. Although Bouteflika—who is now in his third term—has considerable political clout, it is the generals who remain the real power behind the veil. The regime is completely opaque, such that Algerians do not know who really pulls the strings in their capital, and outsiders are even less informed about *le pouvoir,* or the power, as the generals' inner circle is known.

JANUARY PROTESTS BURN OUT AFTER LIBYA

In January 2011 demonstrations broke out across the country largely over economic issues and rising prices. Every major Algerian city was the scene of large and nonviolent protests, the most significant since 1991. Four Algerians followed Bouazizi's example and died by lighting themselves on fire—more than in Tunisia—to protest living conditions. In response, Bouteflika promised economic improvement and political reforms, ending emergency rule in February. Gradually the demonstrations petered out, with fewer and fewer participants. An uneasy calm followed.[3]

Most observers believe the specter of a return to the chaos and violence of the 1990s checked the impulse for protest, especially after the unrest in Libya, Yemen, and Syria turned into armed clashes and civil war. The Libyan war was especially disturbing for Algerians. Like the rest of the world, Algeria has no affection for Muammar Qadhafi and his regime. But the division of Libya between Tripolitania and Cyrenaica and the intervention of NATO forces, especially French aircraft, are viewed with alarm in Algeria. Like Libya, Algeria has a history of strong regional rivalries and city-state rule. The thought of European and American forces fighting next door has reopened deep and bitter colonial memories among many Algerians. Algerians did not like what they saw happening in Libya and do not want it repeated in their country.

As a result, Algiers effectively backed the Qadhafi regime against the rebels, criticizing the NATO operation and voting against the Arab League resolution that supported the creation of a no-fly zone. Algeria has expressed particular concern that the unrest in Libya could lead to the development of a major safe haven and sanctuary for AQIM and other extremist jihadists. Reports that Libyan military bases have been ransacked by extremists and arms distributed on the Saharan black market have been especially worrisome for the Algerian regime.[4] So, too, are reports that the rebels include members of the Libyan Islamic Fighting Group, a jihadist group closely tied to al-Qaeda.

The Algerian military is also alarmed by the Yemeni example. Al-Qaeda in the Arabian Peninsula (AQAP) has taken advantage of the chaos in Yemen to strengthen its position in the southern and eastern parts of the country, even briefly taking control of large towns. AQIM is probably not strong enough to do the same in Libya, but the Algerian generals know that AQIM has strong connections to Qadhafi's traditional enemies in Cyrenaica that date back to the Afghan jihad in the 1980s.

AQIM—BOGEYMAN OR THREAT?

In 2003 Ayman al-Zawahiri, Osama bin Laden's deputy, sent a delegation to Algeria to meet with the GSPC and discuss coordination between the two terror groups. Abu Musab al-Zarqawi, the late Jordanian leader of al-Qaeda in Iraq, also reached out to the GSPC to lay the groundwork for unifying GSPC with al-Qaeda. After prolonged discussion in September 2006—the fifth anniversary of 9/11—Zawahiri announced in a video message from al-Qaeda's media center (al-Sahab) that the GSPC was becoming the North African wing of al-Qaeda. In January 2007, the GSPC formally renamed itself al-Qaeda in the Lands of the Islamic Maghreb, and it soon attacked UN headquarters in Algiers and attempted to assassinate Bouteflika.[5]

But after a violent start, AQIM receded as a threat. Its attempts to carry out terror attacks in France, where the GSPC had a significant following in the large émigré Algerian community, were foiled by the French security forces. In addition, it failed to attract significant support outside Algeria in either Morocco or Tunisia. It did have some success in kidnapping foreigners and attacking French interests in the Sahelian states of Niger, Mauretania, and Mali, but these were mostly of nuisance value, not mass casualty attacks or existential threats to the regimes.

Of course, much of the failure of AQIM to live up to its potential has been a result of the ruthless but effective Algerian counterterrorism effort against the group. The Algerians have mobilized not only their own resources to fight al-Qaeda in the Maghreb, but they have also organized the region's intelligence services to fight together and enlisted the support of France, Spain, Italy, and the United States in the effort. Unfortunately, the demise of the Ben Ali and Qadhafi regimes threatens to imperil this effort, and for the Algerian generals, the rise of Islamic parties in Tunisia and Libya, even relatively moderate ones, is a threat to the stability they have forged since the 1990s.

Algeria's Underlying Crisis

The ruling elite's fears are well justified. Beneath the widespread desire for peace in Algeria lurk the same sets of problems that have torn apart its Arab brethren—and that were the underlying cause of Algeria's own civil war in the 1990s. Algeria shares the same demographic time bombs as its neighbors to the east. Seventy percent of its 35 million people are under the age of thirty; 30 percent are under the age of fifteen and thus have no memory of the 1990s. Unemployment among young men has been a major problem since the 1970s, despite vigorous efforts to reduce it. While women can participate in the workforce and are well educated by regional standards, they, too, are often unemployed or underemployed. University graduates often find they cannot get jobs commensurate with their education levels. Groups of aimless, angry young men can be seen every day in every Algerian city.

Part of the problem is that the oil and natural gas industry provides only a small number of jobs. In addition, while tourism could produce many more jobs, the country is not tourist-friendly despite its beaches and Roman ruins. Its reputation as a violent and dangerous place discourages Europeans looking for sun, while the regime fears opening the country up to outsiders.

The economy is further disadvantaged by the fact that regional economic cooperation has always been hampered by Moroccan-Algerian rivalry. The two fought a brief border war in 1963 and have been at loggerheads over the status of the Western Sahara since the 1970s. Algeria supports the Polisario group that has fought Morocco for control of the region for decades. The upheavals in Tunisia and Libya will only serve to further hinder regional cooperation.

Economic help does not seem to be on the way any time soon. Greater trade and economic investment from Europe seem unlikely, given the economic crises in Spain, Greece, and Portugal. Europe has to get its own house in order before it will assist Algeria. Pious commitments to greater Mediterranean cooperation or an enhanced Barcelona Process are to be expected but should be regarded as purely rhetorical.

ALGERIA AND AMERICA

The United States has a mixed history with Algeria. American troops helped liberate Algeria from Vichy France and the Nazis in 1942, but the Eisenhower administration staunchly backed the French in the colonial war in the 1950s. Things got better when Senator John F. Kennedy urged France to quit Algeria in his election campaign in 1960 and Algerians saw him as a friend. But the cold war and American support for Israel after the 1967 Six-Day War soured U.S.-Algerian relations again.

The first Bush administration tacitly supported the generals' coup in 1991 and backed their argument that the FIS could not be allowed to take power. Washington said it was worried that an Islamist election victory would pave the way for an extremist state. The Clinton administration followed the same course for the most part. Bouteflika's election toward the end of Clinton's second term opened the door to greater cooperation, and the two presidents met in Rabat in 1999 while attending King Hassan's funeral. Two years later, George W. Bush welcomed Bouteflika to the White House, and after 9/11 counterterrorism cooperation against al-Qaeda helped strengthen U.S.-Algerian ties further. But the 2011 NATO operation in Libya has revived Algerian suspicions of Western motives in oil-rich North African countries. Algiers is likely to have little real sympathy for President Barack Obama's calls for political reforms in the Arab world, and given the legacy of the 1990s, Algerians are unlikely to see the United States as a sincere friend of freedom in their country.

So Algeria is caught between its fear of returning to chaos and violence if the army and the regime loosen up and its underlying socioeconomic difficulties that cry out for political and economic reform. The United States is not a major player in Algerian affairs; Europe could be, but probably is too broke to do so, leaving Algerians to face their dilemma largely on their own.

PART IV

STATES IN CRISIS

24

STATES IN CIVIL WAR

Challenges for the United States

DANIEL L. BYMAN

The Arab Spring has already produced at least one civil war, in Libya, and has exacerbated the one already burning in Yemen. As of this writing, Syria is teetering on the edge. The wave of unrest unleashed in the Maghreb in January 2011 could easily produce more, especially because civil war is no stranger to the Middle East. Since the end of the colonial period, Algeria, Egypt, Iran, Iraq, Jordan, Lebanon, Libya, Oman, Syria, and Yemen have all suffered significant rebellions or civil wars that claimed hundreds of thousands of lives.[1]

Unfortunately, the Arab Spring makes further civil wars more likely. The region's many grievances can easily lead people to take up arms, and new grievances may become politically salient as change sweeps the region. As new governments emerge and surviving ones suffer legitimacy crises, citizens will be able to organize where once they were fearful and passive. By the same token, regimes rocked by internal revolt may choose not to go quietly but to fight back with whatever military forces are left at their disposal, as was the case in Libya.

The outbreak of a civil war is dangerous for many reasons, not least because such a conflict tends to completely remake the politics of a country. It can radicalize segments of the population, causing them to espouse ideas they once shunned or to shed aspirations they once held dear. It can raise up heretofore obscure leaders and knock down men and women who, in more peaceful circumstances, might have shone. Communities that evinced little animosity in the past may become divided and emerge more suspicious and hostile and thus undermine the prospects for social harmony. A government may collapse under the strain or, conversely, may use the war to mobilize the population and become stronger. In many cases, civil wars can recur, creating a cycle of violence that can last for a decade or more.

A civil war can also have "spillover" effects on surrounding states, particularly if the conflict causes significant bloodshed. It may lead to large-scale refugee flows, spawn new and more radical terrorist groups, trigger regional economic dislocation, radicalize neighboring populations (especially those with ethnic, religious, tribal, or even political ties to some of the groups waging the civil war), and prompt various groups to attempt to secede from the country gripped by the war. Some neighboring states will be tempted to prey on a suddenly weak neighbor, while others will fear that some third country will do the same—or that the problems the war creates for their own domestic politics are so grave that they must intervene to end the conflict lest it consume them too. This is how civil wars spread, and how civil wars grow into regional wars.[2]

Inevitably, the problems created by civil wars push the international community to respond as well. At the very least, outsiders may be forced to care for refugees. But, as Libya shows, countries may also choose to get involved militarily to prevent the worst problems from spilling over. Such intervention can help end a civil war or prevent the worst abuses from occurring, but it can also suck in foreign powers, exacerbate the violence, and forfeit a great many lives and much treasure.

THE CAUSES OF CIVIL WARS

As the chapters in this book make clear, grievances abound in the Arab world. Arab publics throughout the region share concerns about corruption, repressive governments, and poor economic growth. In some countries, like Iraq and Lebanon, ethnic and sectarian divisions complicate politics and elicit antigovernment sentiment. As the Arab Spring showed, demonstrations against grievances and their success in one country can catalyze revolt in another.

Not all rebellions lead to civil war, of course. After widespread unrest breaks out in a country, the turmoil can go in four different directions: it can be repressed, as in Bahrain; it can be accommodated (perhaps only temporarily) through reform, as in Morocco; the regime can surrender, as in Egypt and Tunisia; or the regime can attempt to repress the uprising but fail to do so. Only the last path results in civil war.

A crisis within the elite is often a catalyst for unrest in general but can also make civil war more likely once unrest breaks out. A crisis of this nature may arise from a dispute over succession or a power struggle unrelated to popular grievances. When a crisis occurs in an environment of popular unrest, however, the elite may become paralyzed or may respond slowly to limited unrest rather than heading it off with repression or reform.

Unrest then snowballs as part of the elite responds. But the repression may not be too effective if the regime's initial response is clumsy. In some cases, as in Yemen and to a lesser extent in Libya, part of the old guard may join the protesters, helping them offset their own initial military weakness and reducing the power imbalance that the government usually enjoys.

Perhaps the most extreme form of elite paralysis occurs when the military and security services stand back—either because they have been told by their leaders not to fire or choose not to fire of their own accord—and the revolt succeeds. The military may decide not to act because its officers believe the political winds are blowing against the current regime, because they disagree among themselves about the proper response, or because for their own corporate identity reasons they do not want to kill the citizens they are supposed to protect. However, if a regime is determined and able to use force at the outset and slaughter its own citizens in large numbers, the revolution will be very difficult to sustain without outside assistance.[3]

The elite's response to unrest is more likely to be coherent if society is divided and the regime represents only a minority within society. In Bahrain, where a Sunni monarchy rules over a Shi'i majority, in Jordan, where the Hashemite monarchy rules over a majority-Palestinian society, and most markedly in Syria, where the Alawi sect of Bashar al-Asad dominates many key positions, the minorities fear that either reform or regime surrender could lead to catastrophe for the whole community. They will hang alone if they do not hang together.

Outside intervention can often stiffen the spine of a regime opting for repression and increase its repressive capabilities. For instance, as Mike Doran and Salman Shaikh describe in chapter 21, Saudi security forces and political support played a major role in the Bahraini government's crackdown on demonstrators. The U.S. government claims that Iran has helped Syria contain unrest, with some media reports suggesting Tehran is teaching Damascus techniques to control crowds and block communications technology, and perhaps is contributing its own personnel to aid in extinguishing the uprising.

Outside intervention can also contribute to a civil war's outbreak and expand its duration. In Libya, the Qadhafi regime had contained the initial unrest and begun a methodical campaign to reconquer territory lost to the rebels. Had NATO not intervened, the regime would have won out through force, much like what happened in Bahrain. NATO's intervention, by stopping Qadhafi's government from winning outright but not taking decisive action to remove him, initially just prolonged the civil war (although it almost certainly saved many lives in Benghazi), before contributing to the opposition's eventual victory.

At its most extreme, the collapse of a government can cause a power vacuum and pose a serious threat to the stability of the state. When citizens believe their government can no longer protect them, they may organize and arm simply for self-defense. This, in turn, creates a dangerous spiral as other groups, often with memories of violence from past conflicts, see this mobilization as proof of aggressive intentions and respond by arming as well. Even without such precedents, small groups of individuals may turn to violence simply to gain power over a local community and pillage property.[4]

How Civil Wars Change Politics

Civil wars can fundamentally reshape societies, often in negative ways.[5] At times, war can prove an opportunity to strengthen the government. To fight effectively, a regime must mobilize financial resources, draw on its citizenry, govern efficiently, and convince citizens it is worth defending the country—all tasks that can make a regime stronger after the fighting stops. Frequently, however, civil war weakens the regime. The constant drain of fighting is costly and can embitter citizens. Military failures can discredit the government among nationalistic citizens, and lingering divisions can make it harder for the government to mobilize and channel the nation's collective resources.

One of the most negative long-term effects of a civil war is the bad blood that lingers and the hardening of identities because of the inevitable civilian bloodshed that accompanies internal conflict.[6] Memories of violence, often distorted in subsequent years by both sides, poison politics, allowing demagogues to win elections over moderates. As William Faulkner said of the American South, "The past is not dead, it's not even past." Wars involving ethnic or religious communities can "harden" them, making assimilation and other measures to bring people in a country together less likely.[7]

As a war continues, new leaders may arise. In some cases, they may be warlords who have displaced political figures or traditional elites and are militarizing society. Power then often flows from the barrel of a gun rather than from political popularity or technical competence.

Civil wars often recur, with roughly half of civil wars recurring within five years according to some studies. A recurrence is most likely when the country in question possesses valuable—and thus easily lootable—natural resources, like diamonds, gold, or oil. As discussed below, the recidivism rate falls considerably if a credible peacekeeping force from outside becomes and remains engaged.[8]

The Problem of Spillover

One problem that the Middle East, the United States, and its allies must be prepared to confront is the spillover effect of a civil war—when the conflict in one state triggers instability or war elsewhere in the region. The social and cultural connections that bind regional states and make a democratic contagion effect powerful can also work in negative ways. In Lebanon, the civil war that began in 1975 eventually led to intervention by Israel, Iraq, Iran, and of course Syria and fostered terrorism and other problems. It also produced a civil war in Syria and a regional war between Israel and Syria. The civil war in Iraq triggered massive refugee flows and created political instability in neighboring states.[9]

Indeed, refugees are one common form of spillover. Innocent civilians fleeing civil war give rise to both humanitarian and strategic problems. They represent large groupings of embittered people who serve as a ready recruiting pool for armed groups still waging the civil war. As a result, foreign countries frequently become involved in the war: a neighboring government, for example, may try to prevent refugee-based militias from launching attacks back into their country of origin, or it may have to protect refugees from attacks by their civil war enemies. Moreover, large refugee flows can overstrain the economies and even change the demographic balances of small or weak neighboring states.

Terrorists often find a home in states wracked by civil war, as al-Qaeda did in Afghanistan. However, a civil war itself can breed new terrorist groups—Hizbal-lah, Yasir Arafat's Fatah, Hamas, the Groupe Islamique Armé (Armed Islamic Group) of Algeria, and the Liberation Tigers of Tamil Eelam were all born of civil wars. Many of these groups start by focusing on local targets but then shift to international attacks—usually against those they believe are aiding their enemies in the civil war.

In the Muslim world, foreign fighters often flock to civil wars, particularly if the conflict involves fighting non-Muslim forces. Not all of these fighters end up becoming terrorists, but participation in a civil war is at times a gateway for individuals to join groups like al-Qaeda.[10] One reason for this is that in these wars, groups and individuals often develop networks and learn tactics from one another.[11]

Neighboring populations often become highly agitated and mobilized by developments in the civil war next door, especially if they identify with people embroiled in the war because they belong to the same religion, ethnic group, or tribe. A civil war may also encourage groups in neighboring states to demand, or even fight for, a reordering of their domestic political arrangements. Iraq, for example, saw demonstrations and protests against the Saudi-led crackdown on Shi'i dissent in Bahrain, even though the scale of the violence could hardly be considered a civil war.

Secessionism is another form of spillover.[12] Some civil wars erupt when one group within a country seeks independence, while others may lead a warring group to seek independence as the solution to the mounting problems. Groups in similar circumstances (either in the country engaged in civil war or in neigh-boring countries) may follow suit if the first group appears to have achieved some degree of success. Slovenia's secession started the first of Yugoslavia's civil wars, but it also prompted Croatia to declare its independence, which caused Bosnia to follow suit, and later convinced Kosovar Albanian nationalists to try for the same, eventually provoking a secessionist movement among Albanians in Macedonia. During the height of civil war in Iraq, its neighbors worried that secessionist sentiment would grow among Iraq's Kurds and spread to nearby Kurdish populations.

The problems created by these forms of spillover—and the weakness of the government in the country consumed by war—often provoke neighboring states to intervene. In some cases, this intervention is intended to stop terrorism, as Israel tried to do repeatedly in Lebanon; in other cases it is meant to halt the flow of refugees, as the Europeans tried to do in Yugoslavia; and in still other cases, it is meant to end (or respond to) the radicalization of their own population, as Syria did in the Lebanese civil war. These interventions usually turn out badly for all involved. Local groups are typically poor proxies and are often unable or unwilling to accomplish the objectives of their backers. This often provokes the intervening state to use its own military forces to do the job itself. The result is that many civil wars become regional wars because once one country invades, other states often do the same, if only to counter the initial intervener. The most tragic example of this phenomenon is the violence that spilled over from Rwanda's civil war into neighboring Congo and led to civil war there, which prompted seven of Congo's neighbors to intervene, precipitating what is commonly called "Africa's world war" in which several million people were killed.

INTERNATIONAL INTERVENTION

When neighboring states and major powers intervene in a civil war, they typically do so to resolve it, contain it, or help one side win. At times, multiple states may intervene with competing or conflicting agendas. Intervention can bolster a government's power, enabling it to resist opposition and eventually suppress it, as the Saudi intervention in Bahrain appears to have done. Conversely, intervention—as has been the case in Libya—can help a weak, disorganized opposition survive a government onslaught and, perhaps, over time develop its own capacity.[13]

One common goal of intervention is to care for refugees. This is both a humanitarian gesture and a means of limiting spillover. However, aid for refugees and other humanitarian assistance can at times pour fuel onto the flames of the conflict by increasing the lootable resources available to groups and allowing combatants to use refugee camps as havens from which to organize.[14]

On the other hand, foreign troops can help a negotiated settlement work by ensuring that both sides keep the promises made at the negotiating table, promises that the other side may not trust thanks to the bad blood built up during the civil war—although foreign troops from more disinterested countries (and therefore typically farther away) tend to play this role better than those of neighboring states. Such a foreign peacekeeping force can monitor both sides and at times even use force to prevent "spoilers" from shattering any peace.[15] In general, the presence of peacekeepers reduces the likelihood that a war will recur.[16] Moreover, once a settlement is negotiated, foreign troops can help with demilitarization and demobilization, removing one obstacle to the resolution of a civil war. In addition, they can police a country to prevent reprisals until the government is able to establish a measure of trust. But successful intervention is usually a long-term affair, for the trust and institutions that must be put in place take years, not months to build. Indeed, intervening states are unlikely to sustain their commitments or shoulder the heavy financial or human costs unless they have a compelling national interest, and any state that has a compelling interest is more likely to be considered biased toward one party or another.

ISSUES FOR THE UNITED STATES

For the United States, more civil wars will mean more decisions about whether (and when) to intervene to guard vital U.S. interests, secure allies, enable political change, and prevent humanitarian catastrophes. These decisions will not be easy. There are limits to America's ability to intervene overseas, particularly at a time when the U.S. public is increasingly focused on economic and political problems at home. Yet the calls for its intervention will continue, if only because of America's unmatched military power and ability to perform logistical and diplomatic feats that no other nation can. Moreover, in some cases there may be good reason for America to intervene. Thus sorting out decisions of when to intervene in civil wars could be an ongoing policy challenge for Washington. One complication is that U.S. interests in the Middle East are not uniform. In some areas, such as Algeria and Yemen, the United States has historically played a minor role. Other countries, like Saudi Arabia, are vital to U.S. interests. Stopping a civil war in some countries would thus be critical to safeguarding American interests, whereas in others, the focus might be entirely humanitarian or related to a general desire to see that legitimate voices of opposition are not simply crushed by a brutal autocrat. The intervention in Libya was apparently motivated by both of the latter concerns, but because it did not engage vital U.S. interests, the White House sought to place strict limits on the extent of American involvement.

This brings up another key consideration. The United States is already committed to two large-scale interventions in Afghanistan and Iraq. Although American forces are being withdrawn from both (more quickly in the latter than the former), U.S. forces are still stretched, and there is little appetite at home for further intervention in the troubled Middle East.

U.S. willingness to intervene will be further complicated by the nature of the sides in any Middle Eastern civil war. A key question for Americans will be: What kind of regime are we opposing and what kind of opposition are we supporting? A new opposition regime may be neither democratic nor a U.S. ally (though U.S. support for the opposition can make both more likely). The Arab Spring has brought new groups of mostly secular, democratically inclined people into the politics of the Arab world, but in the midst of a civil war, they are often the worst equipped to prevail. In Iraq (as well as Lebanon, the former Yugoslavia, and elsewhere), such people were quickly shunted aside by extremists and warlords when civil war broke out. The alternative may not always be unequivocally better than the existing regime, if the alternative is a fractious group of tribesmen and terrorists. In any civil war in the Middle East, there will be a temptation to pick winners, but doing so can be disastrous. Other states might ramp up their own intervention to counter U.S. efforts, and the oppositionists the United States aids might prove hostile to U.S. interests in the end. Unfortunately, the United Nations is rarely up to the job of addressing an outbreak of civil war—by itself, it can play a symbolic role, but it needs the great powers to contribute troops or otherwise involve themselves heavily in order to make progress on the most difficult issues. To avoid the costs of large-scale intervention, the United States might try to manage the spillover of a civil war rather than try to solve the conflict itself. Some of the most productive efforts may involve trying to inoculate neighboring states, both to reduce the risk of instability spreading and discourage them from intervention. The proper medicine varies by state, but caring for refugees, providing economic assistance, and sending a strong message that unilateral intervention is unwelcome are important steps. At the same time, the United States should be prepared to take unilateral steps should terrorists seek to set up shop in the country in question.

While a reasonable approach in theory, in practice managing spillover is exceptionally difficult. In some cases, the United States might find that containment is its only realistic option for dealing with a state in civil war but should not be fooled that it will be pretty or easy or have a high likelihood of success. Many other states have tried to contain the spillover from civil wars only to fail with disastrous repercussions.

As this overview makes clear, civil wars are deadly and destabilizing events not only for the countries in question, but also for their neighbors and the international community. Unfortunately, the many grievances and the weaker governments of the Middle East increase the chance that new civil wars may break out in the years to come.

25

YEMEN

The Search for Stability and Development

IBRAHIM SHARQIEH

Despite the fact that the Romans knew it as Arabia Felix, or "Happy Arabia," Yemen has witnessed a long procession of internal conflicts, particularly in recent decades. In the twentieth century alone, Yemen experienced clashes between Nasserists and royalists in the 1960s, between nationalists and communists in the 1970s, among various political factions in South Yemen in the 1980s, and between north and south in the 1990s. The twenty-first century has been similarly turbulent, with continued strife among an array of political and religious groups. Today, Yemen is wracked with multiple internal conflicts that threaten the future stability of the country.

The Arab Spring has added a new dimension to this already complex situation. Inspired by the successes of other uprisings in the region, Egypt and Tunisia in particular, Yemeni youth have gathered in the streets of almost every city demanding freedom, justice, dignity, and regime change. The gatherings of young people taking political matters into their own hands in Sana'a's al-Tagheer Square are responses to the failure of the traditional opposition parties to enact reform while the country slowly devolved into instability. The Yemeni people who have taken to the streets are demanding not just changes in the rule of President Ali Abdullah Saleh's regime, but also the complete overhaul of the political system. Therefore, regardless of the outcome of the Arab Spring in Yemen, there is one important fact to keep in mind: the situation before the uprisings cannot be recreated. Change has happened.

The Arab Spring in Yemen presents both an opportunity and a risk for the country. The nonviolent youth movement offers the chance of transforming a dysfunctional system. However, for a country that is overwhelmed by internal conflicts, there is serious risk of state failure and full-fledged civil war.

For the international community, particularly the United States and Saudi Arabia, stability and development in Yemen is their core interest and their most pressing concern. Neither Riyadh nor Washington has taken a strong stance in support of the youth protests, which has only prolonged the crisis, creating a potentially chaotic and uncontainable situation. For the Arab Spring in Yemen to satisfy their strategic interests, Saudi Arabia and the United States need to apply enough pressure on embattled President Saleh to agree to a transition of power. An orderly transition that responds to the protesters' aspirations will go a long way toward establishing a foundation for peace, stability, and development in the future.

A History of Instability

Yemen has endured numerous civil wars, coups, and political unrest since the 1960s. In September 1962, when Yemen was divided between north and south, Colonel Abdullah al-Sallal, a Nasserist, led a coup d'état that overthrew Imam al-Badr of North Yemen, and proclaimed it the new Yemen Arab Republic (YAR). Royalist forces, supported by Saudi Arabia, responded with an insurgency that continued periodically until 1968, when the parties reconciled in the aftermath of a final royalist siege of Sana'a. Saudi Arabia recognized the YAR in 1970, and a cease-fire was declared.

In 1978 the president of the YAR, Ahmad Hussein al-Ghashmi, was murdered, and soon after, Lieutenant Colonel Ali Abdullah Saleh assumed the presidency.[1] While Saleh received the support of the parliament and was popular in urban centers, Sheikh Abdullah al-Ahmar, leader of the Hashid tribal federation, held power in the countryside. The result was an uneasy accommodation, where Saleh's regime tried to increase its own support, particularly in the cities, while balancing other power centers in the country.

By the late 1980s, quasi-communist South Yemen was plagued by violent infighting. When it suffered the devastating loss of its Soviet sponsor, it decided to unite with North Yemen in 1990. Serious challenges complicated the unification, however, leading the South to reconsider its decision and instead go to war in May 1994 with the North to reverse the unification. This civil war ended two months later, on July 7, with northern forces capturing the southern capital of Aden in bloody fighting.[2]

Discontent continued to simmer for years, and in 2007 lingering animosities led to the creation of the Southern Movement, a political catch-all group for southerners to protest against what they considered to be economic neglect, political oppression, and threats to their national identity from the northern-based government. Rather than addressing the southerners' grievances, however, Saleh tried to quash the movement with force.

Meanwhile, in the northern Yemeni district of Saada, al-Houthis presented yet another challenge to the country's unity. The Houthis are an insurgent group drawn from Yemen's Zaydi population—a moderate Shi'i sect that makes up roughly 35 to 40 percent of Yemen's population and is concentrated north of Sana'a, in the northern and northeastern areas of the former YAR.[3] The Houthis have been waging a guerrilla campaign against the government since 2004 to oppose various forms of perceived discrimination—economic, cultural, and political—by the government.[4] Thus far, the Houthis have not been able to extend their revolt beyond their homelands, but they have proved to be a major security concern for the government and have also caused a spillover of violence into Saudi Arabia.[5] The conflict between the Houthis and the government has already resulted in thousands of casualties and hundreds of thousands of internally displaced persons.

THE IMPACT OF THE ARAB AWAKENING IN YEMEN

Today, one of the biggest challenges in understanding Yemen's conflict is accurately mapping all of its fractious parties, alliances, and issues.[6] Before the Arab Spring began, the central government in Sana'a was challenged by multiple players, including, but not limited to, the Houthis in the north, the Southern Movement in the south, al-Qaeda in the Arabian Peninsula (AQAP), traditional opposition parties represented by the Joint Meeting Parties (JMP), and tribal forces across the country. The Arab Spring, however, added a new dimension to Yemen's turmoil. Thousands of peaceful, largely secular, urban Yemenis—many of them young—took to the streets, like thousands of others elsewhere across the region, to protest the same kinds of problems that inspired the unrest in other Arab countries. The protesters called for jobs, education, social welfare programs, equal rights for women, an end to corruption, and the removal of Saleh from power.

The spread of protests throughout the Arab world has undoubtedly had an impact on Yemenis. Many have taken to the idea that there is strength in peaceful protest—a notion that previously did not garner much support among Yemen's heavily armed population.[7] As Sana'a University professor Ahmed al-Kibsi put it, "Just as you have your tie, the Yemeni will carry his gun."[8] Thus, while in the past political opposition was invariably expressed through violence, in 2011 the protests are taking on a different cast, one far more peaceful than any Yemeni has ever seen before. This change was largely the doing of Yemen's urbanized youth.

Surprisingly, the relative success of Yemen's peaceful protests has begun to alter the behavior of some tribes as well. At the very least, some tribal leaders have begun to see value in resolving their differences peacefully, or appearing to do so. For instance, Sheikh Sanan al-Iraqi, one of the al-Jawf tribal leaders, announced that his tribe and its traditional enemies, the al-Otmi, "have ended the revenge killings that have been on-going for 30 years. Their common opposition to President Saleh was what allowed mediation to occur between the two tribes."[9]

This mantra of nonviolence and compromise also seems to have infected Yemen's Southern Movement, which shifted from demanding outright secession to calling for a federal arrangement with Sana'a. On May 11, 2011, a group of 200 of the South's leaders, including former president Ali Nasir Mohammed and former prime minister Haider Abubaker al-Attas, held a three-day meeting in Cairo after which they called for a "two-state federation in Yemen, a unified vision for the Southerners to solve the Southern Cause in line with the youth revolution for change in Yemen."[10]

Even the Houthis have softened their rhetoric and decided to participate in Yemeni political life by forming a political party. Former prime minister Abdulkarim al-Iryani stated that the "Yemeni youth revolution has caused deep impact in Yemen and among those impacted were the al-Houthis who recently accepted to form a political party, and stay away from wars that they fought in the past. I myself negotiated with them forming a political party two years ago, and they rejected that at the time."[11] Since the uprising began, the Houthis have protested peacefully several times in their district of Saada. The fact that nonviolent protest has replaced the gun in Saada, at least for now, represents an important change for Yemen and a hopeful sign for the future.

One additional factor to be noted is the role of women in the protests. Due to its peaceful nature, the uprising allowed for the widespread participation of women, many of whom emerged as leaders. Tawakul Karman, a mother and activist, was one of the first to be arrested and has been a key figure throughout the protests. The uprising empowered Yemeni women by allowing them to mobilize, organize, and lead, something they had previously not done in the country's conservative society.

CIVIL WAR IN YEMEN: CAUSES OF CONCERN

Many Yemenis hope that these developments will prevent the outbreak of violent civil strife. The belief is that if Yemen's many warlords see that bloodshed will cost them popular support, they will be far more likely to restrain themselves. Nevertheless, warlords and other elites might choose to incite violence for a variety of reasons related to their own interests. This in turn could drag reluctant groups and individuals into a broader conflict.[12] Indeed, because of the issues at stake and Yemen's history of instability since the 1960s, a full-fledged civil war remains a real possibility. Robert D. Burrowes, the president of the American Institute of Yemeni Studies, has argued that "regime change in Yemen is likely to lead to state failure—and, at best, civil war (Lebanon, 1975–90) or, at worst, prolonged chaos and anarchy (Somalia, 1990–today)."[13]

Ultimately, Yemen has a fragile state system. An estimated two-thirds of the country's territory was outside the central government's control *before* the recent uprisings.[14] The unfortunate reality of such circumstances is that civil war and state failure are common scenarios. Add to this the prevalence of poverty, the lack of security, tribalism, and a variety of historical and sectarian grievances, and the propensity toward civil war becomes more acute.

Poverty and Lack of Resources

Unemployment in Yemen is a staggering 35 percent, and 45 percent of the population lives below the poverty line.[15] The problem of unemployment is more alarming when one recognizes that 43 percent of the population is below the age of fourteen and will soon be looking for jobs that simply do not exist.[16] A lack of water and poor agricultural practices combine to create another major cause of poverty in Yemen—an estimated 30 percent of the country's meager water supply goes to cultivate the drug qat.[17] Such a strain on resources, coupled with people's expectations that a new government will be able to quickly alleviate these problems, could cause underlying tensions to escalate into civil war. Former U.S. ambassador to Yemen Barbara Bodine has explained the dangerous mix of high expectations and difficult problems in Yemen: "The basic challenges facing Yemen will not be alleviated by a change in government to anyone. It is when the new government cannot meet these expectations that the potential for serious violence could occur, as different regions demand and compete for resources."[18]

Tribalism

The structure of a tribal society, like the one found in Yemen, can contribute to sparking and prolonging civil war. If heavily armed, as in Yemen, tribes furnish a ready source of military power that can be used for or against the regime, or any other group. Because it is relatively easy to mobilize a tribe's military power, and because doing so before an adversary confers an important "first-strike" advantage, tribal leaders—or political figures able to call on the backing of tribal leaders—have an incentive to deal with problems by quickly resorting to force. Cultural factors also often contribute to the tendency of tribal societies to engage in violence. The Saleh regime tried to use tribal affiliations to secure support and divide the opposition, and the president's tribal loyalists may fight to preserve their privileged position. In the future, competition between tribes may also contribute to the escalation of civil war, as tribes seek resources and power while trying to prevent their rivals from doing the same. Towson University professor Charles Schmitz explains, "Yemen's tribesmen are individuals first, concerned with their own honor and survival: If their neighbor is gaining influence, they will look for anybody who can help restore the relative balance of power, regardless of politics and ideology."[19]

Regional Divisions

In addition to tribal cleavages, Yemen suffers from strong geographic divisions that have led to numerous conflicts over the years and, as noted above, have already been stoked again as a result of the Arab Spring. The Houthi revolt may continue or even grow if their rights and grievances are not addressed properly. Similarly, in the context of a deteriorating security situation in Yemen, the Southern Movement may find itself forced to abandon nonviolence and take up arms to defend itself—and given the backing of numerous southern tribes, it could do so very quickly.[20]

Security

A major area of concern for Yemen is the deteriorating security environment. Non-state actors thrive in power vacuums, where there is anarchy, instability, or civil war. AQAP, Ansar al-Shariah, and several other local groups are reported to be active in Yemen, especially in Abyan, a southern province. Al-Qaeda in the Arabian Peninsula was formed as a merger between the Saudi and Yemeni branches of al-Qaeda largely because Saudi Arabia successfully cracked down on the group following a series of attacks in Riyadh in 2003.[21] This drove the Saudi branch into the arms of its Yemeni counterparts. But the actual strength of AQAP and its ability to operate in or outside Yemen is uncertain. Some analysts have argued that AQAP has fragmented, and that there are other more significant security threats.[22] Izzedine al-Asbahi, president of the Human Rights Information and Training Center, has explained that "Saleh has manipulated the threat of AQAP to serve his own political agenda, in particular to sustain his regime through direct financial and military assistance."[23] While remaining a definite danger to Yemen's security, AQAP is too divided to be the gravest danger to the nation's embattled government. Still, the group is likely to try to exploit the growth of unrest to expand its influence within Yemen and increase its freedom of operation.

Alternative Futures for Yemen

Today, a wide variety of scenarios are possible for Yemen. Saleh's sons and regime loyalists might succeed in playing off the differences among the various opposition groups to keep themselves in power in a weak, fractious Yemen that teeters on the brink of collapse. Alternatively, either the regime's loyalists or elements of the opposition might decide that restraint is not gaining them anything and so might opt to use force—something that started to occur as of this writing, with government forces attacking protesters—which could produce large-scale civil war. In still another scenario, opposition forces might be strong enough to finally bring down the government, but their differences are so pronounced that they are unable to agree on a new governing structure for months if not years. This scenario could plunge the country into a stalemate that could trigger a military coup or a resort to violence by one faction or another. Of course, it is also possible that the opposition could oust Saleh's family and loyalists and remain cohesive enough to forge a power-sharing agreement and a constitutional committee to frame a new, inclusive Yemeni state. The last scenario is obviously the most desirable, but at this point there is no credible evidence to suggest which way the country is going to go.

THE SAUDI ROLE IN YEMEN'S FUTURE

It would be difficult to imagine a large-scale conflict in Yemen that did not involve Saudi Arabia. The Saudis fought a war with Yemen for control of Asir Province in the 1930s and have always feared Yemeni irredentism. Ties between North Yemen and the Asir remain close, and the Zaydi population spans the mountainous border, creating the possibility of any turmoil in Yemen to spill over through this channel. In addition, Yemen's large, impoverished population has always been a security concern for the Saudis. The imbalance between Saudi wealth and Yemeni poverty makes some Saudis concerned that the inequity could spur a conflict between the two countries. Indeed, the Saudis have frequently involved themselves in Yemen's various civil wars in hopes of preventing spillover.

Moreover, the regrouping of AQAP in Yemen after Riyadh's massive campaign against it has added another item to the kingdom's long list of concerns. The Saudis fear that if AQAP is able to operate independently—and particularly if it is able to gain power in Yemen—it will be able to launch attacks against the kingdom. Of course, bin Laden was himself a Saudi whose family is of Yemeni origin, and his foremost goal was to overthrow the House of Sa'ud.

Riyadh involved itself in Yemeni civil strife in 2009, in response to the fifth (annual) Houthi campaign against Yemen's government. Although the Saudi regime was not close to Saleh, it feared that a Houthi victory would stir up their own Zaydi population in the Asir, and so began to provide money, intelligence, and, by some accounts, limited direct military support to Yemeni regime operations. Riyadh's actions also stem from a fear that the Houthi presence in Saada creates an opportunity for Iran to exert influence along the southern border of Saudi Arabia. Indeed, the Houthis are believed to have ties to Tehran, and to have received various types of support from the Iranians in their 2010 war (the sixth campaign) against the Yemeni government and Saudi Arabia.

When the widespread popular uprising began in Yemen in 2011, the Saudis found themselves on the horns of a dilemma. On the one hand, they wanted Saleh out of power and wanted to prevent the fragmentation of the country—which they feared a protracted fight between Saleh's regime and the opposition would cause. On the other hand, they did not want to see yet another Arab leader overturned by a popular revolution, and they certainly did not want to see chaos in Yemen.

On June 3, 2011, Saleh was badly injured in a rocket attack on his presidential palace and had to be evacuated to Saudi Arabia for medical treatment. Many Yemenis took Saleh's flight to Saudi Arabia as further proof that the Saudis were colluding with Saleh, but it is far more likely that Riyadh saw this as an opportunity to remove a troublesome neighbor and pave the way for a resolution to the strife. The Saudis privately signaled that Saleh would not be allowed to leave the kingdom even if he made a miraculous recovery, while attempting to broker a deal to resolve the standoff between Saleh's sons and the opposition. But surprising almost everyone, Saleh did return in late September 2011, and violence between the opposition and Saleh loyalists quickly ensued.

Because the kingdom is so invested in Yemen's domestic affairs, a civil war in Yemen would make Saudi involvement highly likely. This in turn could subject the kingdom to possible spillover, which the Saudis would doubtless attempt to prevent by intervening. The Saudis could find themselves dealing with large numbers of refugees fleeing to the Asir,[24] the resumption of attacks by AQAP and other militia groups participating in the civil war, radicalization of their own population, and potential strains on Saudi finances.

Preventing a Civil War in Yemen

All of these possibilities indicate both the potential for an escalation of Yemen's internal conflict and the desirability of forestalling such an outcome. Inevitably, a collaborative effort from local, regional, and international players will be required to prevent it. This is a tall, but not impossible, order.

A smooth and coordinated transition of power in Yemen must be put into place as soon as possible. Both the United States and Saudi Arabia have contributed to prolonging the crisis in Yemen—aiming for "regime renovation" rather than "regime change"—by not pressuring Saleh sufficiently to engage in measures that transfer power and respond to the legitimate demands of the protesters. This approach has made the political environment in Yemen more vulnerable to potential civil war and long-term instability.

The first step to preventing a civil war would be to initiate a national dialogue about a peaceful transition away from the Saleh government, one that involves *all* political parties committed to nonviolent change. An all-inclusive dialogue among these parties is the only hope for a larger reconciliation process and, eventually, the drafting of a new constitution—one that recognizes the concerns of groups like the Houthis and the population of South Yemen. Local councils in the various Yemeni governorates would also need to be involved and empowered to grant legitimacy to the new system, help provide basic services that the central government is too weak to deliver, and give Yemenis experience in self-governance. Tribes could also contribute to the overall stability of the country, especially in a transition period. In a new system, tribal representatives should be allowed to express views through political parties or civil society organizations, limiting the need for them to resort to violence for their political demands.

It is also important for the United States and its allies to approach Yemen from a development, rather than merely security, perspective. In 2010 U.S. aid to Yemen was only $58.4 million, a small amount relative to how much other countries in the region receive from the United States.[25] This must change. A development approach would address the underlying causes and conditions of conflict in Yemen—including the need for jobs among Yemeni youth—whereas a security approach can potentially exacerbate the existing problems by promoting violence—even if the violence is limited to the perpetrators of violence.

The United States should encourage nongovernmental organizations and foreign governments alike to provide the development assistance that Yemen needs. Although the U.S. Congress is unlikely to provide massive development aid to Yemen, making such a goal the focus of U.S. policy toward Yemen and investing substantial diplomatic attention would be a good start. Saudi Arabia and other oil-producing Arab states could certainly play an important role in that process, and they should begin to do so as soon as possible. This might be hard for Yemenis, who are sometimes suspicious of their northern neighbors. It will also be hard for the Saudis, who are reluctant to invest heavily in their backward southern neighbor. Riyadh will have to be convinced that investing in Yemen today will help avoid what could become a very costly civil war in the future.

The Arab Spring and the nonviolent protests in Yemen have created a valuable opportunity to help build a new Yemen. So far, U.S. policy toward Yemen has been behind the curve. The United States has based its Yemen policy on the same narratives and goals that drove its Yemen policy over the past ten years: treating Yemen as nothing but an issue of terrorism. One Yemeni analyst has argued, "The U.S. is creating heroes of al-Qa'eda in Yemen. You chase them, bomb them, and the result is a tense country environment that creates many sympathizers and listeners to their message."[26]

Over the past ten years, and particularly over the past nine months, Yemen, like the rest of the Arab world, has changed dramatically. Today, there are millions of young people in the streets of Sana'a loudly and persistently demanding justice, dignity, freedom, and better opportunities. They want stability and are terrified of civil war, as is the international community. Comprehensive and sustainable development that responds to the aspirations of these young people is the only guarantor that Yemen will not slide into such a civil war in the future.

26

SYRIA

The Ghosts of Hama

MICHAEL S. DORAN AND SALMAN SHAIKH

The revolutionary wave of 2011 was slow to reach Syria. Public disobedience did not show its face until mid-March, a full month after the fall of Hosni Mubarak. When demonstrations did finally emerge, they focused on the grievances of Dara'a, a middling-sized town near Syria's Yarmuk River border with Jordan. The citizens of Dara'a were outraged over state security service atrocities so heinous as to be excessive even by Syrian standards. In early March, a group of fifteen boys, aged ten to fifteen, imitated the crowds in Tunisia and Egypt and sprayed anti-regime graffiti on the walls of public buildings. Agents of the secret police working for General Atef Najeeb, a cousin of President Bashar al-Asad, detained the boys and tortured them by pulling out their fingernails.[1] Angry citizens of Dara'a took to the streets in protest. The regime reacted to the demonstration with lethal force. The Arab Spring had come to Syria.

The conflict between Dara'a and Damascus soon came to symbolize the grievances of all disaffected Syrians against the Asad regime. Across the country, a weekly cycle of solidarity protests soon erupted. After Friday prayers, as worshipers flowed out of the mosques, demonstrations would erupt in different cities all at once. The authorities would respond with lethal force, sniping from rooftops and sweeping individual protesters off the streets and into its dungeons. On Saturdays, the funerals of new martyrs generated still more protests and more killings by the authorities.

At the end of April the regime attempted to break this cycle and reestablish its deterrent capability with a show of gruesome force. It laid siege to Dara'a, cutting off electricity and water, conducting house-to-house searches, and shooting anything that moved on the streets.[2] It was during the siege that security forces tortured, murdered, and partially dismembered a thirteen-year-old boy named Hamza Ali al-Khateeb, who almost instantaneously became a global media martyr. The city suffered greatly but did not back down. Nor was the rest of the country cowed. Protests continued unabated.

The contrast with Egypt was striking. In Cairo, protesters quickly paralyzed public life, and the military, for its part, refrained from firing on civilians. In a matter of days, foreign and domestic pressure forced President Hosni Mubarak to step down. In Syria, however, Asad managed to keep the biggest cities, Damascus and Aleppo, relatively calm largely by resorting to the killing of civilians in cold blood, some targeted but some seemingly selected at random. Several provinces nevertheless slowly slipped out of control. Hama, the fourth largest city in the country, and Homs, the third largest, displayed an unprecedented autonomy from Damascus.

By September at least 2,600 people had been killed and tens of thousands were missing (informally, many observers believe that the real casualty figures may be four or five times higher). These numbers are bound to grow. Though still in power, Bashar al-Asad had proved incapable of vanquishing the protesters—not, evidently, because he has been less ruthless than his father but because Syrian society itself has changed. His regime is now locked into a grindingly slow process of irreversible decline.

A Most Peculiar Regime

What accounts for the "slow-motion" quality to the erosion—perhaps eventual collapse—of Asad's rule? The answer begins with the fundamental character of the regime. During its four-decade life, outbreaks of domestic unrest have been few and far between. Prior to the Asad era, however, instability was the norm. From independence in 1945 until November 1970, when Bashar's father, Hafiz, took power, Syria was a state plagued by chronic political unrest. In just one year, 1949, the country witnessed three separate military coups within an eight-month period. Egypt, by comparison, was tranquil. This difference arises from the fact that in Egypt the state and the society fit together comfortably as a cohesive unit. The Syrian state, in contrast, sits atop a heterogeneous society characterized by deep horizontal fissures.

The rise of the House of Asad undeniably brought stability to Syria. However, this achievement (if that is the appropriate term) came at a high price. Nothing better exemplifies that price than the events of 1982, when the regime brutally confronted a Muslim Brotherhood–led insurgency centered on the city of Hama. In a successful bid to suppress the revolt, Hafiz al-Asad perpetrated one of the worst atrocities in modern Arab history. The military laid siege to the city and unleashed an artillery barrage that leveled an entire civilian quarter. The death toll is unknown, but estimates range from 10,000 to 40,000. Contemporaneous accounts describe the stench of rotting corpses wafting out of the rubble.[3]

The Hama massacre highlights the most salient feature of Syrian political life: the mailed fist of the state. Prior to the March 2003 invasion of Iraq, Saddam

Hussein was universally regarded as the most brutal dictator in the Arab world. He was that, but Hafiz al-Asad ran a close second, the difference between them reputedly being that while Saddam actually enjoyed torturing and murdering people, the elder Asad did similar deeds out of perceived necessity, without excess or flamboyance. Bashar al-Asad has continued his father's approach, adding a veneer of forced geniality to the same basic approach. It is impossible to explain the longevity and stability of the Asad era without reference to the totality of the regime's police state and its ability to smother all forms of independent political activity through continued use of violent repression.

However, as is the case in any successful police state, violence must be rationalized and routinized if it is to bring stability to a deeply divided society. In Syria, the Ba'ath Party provides this service. The Syrian political system, a single-party state, is something of an anachronism, a throwback to the heyday of the cold war. The Ba'ath, like the Eastern European communist parties of yesteryear, is the sole legitimate political organization in the country.

On paper, the Ba'ath is the vanguard of a populist pan-Arab movement, and, to be sure, Ba'athist values are not entirely irrelevant to the regime's behavior. An extreme nationalism that stresses the unity of all Arabs and hostility to American imperialism and Zionism does have its practical uses. Ba'athist rhetoric serves, for example, to deflect attention from the fact that the ruling family and most of its closest associates are members of the Alawi religious community, which constitutes only 10 to 12 percent of the population.[4] Historically, this community was despised by Syria's Sunni Arab majority, which outnumbers it by a factor of at least five to one. The regime is perpetually vulnerable to the claim that it is a tool used by an unrepresentative Shi'i minority to dominate a Sunni majority. Ba'athist ideology allows the Asad family to disprove such claims by arguing that it is the staunchest representative of common "Arab" values and a fierce opponent of the recognized enemies of all Arabs.

However, the party's primary function is to preserve the ruling family's monopoly on political activity. When ideology is not enough (and it rarely ever is), other means of control avail. Overlapping and ubiquitous security services enforce the Ba'ath Party's authority. The capriciousness and venality of these services shape every sphere of public life, including business. In recent years, the regime, seeking to attract foreign investment, has trumpeted modest reforms designed to develop "the private sector." Massive corruption and the absence of the rule of law, however, make the term essentially meaningless. Powerful barons whose status derives directly from political connections dominate the economy. These barons have an undisputed leader: not coincidentally, Bashar al-Asad's maternal cousin, Rami Makhlouf, who, despite his lack of official government position, is one of the most feared men in Syria. Makhlouf owns a share of many of the significant "private" companies in the country. His ties to the coercive apparatus of the state mean that his share of any business, no matter how small on paper, is always a controlling interest. The Syrian public understands perfectly the methods that elevated this "tycoon" and knows that he is no mere private citizen. During the uprisings in 2011, demonstrators have repeatedly chanted slogans against him personally and have torched some offices of Syriatel, the telephone company he controls. In an effort to blunt popular anger, Makhlouf announced in May that he was divesting his share of the company. His special status, however, means that he will continue to play a major role in Syrian business life, if not in Syriatel itself.

Makhlouf's emergence as Syria's answer to Bill Gates and Warren Buffett reminds us that behind the populist veneer, the state is very much a family enterprise. Besides Makhlouf and the president, four other family members constitute the inner core of the regime. The first is Bashar's younger brother, Maher, who leads the Republican Guard, which has spearheaded the suppression of the demonstrations. The second most notable family member is Asef Shawkat, a career army officer and former chief of military intelligence. Shawkat is no doubt talented in his own right, but his rise to power has turned on his marriage to Bushra al-Asad, Bashar's older sister and the third family member of note. She wields significant influence over her presidential brother, to whom Shawkat is also personally close. In the eyes of some, he serves as an éminence grise, with significant influence on the president. Shawkat's relations with Hafiz's other two sons, however, have been stormy. When Basil al-Asad, Bashar's older brother, learned of Shawkat's love affair with Bushra, he opposed the courtship, which he saw as a crass power play by a wily social climber. When Basil died suddenly in a car crash in 1994, Shawkat and Bushra eloped. Eventually, Hafiz al-Asad came around to blessing their marriage, but that did not end Shawkat's problems with the family. In 1999 Maher al-Asad reportedly shot Shawkat in the stomach in the midst of a heated argument.[5] More than a decade after the gunplay, the two men are said to have repaired the rift between them.

The final personality of note is Bashar's wife, Asma. She is the daughter of Fawaz al-Akhras, a Syrian doctor and businessman based in the United Kingdom. Raised in England, she briefly pursued a career in high finance. As first lady of Syria, she has sought to carve out a role modeled on that of Britain's Princess Diana, or Jordan's Queen Noor and Queen Rania. Beautiful, stylish, and worldly, Asma sponsors charities and "civil society" organizations in an effort to depict the Syrian ruling family as everything that it is not: progressive, cosmopolitan, and, importantly, nonsectarian (the al-Akhras family, from Homs, is Sunni).

Situated around the ruling family is an Alawi-dominated network—a loose but real grouping that constitutes the Alawi "deep state," to borrow a phrase from the Turkish experience. The deep state gives Asad a solid power base that, for instance, Hosni Mubarak never enjoyed. In Egypt, when push came to shove, the top brass withdrew their support from Mubarak to safeguard their own interests. In Syria, however, the generals cannot offer up the ruler to the mob, because the military's top ranks are permeated by family members. Second, the sectarian logic of Syrian politics dictates that when Asad falls, the generals will go down with him. In fact, even Alawites who lack regime connections fear reprisals. Having noted well the sectarian score-settling that followed the fall of Saddam in Iraq, they fear an analogous scenario will play out in a post-Asad Syria.

Similar worries beset other significant groups. Taken together, the Arabic-speaking minorities (Alawites, Christians, Druze, and Ismailis) constitute about 25 percent of the population. Because all of them fear instability and the threat of retribution at the hands of the oppressed Sunni majority, they typically support the regime (actively on the part of most Alawites, tacitly on the part of many other minorities) as their only protection against a potential bloodbath. Asad understands this sectarian dynamic and cleverly plays on minority fears. Time and again, the regime has falsely claimed that armed "Wahhabis" have fired on the security services. While these Sunni terrorists are fictions, flesh and blood Alawi gangs known as the *Shabbiha* terrorize the cities of the western coast, where Sunnis live side by side with Alawites.[6] The Shabbiha are known to enjoy friends in high places. Several years ago, it came to light that one gang in Latakia was actually led by a cousin of Bashar, who was caught on tape, Kalashnikov in hand, robbing a bank.[7] Though he went to jail for the crime, he reportedly managed "to escape," presumably with the aid of powerful friends.

President Asad is adept at playing arsonist and fireman simultaneously. While his security services create an atmosphere of lawlessness, he whispers to domestic and foreign constituencies alike that the fall of the regime will doom "secularism" in Syria. He calculates that raising the specter of civil war will encourage minorities to run to the state for cover. For some time, the regime's fanning of sectarian fires had not appeared to gain much traction. In mid-July 2011, however, an episode of sectarian-motivated killings in Homs, a Sunni-dominated city with a large Alawi minority, increased fears of sectarian conflict.[8] Since then, wise to these attempts, residents throughout the country have been marching and chanting slogans like "one, one, the Syrian people are one" in an attempt to take the sectarian edge off their conflict with the regime.

Meanwhile, Asad does all he can to persuade foreign governments to see his regime as the only barrier to regional conflagration. He also constantly dangles the prospect of Syrian participation in a comprehensive Arab-Israeli peace, even as he does whatever is required to keep that prospect as far away from realization as possible. The regime exploited the tactic of spreading unrest (and bludgeoning any slim prospects for peace at the same time) on its borders in late spring and early summer, exporting the instability within to its neighbors in Turkey, Lebanon, and, most egregiously, Israel (with the Nakba and Naksa-day protests on the Golan).

A DYING PARTNERSHIP

There is of course no evidence to support the regime's claim that armed Sunni extremists are a significant cause of the unrest. Nevertheless, sectarianism is a powerful undercurrent in Syrian politics. Not surprisingly, Sunni protesters have on occasion depicted the regime as part of a Shi'i cabal. In Dara'a in March 2011 protesters chanted: "No to Iran, no to Hizballah, we want a Muslim who fears Allah!" The chant expressed the hope that a "true" Muslim—that is, a Sunni—will replace Asad, and that Syria will ally with Sunni powers. Crude sectarian expressions such as this have not been the norm, however; the protesters' primary grievance has been the government's failure to provide dignity, justice, and jobs.

Many often refer to the entire regime as Alawi, but this kind of political short-hand can be misleading. The Alawi deep state has always succeeded in co-opting significant numbers of Sunnis. The Alawi community is large enough to man the top levels of the government and to fill the ranks of the shock troops in the army and intelligence services, but even in alliance with Syria's other minority groups it is too small to populate the machinery of the state and the Ba'ath Party, let alone the entire military. The iron laws of demographics force the deep state to share power. It functions, therefore, as the leading element in what is essentially an Alawi-Sunni partnership, symbolized by the Bashar-Asma marriage. That partnership leaves Syria's other minority groups nowhere to go for favors and protection except to the state.[9]

The Arab Spring threatens to destroy the Sunni-Alawi condominium. The current generation of Sunni elites is proving incapable of reaching down to the grass roots, not just in Dara'a but also in big cities such as Hama and Homs. For the first time, an opposition has emerged that the regime can neither crush nor co-opt. The tools of social networking have enabled civil society for the first time in modern Syrian history essentially to out-organize the state—to act inside its decision cycle and thus remain invulnerable to state efforts at intimidation, disruption, and sabotage. The opposition network has three salient traits: it emerged spontaneously from below, it is nationwide in scope, and its complexion is predominately Sunni. Taken together, these three traits constitute an existential threat to the regime. The new opposition network threatens the status of the Alawi deep state as the gatekeeper to the political and economic arena. Once that status is lost, the regime will collapse.

This will happen despite the fact that, at present at least, the opposition network is fragmented, leaderless, and lacks a common ideology. These deficits have actually been a kind of advantage in the short term, because the regime has found it difficult to identify the revolution's leaders. However, there are rising demands for the opposition to better organize itself and articulate a program, and not the least of these demands come from anti-regime elements in exile. That exiled opposition has begun a "process of consolidation" that led in mid-July 2011 to the formation of a National Salvation Council at a meeting in Istanbul, where some 350 activists represented a variety of groups from liberal secularists to the Muslim Brotherhood.[10] It remains a major challenge to ensure that this movement connects with the demands of the protesters on the ground in Syria and remains credible with opposition figures within the country itself.

Asad is gambling that he can exploit the opposition's in-country weaknesses and insider/exile tensions with tried-and-true methods: brute force and a policy of divide and rule. Instead of establishing "a true dialogue" as U.S. ambassador Robert Ford demanded, Asad has behaved like a monarch receiving petitions from individual supplicants. He has met regularly with delegations from all across Syria in an effort to tacitly define the protests as a series of highly localized complaints, each one requiring its own unique solution.[11] Asad has also generated government-sponsored "opposition dialogues," such as a National Dialogue led by Vice President Faruq al-Shara'a and even a meeting of independent figures in late June. Most true opposition leaders have either boycotted these meetings altogether or treated them with healthy doses of skepticism. Clearly, they are an effort to simultaneously divide the opposition, preserve the status of the state as the sole arbiter of political life, and fob off the demands of foreign powers such as the United States, Turkey, and Saudi Arabia, which are calling for dialogue.

By avoiding systemic solutions Asad has protected the supreme status of the deep state, but his strategy has scored no major successes. Time and again, the opposition network has shown the ability to call demonstrators out to the streets in many different cities simultaneously. Consequently, Asad has found himself confronting twin specters of rising Sunni power: the creeping independence of the provinces from Damascus and a crisis of morale among soldiers in the regular army.

It was precisely to halt the spread of provincial autonomy that the regime dispatched its loyal security units to Dara'a at the end of April 2011. Despite the brutality of the operation, it subdued Dara'a only temporarily. Moreover, it did so at a tremendous cost. The operation horrified a segment of Sunni opinion at home, while abroad it mobilized international opposition. Qatar and Turkey, two traditionally friendly states, both quickly distanced themselves from Asad. Worst of all from the regime's perspective, the Dara'a operation failed to reestablish the deterrent power of the state. Thus by mid-July the local authorities in Hama were exercising unprecedented autonomy. Al-Bukamal, on the Syrian border, also flaunted its independence—a particularly worrying development, given the tribal ties that link its inhabitants to their brethren in Iraq. All told, the cycle of worsening brutality and widening protest saw as many as 250 towns join the movement, while those on the streets came from ever-broadening sectors of society. On July 15, for the first time, major protests broke out in Damascus and have continued on a weekly basis since.[12] Flames are now licking at the palace gates. The second specter Asad now confronts is the fracturing of the military along sectarian lines. After the Dara'a operation, very credible reports of Sunni defections from the military came to light. They pointed to the fact that the Alawi deep state must refrain from forcing Sunni conscripts to carry out atrocities against their coreligionists. If regular units were to defect from the military in significant numbers and make common cause with the demonstrators, the balance of power between state and opposition would tip. In order to prevent a split in the military along sectarian lines, therefore, the regime had no choice but to rely primarily on its Alawi regime protection forces to suppress a nationwide rebellion. But these troops are limited in number; they cannot be everywhere at once. Meanwhile, the sheer magnitude of the demonstrations has increased the likelihood that more and more Sunni cities will develop ever-greater autonomy from the central authorities. The ground is slowly eroding from under the regime.

THE COMING ANARCHY

The Syrian status quo, whatever is left of it, is not sustainable. The transformation of Syrian politics will follow one of three different paths. The first of these is the scenario that was originally favored by Washington, which supported a regime-led transition to democracy. This scenario had little chance of success, and in August 2011 the White House changed course and finally called for Asad to step down. The Asad regime never had any interest in instituting real reforms; any serious accommodation of the opposition would spell suicide (certainly political, if not literal) for Bashar, the family, and the deep state, which together form the central pillar of the regime.

Perhaps the regime will simply disintegrate, Ceaușescu-like. This second scenario, however, is equally unlikely. The entrenched nature of the deep state, the sectarian dynamics of Syrian politics, the fears that significant portions of the population feel for the unknown—all these factors and more will likely compel Asad to cling to power to the bitter end.

Consequently, we should expect the regime to collapse in ultra-slow motion, at least compared with how matters developed in Tunisia and Egypt, and even, in the opposite direction, in Bahrain. The uneasy balance between the protesters and the security services will continue. Cities such as Hama and Homs and tribal regions such as al-Bukamal will probably grow incrementally more autonomous. At some point or in some places, protesters might take up arms—perhaps in response to amplified government attempts to restore its control by force before the process of devolution goes too far. (Indeed, this process may have already begun as of this writing.) In that case, the conflict on the streets will begin to look more like a civil war than a contest between security services and rock-throwing protesters. As the Ba'athist regime loses strength and the power to intimidate, the power vacuum will continue to grow. As Dan Byman warns in chapter 24, a power vacuum, a civil war, or both will have significant destabilizing implications for Syria's neighbors.

Either way, regional powers will work to shape the battle on the ground to their advantage. The Turks, who are deeply concerned about the flow of refugees, especially Kurds, across their border, now seem tempted to intervene directly, if only to establish a buffer zone so that refugees can be sheltered on Syrian territory. Turkey has already taken an active role by hosting opposition conferences and providing a base for, among others, Muslim Brotherhood elements. The Iraqis will inevitably grow concerned about the creeping autonomy of the tribal regions on their border. Meanwhile, the Iranians will continue to support the regime, which is Tehran's closest ally in the region and the gateway to its proxies, Hizballah and Hamas. In sum, Syrian domestic politics will become enmeshed with regional politics, according to a pattern now familiar from the experiences of Iraq and Lebanon.

An American Role?

The question for Washington, then, is this: How can the United States compress the timeline of collapse so as to minimize human suffering and ensure the speediest rise of a new order hospitable to the United States? Washington was right to jettison the completely unsupportable pretense of a regime-led transition toward democratic reform. This policy only encouraged Asad to think that he could ride out the protests. The United States should be working assiduously to convince Asad to go, and go soon. This task of persuasion, which will not be easy, should entail five steps:

1. The United States must issue a strong declaratory policy announcing that it is now working to build the best possible bridge to a post-Asad Syria.

2. Washington should then convene a conference of interested powers, in conjunction with Turkey and France, to develop a Syrian "contact group" devoted to establishing a stable order and preventing a power vacuum. Crucially, this contact group should seek to involve Arab states such as Saudi Arabia and Qatar.

3. The United States must work with other key actors to help turn the Syrian opposition into the nucleus of a transition government. As the experience with the Libyan opposition forces has shown, engagement with the Syrian opposition movement would prove invaluable to efforts to increase its effectiveness and professionalize its efforts.

4. The United States must encourage defections from the Syrian security services with an eye both to convincing Asad to leave and to preserving the Syrian

armed forces as a future national institution. In doing so, Washington must warn officers, down to the brigade level, that they are being monitored and that they will be held personally accountable for the atrocities committed under their command.

5. The contact group should take all available steps to starve the regime of cash and other resources, including taking a leadership role on preventing the regime from generating revenue from oil exports.

Taken together, these steps may not stop the flow of blood immediately, but over the long run they will reduce the number of needless deaths. They will also hasten the rate of defections that will be crucial to reigning in the government crackdown and allowing a genuine process of transition to begin.

PART V

OTHER REGIONAL ACTORS

27

REGIONAL ACTORS

The Changing Balance of Power in the Middle East

DANIEL L. BYMAN AND KENNETH M. POLLACK

The impact of the Arab Spring reaches far beyond the countries in transition, and perhaps no outside powers are more affected than those that border the Arab world. They are fast finding that—through geography, history, national interest, or ideology—the Arab Spring is reshaping the region in which they live. Of these states, Iran, Israel, and Turkey stand out: all are powerful nations, and all have fundamental interests in the Arab world and the fate of the Arab Spring.

These countries have watched the Arab Spring unfold with a mixture of glee, opportunism, and fear. The events of 2011 have shattered important geopolitical alignments, causing new ones to emerge. Diplomatic relationships, such as those between Turkey and Syria and between Egypt and Israel, are under strain. Some states are hopeful that the stunning changes will increase their influence and popularity in the region, and even the world. Egyptians are hopeful that the Arab Spring will rejuvenate their proud nation and make it the leader of the Arab world once again, while the Saudis fear that they will lose a strategic situation they found exceedingly comfortable—at least in retrospect.

One of the most profound geostrategic shifts wrought by the Arab Spring is that the new regional politics will rest much more firmly upon domestic politics and public opinion. Arab opinion always influenced regime behavior; indeed, the Qadhafis and the Asads tried to court their publics even if they never let public opinion dictate their foreign policies. Now, however, in Egypt, Iraq, and Tunisia—and perhaps in other countries—governments may emerge that reflect the will of the people, with earth-shaking consequences for regional politics. The Middle East's powers, in turn, are reshaping their relations with the United States to reflect the pressures and opportunities of the Arab Spring.

PUBLIC OPINION AND REGIONAL POLITICS

One of the biggest potential shifts in regional politics, and one of the biggest unknowns, is the role public opinion will play in the Arab world. Should Egypt, Tunisia, and Libya become successful democracies, public opinion could well shape foreign policy more than it did for Qadhafi, Ben Ali, and Mubarak. This could translate into a a variety of changes. For instance, since the 1978 Camp David Accords, Egypt's public relationship with Israel has been cold, but beneath the surface there has been considerable cooperation. In the future, reflecting a more anti-Israel (indeed, anti-Semitic) public, Cairo might distance itself from Jerusalem. But this may not be the full extent of the change. Nascent democracies are particularly susceptible to the siren song of demagogues. Irresponsible populist leaders have gotten the Middle Eastern states into trouble before by recklessly provoking a hated enemy in hopes of rallying the public to their banner, only to find that in so doing, they crossed an important red line and brought down destruction upon their country. Gamal Abdel Nasser's mishandling of Israel before the 1967 Six-Day War is the best example of this, but Syria's Salah Jadid and Iran's Mohammad Mosaddeq also made similar miscalculations. All three sought popular acclaim by poking a hated enemy (Israel, Britain/America), went too far, and suffered the consequences.

Even those regimes that the Arab Spring does not topple may choose to be more solicitous of public opinion than they have been in the past so as to avoid provoking new waves of popular unrest. Some may blame external states for their internal problems as a way of diverting popular antipathy and simultaneously rallying the people around the flag. The fact that the Bahraini government truly believes that Iran is responsible for its problems does not negate the fact that it is acting in a dangerous manner—dangerous both because it misidentifies the real source of Bahrain's problems and because it could end up provoking a dangerous adversary.

That said, the most likely response to the Arab Spring by all of the countries of the Arab world is bound to be a greater focus on their internal state of affairs. With the exception of those absolutely determined to stick their heads in the sand, the regimes of the region understand that the terrifying wave of popular upheavals was provoked by the economic, social, and political problems of the Arab states themselves. In response, all of the leaders will doubtless focus heavily on dealing with these internal problems in some way or another. The first governments of the newly democratizing states will have to show their constituents that they are doing better than the autocrats they replaced, and that will mean grappling with unemployment, underemployment, income gaps, investment flows, and the rule of law. Even the surviving monarchies and autocracies are likely to try to address their economies—and perhaps reform their political and social systems as the king of Morocco has proposed doing—at least for some period of time.

Of course, that internal focus does not necessarily mean that these states will pay no attention to foreign policy. But instead of security threats and terrorism steering their foreign policies, economic growth may become the primary motivating force. Such a shift could be beneficial regionally: it could drive the states toward greater regional economic coordination and might convince the Arab world to develop closer ties to the powerful Israeli and Turkish economies. However, it could create new splits as well. In particular, the Arab states without major oil resources might begin to demand greater assistance from their oil-rich brethren. Such a "haves versus have-nots" schism would represent a major reorientation of Middle Eastern geopolitics.

New Uncertainties

This influence of public opinion on foreign policy will inject important new unknowns into the international relations of the Middle East. Publics are notoriously fickle, and especially in the early years of a state's development, it is not clear exactly what they think. Many citizens have been so fearful of their autocratic regimes that they have never honestly expressed themselves in polls, let alone elections. Consequently, one of the most unpredictable aspects of the new Arab states may lie in simply finding out what their publics actually believe.

That is not likely to be where the uncertainties will stop. Another major unpredictable element in the new Middle East's regional balance will be the new leaders themselves. New politics, especially more pluralistic politics, will allow new men and women to emerge to lead their countries, bringing with them new ideas and new experiences. In the past, Middle Eastern states were heavily top-down structures: the king or president and inner circle dominated decisionmaking, and policy typically did not change much from year to year, or even decade to decade. Pluralistic systems will allow more people from far more diverse backgrounds to emerge and take a role in policymaking. A more bottom-up process of foreign policymaking could produce courses of action very different from those the country pursued in the past.

For similar reasons, the emergence of new leaders could actually inject a great deal of instability into the regional system. For the past thirty to forty years, most of the leaders of most of the Arab states remained stunningly unchanged. As a result, they got to know one another and came to understand the rules of the Middle Eastern game. It was a rarity when one of them broke the rules—as Saddam Hussein did by invading Kuwait in 1990—and when one did, all the rest would unite against the violator to enforce the rules. This has been one of the reasons that there have been relatively few interstate wars in the Middle East, despite the prevalence of interstate skirmishes. All of the Arab rulers knew what to expect of one another, and what they could and could not do. They were generally quite careful to avoid crossing one another's well-understood red lines.

This paradigm may soon become a thing of the past, as new leaders take over in important Arab countries. These new leaders will not know their counterparts, and their counterparts will not know them. It is worth reflecting that many of the Middle East's worst wars and crises were a product of the miscalculations of relatively new leaders. The longer that a leader was in office, therefore, the less likely it was for him to launch a war (again, with the notable exception of Saddam Hussein—the exception that proved the rule because he was such an exceptionally aggressive and reckless leader).

There is also the unpredictable element of civil wars. As Dan Byman notes in chapter 24, the incredible changes of the Arab Spring produced at least one new civil war (Libya) and may produce more (with Yemen and Syria both teetering on the brink). Civil wars have a very bad habit of spilling over into neighboring states, and that spillover often produces external intervention in the states in civil war. In the worst cases, regional intervention can then lead to regional wars—just as the Lebanese civil war sparked a war between Israel and Syria in 1982, and the Congolese civil war triggered what is often called "Africa's world war."

If the Arab Spring does produce more civil wars, these wars will create power vacuums that will suck in other states. So far, neither Yemen nor Libya has touched directly on the core interests of regional powers, although the Egyptians are watching Libya closely, as the Saudis are Yemen. Other weak states, however, would be far more likely to invite regional intervention. Should Iraq (again) fall into chaos, for example, Iran, Turkey, and even Saudi Arabia and Jordan may feel compelled to intervene, deepening the mayhem and raising the risk of regional war. Chaos in Syria, too, raises the risk of Israeli, Turkish, Iranian, and Saudi intervention. Already, Iran has stepped up support for the Asad regime to preserve its closest Arab partner.

Even successful efforts to quell unrest may incite rivalries between Arab and non-Arab powers. The quashing of the revolution in Bahrain infuriated Tehran, which has stepped up its criticism of the Bahraini and Saudi regimes. Riyadh, for its part, blamed much of the unrest on Iran, and even thinks Tehran is responsible for many of the problems in Yemen.

New Balances of Power

New alliance blocs have yet to emerge in the Middle East, but several possible configurations deserve close consideration. One of the most obvious is an alliance of new democracies against surviving monarchies, but it might also include any dictatorial "republics" that survive the upheavals, like Algeria or Syria. Already Saudi Arabia's move to expand the Gulf Cooperation Council to include not only Jordan but also faraway Morocco suggests that the Saudis are thinking in terms of regional blocs of conservative powers. In the 1950s, an "Arab cold war" broke out between the monarchies and the then-new Arab nationalist regimes. Today the publics that reject dictatorship at home may well look askance at a close alliance with dictatorships abroad, and perhaps even support their overthrow by working with like-minded democrats in those countries. Some regimes may try to reach over the heads of neighboring leaders, appealing directly to the people.

Tension between nascent democracies and established autocracies could be exacerbated if economics proves to be a bone of contention. Most of the Arab states that have begun the transition to democracy (Egypt, Tunisia) or seem to be embracing reform in a more serious way (Morocco, Oman, and perhaps Jordan) are not oil producers.[1] Their poverty was part of the reason that their regimes either fell or felt intense pressure to change. It is still too early to tell whether these countries will make anything like a significant transition to pluralism. But if they do, and if their leaders increasingly demand that the oil-rich Arab states provide greater support to share the wealth more equitably across the Arab world, this could amplify tensions arising from their different political systems. Rich monarchies and poor democracies might find a lot to dislike about one another.

The role of Islam could prove another fault line. Tehran believes that if Islamists come to power in Egypt, Iraq, and elsewhere they may be more inclined toward good relations with Iran. However, Islamists in power might increasingly identify by sect, making Sunni-Shi'i identities the key to their regional alignments. This might bring Iraq closer to Iran but would likely push Egypt into a new alliance with the Saudis and other Sunni states. Depending on the type of Islamist voices that emerge, Turkey may be best positioned in the region, with its successful blend of Islam and democracy under the Erdoğan government.

AMERICAN DILEMMAS

The United States has no shortage of challenges emanating from the Arab Spring, and no shortage of opportunities either. This mixed outlook stems from the elements described in the preceding pages—potential changes in the overall balance of power, the possible shifts in regional alignments, and the new dynamics that will drive the geopolitics of the Middle East. Because the ground is shifting in the Middle East, the United States must be adept at shifting as well. If the United States can, it will be much better positioned to see its interests secured in the region than it is today. But the converse will also be true if the United States gets things wrong.

Washington will face a particularly acute dilemma if a group of democratic Middle Eastern states pit themselves against a group of autocratic states that includes key U.S. allies like Saudi Arabia and the United Arab Emirates. The United States should never turn its back on democracies, both because that is where American values lie and where America's long-term interests are best served. But it would also be extremely distasteful and potentially damaging for the United States to part ways with its strong allies. As the separate chapters on each of these countries have explained, the best solution to this problem lies in helping these states embrace meaningful, deliberate reform. If successful, this would create a different, much more positive division in the region between those states moving (perhaps at different paces) to bring their economic, social, and political systems more into line with what their people want—which could include nascent democratizers like Egypt and Iraq as well as reforming countries like Morocco and, *insh'allah*, Saudi Arabia—and those states adamantly determined to rule through old-fashioned repression. Iran and Syria (if the Asad regime survives) would obviously be charter members of the latter.

Indeed, one of the opportunities created by the region's potential realignment is the chance for the United States to weave a new narrative. Specifically, Washington should frame the divisions of the Middle East in a new way and articulate which side the United States is on. To do this, it should define the new regional struggle as one based on internal politics and the aspirations of its people. It should make clear that the region is now clearly divided between states that have acknowledged the desires of their people for a better future and are taking concrete steps to improve their peoples' lives through political reform, economic transformation, and social adaptation, and those that have not. Doing so will strip the veneer of authenticity from Iran, Syria, Hizballah, and other violent rejectionists by making clear that what they stand for is not what the people of the Middle East want.

As Suzanne Maloney explains in chapter 29, the Iranians have their own narrative and will be working just as hard to convince Middle Easterners that they have it right. Iran will doubtless try to exploit the fall of pro-American stalwarts like Hosni Mubarak and fill power vacuums that emerge in Iraq or elsewhere. The suspicions, and at times paranoia, of regional states that Iran is meddling in their affairs will limit Iran's power. But the message that Tehran is peddling— that the region is rejecting pro-U.S., anti-Islamic regimes—may find some takers. Whether the Arab Spring succeeds in transforming the region depends not just on the courage and resourcefulness of Arab publics, but also on how the Arab world's neighbors respond. As the initial surprise wears off and a hard-headed appraisal of the new landscape begins, these powers can be expected to play an increasingly important role in trying to shape the course of regional politics, defending their interests, and exploiting opportunities as they arise.

The challenge for the United States will be to balance the concerns of its existing allies in the region with the new demands that the Arab Spring brings. Some of these demands are opportunities offering the United States the chance to deepen existing friendships or create new ones. In many instances, however, policymakers may have to factor in an uncertain future when weighing how to respond to the challenges of today.

28

ISRAEL

A Frosty Response to the Arab Spring

DANIEL L. BYMAN

Americans took heart as they watched Egyptian demonstrators rally in Tahrir Square and topple the regime of Hosni Mubarak in a peaceful revolution.[1] Next door in Israel, however, the mood was somber. Addressing the U.S. Congress a few months later, Israeli prime minister Benjamin Netanyahu warned, "These hopes could be snuffed out as they were in Tehran in 1979."[2] As unrest spread from Egypt to Bahrain, Jordan, Syria, and Yemen, the gloom among Israelis only seemed to deepen.

The new regimes and the chaotic regional situation pose a variety of political and security challenges to the Jewish state. These challenges, and the Israeli reactions to them, are likely to worsen the situation in Gaza and make the prospects for peace between the Israelis and Palestinians even more remote. The new revolutions also have the potential to complicate the relationship between Israel and the United States further and make it harder for the United States to benefit from the Arab Spring. In the end, however, it is in Israel's interest, as well as Washington's, that the regional transformation is peaceful and that democratization succeeds.

FEAR FACTORS

The list of Israeli concerns about the wave of revolution sweeping the Arab world is long. Some are overstated or erroneous, but others are understandable and legitimate. And because both the irrational and rational fears will drive Israeli policy, both sets deserve serious attention.

When Friends Become Enemies

The biggest question for Israelis, and the one that has gotten the most attention, is what will replace Mubarak's regime in Egypt. For much of Israel's history, Egypt was its most dangerous foe, and the two countries fought bitter wars in

1948, 1956, 1967, 1969–70, and 1973. Egyptian president Anwar Sadat upended this seemingly constant belligerency when he made peace with Israel, transforming its greatest foe into a partner. Hosni Mubarak did not win the goodwill of ordinary Israelis as Sadat or the late King Hussein of Jordan did, but he maintained the peace treaty, cooperated on counterterrorism, opposed Iran, and otherwise shared strategic objectives with the Jewish state. And he and his regime seemed immovable. As Israeli analyst Aluf Benn points out, "Israel has replaced eight prime ministers, fought several wars, and engaged in peace talks with multiple partners, and Mubarak was always there."[3]

Netanyahu and others are particularly fearful that Islamists, led by the Muslim Brotherhood, will gain power in Egypt, either legitimately through democratic elections or by seizing power during a time of chaos. The Brotherhood often criticized Sadat and then Mubarak for making peace with Israel, pointing to this as one (of many) factors that delegitimized the regime. In February 2011, days before Mubarak stepped down, Rashad al-Bayoumi, a Brotherhood leader, declared, "After President Mubarak steps down and a provisional government is formed, there is a need to dissolve the peace treaty with Israel."[4] Other Brotherhood leaders are more conciliatory (or evasive), but none are fans of the peace treaty. Israel is leery of a Brotherhood-influenced regime in Egypt because of the effect it would have not only on the peace treaty but also on events in the Gaza Strip, where Hamas—whose own history is rooted in the Muslim Brotherhood—rules.

Israel's bigger problem is that the Brotherhood is not alone in its anti-Israel sentiment. Israelis focused less on the many Tahrir Square demonstrators whose uplifting pleas for liberty inspired Arabs throughout the region and more on the few who also hanged a puppet with a Star of David on it to symbolize Mubarak while chanting, "God is great."[5] Even more troubling for Israel is that moderate Egyptian leaders who enjoy support in Washington, such as Ayman Nour and Nobel laureate Mohamed ElBaradei, have also called for revision of the peace treaty or a referendum on it. Amr Moussa, formerly Egypt's foreign minister and now a leading presidential candidate, has long criticized Israel. He enjoys the distinction of being mentioned in a top pop song with lyrics declaring, "I hate Israel and I love Amr Moussa."[6] Nour even proclaimed, "The era of Camp David is over," though he claims to favor revising, not abrogating, the treaty.[7]

It is easy to dismiss statements like Nour's as empty posturing in the run-up to elections. And, more encouragingly, Brotherhood leaders have also made statements to the effect that what is signed is signed—they oppose the peace treaty with Israel, but will not do anything to change it. Therefore much of the anti-Israel rhetoric is likely to be honored largely, if not entirely, in the breach. However, in a true democracy, politicians cannot always escape their campaign promises. This may be especially true in this case because anti-Israel sentiment is strong in Egypt. A Pew poll taken after Mubarak's fall found that Egyptians favored annulling the peace treaty with Israel by a 54 to 36 percent margin.[8]

Ultimately, the peace treaty is likely to endure because Egyptian elites generally recognize its enormous benefits to their country. Therefore it is easy for many to dismiss Israeli fears without acknowledging that some are valid. The Egyptian peace with Israel, always cold, could become even chillier. Egypt has already made overtures to Iran, which Israel considers its nemesis. On March 29, 2011, acting Egyptian foreign minister Nabil al-Arabi announced that Egypt would eventually normalize relations with Iran and its Lebanese ally Hizballah. The previous month, Egypt allowed two Iranian naval ships to transit the Suez Canal, sending a clear message that Mubarak's anti-Iran position was over.

Other countries worry Israelis as well. Jordan, which has also signed a peace treaty with Israel and cooperates closely on intelligence matters, is of particular concern. Jordan has been especially helpful to Israel in stopping infiltration into the West Bank and otherwise assisting Israeli counterterrorism efforts. King Abdullah II, like his father King Hussein before him, is a staunch friend of Israel. However, he rules over a restive, Palestinian-majority population that does not take well to his openly pro-Western and pro-Israeli stance.

Palestinians, both moderate and militant, are also vulnerable to unrest, and Israelis fear the change sweeping the region will create instability and bolster extremists. Some Palestinians depict President Mahmoud Abbas, whose moderation makes him so prized in Washington, as a Mubarak clone. While Israelis often scorn, belittle, or ignore Abbas, they also recognize that he is willing to make peace and, perhaps more important to many Israelis, is willing to crush Hamas and other enemies of Israel on the territory he controls. A new Palestinian leader may not be so conciliatory.

To offset pressure for democratic change, the Hamas and Abbas governments did the unthinkable: they united, at least on paper. Whether this unity lasts is an open question, but Israelis have reacted harshly to it. Many observers in the United States believe Palestinian unity is necessary for peace: Abbas now claims he can negotiate on behalf of all Palestinians, and if Hamas uses terrorism against Israel it risks disrupting intra-Palestinian peace as well as provoking an Israeli reaction. However, on May 3, Netanyahu called on Abbas to jettison the agreement, contending that Israel could not make peace with a Palestinian government that included a terrorist organization.

Devils You Know

One of the most surprising Israeli reactions to the Arab Spring is the apparent concern that unrest could topple adversaries like Bashar al-Asad in Syria. Asad supports Hamas and Hizballah, rejects peace (or at least has not embraced negotiations, as has Abbas), and is a close friend of Iran. In 2007 Israel even bombed a suspected nuclear facility in Syria.

But Syria's past suggests the danger of instability to Israel. Salah Jadid, who ruled Syria before Bashar al-Asad's father, Hafiz, whipped up popular sentiment against Israel, agitating on behalf of the Palestinians to the point that the situation spiraled into war in 1967—a conflict that Damascus was not prepared to fight and that resulted in the loss of the Golan Heights to Israel. Hafiz, who consolidated power in 1971, learned this lesson and controlled and manipulated popular sentiment. At times he went against it, but always—after he had satisfied the demands of honor by attacking Israel in 1973—to avoid a conflict with Israel. His son Bashar takes more risks, but he, too, recognizes that an open clash with Israel would be disastrous for Syria and his regime. Relations between Syria and Israel are governed by many rules, most of which are unspoken but nevertheless quite real. So while Damascus supports Hamas, and hosts its leadership on Syrian soil, it also places limits on the Palestinian group's activities. Similarly, Syria backs the anti-Israel Hizballah in Lebanon, but also keeps its activities against Israel in check to avoid escalation. Changes in Syria could bring to power a new government that does not understand these subtle rules and, again, plays to popular opinion rather than strategic reality.

Even if Asad stays in power, he may feel compelled to stir up anger against Israel to divert the pressure of popular opinion. If Syria's economy continues to stagnate, Asad may try to seize on anti-Israeli sentiment to divert popular anger and adopt more confrontational policies. Already, in May and June 2011, as unrest swept across Syria, the Asad regime encouraged (some reports say coerced) Palestinians to march across the Syrian border into the Golan Heights, leading to over a dozen deaths (Syria claims far more).[9]

The Arab Spring has also diminished the possibility of an Israeli-Syrian peace agreement. A deal between Syria and Israel was always seen as easier, though less important, than an Israeli-Palestinian agreement. As a result, American (and Israeli) negotiators often urged a "Syria first" approach to a comprehensive peace. However, the weakness of the Asad government, as well as the likely position of any conceivable replacement, makes peace even less likely.

Down with the People

In the past, Israel used the lack of democracy in the Arab world to justify its closeness to the United States and its isolation in the region. Israel was an island of democracy in a sea of dictatorship, and as such had a strong relationship with the United States, the world's oldest and most powerful democracy. Netanyahu used to argue that democracy was vital for true peace, as undemocratic countries were not trustworthy and thus might not honor any treaty they signed. He tempered these views after Hamas won the 2006 Palestinian elections and now seems to have shelved them completely.[10] Now Israel's rhetoric has shifted to emphasize liberal values. As Netanyahu contended in his May 2011 speech to Congress, "In a region where women are stoned, gays are hanged, Christians are persecuted, Israel stands out. It is different."[11]

Given how strong anti-Israel sentiment is in much of the Arab world, Israelis do not trust Arab publics. A 2010 University of Maryland/Zogby poll found that almost 90 percent of Arabs saw Israel as "the biggest threat to you."[12] "The ugly facts," said former defense minister Moshe Arens, "are that the two peace treaties that Israel concluded so far—the one with Egypt and the other with Jordan—were both signed with dictators: Anwar Sadat and King Hussein."[13] In other words, Israelis fear that the Mubaraks, Husseins, and other dictators are as good as it will get for Israel *because* these leaders are outside the mainstream of their societies.

CRISIS POINTS

In the near term, the dramatic changes in the Arab world are likely to exacerbate two important security issues for Israel: its confrontation with the Hamas government of the Gaza Strip and the status of the peace process.

Gaza

Since Hamas took control of Gaza in 2006, Israel has tried to contain and undermine the Islamist regime with a mix of diplomatic isolation, economic pressure, and occasional military strikes. Under Mubarak, Egypt quietly helped Israel against Hamas, much to Hamas's outrage. Egypt kept the Rafah border crossing between Egypt and Gaza by and large closed, helping Israel restrict the flow of goods and people into and out of Gaza. Over time, smugglers and terrorists dug a massive tunnel complex between Egypt and Gaza, and Israeli officials complained that a mix of incompetence, corruption, and sympathy kept Egypt from shutting it down. Israelis, however, recognized that Egypt could be far more helpful to Hamas, and thus muted their criticism even as they pressed Cairo to be more aggressive. In the last months of Mubarak's rule, Egypt heeded Israel's call, building a barrier on the border that extended deep underground to make tunneling much harder.

The revolution in Egypt and unrest elsewhere in the Arab world have shaken this always-fragile equilibrium. Sympathy for Gazans is high in Egypt, and Hamas's resistance to Israel is also popular. The influential commentator Rami Khoury finds "widespread indignity felt by Egyptians who see themselves as the jailers of Gaza on behalf of Israel and Washington."[14] The Egyptian government has already announced that it will open Rafah and no longer cooperate with the economic isolation of Gaza, for in the words of Egyptian foreign minister Nabil al-Arabi, "Egyptian national security and Palestinian security are one."[15]

Should pressure ease, and should Hamas—as is likely—exploit this to acquire weapons and send personnel in and out for training, Israel will be tempted to take unilateral action. This may involve operations on or near the Egyptian side of the Gaza border and an increase in the pace of killing Hamas leaders in Gaza. Such actions, in turn, would inflame popular sentiment in Egypt against Israel and increase pressure on any regime in Cairo to further aid Hamas.

Already, in August 2011, a bloody terrorist attack on Israel almost sparked a broader confrontation. Terrorists from Gaza infiltrated Egypt via the Sinai, and, in conjunction with Egyptian radicals, killed eight Israelis near the vacation town of Eilat. Several of the surviving terrorists fled back into Egypt. Israeli forces entered the Sinai in hot pursuit, killing six Egyptian security officers who engaged the Israeli forces. In response, angry crowds demonstrated outside Israel's embassy in Egypt, demanding that Egypt sever relations. Fortunately, cooler heads in Egypt and Israel prevailed and leaders backed away from a confrontation, but such events can excite public passions and make it hard for leaders to avoid escalation.

Hamas, too, may become bolder. Where Israel sees a loss of an ally in Egypt, Hamas sees a potential friend, particularly if the Muslim Brotherhood gains influence there. Hamas can now play to the Egyptian people even if the Egyptian military and any elected leaders prefer to avoid a confrontation with Israel.

Hamas may seek to burnish its resistance credentials in order to counter any legitimacy it loses from its authoritarian ways. Because of this, Hamas will find it harder to back down from its on-again, off-again confrontations with Israel. But even if Hamas itself does not engage in attacks, more radical groups like Palestine Islamic Jihad and Salafi jihadists will still attack Israel, and Hamas may fear that cracking down on them would hurt it politically.

Poor Prospects for Peace

Beyond the usual reasons that peace is desirable—security for Israel, justice and dignity for the Palestinians, and greater stability for the region—a successful peace process would take away one of the greatest rhetorical weapons of extremists and make it harder for demagogues to create an escalatory spiral of extremism. It would also improve Israel's relations with the United States and Europe at a key moment in the region's history. In the wake of the Arab Spring, however, Israel will be even more skeptical of taking risks for peace. For now, the long-term identity of Netanyahu's peace partner is an open question. If Mubarak can go, so too can Abbas or Asad. So why, Israelis ask, take risks for peace if your partner may be gone tomorrow?

Nor are Arab leaders likely to extend a hand. New leaders of nascent democracies are not likely to risk their popularity by embracing a peace that under most conceivable scenarios would be seen by their own people as selling out the Palestinians. Battered, surviving regimes are also less likely to embrace—much less push for—a peace that would not be popular with their constituents. Palestinian leaders will be less compromising. Abbas, for example, is already under pressure because of his authoritarian ways in the West Bank, and the charge of "sellout" might topple his regime.

Should actual negotiations commence, Israeli demands for security guarantees are likely to grow. One Israeli analyst called for any agreement to include "a demilitarized Palestine, Israel's right to respond to terror attacks, and an Israeli military presence along the Jordan River."[16] Some of these demands (like a demilitarized Palestinian state) have been accepted in a de facto way by Palestinian negotiators, but others represent a more hard-line stance than previous Israeli positions.

Given Israel's overwhelming conventional military superiority, and the unlikely prospect that impoverished Syria or a new, revolutionary regime in Jordan could suddenly field a strong conventional military, these demands are based more on political, rather than security considerations, meant to reassure the Israeli public in an uncertain time. But they are political on the Palestinian side too, and acceptance of additional Israeli security demands would tell many Palestinians that their sovereignty means little in practice—so little, in fact, that Israeli troops could stay along their borders and go into their cities without interference.

AMERICA CAUGHT IN BETWEEN

The United States will be caught between its commitment to Israel and its desire to advance democratization in the region and gain the goodwill of the new Arab leaders. U.S. regional interests go well beyond the security of Israel, of course, and include counterterrorism and energy security—areas in which strong ties with Arab countries are vital.

The peace process will be an obvious challenge for the United States. As Khaled Elgindy and Salman Shaikh argues in chapter 6, one way to make the success of the Arab Spring more likely is to remove one of the greatest radicalizing forces in the region—the Palestinian question—from the agenda. New governments and old will want the United States to once again exert itself in hopes of a breakthrough. Yet well before the Arab Spring began, the Obama and Netanyahu administrations had locked horns on this issue.

The divisions within the Palestinian camp, the rightward shift in Israeli politics, and the upcoming 2012 presidential election in the United States have already made this peace-process season unlikely to bear fruit, but the Arab revolutions mean it will be almost impossible. The result is likely to be the triumph of form over substance. As Aaron David Miller contends, "In the coming months we'll see a lot of process but not much peace."[17] Even an empty process—perhaps especially an empty process—can lead to disputes, particularly if the Obama administration believes Netanyahu and company are refusing to put a serious proposal on the table.

In addition, Gaza offers the risk of a high-profile crisis that both the new leaders of the region and the United States would rather avoid. Washington, however, will find it hard to press Israel to restrain itself in Gaza if Hamas becomes more aggressive. Mortar attacks and shootings from Gaza deserve an Israeli response, but a new regime in Egypt, unlike Mubarak, may not sit quietly by.

Yet the greatest danger is if the progress of the Arab Spring hits a wall. Israel's fears are much more likely to become reality if reform efforts stall or fail. Failure would empower radicals in Egypt and throughout the region, "proving" that a Western, democratic model is not right for the Arab world. Reformers would point to a lack of Western support, while critics would use U.S. support for Israel as a cudgel to beat back moderates. More extreme voices would only gain resonance.

If new Arab governments start to fail, the likelihood that they and their supporters will scapegoat Israel will rise proportionately. Anti-Israel sentiment has long been a way for Middle Eastern dictatorships to deflect popular dissatisfaction with their regimes, and new rulers will use this tool too. If these new governments suffer economic and political problems, the political logic of blaming or provoking Israel grows. Conversely, if regime legitimacy grows because new leaders enjoy the consent of the governed and are showing material progress on political and economic grounds, the need for scapegoating diminishes. Scapegoating is more likely to succeed, however, if Israel's policies are widely seen as provocative and uncompromising on their own. The success of democratization in Egypt is particularly important here. Israeli fears that Iran will exploit the void can best be countered by a politically strong Egypt that enjoys credibility with the Arab people and offers a more powerful message than what Tehran promotes. Under these new circumstances, Egypt's peace treaty with Israel could become particularly important. No longer would the treaty be a deal between elites. Rather, the Egyptian nation would be embracing it de facto, not just de jure, making it easier for leaders in other countries to convince their own people that an unpopular peace may be the best they can hope for given today's political and strategic realities.

In the end, regional revolutions can eventually work to Israel's benefit. But Israel must recognize the new regional dynamics, including the potential for escalation and the political realities of its neighbors and potential peace partners. Such recognition will not make the new challenges go away, but they should allow Israel to seize opportunities for peace and diminish the likelihood that Jerusalem will engage in dangerous behavior that could spiral into disaster.

29

IRAN

The Bogeyman

SUZANNE MALONEY

The specter of Iran looms large over the upheaval sweeping the Middle East. Although it has by and large escaped the explosion of unrest that has evicted several Arab dictators and unsettled many others, Iran is very much a central protagonist in the ongoing regional transformation and the future of American policy toward the region. Its revolutionary theocracy is the product of the first popular revolution in the Middle East, and its 1979 ouster of a pro-American monarch remains the single enduring regional experience with a peaceful mass mobilization against a seemingly stable autocracy. The outcome of that revolution also stands as the cautionary tale of how the best-laid intentions of a popular movement for democratic change can go badly awry. More immediately, the ongoing and unpredictable process of transition taking place across the region presents Tehran with new opportunities as well as challenges—and the evolving shifts in the balance of power require a careful, realistic reassessment of Washington's options and approach.

IRANIAN CALCULATIONS

Contrary to the expectations of some observers, Iran's dominant conservative faction did not view the eruption of popular agitation for government accountability and democratic representation as a threat to its control or an indictment of its own autocratic tendencies. Rather, Iran's dogmatic theocrats perceive the Arab uprisings as both a reverberation of their own revolutionary experience and a vindication of their belief in their own ascendance and the concomitant demise of Western influence. For this reason, Iranian leaders greeted the earliest stirrings of the Arab Spring with enthusiasm, applause, and encouragement.

This initial response—which has remained consistent over the course of the upheaval, except in reaction to the developments in Syria—reflected Tehran's shrewd recognition of the prospective costs and benefits of change in the region.

Since its inception more than three decades ago, the Islamic Republic of Iran has resented and rebelled against the prevailing balance of power in the Middle East. Therefore the region's recent implosion, enacted through no expenditure of resources or political capital by Tehran, came as a windfall.

From the vantage point of Tehran, the balance sheet has been overwhelmingly positive: several of Iran's most determined regional adversaries were dispatched into exile, prison, or at minimum into a defensive crouch. Having long experienced the constraints and indignities of isolation, Iranian authorities exulted in the possibility of new diplomatic access to the historic heart of the Sunni Arab world. Even the possibility of new inroads presents a significant net gain for a state that has long had far more enemies than friends in its own neighborhood. Instead of the creeping isolation that the Obama administration has sought to impose on Tehran as a price for its nuclear noncompliance, Iran's regional prospects suddenly look downright rosy.

There were other advantages to be tallied. Regional insecurity helped ratchet oil prices back up to $125 per barrel, at least briefly, and the persistence of tensions in the neighborhood offers a fairly reliable insurance policy against a repetition of the 2008 price crash that for the first time in a decade had directly impinged upon the theocracy's financial viability. Oil remains the Iranian regime's economic lifeline, and the prospect of a sustained $80 to $100 per barrel price band provides a substantial cushion against the creeping costs of Iran's estrangement from its traditional trade partners and the impact of unprecedented international economic sanctions adopted by the United Nations, the European Union, and other states in 2010.

In addition, the uncertainty that is an unfortunate offshoot of the dramatic changes sweeping the region is favorable to Iran's interests. Although the crowds that have shaken the Arab status quo have focused primarily on domestic issues and grievances, an undercurrent of mistrust for Washington is clearly identifiable. Should the democratic dreams of Arab masses end in despair—with instability, renewed autocracy, or merely dashed economic expectations—the disillusioned will be particularly ripe for the kind of manipulation that the Iranians know best.

And perhaps most important, Iran's triumphal reaction to the Arab Spring reflects its leadership's zero-sum logic of the strategic competition with Washington. The uprisings eliminated or strained long-standing American partners in the Arab world, and inevitably complicated each of the fundamental priorities that have animated American regional policy for three decades, including the containment of Iranian influence. Without lifting a finger, the Islamic Republic sensed that it had achieved one of its foremost strategic objectives—weakening American influence across the Middle East.

The Syrian Exception

The single dark cloud looming on the horizon for Tehran's gloating clerics is Syria, the only Arab state that has proved to be a reliable ally for the Persian theocracy. Syria's slow simmer over the course of the early months of 2011 meant that the Iranian leadership was caught off guard in late spring by the ferocity of the violence that wrought havoc there in the second half of the year. Unlike the prospective opportunities to be seized in almost every other Arab state, unrest in Syria must engender deep-seated angst among Iranian decisionmakers. Should the Asad regime collapse, Tehran would lose its most trusted regional partner and its most reliable mechanism for resupplying Hizballah and maintaining direct access to the political dramas of the Levant. Moreover, the scope and pace of Syria's descent must be unnerving for Iran's confidence in its own ability to preserve control.

For all of these reasons, it is hardly surprising that, according to senior U.S. officials, Tehran has assisted Syrian leader Bashar al-Asad in his brutal campaign to quell the uprising. Iran maintains a contingent of Revolutionary Guard forces in Syria, and its security cooperation with Syria has always been oriented toward mutual defense, with the utilization of violence against civilian populations through terrorist groups such as Hizballah, and more recently Hamas, a primary method. Tehran's official dogma insists that unrest in Syria is the product of Western subversion in collaboration with Saudi (or "Wahhabi") interests, intended to avenge their loss of influence and penalize the apparent "victors" of the shift in the broader regional balance of power (namely, Iran and its allies). As the situation in Syria degenerates and the international outcry over civilian casualties mounts, Iranian leaders have begun drawing a line in the sand, so to speak, that they would not accept direct Western intervention in Syria. This sets the stage for a possible confrontation not only between Iran and the international community, but perhaps more importantly between Tehran and the broader Arab constituency that it has long sought to cultivate.

The Iranian discussion of the events in Syria has elicited some surprising nuances, however. These can only be intentional on the part of the regime, given the severely restricted domestic political climate. Although Iran's reformist press is a pale shadow of its former glory, it still voiced increasingly sharp criticism of the Asad regime's approach to Syria's domestic difficulties. It even criticized the Iranian state media's coverage of events in Syria.[1] In addition, several former officials aligned with the more pragmatic wing of Iran's regime have openly diverged from the government line. Former president 'Ali Akbar Hashemi Rafsanjani reportedly compared the Syrian unrest with the popular movements that brought down the Tunisian and Egyptian regimes, while former foreign minister Manouchehr Mottaki proclaimed that the uprisings reflected the "hidden anger" of Arabs toward their governments and recommended that

Damascus open a dialogue and demonstrate leniency toward the opposition.[2] As Syria's situation grew more bloody, even President Ahmadinejad critized the crackdown, a bitter irony considering his own means of maintaining power. These refrains suggest divisions within the Iranian establishment over Syria, as well as more broadly mirroring the fissures that emerged over Iran's own disputed 2009 presidential election.

IRAN'S POWER PLAYS

Interestingly, although Iran's assessment of the regional context and the tone of its rhetoric have tended toward the exuberant, its initial diplomatic forays into the new regional context outside of Syria have been relatively prudent. This has not been wholly atypical for a regime that often talks bigger than it acts, and that in recent decades has made some effort to mollify the long-standing fears of some of its neighbors.

It also has reflected the maturation of an Iranian leadership from the heady first decade of the revolution, when Tehran engaged in a noisy and often violent campaign to subvert its neighbors under the guise of "exporting the revolution." Since the 1990s, Iranian leaders of divergent factional orientations have remained broadly committed to maintaining a tepid peace and modest trade relations in the region. This did not entail an abandonment of the theocracy's predilection for sowing instability or utilizing unconventional instruments, but rather a retreat to a more nationalist interpretation of its interests and a hard-won recognition of the limitations of its capabilities.

The theocracy's experience in post-Saddam Iraq has further refined its approach to the region, demonstrating the sufficiency of the eviction of an old antagonist and the utility of democracy and its attendant openings for the purposes of enhancing Iranian influence. Based on the Iraqi precedent, Tehran readily welcomed the embrace of democratic principles in Tunisia, Egypt, and elsewhere, confident that regime change will almost inevitably produce governments in key Arab capitals that will be less compliant to Washington's wishes and less hostile toward Tehran than their predecessors. And that outcome would be more than sufficient for Iranian purposes.

This pragmatism underpinning Iran's approach to its neighborhood has generated a somewhat bifurcated set of tactics in response to the Arab Spring. On the one hand, Tehran has sought to impose its own narrative on the unfolding changes—one that tends to be provocative, misleading, and toxic. According to its official line, Iran and Islam are central to the ouster of Arab autocrats, as well as to sowing suspicions of American aims and policies. Iranian leaders have postured as the region's most ardent defenders of democracy and as the inspiration for the popular mobilization against repressive regimes, while blaming the West for the violent reprisals against oppositionists in Libya, Yemen, and Bahrain. One final important element of the Iranian public diplomacy campaign has been to link the Arab uprisings with the plight of the Palestinians—despite the Palestinians' relative quiescence over the course of the tumultuous year—in order to misrepresent Arab activism as being aimed at Israel.

Iran's posture on the Arab Spring is deceptive and deliberatively infuriating for its neighbors and adversaries, but in practice it belies the relative discretion of Iranian policy. To be sure, Tehran has sought to flex its muscles and test the boundaries of its new access to various Arab governments and populations in the wake of the Arab upheaval—as epitomized by its dispatch of warships to transit the Suez Canal in February 2011 for the first time in three decades.

Yet beyond its initial attempts to expand its formal contacts with old adversaries such as Egypt, Iran has proved more reactive than proactive, at least over the early months of the upheaval. Even in Bahrain, where the Sunni government and its Saudi ally crushed peaceful protests by the disempowered Shi'i majority, the Iranians have for the most part countered with oratory rather than intervention. Even a much-hyped convoy of Iranian aid ships, aimed at providing supplies to Shi'i Bahrainis and meant as a parallel to the May 2010 "Gaza Freedom Flotilla" that was attacked by the Israelis, was quickly turned back to avoid inflaming an already-tense situation. Besieged governments across the region have wailed about Iranian interference, either directly or via its Lebanese ally Hizballah, but there is little publicly available evidence of a meaningful Iranian role in any of the upheavals, except in Syria.

At least in relation to its past troublemaking, Tehran's restraint so far in exploiting the Arab upheaval, in deed if not in words, suggests that the Iranian regime is hedging its bets. Just as it did in the aftermath of the collapse of the Soviet Union, the Islamic Republic may be seeking maximum impact with minimal outlay, in recognition of the very real limitations on its capabilities and resources, particularly in comparison with competitors like Saudi Arabia. Just as Iran's more aggressive factions derided its Central Asian outreach as *siyasat-e dast-e gul* (roughly translated as a foreign policy of distributing flower bouquets), its hard-liners are already questioning the capabilities of the relatively staid foreign ministry to take maximum advantage of the new regional opportunities. The stakes are considerably higher in the Middle East, which has long served as Iran's preferred arena for power projection. Still, it remains to be seen whether Tehran's bite will prove as fierce as its bark.

Whatever the actual extent of Iranian activism in the Arab upheaval and nascent democratic transitions, its neighbors have not been inclined to look the other way. Stoked by a decade of growing frustrations with Washington's Middle East policy, the Saudis were shocked by what they saw as America's casual willingness to abandon a long-standing ally, Hosni Mubarak. In response, they wasted no time sounding the alarm about what they saw as a seemingly inexorable Iranian march toward regional hegemony as a result of American blunders, naiveté, and weakness. "As Riyadh fights a cold war with Tehran," a well-known Saudi surrogate proclaimed in the *Washington Post* in May 2011, "Washington has shown itself in recent months to be an unwilling and unreliable partner against this threat. The emerging political reality is a Saudi-led Arab world facing off against the aggression of Iran and its non-state proxies . . . Saudi Arabia has the will and the means to meet its expanded global responsibilities."[3]

For their part, Iranian leaders have warned darkly that efforts by the Saudis and other Arab states would only come back to haunt them. One of the Islamic Republic's most senior military officials predicted that the Saudi incursion into Bahrain would undermine its own security, while Ayatollah Ali Khamenei, Iran's supreme leader, thundered that "the Saudi government made a mistake and should not do such a thing. They make themselves reviled in the region. . . . [T]he Saudis are living in this region, and if they become reviled, it will cause very heavy damage to them. They made a mistake in doing so."[4]

The corresponding tensions have played themselves out across the region, with frequent accusations of Iranian "meddling," particularly in Bahrain and Yemen where Iran has a history of involvement because of their Shi'i populations. In Egypt, an Iranian diplomat was arrested in mid-May 2011, but quickly released, and both governments quashed rumors of a speedy reestablishment of full diplomatic relations, lapsed since Iran's 1979 revolution. In the Gulf, the tenor of rhetoric on both sides has veered toward the histrionic, and accusations of Iranian weapons-smuggling and espionage activities in Kuwait and Bahrain have precipitated diplomatic expulsions and breaches in the bilateral relationships. There are reports that Kuwait is denying entry visas to Iranian business travelers, while the Bahraini state-sponsored business association has clamored for the entire Arab world to boycott Iranian products and businesses. In typical tit-for-tat fashion, Iranian officials have threatened to boycott pilgrimages to Mecca on the grounds that "the money that Iranian Muslims spend on the *umrah* is used to buy weapons to massacre Bahraini Muslims."[5] If left unchecked, Iran's escalating frictions with its neighbors—as demonstrated by the October 2011 indictment of Iranian agents in a plot to assassinate the Saudi ambassador to the United States—could prove deeply destabilizing for the Gulf, and have troubling implications for U.S. security interests and the global economy.

Iran's Internal Drama

The improbable success of peaceful protests in the Arab world sparked hopes and some expectations that the contagion effect might galvanize Iran's besieged and inchoate opposition. After all, Iran benefits from a century of popular agitation for representative government, considerable direct experience with elections, and a relatively sophisticated internal discourse around questions of authority and legitimacy. More immediately, as President Barack Obama noted in his May 2011 speech on the Arab Spring, it was only two years ago that Iran itself was engulfed by mass upheaval in the aftermath of the 2009 presidential election that was widely perceived as rigged. And yet, with the exception of a few early protests, Iran has experienced very little of the upheaval that has beset its neighbors. With gallows humor and evident frustration, U.S. government analysts invoke the description used by President Jimmy Carter in late December 1977, when he referred to Iran as an "island of stability" only months before the eruption of the sustained unrest that led to the 1979 revolution.

Iran's unexpected quiescence can be traced to a variety of factors, including the depoliticization of a population that appreciates all too well the risks and uncertainties inherent in any act of rebellion. Certainly, the spirit of protest has been beaten down by Iranian dissenters' inability to achieve meaningful results and the high price paid for each failure. Iran's unique history, its ethnic and religious divergence from its neighbors, and the central role of long-time regime insiders in leading the proto-opposition that has existed since 2009 also contribute to the surprising quiescence of the Islamic Republic. The primary factor, however, is the resourceful campaign by the Iranian regime to prevent the resurgence of any significant popular opposition. Yet many media analysts have perpetuated a basic misconception about the nature of the Iranian domestic response to the Arab Spring, conflating Iranian repression with that of other authoritarian adversaries of Washington such as Syria and Libya. Although Washington's accusations that Tehran has been directly complicit in the Syrian repression are well grounded, at home the Iranian leadership has adopted a substantially different approach to managing domestic instability. In direct contrast to Bashar al-Asad and Muammar Qadhafi, Tehran has not engaged in mass killings of protesters or indiscriminate violence against civilians. Even Egyptian security forces proved more deadly in 2011 than Iran's reviled Revolutionary Guards in 2009. Approximately 850 Egyptians were killed during Mubarak's ouster, whereas the best estimates put the deaths in Iran during the protests after the 2009 elections at less than 100, although there are no authoritative sources. Compared with the brutality employed by the regimes in Yemen, Libya, and Syria, the Iranian approach appears significantly more subtle.

The purpose of drawing this distinction is not to exonerate the Islamic Republic, but to highlight its preference for dealing with popular dissatisfaction through tactics that appear to be more effective and more durable over the long term. Tehran's approach does not reflect a more humane leadership, but one that appreciates the escalatory impact of wide-scale crackdowns as a result of direct experience. Rather than mow down its opposition, Tehran has engaged in a more multifaceted and shrewd set of measures. Repression plays an important role, but one that is utilized selectively to eliminate prospective leaders, decapitate opposition organizations, and disillusion the wider array of Iranians who were willing only two years ago to risk their lives to protest the regime. In this sense, the Arab Spring proved an impediment to the Iranian opposition, as the dramatic developments in Egypt and elsewhere diverted the world's attention from Tehran's shameless and shocking move to effectively "disappear" two long-time regime insiders who had become the titular leaders of the Green Movement.

Intimidation has constituted an equally or even more important dimension of Tehran's approach to instability; the Iranian regime has targeted relatives of activists simply to send a chilling message to any aspiring oppositionists and has instituted much more stringent political vetting of the wide range of employment opportunities available in the public sector. These measures, together with significant investments to enhance mobilization of regime supporters and buy off dissent through social spending and direct distribution of oil revenues, have insulated the Iranian regime and undercut the capacity of the nascent opposition to threaten its perpetuation.

In addition, it is worth noting that the Arab Spring began unfolding at the precise moment that the conservative camp, which has come to dominate the institutions and political debates of the Islamic Republic, began to turn on itself in an unpredictable fashion. Somewhat paradoxically, while Iran's opposition remained largely dormant throughout the early months of the Arab Spring, the political frictions within the regime ramped up sharply. The long-standing resentment and suspicion toward President Mahmoud Ahmadinejad harbored by traditional stalwarts of the regime exploded into public view as Ahmadinejad sought yet again to assert himself beyond the scope of his limited responsibilities. For the first time, Iran's supreme leader publicly undercut his presidential protégé, a move that only inflamed the antagonisms within the Iranian leadership.

It is possible, albeit unlikely, that the opposition and its more prudent allies such as former presidents Rafsanjani and Mohammed Khatami will take advantage of the clash among their conservative allies to regain the advantage. Nevertheless, the chaos at home and on the regional stage does not substantially alter the primary obstacle to resurrection of either the reform movement or its Green Movement successors: the fierce adherence to absolute authority by the supreme leader. If anything, the regional upheaval appears to have reinforced Khamenei's determination to eradicate any dissent and confront any potential external adversaries.

AMERICAN OPTIONS

For Washington, the resistance and persistence of the Islamic Republic presents a complicated set of dilemmas that have only been exacerbated by the Arab

Spring. Iran today presents a greater concern within the region than at any time in the past two decades, yet American influence and allies are in flux. Moreover, regional developments almost surely undercut the Obama administration's effort to persuade Iran's leader to bargain away its nuclear program. Having watched the international community bombard Libya, it is hard to imagine that the Iranian leadership would ever concede its nuclear advantage in exchange for rapprochement and trade ties. Nor would a regime that sees the United States as both weakened and distracted by the multiple, simultaneous crises of the Arab world fear subsequent American moves.

The current American approach is minimally sufficient for dealing with Iran, in the sense that it has successfully impeded Iran's most problematic policies without actually generating much progress toward reversing them or altering the regime's political calculus. But without a viable endpoint, Washington's strategy is simply too reliant on economic sanctions, the efficacy of which is progressively declining, to successfully resolve the most urgent American concerns about Iranian policies.

There is no magic bullet for taming Tehran, but in the wake of the Arab uprisings a few general principles should be considered:

—The Islamic Republic's greatest advantage stems not from its own achievements or influence, but from opportunities created by American missteps in the region. Ensuring, to the extent possible, that the Arab states successfully navigate this transitional period will provide the best defense against further Iranian inroads.

—The United States should resist the bait of Tehran's zero-sum articulation of regional influence. American relationships with the transitional Arab democracies are robust enough to withstand competition, while the reality is that Iran's efforts to expand its relationships with the emerging Arab democracies are inherently self-limiting. Over time, there is no question that the reputation and influence of the Islamic Republic will be devalued as a result of the Arab uprisings.

—Washington must find a new sustainable center for dealing with Riyadh that facilitates cooperation on common interests, including the threat from Iran and energy supply/pricing, while mitigating the impact of the very real conflicts that have arisen and will continue to arise as a result of divergent interests in regional reform.

—The U.S. government should develop strategies for avoiding conflict that are specific to prospective flashpoints between Tehran and Washington such as Gaza and Bahrain.

—Washington should rethink the universe of possibilities for advancing political change within Iran. In practice, American assistance to the Iranian opposition should focus first on facilitating access to technology that enables Iranians to circumvent the regime's control over the flow of information, for instance, by offering targeted sanctions relief, investing in filter-busting technology, and providing some tech products to Iranians.[6] Second, efforts could be made to enable greater contacts between Iranians and the rest of the world. Initial measures have included multiple-entry visas for students and a new emphasis on public diplomacy toward Iran through the appointment of a Persian-speaking State Department spokesperson; however, more can be done to enable Iranians to travel to the United States or access opportunities abroad. And third, programs could be initiated to support and protect dissidents who have already fled by helping them gain expanded access to visa and refugee status.

30

TURKEY

An Interested Party

ÖMER TAŞPINAR

The Arab Spring came at a time of significant turbulence in Turkey's relations with the United States, Israel, and Europe. The uneasiness emanated in part from growing Western concerns about an "Islamist" turn in Ankara's foreign policy. Tensions began mounting in 2010 with the Gaza flotilla crisis, which ended with Israeli forces killing nine Turkish citizens. Weeks later, Turkey's "no" vote to a new round of UN sanctions against Iran triggered a heated "who lost Turkey?" debate in Washington. As relations with Israel and Washington continued to sink, Turkey appeared to find new allies in Syria, Russia, and Iran. The resulting perception of an Islamist "axis shift" in Turkey led observers like columnist Thomas Friedman to suggest that Ankara was now joining the "Hamas-Hezbollah-Iran resistance front against Israel."[1]

What a difference a few months make. When the Arab Spring shook the core of the Arab world, it also caused a drastic change in Western discourse about Turkey. Instead of asking "Who lost Turkey?" or complaining about the Islamization of Turkish foreign policy, many Western analysts have now been busy discussing whether the new regimes in the Arab world will be lucky enough to follow the "Turkish model." As the most democratic and secular Muslim country in the region, Turkey has come to be seen in a much more positive light in recent months. Turkey's call for democratic change in Egypt and Syria, as well as its support—after initial reluctance—for the NATO military effort in Libya, has also contributed to a perception that Ankara is playing a constructive role in promoting democratic change in the Middle East. Even the Arab media are commenting on the Turkey model: one of the most discussed questions in the Arab world is whether Islamic movements in Egypt, Tunisia, Yemen, Libya, Syria, and other Arab states will be able to generate political parties that are as moderate as the Justice and Development Party (AKP) of Prime Minister Recep Tayyip Erdoğan.

This rapid turnabout in conventional wisdom, from talk of a "lost" state to one worthy of emulation, shows the confusion surrounding this important country—confusion abetted in part by the mistaken notion of a "pro-Western" versus

"Islamic" divide in Turkish foreign policy. It is easy to see why this misunderstanding arose. Turkey's population is almost entirely Muslim, and the AKP, a party with Islamic roots, has won three consecutive elections. Many thus assume that Turkish divergence from the West—"losing" Turkey—is the product of an Islamic revival or Islamization. While the growing importance of religion in Turkey should not be dismissed, a more nuanced discussion of Turkish foreign policy should instead focus on the new dynamics in Turkey such as neo-Ottomanism and the rise of Turkish "Gaullism."[2]

NEO-OTTOMANISM AND THE AKP

Since the AKP came to power in late 2002, its foreign policy has been based on what Prime Minister Erdoğan's top foreign policy adviser and now foreign minister, Ahmet Davutoğlu, calls "strategic depth" and "zero problems" with its neighbors. As Davutoğlu sees it, Turkey is a great power that has long neglected its historic ties and diplomatic, economic, and political relations with the Middle East, North Africa, the Balkans, and Central Asia. Since Turkey's new-found self-confidence and activism are evident for the most part in formerly Ottoman territories, the AKP's foreign policy is sometimes referred to as neo-Ottomanism.

The neo-Ottoman tendencies of the AKP are evident principally in three different aspects of Ankara's current policies. First, Ankara has a newfound willingness to come to terms with Turkey's Ottoman heritage at home and abroad. This does not mean pursuing Turkish imperialism in the Middle East and beyond or seeking to impose an Islamic legal system on Turkey itself. Instead, neo-Ottomanism favors a more moderate version of secularism at home and a more activist role in foreign affairs, particularly as a mediator in regional conflicts, such as between Israel and Syria. In this neo-Ottoman paradigm, Ankara exerts more "soft power"—political, economic, diplomatic, and cultural influence—in formerly Ottoman territories, as well as in other regions where Turkey has strategic interests.

Neo-Ottomanism is also relevant for Turkey's number one domestic problem, the Kurdish question. Since it is at peace with the imperial and multinational legacy of Turkey, neo-Ottomanism opens the door for a less "ethnic" and more multicultural conceptualization of "citizenship." As a result, compared with the Kemalist principles of the nationalist Turkish Republic, neo-Ottomanism is much more tolerant of Kurdish cultural rights and expressions of Kurdish national identity, as long as the Kurds' loyalty to the Republic of Turkey remains ironclad.

The second characteristic of neo-Ottomanism is a sense of *grandeur* and self-confidence in foreign policy. Neo-Ottomanism sees Turkey as a regional superpower, whose strategic vision and culture reflect the geographic reach of the Ottoman and Byzantine Empires. Thus, as a pivotal state, and one situated at the center of the Middle East, it should play a highly active diplomatic, political, and economic role across the region. In keeping with such grand ambitions, Turkey must be at peace with its multiple identities, including its Muslim and multinational past.

The third feature of neo-Ottomanism is a desire to embrace the West as much as the Islamic world. Like the imperial city of Istanbul, which straddles Europe and Asia, neo-Ottomanism is Janus-faced. In that sense, the European legacy matters a great deal to neo-Ottomans.

In the past eight years, the AKP government has followed its neo-Ottoman instincts and taken a more active approach toward the greater Middle East. Turkey has taken uncharacteristically strong positions on the Israeli-Palestinian conflict; sent troops to the NATO mission in Afghanistan; contributed to UN forces in Lebanon; assumed a leadership position in the Organization of Islamic Conference (now the Organization of Islamic Cooperation); attended several Arab League conferences; established closer ties with Iran, Iraq, and Syria; and improved its economic, political, and diplomatic relations with most Arab and Muslim states.

THE TURKISH MODEL AND THE ARAB SPRING

The Arab Spring presents a decidedly mixed blessing for the neo-Ottoman ambitions of Turkey. To be sure, most Turks feel a sense of pride in hearing their country regularly referred to as a model for democratizing Arab states. Yet the dizzying pace of events is rapidly changing the balance of power in the Middle East and challenging Foreign Minister Davutoğlu's zero problems with neighbors policy. In an immediate sense, Syria is one of the challenges, as Ankara must cope with the Asad regime's brutal response to its internal challenges—which has created a range of problems for Ankara, from humiliation to refugees. Over the longer term, however, Egypt's reemergence as a regional leader may ultimately prove to be the greater complication for neo-Ottoman Turkey.

Until recently, the AKP's neo-Ottomanism had the advantage of operating within the vacuum of strategic leadership in the Arab world. It was the dismal failure of Egyptian leadership in the region that was at the heart of the Arab strategic predicament, and that also translated into Arab admiration for Turkey's growing influence. With the Arab Spring and Egypt's revolution, Cairo is now reemerging as the most likely candidate to fill the vacuum of strategic leadership in the Arab world. Consequently, a successful Egypt could pose an alternative "model" for other states of the region. This means that the Arab Spring's impact on the region, especially on Egypt, could have important implications both for the Turkish model and for Turkey's Middle East policy.

The potential opportunities that the Arab Spring may open for Turkey will obviously depend on the overall relevance of the Turkish model for the Arab world. On closer inspection, it seems there are actually two Turkish models for Arab states to consider. The most familiar one, touched on by Shadi Hamid in chapter 4, centers on the AKP. The question is whether the AKP would serve as a model for the potential evolution of Islamist parties and whether the Muslim Brotherhood in Egypt and factions in other Arab states may adopt it. The second variation of the model, as Ken Pollack explains in chapter 7, focuses on the military, which plays a large role in shaping the political system. In both Egypt and Tunisia, the army played and continues to play a crucial role in the ongoing transition to post-authoritarianism. It should not come as a surprise that whenever the military becomes the most important factor shaping the political environment, people think of the Turkish model. After all, the Turkish military played a crucial role in the formation of the republic and has been the self-declared guardian of the Kemalist regime in Turkey since 1923. The duality of the Turkish model, however, creates a paradox for its potential emulators: How to build a new order founded on both an activist military and a moderate Islamic movement? The answer in Turkey's own case lies in some historical characteristics of the Turkish political system.

The Turkish state has a tradition of political supremacy over Islam that goes back to Ottoman times. In many ways, the Ottoman state was based on political supremacy over Islam. A body of law known as *Kanuns* was promulgated by the sultan outside the realm of Shari'a and had no direct Islamic justification. Its laws were based on rational rather than religious principles, and they applied in the public, administrative, and criminal spheres, as well as in the state's finances. Whenever there was a clash between such "raison d'état" and Islamic law, the sultan's law, or raison d'état, emerged victorious.

After the founding of the modern Turkish Republic under Ataturk, the staunchly secularist military continued this tradition of political supremacy over Islam. Political Islam, in its Turkish form, had to respect the red lines of Turkish secularism or suffer the consequences. In that sense, the moderation of Turkish political Islam was dictated in part by the presence of a strong secular state and an interventionist military. Today, the AKP is the fourth reincarnation of political Islam in Turkey. Not surprisingly, it follows much more moderate policies than earlier ones banned by strictly secularist Turkish constitutions in the 1970s, 1980s, and 1990s. This also helps to explain why Turkish Islamists, unlike some of their Arab counterparts who dream of a caliphate under Shari'a law, have less ambitious agendas limited to things like decriminalizing the use of Islamic headscarves by state employees or ending the ban on headscarves in public universities.

Yet the military and the secular state tradition should not get all the credit in explaining the emergence of the AKP. Turkey's transition to democracy in 1950 was equally crucial. Democracy is often the best antidote to political Islam. In the absence of freedom of expression, freedom of the press, free political parties, and free elections, in the Arab world, the mosques and politicized Islam became the only outlets for dissent; Islam became the only language of resistance against tyranny and the solution to everything. Unsurprisingly, "Islam is the solution" is the motto of the Muslim Brotherhood, the most powerful Islamic movement in the Arab world. Turkey managed to avoid this situation by transitioning to a multiparty democratic system in the 1950s and by allowing conservative Muslims to participate in the political system.

Combined with economic growth and the emergence of a middle class that benefited from globalization, capitalism, and democratic openings, Turkey's political dynamics diverged significantly from those of the autocratic Middle East. Turkey is also blessed by the absence of vast oil and gas resources, which has helped prevent it from going down the same political path as other countries in the region. Energy abundance is a curse that paralyzes the growth of democracy and capitalism in the Arab world. Instead of oil and gas, the Turkish economy is fueled by its highly productive and export-oriented "Anatolian tigers." This upwardly mobile, devout Anatolian bourgeoisie regularly votes for conservative political parties and has a vested interest in political stability. As a result, Turkey's Muslim entrepreneurs dream about maximizing their sales and profits in the global marketplace, rather than an Islamic revolution that will bring Shari'a to Turkey. Another important reason why Islamic fundamentalism is not in Turkey's future is that Turkish Islam has a healthy dose of Sufism. This brings a social, cultural, and mystical dimension to Turkish Islam at the expense of a radical political agenda. The fact that Turkey's most powerful religious movement is more interested in education, media, and interfaith dialogue is a case in point.

As this discussion shows, none of the political, economic, or cultural elements that define Turkey are easily transferable to the Arab world. To be sure, the Arab world is not a monolith. Arab states have different histories, class structures, political regimes, and economic systems. In any case, it is important to keep in mind that Turkey is not an Arab country and that its political evolution and history are unique. Moreover, one can argue that with the Arab Spring and particularly Egypt's revolution, Cairo is slowly reemerging as the most likely candidate to serve as a relevant model for the Arab world.

TURKISH FOREIGN POLICY AND THE ARAB SPRING

Beyond the limited relevance of the Turkish model, the Arab Spring is causing significant problems for Turkish foreign policy in at least two areas: Syria and the emergence of Egypt as the country that will fill the vacuum of strategic leadership in the region. The fact that it was Cairo and not Ankara that brokered the May 2011 deal for Palestinian reconciliation between Hamas and Fatah illustrates Egypt's ascent at the expense of Turkey.

Until recently, the Syrian-Turkish bilateral relationship was a remarkable story of a journey from enmity to friendship. It was also the cornerstone of Turkey's zero-problems strategy. Yet the brutal crackdown in Syria, coupled with the flow of refugees across the border into Turkey, has put a great deal of pressure on Ankara. The events in Syria provided a crucial test for Prime Minister Erdoğan's proclaimed commitment to democratization in the region. This is not a matter of idealism versus realpolitik. Turkey needed to change its zero-problems policy with Syria out of pure Turkish self-interest rather than ideals of freedom and democracy in the region.

Simply put, the destabilization of Syria is not in Turkey's national interest. Yet Ankara fears that the path that the Asad regime has taken will end in just that. It will destabilize Syria and potentially set it on a course toward sectarian civil war. As Syria's only democratic ally, Turkey realized that it had a responsibility to condemn the regime's brutal killing of hundreds of protesters. At the same time, Turkey is uniquely placed to provide some friendly advice to Syria. The obvious problem is that Damascus is in no mood to listen. It should not be too surprising that when a dictator is faced with regime survival, outside pressure seldom works.

As a result, Turkey is now rapidly discovering the limits of its regional influence and zero-problems policy. In case the refugee crisis with Syria gets out of hand and a much larger influx takes place, Turkey is likely to consider establishing a buffer zone at the border, which may turn into a safe haven for the Syrian opposition. The Syrian official news agency has blamed Turkey, a majority Sunni country, for supporting the Sunni Muslim Brotherhood in Syria. These reports are nonsense, but they raise the point that Turkish public opinion would not look favorably on a minority Alawi regime massacring Sunnis in Syria—a manifestation of the common phenomenon of civil conflicts radicalizing neighboring populations and potentially provoking intervention that Dan Byman raises in chapter 24.

Navigating the Shoals of the Arab Awakening

The challenge for Ankara in reacting to the dramatic events of 2011 is not so much to compete with Cairo for strategic leadership, but to find a different niche for itself. Turkey's comparative advantage here is twofold. It was the first and still is the most important Muslim country represented in Western institutions such as NATO and the Council of Europe.[3] It is also the only Muslim candidate to the European Union. As such Ankara has a unique advantage as a "Western" country that can speak on behalf of the Islamic world. Yet to be a strong voice of both the West and the Islamic world, the AKP will have to boost its "Western credentials" as a transatlantic partner and a serious candidate for EU membership. Despite the French and German leaderships' lack of strategic vision, the AKP should realize that Turkey still needs to pursue European Union membership enthusiastically for the sake of its own democratic and foreign policy ambitions. After the AKP's third consecutive electoral victory in June 2011, and as it embarks on its constitutional agenda to solve the Kurdish problem, it should remember that Turkey's EU candidacy has been the engine of past reforms.

Turkey's second comparative advantage stems from its secular and democratic identity. Turkey should try harder to find creative ways to transcend the sectarian and religious divides in the Middle East. Two of the most polarizing issues in the Middle East are the Arab-Israeli conflict and the Sunni-Shi'i sectarian tension. On the Sunni-Shi'i divide, Ankara is already playing a crucial role—Prime Minister Erdoğan's visit to the Shi'i holy sites in Najaf and his two-hour visit with Iraq's most important Shi'i religious leader, Ayatollah Sistani, were a first for the leader of a Sunni country. As the prime minister of a secular country and thanks to his own religious credentials as a pious Muslim, Erdoğan is better placed than any other leader in the Muslim world to speak about the dangers of sectarianism in the region.

Turkey should find a similar strategic vision in transcending its current problems with Israel. A more self-confident and strategically minded Turkey should be part of a solution to the Arab-Israeli conflict and not exacerbate an already tense situation. Turkish-Israeli relations are in the national interest of both countries, and given the stakes involved, Washington should play a much more active role in brokering a face-saving deal between the two estranged allies. To facilitate that, Ankara should continue to discourage provocative actions against Israel, like flotillas to Gaza, while applauding positive trends, such as Israel's partial lifting of its Gaza blockade and the opening of the border with Egypt. Unfortunately, Turkey is in no position to soften its demands for an apology from Israel and compensation related to the 2010 flotilla crisis. Moreover, the Arab Spring seems to have strengthened the Turkish belief that time is not on Israel's side.

It is still too early for a clear account of how the Arab Spring will affect Turkish foreign policy. In the new Middle East, Turkey will remain an important and able player. Yet as the Arab world shows signs of democratic revival, Turkey will probably realize that its comparative advantage lies in its strong ties with the West. Washington can help with stronger support for the normalization of Turkish-Israeli relations and better coordination with Ankara on issues related to Iraq, Iran, Syria, and Libya.

PART VI

The External Powers

31

EXTERNAL POWERS

Riding the Tsunami

KENNETH M. POLLACK

From late January to early April 2011, the daily newspapers, TV news shows, and Internet news sites were packed with stories about the Middle East. Even for those who did not live in the Middle East, the Arab Spring was big news. The biggest news of the year, to say the least. To some extent, that was because journalists and bloggers will chase whatever seems unusual. But to a much greater extent, the Arab Spring dominated the news all across the globe because it was, is, and will be of phenomenal importance to countries all across the globe, even countries that do not share a border with the Middle East, let alone a language, a culture, or even a religion.

The impact of the Arab Spring has been particularly profound for the great powers of the world, both the established and the emerging. Because the Middle East has been important for a long time, the established great powers have had interests in the Middle East for similarly long periods, including eras when parts of the Middle East were under their formal or informal control. Consequently, they have vested interests in the region, which are being threatened, reshaped, or even benefited by the events of the Arab Spring—and often some unknowable combination of the three. What is more, the people of the Middle East, both rulers and ruled, are looking to the great powers—especially to the more established great powers with which they have been dealing with for decades—to help them. And of course, the help that the rulers want is often the diametric opposite of what their people want.

But the emerging powers are also recognizing, increasingly, that their own interests are bound up with the fate of the Middle East as well. For many of them the Arab Spring is proving the first time that they are having to take a long, hard look at the region and their interests in it, and decide what kind of a Middle East they want to see appear from the ashes of Bouazizi's fire. And for many of them, the issues of the Arab Spring that touch their interests are matters of principle that transcend the specific importance of the Middle East itself.

Consequently, as always in the Middle East, the game of nations is being played on many levels. There are the changing relations among the states themselves, which we have treated in many of the chapters of this book, including in particular by Dan Byman and Ken Pollack in chapter 27 on the evolving regional balance. But then there are the changes that are taking place between the states of the region and the great powers as the Middle Eastern peoples seek help from various quarters, and the great powers must sort out what kind of assistance they want to provide to secure which goals. Beyond this, however, there is also a considerable impact on the relations among the great powers themselves, as their actions (and inactions) toward the Middle East affect their interests and relationships with one another. Thus the great powers are influencing the region, the region is influencing the great powers, and the great powers are influencing one another. And inevitably, all of these games are inextricably intertwined so that without seeing the entirety of the field and all of the players and their actions, it is easy to misinterpret why various things happened.

It's the Oil, Stupid

Whenever we talk about the great powers and the Middle East, we have to begin by talking about oil. Of the 87 million barrels of oil per day (bpd) consumed globally in 2010, over 25 million bpd (29 percent) were produced by Middle Eastern countries.[1] Moreover, virtually all of the world's excess production capacity, amounting to about 1 million to 2 million bpd, is located in the Middle East—and nearly all of that is in Saudi Arabia.[2] This excess production capacity is important because it is the only way (other than various national strategic oil reserves, which governments are loath to release) to compensate for lost production in the short and medium terms.[3]

The economies of every developed nation and ever greater numbers of developing nations are addicted to oil. In the words of one recent study, "Oil is the lifeblood of modern civilization. It fuels the vast majority of the world's mechanized transportation equipment—automobiles, trucks, airplanes, trains, ships, farm equipment, the military, etc. Indeed, according to the Department of Transportation, oil accounts for a whopping 97 percent of the energy used for transportation in the United States. Oil is also the primary feedstock for many of the chemicals that are essential to modern life."[4] Petroleum products are a critical input into a modern economy not merely for transportation, but also for industrial production (including plastics), and even power generation. Petroleum accounts for 40 percent of all of the energy used in the United States, far more than either of the next two biggest sources of American energy, natural gas and coal, which account for only 23 and 22 percent, respectively.[5]

Of the great powers, only Russia is self-sufficient in terms of its hydrocarbon needs. Everyone else must import large amounts of oil, and that makes everyone else dependent on the Middle East—not necessarily because they get all of their oil from the region, but because their economies are heavily dependent on the international price of oil. Since oil is fungible, meaning that any barrel of oil can be burned anywhere in the world and have the same effect, the international price is determined by *global* supply in relation to *global* demand. Whenever the demand increases faster than the supply, or whenever the supply unexpectedly drops, the price of oil rises—and it rises for every country, no matter where it gets its oil.

The Arab Spring has raised everyone's fears about oil and oil prices—everyone except other, non–Middle Eastern oil suppliers. Major political upheavals like revolutions, civil and international wars, insurgencies, and the like have a very bad habit of affecting oil supplies and jacking up oil prices in potentially disastrous ways. As just one example, between the dislocations caused by the Iranian Revolution and Ayatollah Khomeini's own personal belief that Iran's oil wealth had been the source of the shah's corruption, Iranian oil production dropped from 5.9 million bpd in 1978 to just 1.3 million bpd before the start of the 1980 Iran-Iraq War.[6] It is an important lesson that regime change and zealotry, especially in the Middle East, can override economic need with calamitous results for all. Iran's production collapse crippled the Iranian economy and helped cause the worst global recession in postwar history before 2008–09. Indeed, as Alan Greenspan has warned, every major postwar recession except one was preceded by a major increase in oil prices.[7] Incidentally, the 2008–09 recession was preceded by a tripling of oil prices between 2005 and 2007.[8] Consequently, a key consideration for all of the great powers save Russia has been making sure that whatever happens with the Arab Spring, it does not affect the vital flow of Middle Eastern oil.

Location, Location, Location

In addition to its vital energy reserves, the Middle East also plays an outsized role in geopolitics because it is perfectly sited for global importance. Sitting at the crossroads of Europe, Asia, and Africa, the Middle East is where a big part of the world comes together. Although its geographic importance is often exaggerated, it would also be a mistake to denigrate it. For the world's great powers, whose interests span the globe, the ability of events in the Middle East to affect other parts of the world because of its geographic centrality is often the nub of many other interests.

The part that gets exaggerated is the Middle East's importance as a transshipment nexus. Although the Middle East has been a passage for East-West trade since the dawn of civilization, and the Suez Canal has preserved—if not expanded—that role, it is just not the case that this makes the region vital to international commerce. The Middle East lost its status as a critical trade route from Asia to Europe back in the eighteenth century, when the maritime revolution made it cheaper to move goods by sea than by land, and the camel caravans of the silk and spice roads were replaced by European sailing ships. Today, very little trade passes over the territory of the Middle East, with the big exceptions of oil and the ships that pass through the Suez Canal. In the case of the oil trade, obviously the issue is principally the region's oil exports, not its geographic position per se. The Suez Canal has strategic value, but not nearly as much as one might think. While a considerable amount of trade still flows through the canal, free access to the canal is largely a matter of cost and convenience, and not a matter of strategic necessity either for the United States or anyone else. If the Suez Canal were closed or blocked (as it was from 1967 to 1975), ships would be rerouted around the Cape of Good Hope, which would mean longer voyages, and that in turn would cost more money. But, as was the case in 1967–75, the increased costs would hardly be crippling.

What does make the Middle East geographically important is how many other parts of the world the region touches. The Mediterranean once seemed a daunting obstacle to travel, but with modern air (and maritime) travel, it is virtually an afterthought. Xerxes once had to build a bridge of ships across the Hellespont to cross from Anatolia into the Balkans, but today the same crossing is effortless. North Africans, Turks, Kurds, and other Middle Easterners emigrate across the Mediterranean and the Bosporus all the time. And because of Europe's past colonial relationships with the Middle East (itself a product of geographic proximity), virtually every Western European country has large Middle Eastern communities that facilitate the immigration of more of their countrymen. Many of Europe's most pressing political, economic, and cultural questions are thus bound up with its relations with its neighbors to the south, and disturbances in the Arab lands often cause powerful ripple effects into European internal affairs, not just their external concerns.

To the north and east of the Middle East lie the Caucasus and Central Asia, which share religious and ethnic ties with many Middle Eastern countries and share many of the same economic and political features of the imploding autocracies of the Arab world, as discussed in chapter 33. South Asia, to the east of Iran, falls into a similar category. Indeed, some of the South Asian states—particularly Pakistan—have so many of the same features as the Arab world that fanatics and troublemakers from the two societies travel easily back and forth, bringing with them hate, violence, narcotics, and perverse ideas about politics and society. Thus what happens in the Middle East, for good and ill, could easily infect the Caucasus and Central and South Asia through the permeable membrane of their multifaceted commonalities, themselves a product of easy geographic access.

Finally, there is Africa. The truth is that the great powers, both old and new, still have only modest interests in sub-Saharan Africa. There are resources there—oil in Nigeria, diamonds and gold in South Africa, coltan in the Congo. There are nascent democracies there as well, and at least one potential great power in South Africa. And, inevitably, there is some degree of competition among the great powers over Africa related to resources and markets. But Africa has still not received focused attention. Nevertheless, the spillover effects from the Middle East and North Africa could be profound, in either a positive or negative fashion. If Middle Eastern states successfully transition from autocracies to democracies, they will give both encouragement and ammunition to African peoples to do the same. Indeed, watching various Arab peoples rise up against oppressive, indigenous dictators might still inspire some African nations to do the same—although sub-Saharan Africa is different enough from the Arab world that the models may not translate easily. That said, if Arab states in North Africa descend into Somalia-like chaos or Congo-like civil wars, the spillover will inevitably affect their neighbors, with concomitant consequences for the rest of the continent.

PUBLIC GOODS AND AMERICAN POWER

Another key issue created by the sudden upheaval in the midst of the world's great oil supply that the great powers have had to address is the role of the United States as the global hegemon. As I discuss further in chapter 36, it is the United States that has taken on the onerous task of guaranteeing the world's supply of oil for the past forty years—basically since the British withdrew their military forces from "east of Suez" in 1971. During this period, the United States has devoted a considerable percentage of its political and diplomatic clout, its military power, and its economic resources to ensuring that the oil continues to flow, and continues to flow relatively cheaply, from the Middle East.

That has been the principal goal of American policy over that same stretch of time. It has been the motive that prompted Washington to develop deep diplomatic and military relationships with the Saudis, Egyptians, and the Iranians (during the shah's era). More than anything else, oil's importance to the global economy is what drove the United States to intervene militarily in the Iran-Iraq War and the 1990–91 Gulf War, and eventually to invade Iraq in 2003. It is why the United States has long based significant air, land, and naval forces in and around the Persian Gulf since 1971 (with considerable augmentations in 1987 and 1990).

Of course, the United States did not do this out of purely altruistic motives. The American economy is heavily dependent on oil, including imported oil, meaning that by ensuring the flow of relatively cheap oil from the Middle East, the United States has been securing its own economic growth and prosperity. But the United States might easily have seized the oil for itself and taken the profit from it—as the British did in the first half of the twentieth century. Alternatively, it might have doled out the oil only to those countries that toed Washington's line, and left those that did not wallowing in the preindustrial mire, as other world empires doubtless would have. In short, America's exertions in the Middle East have come for the sake of providing a public good, and not just any public good, but the most important public good to all of the nations of the world—and especially the most developed of those nations.

America's willingness to play this role, and to play it so unselfishly, has been an enormous boon to the other great powers, particularly to those still emerging. But there is also a potential dark lining to this silver cloud, which the events of 2011 have suddenly highlighted: namely, that because of its political-military dominance in the Middle East, America has the only hand on the oil spigot—the fountain from which every other country on earth must drink.

The Arab Spring has suddenly focused a new spotlight on this issue. In large part because the Obama administration decided to embrace revolutionary change rather than the seeming (and we would argue, tenuous) stability of the old order, many of the other great powers are beginning to ask whether the United States should be allowed to remain the sole guardian of Middle Eastern oil flows. In the past, the question was never answered because Washington's (wrong-headed) support for the regional status quo and opposition to change meant that American thinking coincided perfectly with these countries' own ideas about how the Middle East should be treated. As long as all of the great powers agreed that the old order had to be preserved and any changes to the status quo, whether internal or external, had to be prevented, then America's role in enforcing this approach was a godsend to the others. Now that Washington has decided that change needs to come to the region, that the status quo cannot hold, and, worst of all, that revolutions should be allowed to run their course, suddenly America's predominant position in the Middle East and its exertions to guide the region don't look like such a bargain any more to other great powers that have not come to the same enlightened conclusion.

Conflicting Values and Interests

Growing rifts among the great powers over America's guardianship of Middle Eastern oil has also become entwined with another difference of opinion over the tension between state sovereignty and basic human and civil rights. In Libya, Bahrain, Yemen, Syria, and elsewhere across the Arab world in 2011 (and Iran in 2009), sovereign governments decided to employ force against their people to prevent them from gathering and registering their political demands. These political demands grew from the outrageous corruption, oppression, and mismanagement of these countries' political, social, and economic systems by their autocratic regimes. In case after case, the United States and its Western allies took the side of the people, championing their basic human rights as the highest international obligation. In the case of Libya, this led to military intervention. In the case of Syria, it led to sanctions on the regime. Even where it was nothing but rhetoric, as in Bahrain, the Western position favored human rights over all else, even at the expense of state sovereignty.

More than a few countries took a very different line. China and Russia, in particular, consistently prioritized state sovereignty over the rights of citizens. Many other emerging powers, though less vocally and consistently, sided with sovereignty as much or more than they sided with human rights. When this debate also engaged the question of American military hegemony in the Middle East and Washington's right to employ its military might, the divisions seemed to clarify quickly, with the emerging states lining up squarely behind Russia and China. It is noteworthy that Brazil, Germany, and India (along with Russia and China) all abstained from the March 2011 vote on UN Security Council Resolution 1973, which authorized the international military intervention in Libya that everyone knew would be led by the United States.

Of course, this debate over values can also be seen as a debate over interests. As Pavel Baev and Jonathan Pollack explore in chapters 33 and 34, respectively, Moscow and Beijing both fear that they will have to launch crackdowns of their own in the future, and they want to establish an international consensus that state sovereignty trumps every other consideration so that they will not have to fear international interference when they do so. For their part, the United States and its (democratic) Western allies have no such concerns. However, they do worry about the Middle East and its ability to affect their domestic affairs through oil, immigration, terrorism, and the like. As I explain in chapter 36, the United States has finally concluded that its long-term interests in ensuring the flow of Middle Eastern oil is best served not by the prior, misguided notion of achieving stability by helping the Arab autocracies to further calcify. Instead, Washington—and its Western allies—is now attempting to create a "dynamic stability" in which change comes to the Middle East to address the pent-up grievances of the people, but this change is peaceful, deliberate, and channeled in directions that will increase stability (and remove the irritant of anti-Americanism) over the long term. This is another important difference between the United States and its allies on the one hand, and many of the emerging great powers on the other.

To Be Continued. . . .

For most of the postwar era, the Middle East has been a cockpit of great power competition. But when the Berlin Wall and the Soviet Union fell—and America demonstrated its astonishing military power during the 1991 Gulf War—all of that ended, at least for a time. Between 1991 and 2011, the Middle East was largely an American preserve where Washington was effectively the only great power with influence, and the other great powers could play in the region only insofar as they were willing to complement Washington's initiatives. Paradoxically, it seems likely that later historians will date the end of that brief era to the Arab Spring. As we have discussed throughout this book, part of the reason for this is that in standing up for themselves and throwing off the shackles of their own indigenous autocratic oppressors, the Arabs have stated very loudly that they mean to take a more independent role in all things, explicitly including their foreign affairs. Thus, America is likely to face an even more fractious and willful group of Arab states than it has in the past, and the past was certainly no picnic. That may well be bad for the Middle East too, because much that the United States sought to do in the region was actually beneficial to the Arab world. Regardless, it will certainly be very problematic for the United States and a damper on the exercise of American power.

Another aspect of that change, however, will doubtless be the reinvigorated interest of other great powers in the events of the Middle East and their greater willingness to try to actively shape events there. Part of this phenomenon is a product of their own growing influence, and of the relative diminution of American sway for a number of reasons. But this shift will also derive from the fact that the events of the Arab Spring have sounded alarm bells in capitals across the globe, which now recognize that they have compelling interests in the Middle East, a greater ability to protect those interests, and some very important differences with the United States over how to protect those interests.

The more that this is the case, the more that the Middle East will see the intrusion of more and more foreign great powers, deepening the complexity of its international politics. As always, the Middle East is likely to get curiouser and curiouser.

32

EUROPE

Muddling Through

RUTH HANAU SANTINI

Because of its proximity, Europe has a lot at stake in the future evolution of the Arab world, particularly that of North Africa. Promoting prosperity and stability in this region has been a European foreign policy goal over the past two decades as Europe has wrestled with the issue of immigration from the southern Mediterranean coast and the integration of these and other immigrant communities from the Arab world.[1] Because of these concerns, the prevailing discourse during the Arab Spring has become suffused with security concerns, especially terrorism and illegal migration. Equally important is the fact that Europe is the main trading partner for most countries undergoing transitions: 17 percent of exports from the Middle East and North Africa (MENA) region go to Europe, with higher percentages for certain individual countries.

EUROPEAN APPROACHES TO THE SOUTHERN MEDITERRANEAN

The Euro-Mediterranean Partnership (EMP)—or Barcelona Process—was born in 1995, and it provided a multilateral framework for relations between the European Union and fourteen Mediterranean partners. Its main goals were to create a free trade area between Europe and the south, and to promote democracy. Enshrined in the EMP were negative conditionality clauses, which would allow the freezing of the agreement in cases of democratic backsliding or human rights violations. These provisions, however, despite numerous instances that would have justified a freeze, were never implemented. The EMP was articulated in three baskets of cooperation between the European Union and the southern Mediterranean: political, economic, and cultural. The idea of the Barcelona Process was that through a gradual approach, where progress in economics, rule of law, and political liberalization would reinforce one another. This strategy stumbled over the breakdown of the Israeli-Palestinian peace process, which blocked progress in all other dimensions of cooperation.

When the European Commission was formulating the European Neighborhood Policy (ENP), addressing relations with many of its eastern neighbors who
did not have the prospect of becoming members of the EU, it decided to enlarge
the new framework to include the southern Mediterranean countries. The new
approach, formally launched in 2004, was bilateral, laying the groundwork for
advanced cooperation in several fields between Europe and individual countries
to its east and south. The policy was based on the idea of "positive conditionality," which was to pave the way for increased cooperation and the recognition of
"advanced" status of the cooperation agreement if progress was made on several
dimensions (mainly the rule of law and economic liberalization). The ENP aimed
at "developing a zone of prosperity and a friendly neighborhood—a ring of
friends—with whom the EU enjoys close, peaceful and co-operative relations."

Creating "an area of shared prosperity and stability," however, did not imply
that the European Union would consistently engage democratic homegrown
forces and promote the respect of human rights. The priority was mainly attrib-
uted to a "stabilizing liberalization," through which European security would
be granted.[2] At the heart of cooperation in noneconomic areas was rule of law
reform rather than more contentious issues revolving around wider political and
civil liberties. In most MENA states, even those in which Europe had strong
economic leverage (as in Ben Ali's Tunisia), Brussels refrained from exerting
pressure to open up space for political reforms.[3]

In 2008 France proposed a new approach that would focus on enhancing economic relations with MENA countries. The Union for the Mediterranean (UfM)
was initially thought of in isolation from the Euro-Mediterranean Partnership
and the existing frameworks of contractual relations with MENA countries, but
was later subsumed under the EMP umbrella. Initially, the UfM was designed
as a free trade scheme that would replace the abandoned vision of a free trade
area between Europe and MENA countries, which should have been reached
by 2010 under the EMP. The new approach added security as a fourth basket,
alongside economic, political, and cultural cooperation. Under the rubric of
security cooperation, the European Union intended to tackle both hard security
challenges (mainly terrorism) and soft security challenges (controlling migratory
flows to Europe). Six concrete projects have been discussed so far within this
initiative: de-pollution of the Mediterranean, maritime and land highways, civil
protection, alternative energy, Euro-Mediterranean University, and a business
initiative. Many argue that structurally the UfM has limited political transformative potential, mainly because it focuses on governmental relations rather than
engagement with civil society organizations and because it is not based upon
a political vision of the region and its political development. The main goal of
the UfM could be described as fostering economic development. These different policies partly overlap in their mission: both the ENP and the UfM strive

for increasing southern Mediterranean economic progress and cooperation in soft and hard security fields, whereas the Barcelona Process used to be more concerned with the promotion of political democracy. On the ground, however, progress in democracy and human rights issues, albeit limited, has mainly been secured through ENP agreements.[4]

Overall, despite a long history of engagement, Europe has failed to formulate consistent approaches to explain the links between the promotion of democracy and security interests in the Arab world. For the most part, it has let the latter trump the former whenever they clashed.

RETHINKING EUROPEAN VIEWS OF THE ARAB WORLD

The Arab uprisings have forced Europeans to rethink their policies. The uprisings have signaled the end of Western-led, top-down models of reform in the Arab world. Proposing packages of rule-of-law reform that a state has to implement in order to improve cooperation with Europe seems to be an outdated approach for advancing progress in neighboring countries. Europe is slowly acknowledging that political change has to start endogenously and that it should be based on indigenous understandings of democracy if it is to be sustainable. This acknowledgment, however, is far from having been substantiated in any concrete new political approach to the region or even the post-revolutionary countries.

Europe, like the United States, had also considered friendly authoritarian regimes to be stable and politically sustainable in the long run. The uprisings have not only increased the visibility of Arab populations, transforming their image from passive and subjugated peoples to legitimate and powerful political actors, but have also implied the necessity of engaging with civil society actors in a much broader and more consistent way—actors from across the political spectrum and not just the "usual suspects" (traditionally pro-Western, secular elites, often out of touch with and scarcely representative of the broader public opinion). The power that public opinion will have to influence political decisions, even foreign policy ones, is altering calculations everywhere—Europe included.

RESHAPING THE NEIGHBORHOOD POLICY

The Arab world, for its part, perceives the European Union as a complacent actor—punching below its weight and contenting itself with minor reforms to the rule of law, moves to liberalize the economy, and technocratic progress, rather than with substantial political and economic development. Looking at European policies so far, there is some truth to this perception, and the revised European Neighborhood Policy (still under discussion) focuses on political reforms and improving basic political freedoms.

The EU's rethinking of its Middle East and North Africa policy is characterized by a stronger endorsement of political reform as an integral part of bilateral cooperation. Europe's emphasis is on the development of "deep democracies"—meaning political systems characterized by the rule of law, freedom of speech, respect for human rights, and an independent judiciary—and the calling for free and fair elections as a precondition for negotiation. Europe, therefore, is moving from "electoral fetishism," and focusing on the full spectrum of political rights. The discourse in Europe has started to shift from a procedural conversation (where a democracy is evaluated according to how elections are run) to one that calls for the promotion of a wide range of rights and democratic institutions. Central to these claims will be the future of conditionality clauses: by refraining from using both positive conditionality (through the ENP) and negative conditionality (through the Barcelona Process), the European Union limited its own ability to positively influence political transformations among its southern neighbors.

The absence of clear-cut democracy and human rights benchmarks further constrained Europe's ability to tie funding to specific policy objectives. The current absence of a debate over the shape conditionality could take underlines the slow change of paradigm from a purely top-down approach in how priorities are set to a more inclusive and participatory approach, whereby civil society shapes the debate surrounding the list of priorities that should be pursued.

The enhanced "more for more" logic of the reframed ENP should imply a closer relationship between political progress and funding. However, the continuing absence of benchmarks does not bode well for an effective implementation of the policy. The reference to "mutual accountability" between the EU and third parties—aimed at countering power asymmetries by making the EU accountable as well—could further diminish conditionality claims. Above all, because it was an outgrowth of the initial Neighborhood Policy aimed at Europe's eastern countries, the EU's southern policy lacks a political vision for the North Africa region. The southern Mediterranean was added to the ENP by the former president of its commission, Romano Prodi, almost as an afterthought.

From that vantage point, the May 2011 review of European Neighborhood Policy shows little change. The resolution of regional conflicts will continue to be dealt with in isolation from bilateral action plans, the MENA region will continue to suffer from insufficient intraregional cooperation, and, more broadly, there will be no strategy to define the kinds of relations that Europe wants to develop with North Africa and the Middle East in the medium to long term. The purely reactive logic, working in the aftermath of a crisis and doing what the European Union does best, namely capacity and institution building, without setting a broader political horizon, will hardly be an effective recipe for closer, more comprehensive relations with the EU's southern neighbors. One challenge will be that with the ENP, Europe had focused its aid more on governments than on nongovernmental organizations (NGOs). Moving forward, it is unclear to what extent it will engage Islamists and/or anti-Western political and civil society actors.

INSUFFICIENT ECONOMIC ENGAGEMENT

High Representative Catherine Ashton's "three Ms" approach for the future of the region centers on market access, money, and mobility. Market access refers to the need for Europe to open up its (mainly agricultural) market to its southern neighbors in a more consistent way and in accordance with these countries' needs and readiness. Money refers to the resources needed in the short to medium term when transitions are more challenging and instability risks are higher, something Europe will be hardly in a position to substantially contribute to, given its own financial weakness. And mobility stands for the EU's intention to open its doors to more young people and professionals coming from MENA countries. And yet, in the first phases of their outreach to MENA countries, the United States and the European Union together allocated only $2 billion for Tunisia and Egypt.

In the meantime, regional stakeholders will not hold their breath—Saudi Arabia alone has pledged $4 billion in aid to Egypt. If this comes with any strings attached, as seems probable, they will likely differ from European political conditionality. Most of the U.S. and European activity is concentrated on increasing the role of international financial institutions that are expected to step in with long-term loans: the World Bank, the International Monetary Fund, the European Bank of Investment (EIB), and the European Bank for Reconstruction and Development (EBRD). At the G20 summit in Deauville in May 2011, $20 billion in aid was pledged for the Tunisian and Egyptian transition under the guise of loans by multilateral financial institutions. Both the United States and Europe have underscored that the loans are more focused on trade and investments than on aid and assistance, and that these loans will be tied to the democratic reforms the two countries are expected to undertake. The EBRD, which was created at the end of the cold war to help the transition of communist countries to developed market economies, will extend its mandate to grant aid to MENA countries committed to the core principles of democracy, political pluralism, and a free market.

In June 2011, Europe acknowledged the urgency of helping economic reconstruction, as signaled by the creation of a European task force for the southern Mediterranean, which is composed of members of the European External Action Service, the European Commission, the European Investment Bank, the EBRD, and other international financial institutions. The challenge ahead for an effective European economic engagement in MENA countries will be to focus on helping to enhance intraregional trade (today, only 10 percent of MENA exports are intraregional) and contributing to the development of regional economic integration. A broader challenge for the European Union will be to increase its share of the budget for foreign policy (in the current financial framework, 2007–13, this was only 6 percent of the overall EU budget, as compared with 40 percent for agriculture), so as to increase its leverage, provided a clear foreign policy trajectory is envisaged.

DOES THE CURRENT RETHINKING GO FAR ENOUGH?

Some in Europe are challenging the whole foundation of the Neighborhood Policy, which gathers sixteen very different countries across Eastern Europe, the South Caucasus, and the Middle East and North Africa. Despite the fact that the European Union has tried to tailor its individual sets of bilateral relations, according to some critics there should be completely different frameworks to deal with the social, economic, and political diversity across the southern and eastern region, not one overarching framework.

A way to strengthen Europe's Neighborhood Policy would be to differentiate between sub-regional clusters, identifying one approach for the Maghreb and one for the Mashriq. Within each cluster, cross-case comparisons and the sharing of best practices should then be carried out. Such a sub-regional approach would allow for linkages to be created for specific issues, focusing, for example, on conflict resolution dynamics based on confidence-building measures and intraregional integration schemes to bring together different parts of the European Neighborhood Policy.

What has also been lacking in the European rethinking is a way to tie together the Neighborhood Policy and the Union for the Mediterranean. While the former will now focus more closely on political reform, the latter ignores the political dimension of Arab polities and of Euro-Med relations and so far has pretended it could foster economic and environmental projects with its southern partners in isolation from the broader political context.

33

RUSSIA

Moscow Does Not Believe in Change

PAVEL K. BAEV

The ongoing, spectacular changes in the Middle East have Russia worried. This despite the fact that Moscow has discovered that the turmoil has created a range of new opportunities to further its interests. Where President Barack Obama finds a "historic opportunity" for advancing democratic values, the Russian leadership sees instead an opportunity to prove that revolutions are messy and futile—and to build ties with the extant ruling regimes, despotic though they may be.[1] The key words in the mainstream Russian assessments of the mass uprisings are "destabilization," "turmoil," and "extremism," but a term that is practically absent is "Arab Spring."

Russia's negative perspective on the unexpected change in the familiar political landscape is not shaped by concerns about its material interests in the region. Indeed, Russia, unlike most other major powers, has no stake in the oil supplies from the Gulf and actually benefits from climbing oil prices caused by regional instability—it even gains in reputation because European energy consumers now see it as a more reliable energy source. Nevertheless, Moscow has taken a firm counterrevolutionary stance and shows no intention of switching to the possible, but not definite, winning side. This principled position differs from the familiar fusion of pragmatism and opportunism that has been characteristic of Russia's foreign policy.

EXORCIZING THE SPECTER OF REVOLUTIONS

Russia's pronounced dislike of revolutions is rooted not in its own painful experience going back to the 1917 Bolshevik seizure of power and the chaos and bloodshed that followed, but in the nature of its current regime, which professes commitment to democracy but operates through centralized control. This regime could be defined as "enlightened authoritarian," were it not so corrupt; its unwavering commitment to self-perpetuation makes it side with the forces of authoritarianism and the status quo, and oppose those who demand change to end abuses of power.[2] The current regime will certainly make rhetorical gestures in favor of greater political competition, such as the speech of President Dmitry Medvedev at the St. Petersburg Economic Forum in June 2011. However, Prime Minister Vladimir Putin's creation of the Popular Front—a broad-based bloc of political, private-sector, and civic groups—in advance of elections proves beyond doubt that in the current Russian election campaign, competition is severely curtailed. Thus, it is unlikely that Moscow would encourage it anywhere else.

For Russia's leadership, the events of the Arab Spring hit too close to home. The corrupt bureaucratic superstructure of Putin's regime is extremely rigid and resistant to modernization, making Medvedev's chances of staying in office for a second term slim. It also means that the window for painful but peaceful reforms is closing. As Mikhail Khodorkovsky, the most famous political prisoner in Russia, warns, the urban middle class's anger against corruption is growing much the same way as it did in the Middle East, leaving a revolution as the only possible way to break out of Russia's own trajectory of stagnation.[3]

Russia's elites recognize this looming prospect of revolt more clearly and with a greater sense of imminent danger than they did the wave of "color revolutions" in the mid-2000s, the latest splash of which was the December 2010 rally in Minsk, Belarus, which was brutally dispersed by police. On that occasion, Moscow did not utter a word of criticism to President Aleksandr Lukashenko, even though he is often a target of ridicule in the media because the personal chemistry between him and Putin is chilly. Moscow's implicit support of Minsk corresponds with the sustained effort invested by the Russian leadership in proving that the "Orange Revolution" in Ukraine was merely a senseless disorder sponsored by the West. The election of Viktor Yanukovich as Ukraine's president in January 2010 was interpreted as the ultimate proof of this proposition, but the self-congratulation was cut short by the shocking revolutions in Tunisia and Egypt.

Medvedev's first take on the "very complex events" of the Arab Spring was outright alarmist: "We must face the truth. In the past, such a scenario was harbored for us, and now attempts to implement it are even more likely. In any case, this plot will not work."[4] This conspiracy theory was elaborated in semi-official accusations that social networks like Facebook were exploited to incite unrest. There were also expert analyses that outlined the involvement of Western secret services allegedly keen to stage experiments for their "controlled chaos" strategy—which Russians believe the West intends to employ against them.[5] As weeks grew into months, it became obvious that explaining revolutions away as foreign plots was not very clever, but the idea that authoritarian regimes were organic to the Middle East was never abandoned. Describing Qadhafi's regime as "a warped and ugly monarchy," Putin nevertheless argued that it "on the whole satisfies the local public mentality and political practice."[6]

The fact that educated, urban Arabs were deeply dissatisfied with corrupt presidents-for-life has been edited out of official Russian rhetoric, which emphasizes the risk of power capture by extremists. Experts in Moscow have been as surprised as analysts in Washington that a Libyan opposition supported by al-Qaeda in Libya received air support from NATO.[7] It is not, however, about extremists of this sort that the Russian leadership is concerned, as it has never had qualms about maintaining contacts with Hamas or engaging in a high-level dialogue with President Mahmoud Ahmadinejad.

The real Russian concern, the real groups it sees as dangerous extremists, are students and educated urban professionals who detest the self-serving bureaucracy, cannot be fooled by cheap populism, and have lost their fear of the corrupt, repressive apparatus. This "extremism" is particularly dangerous because, unlike in most "classical" revolutionary situations, charismatic leaders or party organizations are no longer necessary to mobilize masses. The rapid mobilization of populations can now be accomplished by virtual networks. In Russia, the strategy for the regime's self-preservation has been based on denying the opposition a legitimate political space and pushing it underground, but this repression—as the Arab Spring has shown—creates a hidden explosive potential that can detonate. Putin puts himself forward as the leader determined to crush such "extremism," but there is no guarantee that the Russian military, demoralized by painful reforms, would follow a "shoot-to-kill" order.

Sovereignty above Humanitarian Interventionism

There was never any real option for external intervention in the popular uprising in Egypt, but the spread of revolutionary fervor to Bahrain, Libya, and Syria has made it necessary for concerned neighbors and the international community at large to contemplate the hard question of intervention—and three different answers have been supplied. In Bahrain, the swift intervention of Saudi Arabia helped the royal family suppress the revolt; in Syria, in spite of massive and sustained use of force against the rebels, no international action has been forthcoming, but the European Union and the United States have imposed unilateral sanctions; in Libya, the limited NATO intervention mandated by the United Nations ultimately helped force Muammar Qadhafi from power. Russia has no problem with the first case, is firmly against any intervention in the second one, and has been of two minds about the Libya issue.

At first, the uprising in Libya appeared not that different from other revolutions, and the use of force against the motley crowds was seen as the desperate measures of a doomed regime. The motives for launching an intervention were varied and far from solid, but it is clear that the personality of Colonel

Muammar Qadhafi was a major factor, since the common good in removing a not-entirely-sane dictator from power was obvious to virtually every interested party.[8] Russia was not altogether comfortable with the draft resolution that France and the United Kingdom tabled at the UN Security Council, but let it pass, perhaps because Medvedev did not want to act as a spoiler in the gambit initiated by his special "friend" (to the degree such terms are applicable in high-level politics), French president Nicholas Sarkozy. Putin immediately lambasted UN Security Council Resolution 1973 as "flawed and inadequate," but Medvedev reprimanded him publicly for comparing the resolution to "crusades." Only two months later, on May 18, 2011, Medvedev expressed chagrin that the resolution had been "trampled by actions committed by certain countries."[9]

This might seem like petty bickering between co-rulers drifting apart on the election trail but, in fact, the issue here is the difference of opinion among the Russian elite about the incentives for, and limits of, cooperation with the West. Putin dismissed the protection of civilians as a mere "pretext" for the real thing—a military intervention against a sovereign state. Medvedev initially followed the interests of Russian elites who saw the benefits of cooperation with the West as far more important than the safety of some exotic despot, but he gradually came around to Putin's position. Putin's mindset was shaped, or perhaps traumatized, by the 1999 Kosovo crisis that came at the very start of his fantastic rise to power, when NATO launched a military intervention over Russia's strong objections. Fundamentally, however, this obsession with sovereignty originates in the very nature of a quasi-democratic regime, the leaders of which strongly suspect that at some point they will have to protect their supremacy by violent repression, whatever outcry that might generate in the West. Medvedev might fancy himself as the reformer on the ruling team, but he dare not deviate too far from the groupthink on the sovereign right to crush opposition.

In this context, granting NATO legitimacy to halt a counterrevolutionary offensive amounted to a dangerous precedent, which was only partly mitigated by the initial discord the operation caused in the Atlantic Alliance and the length it took to achieve the desired outcome.[10] Qadhafi's dogged resistance provided Medvedev a chance to lament the abuse of the no-fly-zone mandate (the real meaning of which was crystal clear to all voters and abstainers in the UN Security Council) and to assert that the precedent would not be reproduced in Syria, no matter what kinds of brutal repressions are unleashed against the opposition. One of the few affirmative statements he made at the May 18, 2011, press conference was: "I will not support such a resolution, even if my friends and acquaintances were to ask me about it."[11]

It is characteristic that Russia's position on this problem has evolved in sync with China's, which traditionally puts state sovereignty first. This meeting of minds is perfectly captured by a political cartoon that depicted Putin and Hu

Jintao condemning foreign intervention in Libya "because you never know when the occasional heinous crime and despicable act might come in handy."[12]

RESONANCE IN THE CAUCASUS AND CENTRAL ASIA

As Stephen Grand observes in chapter 3, revolutions have a tendency to spread in waves. Of course, there is no way of knowing whether the latest wave will stop at the borders of the Arab world or spread further north into the Caucasus and Central Asia. Quite a few states in these troubled regions share characteristics similar to Arab autocracies and are certain to experience turbulent regime change at some point, although not necessarily in the immediate future. Urban populations in these still relatively young states may or may not get stirred up by the demonstration effect of the Tahrir Square triumph, but the presidents-for-life of their countries are already feeling a changed attitude from their until-recently-amicable Western partners. This is perhaps most unpleasant for Azerbaijan's president, Ilham Aliyev, who used to be treated in Washington and Brussels as an honored guest and now is seen as just another oil despot whose term might expire at any time. It is not impossible that he might try to forestall a brewing revolution by reactivating the conflict around the Nagorno-Karabakh region, perhaps aiming for a limited victory this time, rather than a total war.[13]

For their part, Russia's leaders are not at all concerned about developments in Azerbaijan. They expect that the cold shoulder from the West will push Aliyev closer to his more sympathetic northern neighbor, Turkey. They are, however, rightly worried about instability in the North Caucasus. In fact, the high point of the Egyptian revolution coincided with the peak of rebel attacks in Kabardino-Balkaria, where the tourist season was disrupted, and in Dagestan, from where several suicide bombers organized the explosion at Domodedovo Airport near Moscow. There was certainly no causal connection between the two trends as the escalation of violence in the North Caucasus began in the spring of 2009, but the psychological link between the images of helpless tanks in Tahrir Square and angry Muscovites on Manezhnaya Square brought the Kremlin close to panic.[14] By the summer of 2011, however, that acute fear had almost evaporated, thanks to several successful counterterrorist operations that wiped out a number of prominent leaders and cells. Interestingly, the death of Osama bin Laden at the hands of U.S. Special Forces also had an indirect demobilizing impact on the rebel activity in the North Caucasus. The escalation of instability has been interrupted, but the duration of the pause is highly uncertain.

The situation in Central Asia has shown no visible signs of further deterioration, but the resonance from Egypt can interact with the gradual accumulation of explosive material, first of all in the divided Fergana Valley. Moscow was caught off guard by the violent unrest in southern Kyrgyzstan in the spring and summer of 2010, and had to reckon with the fact that it had no military muscle for enforcing order in that hot spot—or for projecting force in any forthcoming contingencies. Tajikistan is seen as prone to implosion of the same type that Kyrgyzstan is struggling to get out of because the state structures in both are deeply corroded by narco-traffic from Afghanistan.[15] Moscow is now aware that the Russian military base in Tajikistan would not be able to reproduce the intervention that was crucial to terminating the civil war of 1992–95. Meanwhile, the country that appears most ripe for an Arab Spring–type revolution is Uzbekistan, which has no oil revenues to buy compliance from the have-nots and is ruled by an aging despot who is resented by the urban middle class.[16]

Nevertheless, Russia's seeming indifference to the brewing troubles in Central Asia is to a large extent a consequence of the much-reduced EU and U.S. involvement in this region, so that the proposition of a geopolitical competition driven by appetites for energy resources is increasingly irrelevant. The risk that various local disturbances will somehow merge with the war in Afghanistan is certainly a possibility, but Moscow is inclined to see it as Washington's problem more than it its own.

Counting Blessings and Reflecting on Risks

Revolutionary situations often evolve in entirely unpredictable ways, but Russia has good reasons to feel that things have worked out reasonably well so far. It can expect to gain some influence in the wider Middle East by default rather than by proactive engagement primarily because the pro-democracy uprisings have created, paradoxical as it may seem, a series of setbacks for the West. America's great ally, Hosni Mubarak, fell, whereas Russia's close friend, Bashar al-Asad, did not.[17] Washington now also faces a major conundrum reconciling its pro-revolution stance with Saudi Arabia's anti-revolution policy, potentially opening a rift with America's other great Arab ally. Russia has no problems of this sort.

Russia's course in nearly every revolutionary conflict in the wider Middle East goes against the guidelines set by the United States and the European Union (uncertain as these aims and goals often are), and instead has been remarkably compatible with those drawn by China. Moscow is interested in strengthening this counterrevolutionary proto-alliance by building up ties with conservative Arab regimes, including Saudi Arabia, and also by upgrading its strategic partnership with Turkey. A crucial step in this direction could be the Moscow-initiated proposition for Turkey to join the organization known as BRICS (Brazil, Russia, India, China, South Africa), which is seeking to increase its profile as the forum for emerging powers.[18]

Although Russia has harvested unexpected dividends from the turmoil in the Arab world, it cannot ignore the risks of a sudden explosion of revolutionary energy closer to, or even inside, its borders—and neither can it effectively hedge against such risks. As of mid-2011, Central Asia appears critically unstable, but the most likely epicenter for revolution is Belarus, where the street protests after the crudely manipulated elections in December 2010 were swiftly suppressed, and the financial crisis and currency devaluation of May 2011 have vastly increased the potential for discontent. In Russia itself, the relative stabilization of the North Caucasus (albeit with a dangerously high level of violence) makes it possible for the election campaign to proceed in an orderly fashion, and to deliver the result desired by the leadership. This outcome, nevertheless, could turn out to be the beginning of the disintegration of Putin's political order, which is based on levels of corruption that are straining Russia's stagnant economy. The North Caucasus might supply the fuse for such an implosion, perhaps through a new escalation of terrorist attacks or a rise in public protests against corrupt ruling clans and police brutality. The latter could look eerily similar to what started as a minor disturbance in the poor quarters of Tunisia.

34

CHINA

Unease from Afar

JONATHAN D. POLLACK

The political and social turbulence in the Arab world has reverberated well beyond the Middle East, with China deeply affected by the upheavals. Over the past decade, Beijing has pursued closer relations with entrenched authoritarian leaderships in the Middle East, calculating that its interests and needs in the region would be well protected by these ties. China's increasing dependence on energy imports from the Middle East, its central role in the financing and development of major oil fields in the Persian Gulf, and the heightened investment of Chinese multinationals across the Middle East and North Africa all reflect the expanding scope of its interests. In the aftermath of the Arab Spring, China has been compelled to reexamine its policies, protecting its interests where it can while limiting the damage wherever possible. The Arab Spring has also triggered obvious comparisons to China's own internal situation, where political and social grievances continue to fester, even as anxious leaders seek to repress pressures from below. The picture for China is thus very mixed and at times very sobering, reflecting the competing factors and interests at work within the Chinese system.

China's previous policies in the Middle East were dominated by prudence and risk aversion. It cultivated ties with authoritarian leaderships and avoided entanglement in the internal affairs of regional states, accommodating to the expectations and preferences of ruling elites, especially the governments of major oil suppliers like Saudi Arabia. But the stunning developments within the region have upended China's expectations of leadership stability. China is no longer insulated from the upheavals in the Middle East, and its political and financial investments in some instances are at risk. These circumstances are a direct consequence of China's "going out" strategy, by which it has pursued trade, investment, and energy ties across the region. Indeed, the involvement of Chinese state-owned enterprises and private firms in major development projects across the Middle East increased greatly over the past decade. While China is hardly alone in confronting the upheavals of 2011, it now must weigh its interests and future strategies in a politically and socially energized Middle East, where the ultimate outcomes are far from certain.

The civil strife that wracked Libya affords telling examples of the uncharacteristic speed and decisiveness with which Beijing had to act. Hostilities in Libya posed immediate risks to Chinese businesses and to the safety of approximately 36,000 Chinese workers in the country.[1] As Chinese nationals sought to flee civil strife, China undertook humanitarian operations unprecedented in its history, with the People's Liberation Army Navy undertaking its first-ever operational deployment to the Mediterranean. Beijing claims that it will uphold the principle of noninterference in the internal affairs of other states while asserting the need to protect Chinese interests. Over the longer run, it must also determine whether to enter into collaborative arrangements with other involved powers, as distinct from "go it alone" approaches geared to a narrower, self-protective conception of Chinese policy objectives.

The Communist Party leadership sees highly unsettling parallels between the Arab Spring and pressures for political change within China. Internal stability has emerged as an increasingly worrisome issue for China's leaders over the past half-decade. Societal grievances have festered and deepened and local protests across China have mushroomed, with the eminent Tsinghua University sociologist Sun Liping reporting that there were at least 180,000 such incidents in 2010 alone.[2] The party leadership seeks to prevent any political upsurge from below, so upheavals in the Middle East furnish an ominous precedent. Senior leaders have resorted to highly repressive measures to forestall such possibilities. The transformations under way in the Middle East have compounded the challenges to the leadership as it works through its own succession planning, scheduled to take effect in late 2012. U.S. and other Western urgings for Arab leaders to respond to bottom-up demands for political change, and in some cases to step aside, add to Chinese anxieties and suspicions about American intentions.

CONFRONTING THE THREATS TO CHINA'S INTERESTS

Exigencies of the moment left China little time to deliberate its policy options. Immediate risks to Chinese political and commercial interests, threats to the safety of Chinese citizens, and larger concerns about the potential dangers of regional instability were all factors in Chinese decisionmaking during the Arab Spring. China's reaction to events in Egypt—the first Middle Eastern state to establish diplomatic relations with China—illustrates its displeasure with the course of recent events, but also shows its pragmatism in quickly trying to secure its interests for the future. Long before the Arab Spring, Beijing understood Egypt's pivotal strategic position in the Arab world and sought to build close ties with the Mubarak regime. Between 1999 (when China first established "strategic cooperative relations" with Egypt) and 2009, there was a tenfold increase in Sino-Egyptian trade and the beginnings of Chinese investment in Egypt.[3] As Hosni Mubarak's hold on power grew increasingly tenuous in early 2011, Chinese officials expressed open unhappiness over U.S. pressure on him to resign. But ultimately Mubarak's vulnerabilities derived from internal circumstances, not from an orchestrated external campaign to undermine him, and Beijing did not have the means to prevent his fall from power. Following Mubarak's resignation, China moved quickly to establish relations with transitional authorities in Egypt as well as in Tunisia. Nevertheless, the Chinese were clearly perturbed by America's willingness to sever its ties with a leader who had supported U.S. policy goals for nearly three decades.

The potential risks to Chinese interests are even greater in Saudi Arabia, China's leading supplier of oil since 2002. Riyadh currently provides China more than 1 million barrels per day of crude oil, or approximately 20 percent of China's total oil imports—a more than fifteen-fold increase in absolute levels since 1999.[4] (In November 2009, China for the first time surpassed the United States as the leading purchaser of Saudi crude oil, though annual exports to the United States remained greater in both 2009 and 2010.) As China's dependence on Saudi oil supplies has grown, it has solidified its relations with the kingdom. During President Hu Jintao's state visit in early 2009, Saudi authorities pledged to meet China's burgeoning oil import needs, which are projected to more than double between now and 2030. Riyadh thus hopes to limit Beijing's future energy transactions with Iran, currently China's third leading supplier of crude oil. Chinese leaders are hoping to avoid any possible disruption in energy supply; they seem confident about their deepening relationship with Saudi Arabia and (if anything) perceive an opportunity in consolidating these ties at a time of mounting friction in Saudi relations with the United States.

Chinese disquiet over abrupt change in the Arab world, however, entails more than potential threats to its crude oil imports. Internal upheaval in the Middle East has reinforced innate fears of instability within China, including the potential contagion effects of social media as a tool of mass protest. Chinese policymakers recognize that deep internal grievances and societal disaffection triggered the Middle Eastern upheavals. Though some Chinese commentators claim a U.S. "hidden hand" in the Arab Spring, numerous Chinese analysts recognize that recent events derived largely from bottom-up pressures for political change and acute dissatisfaction over economic conditions and pervasive official corruption. China's social and economic conditions differ markedly from those in most of the Middle East, but there are obvious comparisons to political circumstances in the Arab world, in particular the Communist Party's claim to a monopoly on political power. There have been repeated, frequently violent protests in numerous provinces in recent years, not only among alienated ethnic minorities in

Tibet, Xinjiang, and Inner Mongolia.[5] Senior Chinese officials insist that China will not experience its own version of the Arab Spring, arguing that social and economic conditions in China are very different from those in the Middle East.[6] But the leadership's major crackdowns on internal dissent highlight acute worries atop the system, including fears of comparable challenges to political authority within China.

Events in the Arab world have therefore served as a mirror of Chinese leadership anxieties, reinforcing the leadership's determination to stifle the flow of information about protests across North Africa and the Middle East. The Chinese Communist Party was not prepared to permit any public expressions of support for the Arab Spring.[7] Pervasive censorship quickly proved the rule of the day in Chinese media during the uprisings, including blockage of the words "Egypt" and "Jasmine" in Internet searches, and even the banning of the sale of Jasmine flowers from some locations to try to forestall any online equivalent of the Arab Spring within China.[8] Chinese authorities also harshly suppressed the efforts of foreign journalists (including by physical intimidation) to report on the possible effects of the revolutions in the Middle East.[9] The abrupt incarceration of leading human rights advocates further revealed the fears of political contagion, especially as perceived by the internal security services and the government's propaganda apparatus. But Chinese experts acknowledge that mounting social and economic grievances are a growing threat to internal stability. Some see the Arab Spring as evidence that festering tensions and popular disaffection within China will be increasingly difficult for leaders to suppress.[10]

The responses of the United States and other Western powers to the Arab Spring represent a different but also very troubling concern for leaders in Beijing. The Communist Party leadership retains an almost instinctive aversion to and suspicion of Western calls for autocratic leaders to offer concessions to pressures from below, believing such steps could become a slippery slope for even greater challenges to the party's authority—a perspective they share with many of the Arab world's autocrats. Should major protests materialize in China or should Internet activism ultimately contest the party's monopoly on power, many officials see the potential for highly disruptive political outcomes.

THE LIBYAN EXCEPTION

Internal hostilities in Libya represented a very different case from events in Tunisia and Egypt. The outbreak of armed conflict in Libya caused widespread damage and looting to more than twenty-five Chinese projects within the country, which included major undertakings in telecommunications, railway construction, oil exploration, and metallurgical development.[11] With Chinese citizens and business interests at risk, Beijing was prepared to act in rapid and unprecedented fashion, including the establishment of a high-level task force to oversee the evacuation of Chinese workers from Libya.[12] The Arab League's endorsement of a humanitarian intervention was a pivotal factor in Chinese policy calculations. With the league's evident consent for an external intervention, China as well as four other Security Council members opted to abstain from (rather than oppose) UN Security Council Resolution 1973, thereby enabling NATO's rapid employment of air power against the regime. Though this appeared to signify a shift in Chinese readiness to interfere in the internal affairs of another state, it was also a reflection of immediate exigencies (that is, the safety of Chinese citizens) as well as Beijing's desire to avoid international isolation at the United Nations. China's abstention from the resolution was in line with its prevailing practice in the Security Council; it has employed its veto on only six occasions since 1971.[13]

However, Chinese officials and commentators were soon perturbed by NATO's expansive use of force, even though Beijing had consented to the imposition of a no-fly zone. Claiming that continued military actions by NATO would trigger an even larger humanitarian crisis, Beijing soon criticized "action that exceeds the mandate of the Security Council."[14] In essence, China saw mission creep in Libya. But as hostilities persisted, China tried to straddle the fence, establishing working relations with rebel forces, while simultaneously maintaining consultations with the Libyan government. Still, Beijing appeared to focus on the Libyan opposition forces, which it characterized as an "important dialogue partner."[15] Beijing recognized the need to be better positioned in the event of a leadership change, perhaps in the hopes of ultimately recovering at least a portion of its major investment losses purportedly sustained during the civil conflict, with some estimates ranging higher than $10 billion.[16] Immediately following Qadhafi's ouster from power in late August, the Chinese Ministry of Foreign Affairs declared that "we have noticed recent changes in the Libyan situation and respect the choice of the Libyan people," but it deferred formal recognition of the National Transitional Council (NTC) as a legitimate governing authority. The spokesman also noted that "China is willing to work together with the international community and to play an active role in the future reconstruction of Libya."[17] Bowing to the inevitable, in mid-September 2011 Beijing officially recognized the NTC as the "ruling authority of the country."[18]

Beijing's stated objections to the use of force, however, did not reflect any particular affinity for the Qadhafi regime. China's relations with Libya have long been deeply strained, partly due to Tripoli's accusations of Chinese economic domination of Africa and Tripoli's periodic efforts to cultivate ties with Taiwan.[19] But Chinese leaders exhibited ample unease about NATO's freedom of action and by parallel Western efforts to compel Qadhafi's exit from political power. Western moves to displace a sitting government, no matter how loathsome it may be, and even if justified by the "responsibility to protect," did not sit well with leaders in China. Beijing registered its objections even as it was edging toward full ties with Libyan opposition forces, including an early July visit by a senior Chinese diplomat (Chen Xiaodong, director general of the Foreign Ministry's West Asian and North African Affairs Department) to Benghazi.[20]

Moreover, despite Chinese objections to NATO's use of force, Beijing recognized and acted upon immediate risks to its own interests. Following the outbreak of widespread violence in Libya, China moved with atypical speed and interagency coordination to evacuate Chinese nationals. The late February redeployment of the frigate *Xuzhou* (then involved in counter-piracy operations in the Gulf of Aden) through the Suez Canal was unprecedented in China's post-1949 history. This was the first instance of China deploying a frontline naval asset to a distant location to rescue endangered citizens; Chinese authorities also flew IL-76 cargo aircraft to assist in these efforts.[21] China had thus crossed a major threshold in the operational deployment of military forces that would have seemed unimaginable only a few years ago. This could well presage Chinese responses to future nontraditional security missions, ones that military leaders appear increasingly willing to undertake, including multiple extended counter-piracy missions in the Gulf of Aden conducted since December 2008. In the Libyan case, however, China had edged much closer to interfering in another state's internal affairs, garnering public approval in China as a consequence.

CHINA SPREADS ITS WINGS, UNCERTAINLY

Chinese responses to the Arab Spring thus reflect divergent policy impulses and needs. The responses have entailed harsh repression at home, prudent efforts to protect burgeoning overseas interests, tentative but suggestive steps to modify China's longstanding policy of noninterference in the sovereign affairs of another state, and preliminary steps to heighten multinational collaboration, counterbalanced by continued sharp attacks on Western political and military intervention. This portends the development of foreign policy doctrines that are less equivocal about the employment of Chinese power (including military power) to defend Chinese interests, though Beijing will clearly seek UN sanction for such activities. The larger, unanswered question is whether China perceives sufficient common interests with other major powers to pursue a more collaborative strategy. This will depend in significant measure on whether there is additional upheaval across the Middle East that could threaten the interests of all powers. It will also depend on future Western strategy. As states across the region turn to the prodigious tasks of economic rehabilitation and political restructuring in Libya and elsewhere, a larger effort to limit the risks of major instability seems a shared interest around which outside powers could coalesce.

In the aftermath of the Arab Spring, China is no doubt far more mindful of and sobered by the potential liabilities of deeper regional engagement. It is no longer a marginal actor in regional politics, economics, or security and is clearly prepared to make major investments in the region's future. But it has yet to decide on its preferred regional role or on its readiness to work toward a more inclusive conception of development and security. In the longer term, China must also address its continued affiliation with autocratic regimes whose hold on power seems far less certain than in the past, the protection of China's regional trade and investment, and (most important for Beijing) the assurance of unimpeded access to regional energy supplies on which all states, but particularly China, will depend. However, China surely grasps that the upheavals across the Arab world will continue, requiring Beijing to ponder its future strategies in the face of events that it can neither anticipate nor control.

35

THE INTERNATIONAL ORDER AND THE EMERGING POWERS

Implications of the Arab Awakening

BRUCE JONES

Over the past sixty years, American power has underpinned an international system that has limited global conflict and secured the global flow of trade, finance, and energy. The United States has not done this alone: U.S. power has been embedded in a series of alliances, institutions, and arrangements that have helped to mobilize broader action, promote values, and set rules of the game, thereby legitimizing and creating shared interests in the use of American power.

That international order is already facing a series of challenges: from the economic and diplomatic rise of China, India, and Brazil, which are challenging the terms and values of current arrangements; from a dimming of the vibrancy of the transatlantic alliance; from global challenges like climate change that create collective action hurdles that neither U.S. diplomacy nor international institutions have yet mastered; and from the draining of the U.S. treasury by two wars, unchecked entitlements, and the global financial crisis. All this amounts to the early stages of a global rebalancing of power, values, and responsibilities. Now comes a further challenge, for the Arab Spring creates a series of tensions and ironies about the values, alliances, and institutions that make up the changing global order.

VALUES AND THE WEST

For the past several years, the sense of America's dominance (always somewhat exaggerated) has been diminished. The concept of a "post-American world" is equally exaggerated, but doubts about the durability of American preeminence have become more commonplace.[1] The rampant economic success of several centrally planned economies—in contrast to American, European, and Japanese stagnation—has dulled the appeal of the Western model. At the same time, non-Western powers have exerted new influence in global bodies that promote or protect democratic values, human rights, and development.

Against this backdrop, the peaceful, democratic uprisings in Tunisia and Egypt in January 2011 seemed to constitute a triumphal recovery of Western values. The sight of democratic protesters demanding an end to authoritarian rule re-inspired the West, even if it meant the overthrow of longtime allies. That Russia and China both looked at events in the region with concern for their own system heartened those who saw China's rise as a threat to Western values.

The fight for Arab self-determination is genuinely important in the ongoing debate over values in the international system. The idea, though, that events in North Africa and the Middle East represent a geopolitical advancement for the West is too simplistic. If the movements reflected Western values, it does not follow that those who participated in them sought to move their countries toward the West in geopolitical or policy terms. Western commentators who termed this an "Arab Spring" invoked the move of Eastern Europe's former Soviet satellites into the Western fold, politically and institutionally; but there, the United States and the West had been allied to the protesters for decades and had stood in firm opposition to the regimes. Across the Arab world, by contrast, the West—the United States most of all—is tainted by its close association with the region's autocratic regimes. At the same time, America's reaction to events in Cairo created a deep chill in U.S. relations with Gulf states, further constraining American influence.

None of this makes the U.S. reaction to the revolutions irrelevant. Protesters in Tahrir Square were keen to hear what President Barack Obama had to say and parsed every administration statement for evidence of ambiguity.[2] As the first wave of revolution has given way to struggles within elections or transitional cabinets, however, few are looking exclusively to the West for models or for support: a far wider world of models, potential friends, and funding awaits.

A sense that American dominance in the region had suddenly been unhinged created opportunities for other powers. Even before the revolts, of course, China and Russia had been extending their reach in the region through energy and economic relationships.[3] India has important ties to Iran and had begun to deepen its commercial relationships with the Gulf.[4] Even Brazil, together with Turkey, had launched diplomatic initiatives in the region.[5] With the Arab Spring, and the sense of America being unable to shape, let alone control, events, the space for such initiatives seemed to grow. European powers launched a new bid to displace the United States from its traditional role in the Middle East peace process.[6] Indonesia launched a diplomatic initiative in North Africa designed to showcase the marriage of Islam and democracy as a model for the region.[7] Russia sought new mediating roles. As for economic models, interviews and workshops in the region in the weeks after Tahrir Square suggested that many had their eyes on China's huge reserves of investment cash and were all too aware that the United States was broke and Europe in debt.[8] The Gulf began to throw money around the region, and whereas even a year earlier the action of Gulf states in the region could be presumed to be closely coordinated with Washington, new strains between Washington and the key Gulf regimes meant that their actions did not necessarily align with U.S. interests.

The Arab Spring may well serve to further Western values. So far, it does not look set to do the same for Western geopolitical interests.

U.S. POWER AND THE GLOBAL ECONOMY

A core part of the relationship between U.S. power and the postwar international order was the manner in which the United States used its global assets to protect the operations of the global economy. There are legal, financial, and technical aspects to this, but the most concrete role is the one played by America's navy in securing critical routes for shipping, a major factor in allowing free trade—on which 31 percent of U.S. GDP and fully 62 percent of China's, 52 percent of India's, and 81 percent of Europe's GDP depend.[9]

U.S. dominance in the Middle East was central to this arrangement. Most modern economies are dependent on global oil markets; this makes them dependent on a stable Middle East; and that has made them dependent on the United States' stabilizing presence in the region and the resulting security.[10] This may be uncomfortable, but it is a reality; and as countries like China, India, Brazil, and Indonesia embraced globalization, their rapid growth and exponential energy consumption are making them *more,* not less, dependent on U.S. global power. The vital role played by U.S. power in securing the global flow of oil and trade gives the United States critical leverage in broader international politics, but it also changes the character of U.S. power, in that it gives other states an interest in its exercise. Dominance is less disturbing when the dominant power uses its assets to secure things that are in your interest too.

This introduces a different dimension to the way in which other powers have reacted to the challenge to U.S. dominance in the region. While American dominance in the Middle East has long been an irritant for other powers (and U.S. dominance of the Middle East peace process produces a visceral sense of injustice), these countries also free ride on U.S. efforts to secure energy and trade markets. Central to all this is the role that the U.S. Fifth Fleet plays in maintaining stability in the Strait of Hormuz from its base in Bahrain. India and China, in particular, are reliant on flows of Gulf oil for their energy needs, and heavily dependent on the U.S. security presence in the Gulf. Knowledge of this dependence has caused both countries to begin investing in naval capacity so as to begin to exert some degree of national influence over their own energy security. However, both countries' capacities are still modest.[11]

This dependence also makes countries like India and China nervous to watch the U.S. fallout with the Gulf monarchies, and to watch the revolutionary dynamics in the region impinge on Bahrain and potentially Saudi Arabia. Were developments in the Gulf to halt the flow of oil and gas from the United Arab Emirates, Qatar, Iraq, and Saudi Arabia, the shock to the global economy would be severe, potentially even catastrophic. As it is, constrictions in the flow of oil from Libya have slowed the recovery from the global financial crisis, and Libya accounts for a mere 2 percent of international flows, compared with the 22 percent that flows from the Gulf.[12] If political developments in Bahrain and Saudi Arabia were to undermine the ability of the United States to sustain its naval presence in the Straits of Hormuz, similar consequences could arise.

For now, these dynamics reinforce other states' interest in U.S. power. Over time, though, discomfort with this arrangement seems likely to lead to calls to broaden the responsibility for providing security in the Gulf.[13] Such calls are already a feature of the changing order in other regions—witness China's offer to share in the responsibility for securing trade through the Straits of Malacca in East Asia. Just as former secretary of defense Robert Gates talked about the need for a multilateral mechanism to deal with naval and trade security in the seas along China's eastern borders, so it is not hard to envisage growing calls for some form of coalition to contribute to security and stability efforts in the Gulf. The readjustment of the relationship between U.S. power, and other actors' power, and the international order more broadly seems set to intensify.

NORMS AND INSTITUTIONS

In addition to influence and responsibilities, the evolving renegotiation of the global order is also about values and norms, and the institutional arrangements in which all these are embedded. Nowhere do these issues come together more sharply than around the questions of UN Security Council–mandated interventions, like the one in Libya. By accident of history, the Arab Spring began to unfold during a year in which Germany, Brazil, India, and South Africa—the four leading aspirants for new seats on the Security Council—happened to hold short-term elected seats in that body, giving them a voice on UN decisions on Libya and beyond. This has provided an unexpected preview of debates to come.

When Qadhafi's regime began its crackdown against its nascent opposition, the UN's first steps were surprisingly far-reaching. Libya was suspended from the UN Human Rights Council.[14] The UN General Assembly then *unanimously* confirmed the suspension.[15] The Security Council moved at unprecedented speed to do three things: impose sanctions, refer Qadhafi and several regime lieutenants to the International Criminal Court (a first for Washington), and invoke the concept of the "responsibility to protect"—the first time this had been invoked in a specific case. Soon, however, fissures appeared among Security Council members.

The United States had at first been reluctant to use military force to deal with Qadhafi. As risks of large-scale atrocities mounted, however, Washington shifted its stance, calling for military action to enforce the responsibility to protect and introducing a resolution to the Council to that effect. Russia and China abstained, arguably a glass-half-full move in that by abstaining they deliberately did not block council action. (Neither regime has any love lost for Qadhafi, either.) Brazil and India also abstained—more of a glass-half-empty move, since abstentions for elected members are simply the equivalent of no votes. South Africa voted in favor of military action.

As the U.S. and NATO's air campaign got under way, though, opposition intensified. The scale of U.S. air power on display in the first days of the campaign appears to have chilled both India and Brazil, and brought South Africa around to their position. Russia and China increased the volume of their opposition. Somewhat later, Russia sought to interpose itself between NATO and the African group, now more resolutely lined up against NATO's action. All those states then opposed UN Security Council action—even rhetorical action—in response to Syria's crackdown on its protesters in the summer and fall of 2011.

Brazil will rotate off the Security Council at the end of 2011, and India and Germany one year thereafter; Russia and China of course remain. But whether on the Security Council or simply in the real world of politics, in most regions of the world and most international institutions, the West will encounter and have to contend with the emerging powers more and more. Glass half full or empty, the debate over Libya is a preview of what is to come.

Looking Ahead

Until this year, the Middle East was the last bastion of unchallenged U.S. dominance. Now, the Middle East looks set to become an open terrain, with European, Asian, U.S., and regional interests competing for space, initiative, and influence. Not all of this will harm U.S. interests. If Europe can move the dial on the Middle East peace process, if Indonesia can offer a model that helps Muslim-majority states find a comfortable path to democracy, if Gulf or even Chinese financing helps revitalize dormant economies, American interests will be served. The United States could help marshal some of these efforts, thereby also shaping them, at least at the margins. For all the new constraints on U.S. power, only Washington has that kind of diplomatic marshaling capacity—what President Obama in London called "catalyzing global action."[16] The United States could, for example, lead the establishment of an informal multilateral arrangement that would sustain investment in democratic and economic reform in the region, linking states and international institutions into a coherent tool for support.

Still, the Arab Spring comes at a time when the international order is in flux. Events in the region will intensify the pace and stakes of the global rebalancing of power and responsibilities. The best-case scenario is the emergence of a new compact that sees the powers coordinating in some spheres, sharing responsibility in others, and finding ways to debate their differences without those spilling out into messier conflicts. The worst case is the uncoupling of U.S. power from international order with nothing to replace it—a result that would put in jeopardy both the operations of the global economy and relations among the great powers. Rationally, no one has an interest in such an outcome, including countries in the Middle East; but as history teaches, rationality does not always dictate policy.

36

THE UNITED STATES

A New American Grand Strategy for the Middle East

KENNETH M. POLLACK

Throughout this book, the United States has been a constant focus and a constant presence, implicitly or explicitly. In every chapter, we have included a variety of observations and recommendations for how the United States ought to handle the events and the long aftermath of the Arab Spring. In the issue-oriented chapters of Part I of the book, we provided ideas about how Washington could handle these matters as they pertain to a variety of countries across the region. In the overview chapters that introduced each subsequent part, we addressed the challenges that the United States would face to help each of these different groups of countries overcome the challenges arising from the different kinds of transformations they were undergoing. Then, in the specific country chapters, we attempted to explain how to turn these wider strategic concepts into more concrete tactics tailored to the unique features of each nation.

At an even higher level of resolution, however, there is a common theme, an overarching or "grand" strategy toward the Middle East that knits all of these detailed recommendations together. To some extent, this strategy should have been implicitly obvious from the tenor of these recommendations—for instance, at no point in this book did we suggest that more repression was the answer to any problem, even though we acknowledged that repression might continue to mask a problem for some period of time, before going on to warn that doing so might easily produce a later explosion worse than the original problem. Indeed, one of the most remarkable aspects of this project for all of the authors was in recognizing how closely our views aligned regarding what the United States needed to have happen in the Middle East, and what steps the United States needed to take to help that transformation. In many ways, this harmonic convergence made it possible to connect and coordinate all of the recommendations, weaving them into a larger whole. The purpose of this concluding chapter is to make that implicit American strategy explicit.

Elements of a New American Middle East Strategy

We believe that to secure America's interests in the Middle East, the United States must embrace a long-term commitment to help the countries of the Middle East pursue a process of political, economic, and social transformation. One that grows from within, rather than being imposed from without. One that reflects the values, traditions, history, and aspirations of the people of the region themselves, not a Western guess at them. One that recognizes that change and stability are not mutually exclusive, but mutually reinforcing—and ultimately mutually essential. But one that also acknowledges that change is most likely to be constructive, rather than destructive, when it is deliberate, planned, and properly resourced. This will be a difficult course to pursue, but it is ultimately the only good path to follow.

Many of the core elements of such a strategy are well understood and previously articulated.[1] Nevertheless, for purposes of clarity, it is useful to lay out the core assumptions and recommendations that would together comprise a new American strategy toward the Middle East. These include:

—Change is coming to the Middle East. The people of the region are demanding an end to the stagnant economic, social, and political orders that have left them miserable and frustrated for decades. The only questions that matter are how change comes to the region and when.

—The United States should recognize the desire on the part of the people of the region for economic, social, and political transformation—including an ardent desire for democratic forms of government. *The United States should commit itself to try to assist those efforts.*

—Although change is coming to the region, it can come in many ways. The best way would be without the risks and bloodshed that invariably attend upon sudden, unpredictable revolution. Therefore the United States should favor a process of peaceful transformation through political reform, economic transition, and social adjustment everywhere across the Middle East. However, these programs will have to be tailored to the unique features and circumstances of each country.

—The United States should acknowledge and applaud the desire of the people of the Middle East to shape their own destinies. Washington should make clear that America wants to help them to find their own path forward, rather than dictate how change should come about or what the end-state ought to be. It should seek *partnerships* with them.

—The United States should indicate a willingness to work with its allies in Europe and East Asia, as well as the wealthier states of the region, to pool its resources, and make them available to those states that need them.

The point that change will come to different countries of the region in different ways and at different speeds underscores another theme of the book, namely, that different Middle Eastern states find themselves facing very different challenges that will require different kinds of assistance from the United States and other members of the international community. Although any grouping inevitably glosses over important variances, we nonetheless believe it is useful to think about the states of the region as currently falling broadly into four groups, each requiring a different kind of policy approach—a different application of the overarching grand strategy—on the part of the United States:

—Some of the states of the region (Egypt, Iraq, Tunisia, and Libya) have already begun the long, arduous, and uncertain transition from autocracy to democracy as a result of successful regime change. These nations need to be assisted in every way and to the greatest extent possible to ensure that they succeed, both because their success would add to the stability of the region and create positive models that others might emulate, and because their failure could badly destabilize the entire region. Particularly noteworthy in this regard is Shadi Hamid's point in chapter 12 that because of Egypt's importance throughout the Arab world, its success is vital in seeing a positive transformation of the wider region.

—Other Middle Eastern states (Morocco, Oman, arguably Saudi Arabia, and perhaps Jordan) are pursuing a program of more gradual reform that will bring change more slowly, but hopefully without the risks of revolution and a rapid transition to democracy. The United States must not only lead international efforts to help these states as well, but must also devise methods to ensure that they do not falter (again) in their efforts to truly transform their own political, social, and economic systems. *If reform is going to be the alternative to repression and revolution, as we believe would be best for the region, then reform must be real, tangible, and meaningful.*

—A different group of states (Bahrain, Syria, Algeria, and Iran) has opted for repression over reform or revolution. These states must be convinced, by positive or negative inducements, that they, too, must change. As with the previous group, they must come to recognize that maintaining the status quo through repression is simply not viable over the long term, and that their only real choices are between peaceful, gradual reform in which the current elites will likely be able to retain a role in the future government, or sudden, violent revolution that will sweep them from power forever.

—Finally, some states (Yemen, possibly Syria, and perhaps Libya still) that attempted to resist the inexorable pressure to change—but maintained enough strength to prevent a successful revolution—have fallen into civil war. In these cases, and potentially others to follow, the United States must make the painful decision whether to intervene to try to end the conflict (as it did with NATO in

Libya) or else to try to help neighboring states to contain it. Ignoring civil wars is a foolhardy choice because of their tendency to create (potentially disastrous) problems for their neighbors through the various manifestations of spillover. And whether the United States and the international community intervene or not, it is critical to recognize from the painful examples of Lebanon, Afghanistan, and Iraq that a major rebuilding effort will be necessary to prevent further problems once the dust finally settles. The United States need not (and should not) own these future nation-building programs as it did those in Iraq and Afghanistan. However, neither is it an option for the U.S. government to simply walk away from them: America still plays a unique role in the world, and when it is not willing to help lead, organize, and support such operations, they frequently fail.

Defining a New Narrative

While it is unquestionably true that the people of the Middle East, those making the revolutions, want to secure their own futures, it is also true that they want to know that the United States supports them and will help them when they ask for assistance. Many suspect that the United States still backs the regimes. For all of them, the United States must articulate and consistently hew to a new American strategy that supports transformation in the Middle East.

But the message is equally important for the rulers themselves. Some hope to simply withstand the popular furor and when passions have cooled (perhaps requiring the sacrifice of certain scapegoats like Mubarak) to go back to the way things were. If they are going to be brought around to making more meaningful change they need to understand that resisting reform is unacceptable to Washington and will place them squarely at odds with what will become a new, long-term American strategy toward the region.

Other Arab leaders fear that the United States will define its interest in change in such a way that it will set them at odds with Washington. For them, America needs to articulate a vision of change that is compatible with their own interests (broadly defined) and that lays out a path forward that they could be persuaded to tread, even if grudgingly at first. Saudi Arabia is clearly paramount in this area. King Abdullah himself appears to recognize the need for change within the kingdom and has begun a number of initiatives to overhaul the Saudi educational, economic, judicial, and social systems, although Riyadh has been notably slower to introduce reforms in the political sphere. Despite this, the Saudis clearly fear that the Obama administration now plans to throw its support behind revolutionary regime change across the region—something very frightening to the Saudis in terms of what they believe it would mean both for themselves and for their allies. To some extent, they even fear that the United States will go so overboard in embracing transformation that it will forget traditional threats like Iran, and will decide that states that are not reforming at revolutionary speeds should become the principal target of American pressure.

For Riyadh in particular, then, it is vital that the United States develop a new strategic narrative that paints developments in the region, and future American policy toward it, in terms that are compatible with Saudi interests. The United States must indicate how it will (1) adjust to the changes sweeping the region, (2) continue to address the residual, or more traditional threats like Salafist terrorism and Iran, and (3) do both in ways that Saudi Arabia and other American allies can accept—even if reluctantly.

The United States should define the new regional struggle as one based on internal politics and the aspirations of the people of the region. In other words, it should accept that the region is now clearly divided. On one side are the states that have acknowledged the desires of their people for a better future and are taking concrete steps to improve their peoples' lives through political reform, economic transformation, and social adaptation. On the other side are the states that are not and that are employing the bad old methods of the old Middle East: repression, violence, fear, totalitarian control over information and expression, and the creation of internal or external scapegoats to blame their problems on— all to deny their people the better future they dream of.

Not accidentally, such a framework places the new Egypt, the new Tunisia, the new Libya, and the new Iraq squarely in the "camp" of those states in which such a change has begun, even if all four are beset by challenges. Despite their daunting problems, all are trying to democratize, all are responding to the desires of their people for better lives. It also places Iran, Syria, and groups like Hizballah—which is slowly gaining control over Lebanon—in the "camp" of those states decidedly in the wrong. In so doing, it should rally popular sympathy and support for Egypt, Iraq, Libya, and Tunisia and should help alienate Iran and Syria, especially in terms of Arab public opinion. Indeed, recent public opinion polls demonstrate that this is already happening now that Iran is no longer seen as championing resistance to the status quo and is instead viewed as supporting it in Syria and Lebanon.[2] It should also reassure the Saudis in particular that the United States will continue to see Iran as a major threat, but in a way that rallies the Arab street to its side and against Iran and is consistent with Washington's new emphasis on reform and transformation.

This strategic framework places a number of other countries exactly where they need to be—right in the middle. Saudi Arabia, Morocco, Jordan, Oman, Bahrain, Algeria, and others have in the past made mostly half-hearted forays at reform. To them, the United States can say that it wants to help them move into the first camp. Indeed, all of them have been frightened by the waves of unrest, and this ought to serve as an important motivation to adopt meaningful change. And an American willingness to help, if not push, such change should also keep them on the straight path and bring them more fully into the progressive camp farther down the road.

RECONCILING ENDS AND MEANS

Today, the United States faces very significant financial problems. Although foreign aid had virtually nothing to do with those problems, the issue of spending cannot be ignored. Today, every nickel the U.S. government spends will be scrutinized, and there is little stomach for disbursing large amounts of new aid.

It is in large part for this reason that, throughout this book, we have stressed the need for the United States to provide assistance that costs little or nothing at all. Most of our recommendations focus on providing technology and knowhow, or a wide variety of diplomatic assistance—from mobilizing NGOs to creating new international institutions to addressing troublesome international issues to convincing other countries or international institutions to provide assistance to the Arab world. Some of that assistance could come in the form of military aid, such as supporting the armed forces of the new Libyan government or retaining a residual American military presence in Iraq if the right terms can be negotiated with the Iraqi government. But in most cases, even the military assistance we recommend involves forces that already exist, and many of their operations could be paid for by the governments themselves. The new Libyan government, for example, might use frozen Libyan assets to pay for American arms and training. In short, most of our recommendations for pursuing a new strategy of enabling transformation in the Middle East are specifically designed to minimize the amount of American resources that would be needed.

Nevertheless, some of our recommendations do call for relatively modest commitments of American dollars. In large part, this is because even small new aid packages could have an outsized impact on the countries of the Middle East struggling to change, especially when they form the kernel of larger packages from U.S. allies and international organizations. Ultimately, the United States cannot lose sight of the importance of the changes that have now begun in the Middle East as a result of the Arab Spring. These are too important to our vital national interests to allow a few billion dollars—an insignificant fraction of the total U.S. budget—to become the difference between success and failure.

OUT WITH THE OLD

Throughout the cold war and the past twenty to thirty years, the United States has seen the Middle East largely through the traditional lens of political power. It was the governments of the region that mattered and interstate conflict was the greatest threat (even if that interstate conflict manifested itself in competing attempts at internal subversion). Because the United States had allied itself with those states that largely benefited from the prevailing geopolitical arrangements, Americans saw the status quo as highly beneficial and any threat to the status quo as correspondingly dangerous. America's great Arab allies—Saudi Arabia, Egypt, Kuwait, the United Arab Emirates, Jordan, Morocco—all liked things the way they were, and because they ensured that the oil flowed and were officially or unofficially at peace with Israel, the United States also liked the way things were. Even Israel, after its victories in 1967 and 1973 and its failed attempt to rearrange the Levantine status quo in its favor in 1982, had itself become a status quo power.

Consequently, the United States became the great champion of the status quo in the Middle East and defined its adversaries—Iran, Syria, Hizballah, Hamas, Libya until 2004—as those states and groups seeking to overturn the status quo. In some sense this was correct, because while those states *did* accept the same state-centric view of the Middle East, they did not like the extant geostrategic order and were attempting to subvert it to create a new one centered on their own interests.

The great problem inherent in this construct was that the people of the Middle East saw the preservation of the status quo as condemning them to eternal misery. Maintaining the status quo against all threats, foreign and domestic, meant keeping the people of the Arab world (and Iran) down. It meant preserving the stagnant economic, social, and political systems of the region that were the source of their frustration. Thus preserving the status quo meant dismissing the aspirations of the people of the Middle East.

This, more than anything else, is why so many Arabs admired Hassan Nasrallah, Mahmoud Ahmadinejad, and even Osama bin Laden. *They* at least seemed to be fighting for change, for an overturning of the status quo. And although most Arabs did not like what they stood for, they loved what they stood against—the traditional order that oppressed them. Because the United States supported the traditional order for geopolitical reasons, this also put it on the wrong side of Arab public opinion. Washington's support for the status quo was based on its focus on the region's geopolitical dynamics, but for the people of the Middle East, whose central concern was the region's domestic political-economic dynamics, that same defense of the status quo became a defense of their oppressors. It was a principal (albeit not the only) cause of the region's pervasive anti-Americanism.

Whether this strategy was "dead on arrival" or merely "overtaken by events" should be left to future historians to determine. Today, it is simply the wrong strategy for the United States to pursue, if it ever was the right one. To return to the themes sketched out in the introduction to this volume, more than anything else, the great Arab Awakening has meant that the people of the region can no longer be dismissed. After the wave of terrifying popular upheavals that rolled across the region in 2011, no Arab or external government can ever again ignore the wishes of its people.

So the old status quo is gone. Parts of it might be preserved for some time, but it will never be recreated. The only wise path that the United States can take at this point is to accept that change is coming to the region, and to help the people of the region shape that change to their ends. If the United States comes to be seen as a willing partner of the Arab peoples in their quest to build a new kind of Middle East, then over time we might find a new status quo emerge—one that is truly peaceful and prosperous, and therefore stable. And if America helps in that effort, perhaps it, too, can be transformed, from the most hated and feared foreign power to one of the most beloved. Certainly, we have nothing to lose. Our past strategy condemned us to endless crises and conflicts in the Middle East, consuming more and more of our blood, treasure, and time as the years passed in return for a volatile oil market and worsening anti-Americanism. It was not a very good deal for us. The great Arab Awakening has offered America a second chance. A new opportunity to remake ourselves in Middle Eastern eyes and become the country we imagine ourselves to be. All of the authors of this volume hope that America will seize this day to make a better tomorrow, for ourselves and all of the people of the Middle East.

Appendix:
Political, Social, and Economic
Indicators of the Middle East

The following appendix presents political, social, and economic indicators for the countries discussed in the book. The data reflect the period prior to the Arab Spring.

Appendix Part 1. Political, Social, and Economic Indicators of the Middle East

	Algeria	Bahrain	Egypt	Iran	Iraq	Jordan	Kuwait	Libya	Morocco
Political indicators									
Political risk index 2010[1]	5.5	7	5.5	3	3.5	6	7	4	6
Freedom ranking 2011[2]	Not free	Not free	Not free	Not free	Not free	Not free	Partly free	Not free	Partly free
Political rights[2]	6	6	6	6	5	6	4	7	5
Civil liberties[2]	5	5	5	6	6	5	5	7	4
Corruption perception index 2010[3]	2.9	4.9	3.1	2.2	1.5	4.7	4.5	2.2	3.4
Terrorist attacks 2010[4]	46	2	3	21	2,687	3	N/A	N/A	N/A
Freedom of the press 2010[5]	Not free	Not free	Partly free	Not free	Not free	Not free	Partly free	Not free	Not free
	64	71	60	89	65	63	55	94	66
Social indicators									
Human development index 2010[6]	0.677	0.801	0.620	0.702	N/A	0.681	0.771	0.755	0.567
Male literacy rate (% ages 15 and older) 2005–08[7]	81	N/A	75	87	86	95	95	95	69
Female literacy rate (% ages 15 and older) 2005–08[7]	64	N/A	58	77	69	89	93	81	44
Refugees residing in the country 2011[8]	94,144	165	95,056	1,073,366	34,655	450,915	184	7,923	792
Internally displaced persons (IDPs) residing in the country 2011[8]	0	0	0	0	1,343,568	0	0	0	0
Refugees originating from the country 2011[8]	6,689	87	6,913	68,791	1,683,579	2,254	988	2,309	2,284
Internet users (per 100 inhabitants)[9]									
2000	0.49	6.15	0.64	0.93	N/A	2.62	6.73	0.19	0.69
2010	12.50	55.00	26.74	13.00	5.60	38.00	38.25	14.00	49.00
Cellular phone subscriptions (per 100 inhabitants)[9]									
2000	0.28	32.24	2.01	1.47	0	8.06	24.53	0.76	8.13
2010	92.42	124.18	87.11	91.25	75.78	106.99	160.78	171.52	100.10

Economic indicators

Real GDP growth rate (%) 2009[10]	2.10	2.88[11]	4.65	1.80	4.20	2.34	−2.66[12]	2.10	4.95
GDP per capita (current USD) 2009[13]	4,028	26,021	2,270	4,540	2,090	4,216	N/A	9,714	2,811
Unemployment rate (%) 2010[14]	22.5	15	10	11.2	25–30	12.5 (official) 30 (unofficial)	2.2	30	N/A
Male youth unemployment (%) 2005–08[15]	N/A	N/A	23	20	N/A	N/A	N/A	N/A	18
Female youth unemployment (%) 2005–08[15]	N/A	N/A	62	30	N/A	N/A	N/A	N/A	16
Net primary school enrollment ratio (% of relevant age group) 2008[16]	95	N/A	94	N/A	N/A	89	88	N/A	89
Net secondary school enrollment ratio (% of relevant age group) 2008[16]	N/A	N/A	N/A	75	N/A	84	80	N/A	N/A
Military expenditures (% of GDP)[17]									
2000	3.4	N/A	3.2	3.8	N/A	6.2	7.1	3.2	2.3
2008	3.1	N/A	2.3	2.9	N/A	5.9	3.2	1.2	3.3
U.S. assistance									
Total U.S. economic assistance (in millions USD) 2009[18]	11.2	0.4	483.2	0.7	2,252.7	578.2	0.1	10.7	236.2
Arms deliveries (in millions USD)[19]									
2002–05	0	300	6,100	0	0	400	800	0	0
2006–09	0	300	4,400	0	1,700	800	1,500	0	100

	Oman	Palestinian Territories		Qatar	Saudi Arabia	Syria	Tunisia	UAE	Yemen
		Gaza	West Bank						
Political indicators									
Political risk index 2010[1]	7	N/A		7.5	5	4.5	6	6	4.5
Freedom ranking 2011[2]	Not free	Not free	Not free	Not free	Not free	Not free	Not free	Not free	Not free
Political rights[2]	6	6	6	6	7	7	7	6	6
Civil liberties[2]	5	6	5	5	6	6	5	5	5
Corruption perception index 2010[3]	5.3	N/A		7.7	4.7	2.5	4.3	6.3	2.2
Terrorist attacks 2010[4]	1	236	60	N/A	1	N/A	N/A	N/A	196
Freedom of the press 2010[5]	Not free 71	N/A		Not free 66	Not free 83	Not free 83	Not free 85	Not free 71	Not free 80
Social indicators									
Human development index 2010[6]	N/A	0.645		0.803	0.752	0.589	0.683	0.815	N/A
Male literacy rate (% ages 15 and older) 2005–08[7]	90	N/A		94	90	90	86	89	79
Female literacy rate (% ages 15 and older) 2005–08[7]	81	N/A		90	80	77	70	91	43
Refugees residing in the country 2011[8]	78	0		51	582	1,005,472	89	538	190,092
Internally displaced persons (IDPs) residing in the country 2011[8]	0	0		0	0	0	0	0	220,994
Refugees originating from the country 2011[8]	63	93,323		112	667	18,452	2,174	424	2,076
Internet users (per 100 inhabitants)[9]									
2000	3.52	1.11		4.86	2.21	0.18	2.75	23.63	0.08
2010	62.60	37.44		69.00	41.00	20.70	36.80	78.00	10.85

Cellular phone subscriptions (per 100 inhabitants)[9]								
2000	7.15	0.22	20.45	6.86	0.19	1.26	47.08	0.18
2010	165.54	45.79 (2009)	132.43	187.86	57.30	106.04	145.45	46.09
Economic indicators								
Real GDP growth rate (%) 2009[10]	2.00[11]	N/A	8.64	0.60	4.00	3.13	–0.70	3.76
GDP per capita (current USD) 2009[12]	16,207	N/A	69,754	14,799	2,474	3,792	50,070	1,118
Unemployment rate (%) 2010[13]	15 (2004)[14]	40 (2009)[15]	19 (2009)[16]	0.5[17]	13	8.3[18]	14.2	35
Male youth unemployment (%) 2005–08[19]	N/A	N/A	N/A	N/A	N/A	31	7	N/A
Female youth unemployment (%) 2005–08[19]	N/A	N/A	N/A	N/A	N/A	29	13	N/A
Net primary school enrollment ratio (% of relevant age group) 2008[20]	68	N/A	N/A	85	N/A	98	92	73
Net secondary school enrollment ratio (% of relevant age group) 2008[20]	78	N/A	79	73	68	N/A	84	N/A
Military expenditures (% of GDP)[21]								
2000	10.6	N/A	N/A	10.6	5.3	1.7	3.4	5.0
2008	10.4	N/A	N/A	8.2	3.4	1.3	N/A	4.5
U.S. assistance								
Total U.S. economic assistance (in millions USD) 2009[22]	10.9	1,039.2	4.0	0.5	18.6	1.9	0.4	171.1
Arms deliveries (in millions USD)[23]								
2002–05	300	N/A	0	4,400	0	0	500	0
2006–09	500	N/A	0	5,000	0	0	600	0

Notes

Chapter One

1. This section draws heavily on Thomas Carothers and Marina Ottaway, eds., *Uncharted Journey: Promoting Democracy in the Middle East* (Washington: Carnegie Endowment for International Peace, 2005); Kenneth M. Pollack, *A Path Out of the Desert: A Grand Strategy for America in the Middle East* (New York: Random House, 2008), esp. pp. 67–120; Tamara Cofman Wittes, *Freedom's Unsteady March: America's Role in Promoting Arab Democracy* (Brookings, 2008).

2. United Nations Development Programme (UNDP), Arab Fund for Economic and Social Development, *Arab Human Development Report, 2003* (New York, 2003).

3. On the "democracy deficit" in the Middle East, see, for instance, Larry Diamond, "Why Are There No Arab Democracies?" *Journal of Democracy* 21 (January 2010): 93–104; Alfred Stepan and Graeme B. Robertson, "Arab, Not Muslim, Exceptionalism" *Journal of Democracy* 15 (October 2004).

4. For overviews of the economic problems of the Arab world, see Marcus Noland and Howard Pack, *The Arab Economies in a Changing World* (Washington: Peterson Institute for International Economics, 2007); Alan Richards and John Waterbury, *A Political Economy of the Middle East*, 3rd ed. (Boulder, Colo.: Westview, 2007).

5. On this phenomenon more generally, see William Aviles, "Policy Coalitions, Economic Reform and Military Power in Ecuador and Venezuela," *Third World Quarterly* 30 (2009): 1549–64.

6. Note that in Egypt, at least, the revolution succeeded in bringing down Mubarak, but whether the wider regime apparatus—particularly the military with its perks and nondemocratic interests—will also succumb remains very much in doubt.

7. On this point, see, in particular, Lisa Anderson, "Absolutism and the Resilience of Monarchy in the Middle East," *Political Science Quarterly* 106 (Spring 1991): 1–15; Shadi Hamid, "Why Middle East Monarchies Might Hold On," *The Atlantic*, March 28, 2011 (www.theatlantic.com/international/archive/2011/03/why-middle-east-monarchies-might-hold-on/72170/).

8. For a sample of the voluminous work demonstrating Arab approval and desire for democracy before the Arab Spring, see, for instance, Asad Abu Khalil, "A Viable Partnership: Islam, Democracy and the Arab World," *Harvard International Review* 15 (Winter 1992/93): 65; Thomas Carothers and Marina Ottaway, "The New Democracy Imperative," in *Uncharted Journey: Promoting Democracy in the Middle East,* edited by Carothers and Ottawa, p. 8; John L. Esposito and James P. Piscatori, "Democratization and Islam," *Middle*

East Journal 45 (Summer 1991): 427–40; John L. Esposito and Dalia Mogahed, *Who Speaks for Islam: What a Billion Muslims Really Think* (New York: Gallup Press, 2008), esp. pp. 31–35, 47–48, 57–58; Abdou Filali-Ansary, "Muslims and Democracy," in *Islam and Democracy in the Middle East,* edited by Larry Diamond, Marc F. Plattner, and Daniel Brumberg (Johns Hopkins University Press, 2003), pp. 199–201; Amy Hawthorne, "The New Reform Ferment," in *Uncharted Journey,* edited by Carothers and Ottaway; Anwar Ibrahim, "Universal Values and Muslim Democracy," *Journal of Democracy* 17 (July 2006): 5–12; Ronald Inglehart, "How Solid Is Mass Support for Democracy—And How Can We Measure It?" *PS: Political Science and Politics* 36 (January 2003): 52; Ronald Inglehart and Pippa Norris, "The True Clash of Civilizations," *Foreign Policy* (March/April 2003): 63–70; Amaney A. Jamal, "Reassessing Support for Islam and Democracy in the Arab World? Evidence from Egypt and Jordan," *World Affairs* 169 (Fall 2006): 54–56; Farhad Kazemi, "The Inclusion Imperative," *Middle East Studies Association Bulletin* (December 1996); Radwan A. Masmoudi, "The Silenced Majority," in *Islam and Democracy in the Middle East,* edited by Diamond and others, pp. 260–62; Dalia Mogahed and Geneive Abdo, "Islam and Democracy," Special Report: Muslim World, Gallup World Poll, 2006, p. 3; Dalia Mogahed, "Understanding Islamic Democracy," *Europe's World* 2 (Spring 2006): 163–65; Ahmad S. Moussalli, *The Islamic Quest for Democracy, Pluralism, and Human Rights* (University of Florida Press, 2001); Pew Research Center, "Support for Terror Wanes among Muslim Publics: 17-Nation Pew Global Attitudes Survey," Pew Global Attitudes Project (Washington, July 14, 2005), p. 22; Curtis R. Ryan and Jillian Schwedler, "Return to Democratization or New Hybrid Regime? The 2003 Elections in Jordan," *Middle East Policy* 11 (Summer 2004): 138–52; David Smock, "Islam And Democracy," Special Report 93 (Washington: United States Institute of Peace, September 2002); Mark Tessler, "Public Opinion in the Arab and Muslim World: Informing U.S. Public Diplomacy," in *"In The Same Light as Slavery": Building a Global Antiterrorist Consensus,* edited by Joseph McMillan (Washington: National Defense University Press, 2006), pp. 15–16; Mark Tessler, "Do Islamic Orientations Influence Attitudes toward Democracy in the Arab World? Evidence from Egypt, Jordan, Morocco, and Algeria," *International Journal of Comparative Sociology* 43, no. 3–5 (2002): 229–49; UNDP, Arab Fund for Economic and Social Development, *Arab Human Development Report, 2003* (New York, 2003), p. 19.

Chapter Two

1. The Anwar Sadat Chair for Peace and Development at the University of Maryland, with Zogby International, polls nearly 4,000 people in cities in six countries. Results are released annually at the Saban Center at Brookings and can be accessed at Brookings.edu and at Sadat.umd.edu.

2. This is particularly ironic: the last time major popular upheavals swept the Arab world was in the late 1950s following the Suez War of 1956, when Egypt's story was being told all over the Middle East in the era of radio, through dominant regional broadcasts that challenged the stories of other Arab governments.

3. As of the 2010 poll, the overwhelming majority of Arabs continue to say that television remains their primary source of news.

4. In the Sadat Chair/Zogby polls after the U.S. invasion of Iraq, most Arabs identified George W. Bush as the leader they disliked most in the world—ahead of any Israeli leader.

5. Steven Kull, *Feeling Betrayed: The Roots of Muslim Anger with America* (Brookings, 2011).

6. International Republican Institute, "Egyptian Public Opinion Survey," April 2011, Question 5.

7. Zogby International, "Arab Attitudes, 2011," July 2011 (http://aai.3cdn.net/5d2b 8344e3b3b7ef19_xkm6ba4r9.pdf).

8. Abu Dhabi Gallup Center, "Egypt from Tahrir to Transition," June 2011.

9. Ibid.

10. Ibid., Question 3.

11. Zogby International, "Arab Attitudes, 2011," Question 1.

12. Ibid., Question 2.

13. Ibid., Question 3.

14. Ibid., Question 4.

15. Ibid., Question 5.

16. Ibid., Question 8.

17. Abu Dhabi Gallup Center, "Egypt from Tahrir to Transition" (exact wording of some questions unavailable).

18. Ibid.

19. Sadat Chair for Peace and Development and Program on International Policy Attitudes (PIPA) poll, April 2011. For methodology and full results, see http://sadat.umd.edu/latestreport.htm.

CHAPTER THREE

1. Samuel P. Huntington, *The Third Wave: Democratization in the Late Twentieth Century* (University of Oklahoma Press, 1991).

2. Arch Puddington, "Democracy under Duress," *Journal of Democracy* 22 (April 2011); Joshua Kurlantzick, "The Great Democracy Meltdown: Why the World Is Becoming Less Free," *New Republic*, May 19, 2011.

3. Pippa Norris, ed., *Critical Citizens: Global Support for Democratic Government* (Oxford University Press, 1999); "World Publics Say Governments Should Be More Responsive to the Will of the People," World Public Opinion, May 12, 2008 (www.worldpublicopinion.org/pipa/articles/governance_bt/482.php?lb=btgov&pnt=482&nid=&id=).

4. Larry Diamond, "Why Are There No Arab Democracies?" *Journal of Democracy* 21 (January 2010): 102.

5. For one explanation as to why this might be occurring, see Christian Welzel and Ronald Inglehart, "The Role of Ordinary People in Democratization," *Journal of Democracy* 19 (January 2008).

6. See, for instance, Seymour Martin Lipset, "Some Social Requisites of Democracy: Economic Development and Political Legitimacy," *American Political Science Review* 53 (March 1959): 69–105.

7. On Moore's groundbreaking work, see Barrington Moore Jr., *The Social Origins of Dictatorship and Democracy: Lord and Peasant in the Making of the Modern World* (Boston: Beacon Press, 1966).

8. Morton H. Halperin, Joseph T. Siegle, and Michael M. Weinstein, *The Democracy Advantage: How Democracies Promote Prosperity and Peace* (New York: Routledge, 2005). Indeed, recall that the protests in Syria were slowest to materialize in the middle-class urban centers of Damascus and Aleppo, which benefited economically from their connections to the Asad regime. Similarly, the Muslim Brotherhood in Egypt has traditionally drawn a large share of its support from the urban upper-middle class. Many of the protesters who filled Tahrir Square may have had middle-class expectations, attitudes, and educations, but it was precisely their inability to attain job opportunities permitting them to have middle-class economic status that was a key factor driving them to the streets.

9. Huntington, *Third Wave.* Not all of these remained so over the long term, however. A number of low-income "consolidated democracies" reverted over time to autocratic rule. In short, there is mounting evidence that any country, no matter the level of per capita income, is capable of becoming an electoral democracy, though wealthier countries are more likely to remain so over time.

10. Welzel and Inglehart, "The Role of Ordinary People in Democratization."

11. An example of this early literature is Guillermo O'Donnell and Philippe C. Schmitter, *Transitions from Authoritarian Rule: Tentative Conclusions about Uncertain Democracies* (Johns Hopkins University Press, 1986). One of the best critiques of the "democracy template" remains Thomas Carothers, *Aiding Democracy Abroad: The Learning Curve* (Washington: Carnegie Endowment for International Peace, 1999), chap. 5. See also Carothers, "The End of the Transition Paradigm," *Journal of Democracy* 13 (January 2002).

12. Freedom House, "Freedom in the World 2011: The Authoritarian Challenge to Democracy" (Washington, 2011).

13. Barrington Moore Jr., *Injustice: The Social Bases of Obedience and Revolt* (New York: M. E. Sharpe, 1978).

14. Thomas Carothers, *Critical Mission: Essays on Democracy Promotion* (Washington: Carnegie Endowment for International Peace, 2004); Steven Levitsky and Lucan A. Way, "The Rise of Competitive Authoritarianism," *Journal of Democracy* 13 (April 2002): 51–65; Fareed Zakaria, "The Rise of Illiberal Democracy," *Foreign Affairs* 76 (November/December 1997).

15. Carothers, "The End of the Transition Paradigm."

16. For more on hybrid regimes, see Ivan Krastev, "Paradoxes of the New Authoritarianism," *Journal of Democracy* 13 (April 2011); Steven Levitsky and Lucan A.Way, *Competitive Authoritarianism: Hybrid Regimes after the Cold War* (Cambridge University Press, 2010); Marina Ottaway, *Beyond the Façade: Political Reform in the Arab World* (Washington: Carnegie Endowment for International Peace, January 2008); Steven Heydemann, "Upgrading Authoritarianism in the Arab World," Analysis Paper 13 (Brookings Saban Center for Middle East Policy, October 2007); Marina Ottaway, *Democracy Challenged: The Rise of Semi-Authoritarianism* (Washington: Carnegie Endowment for International Peace, 2003); Daniel Brumberg, "The Trap of Liberalized Autocracy," *Journal of Democracy* 13 (October 2002).

17. On this phenomenon in the Middle East, see Brumberg, "The Trap of Liberalized Autocracy," pp. 56–68.

18. Rule of law means "a system in which the laws are public knowledge, are clear in meaning, and apply equally to everyone." Thomas Carothers, ed., *Promoting the Rule of Law Abroad: In Search of Knowledge* (Washington: Carnegie Endowment for International Peace, 2006), p. 4.

19. See, for example, Guillermo O'Donnell, "Horizontal Accountability in New Democracies," *Journal of Democracy* 9 (July 1998): 112–26; Andreas Schedler, Larry Diamond, and Marc F. Plattner, eds., *The Self-Restraining State: Power and Accountability in New Democracies* (Boulder, Colo.: Lynne Rienner, 1999); Kimberly Ann Elliott, ed., *Corruption and the Global Economy* (Washington: Institute for International Economics, June 1997). A more recent example is Daniel Kaufmann, Aart Kraay, and Massimo Mastruzzi, "Governance Matters 2009: Learning from Over a Decade of the Worldwide Governance Indicators" (Brookings, June 2009).

20. Ralph Waldo Emerson, "Politics," *Essays,* 2nd ser. (1844).

Chapter Four

1. 'Abd al-Rahman Ayyash, interview with the author, Cairo, Egypt, February 9, 2011.

2. For more on the origins and structure of the Muslim Brotherhood, see Richard P. Mitchell, *The Society of the Muslim Brothers* (Oxford University Press, 1993); and Brynjar Lia,

The Society of the Muslim Brothers in Egypt: The Rise of an Islamic Mass Movement, 1928–1942 (Reading, U.K.: Ithaca Press, 1998).

3. Edward P. Djerijian, "The U.S. and the Middle East in a Changing World," address to Meridian House International, Washington, June 2, 1992.

4. Jillian Schwedler, *Faith in Moderation: Islamist Parties in Jordan and Yemen* (Cambridge University Press, 2006); Mona el-Ghobashy, "The Metamorphosis of the Egyptian Muslim Brothers," *International Journal of Middle East Studies* 37 (August 2005): 373–95; Eva Wegner and Holger Albrecht, "Autocrats and Islamists: Contenders and Containment in Egypt and Morocco," *Journal of North African Studies* 11 (June 2006): 123–41; Lisa Blaydes and Safinaz El Tarouty, "Weapons of the Weak in Parliament: Muslim Brotherhood Activity in Egypt, 1984–2008," paper presented at the 2008 Annual Meeting of the Middle East Studies Association, Washington, November 20, 2008; James Piscatori, *Islam, Islamists, and the Electoral Principle* (Netherlands: Leiden ISIM, 2000).

5. Compare, for example, *Al-Barnamaj al-Intikhabi li al-Ikhwan al-Muslimin fi al-Intakhabat al-Tashri'iya* [The Electoral Program of the Muslim Brotherhood in the Legislative Elections], Cairo, October 2005, with the 1987 electoral platform of the Brotherhood's "Islamic Alliance," *Al-Barnamaj al-Intikhabi li al-Tahaluf al-Islami* [The Electoral Program of the Islamic Alliance], Cairo, October 1987, in Mohammad Muru, *al-Haraka al-Islamiya fi Misr min 1928 ila 1993* [The Islamic Movement in Egypt from 1928 to 1993] (Cairo: Dar al-Misriya li al-Nashr wa al-Tawzi', 1994).

6. For more on the Brotherhood's social service activities, see Ziad Munson, "Islamic Mobilization: Social Movement Theory and the Egyptian Muslim Brotherhood," *Sociological Quarterly* 42 (Autumn 2001): 487–510; and Carrie Rosefsky Wickham, *Mobilizing Islam: Religion, Activism, and Political Change in Egypt* (Columbia University Press, 2004).

7. The basic level of the organization is the *usra*, which is sometimes translated incorrectly as "cell"—with its military and subversive connotations—but is actually a literal translation of "family." As Richard Mitchell writes, the system of families is "the most fundamental of [the Brotherhood's] 'educational' (*tarbiyya*) instruments." Mitchell, *The Society of the Muslim Brothers,* p. 195.

8. Abdel-Moneim Abul-Futuh, interview with the author, August 2006, Cairo, Egypt.

9. Muslim Brotherhood, *"Mashrou' A'ada Taqdim al-Jama'a li al-Gharb"* [Project of Re-introducing the Brotherhood to the West], internal document, 2005. Work on the project lasted a year and involved extensive consultations with outside experts. The white paper, which lists misconceptions on both sides and proposes a plan of action to address them, provides a glimpse into the Brotherhood's strategic thinking.

10. For more on the role of al-Nahda in Tunisia, see chapter 13. See also Marion Boulby, "The Islamic Challenge: Tunisia since Independence," *Third World Quarterly* 10 (April 1988): 590–614; Emad Shahin, *Political Ascent: Contemporary Islamic Movements in North Africa* (Boulder, Colo.: Westview Press, 1997).

11. Notably, though, the Brotherhood's new political party—"Freedom and Justice"— has dropped the offending clauses from its political program.

12. For more on Islamist attitudes on foreign policy, see Shadi Hamid, "The Rise of the Islamists: How Islamists Will Change Politics, and Vice Versa," *Foreign Affairs* 90 (May/ June 2011): 40–48.

13. On this contention, see Jillian Schwedler, "Democratization, Inclusion and the Moderation of Islamist Parties," *Development* 50 (January 2007); and Schwedler, *Faith in Moderation.*

14. Khalil al-Anani, *Al-Ikhwan al-Muslimun fi Misr: Shaikhouka Tassaru' al-Zaman* [The Muslim Brotherhood in Egypt: Gerontocracy Fighting the Clock] (Cairo: Maktaba al-Shorouq al-Dawliya, 2007), p. 93. Khalil al-Anani's "field study" of fifty rank-and-file

Brotherhood activists in Egypt is neither a random sample nor a large one (acquiring either would be nearly impossible under the circumstances). However, his data are worth considering as this is one of the few "base" surveys of any Islamist group in the region and is a product of Anani's access to Brotherhood members at various levels.

15. Muslim Brotherhood, "*Al-Mara al-Muslima fi al-Mujtama' al-Muslim*" [The Muslim Woman in Muslim Society] and "*Moujiz min al-Shura fi al-Islam wa Ta'adud al-Ahzab fi al-Mujtama' al-Muslim*" [Summary on Shura in Islam and Political Party Pluralism in Muslim Society], pamphlet (Cairo: Al-Markaz al-Islami li al-Darasat wa al-Buhuth, March 1994), p. 3. The pamphlet includes both statements.

16. Pew Global Attitudes Survey, "Muslim Publics Divided on Hamas and Hezbollah" (http://pewglobal.org/2010/12/02/muslims-around-the-world-divided-on-hamas-and-hezbollah/).

17. Hamdi Dabash and Hany ElWeziery, "Brotherhood Leader: Media Highlights Mistakes to Disparage Group," *Al Masry al-Youm,* May 28, 2011(www.almasryalyoum.com/en/node/454611).

18. For more on Jordan's Salafi movement, see Quentin Wiktorowicz, *The Management of Islamic Activism: Salafis, the Muslim Brotherhood and State Power in Jordan* (State University of New York Press, 2001).

19. Khalil al-Anani, "The Myth of Excluding Moderate Islamists," Working Paper 4 (Brookings Saban Center for Middle East Policy, March 2010), p. 6.

20. Esam al-Erian, interview with the author, Cairo, July 16, 2008.

21. Malik Mufti, "Elite Bargains and the Onset of Political Liberalization in Jordan," *Comparative Political Studies* 32 (February 1999): 116.

22. For more on why Islamists deliberately lose elections, see Shadi Hamid, "Arab Islamist Parties: Losing on Purpose?" *Journal of Democracy* 22 (January 2011): 68–80; Michael Willis, "Morocco's Islamists and the Legislative Elections of 2002: The Strange Case of the Party That Did Not Want to Win," *Mediterranean Politics* 9 (Spring 2004).

23. Tayseer Fityani, interview with the author, Amman, May 19, 2008; Ruheil al-Gharaibeh, interview, Amman, June 8, 2008; Mohammad Bzour, interview, Amman, May 15, 2008; Abdul Latif Arabiyat, interview, Amman, June 11, 2008.

24. See Shadi Hamid and Amanda Kadlec, "Strategies for Engaging Political Islam," Project on Middle East Democracy, January 2010 (http://pomed.org/strategies-for-engaging-political-islam/).

CHAPTER FIVE

1. Available at http://edition.cnn.com/video/?/video/bestoftv/2011/02/11/exp.ghonim.facebook.thanks.cnn.

2. There is a vigorous debate on the democratizing impact of the Internet. For the optimistic position, see Clay Shirky, *Here Comes Everybody* (New York: Penguin, 2008), and "The Political Power of Social Media," *Foreign Affairs* (January/February 2011). The pessimists are best represented by Evgeny Morozov, *The Net Delusion* (New York: Public Affairs, 2011).

3. Christopher Dickey, "The Tragedy of Mubarak," *Newsweek,* February 13, 2011 (www.newsweek.com/2011/02/13/the-tragedy-of-mubarak.html).

4. Available at www.facebook.com/ElShaheeed.

5. "Interview With Syrian President Bashar al-Asad," *Wall Street Journal,* January 31, 2011 (http://online.wsj.com/article/SB10001424052748703833204576114712441122894.html).

6. See http://astrubal.nawaat.org/2007/08/29/tunisie-avion-presidentiel/.

7. Howard Rheingold, *Smart Mobs* (New York: Basic Books, 2002).

8. Fatima Atfa, "Ghassan Aboud, the Owner of the Syrian Orient TV," April 9, 2011 (www.sooryoon.net/?p=20600).

9. John Kifner, "Rebellion Erupts in Central Syria, Diplomats Report," *New York Times,* February 11, 1982, p. A1.

10. David Goodman, "Video From Syria Shows Military Action," *New York Times,* April 25, 2011, (http://thelede.blogs.nytimes.com/2011/04/25/video-from-syria-shows-military-action) (June 20, 2011); Human Rights Watch, "We've Never Seen Such Horror," June 1, 2011 (http://www.hrw.org/reports/2011/06/01/we-ve-never-seen-such-horror-0).

11. Shirky, "The Political Power of Social Media."

12. "Protest Hero Wael Ghonim Barred from Stage," Agence France-Presse, February 18, 2011 (www.hindustantimes.com/Egypt-protest-hero-Wael-Ghonim-barred-from-stage/Article1-663996.aspx).

13. Hillary Clinton, "Remarks on Internet Freedom," Department of State, Secretary's Remarks, January 21, 2010 (www.state.gov/secretary/rm/2010/01/135519.htm), and "Internet Rights and Wrongs: Choices & Challenges in a Networked World," February 15, 2011 (www.state.gov/secretary/rm/2011/02/156619.htm).

CHAPTER SIX

1. See chapter 28.

2. Shadi Hamid, "Egypt in Middle of Arab Cold War," *National Interest,* April 21, 2011 (http://nationalinterest.org/commentary/egypt-middle-arab-cold-war-5208).

3. The day after the Nakba Day protests, Israeli defense minister Ehud Barak remarked: "The Palestinians' transition from terrorism and suicide bombings to deliberately unarmed mass demonstrations is a transition that will present us with difficult challenges." Quoted in Karin Laub, "Palestinians Test Tactic of Unarmed Mass Marches," Associated Press, May 16, 2011. See also Ben Frankel, "Palestinian Non-violent Resistance Will Challenge Israel," Homeland Security Newswire, July 8, 2011 (www.homelandsecuritynewswire.com/palestinian-non-violent-resistance-will-challenge-israel): "For Israel, a third intifada, with its violence and rockets and suicide bombing, will be more painful but easier to deal with. A non-violent, peaceful resistance will make life much tougher for Israel, and force it into making decisions which otherwise it would not make."

4. For the full text of Netanyahu's speech before Congress, see "Transcript: Israeli Prime Minister Binyamin Netanyahu's address to Congress," *Washington Post,* May 24, 2011 (www.washingtonpost.com/world/israeli-prime-minister-binyamin-netanyahus-address-to-congress/2011/05/24/AFWY5bAH_story.html). Interestingly, in his first address to Congress in July 1996, Netanyahu's support for Arab democracy was far less equivocal, as he called on neighboring Arab autocrats "to put the issues of human rights and democratization on their agenda" as an essential "pillar of lasting peace."

5. Aluf Benn, "Israel's Lost Chance," *New York Times,* July 29, 2011 (www.nytimes.com/2011/07/30/opinion/netanyahu-missed-opportunity.html?_r=1).

6. PA foreign minister Riad Al-Malki quoted in Tovah Lazaroff, "'The Window for a Negotiated Peace Ends in September'," *Jerusalem Post,* March 23, 2011 (www.jpost.com/MiddleEast/Article.aspx?id=213386).

7. See Palestinian Center for Policy Studies and Research, Palestinian Public Opinion Poll 39, April 10, 2011 (www.pcpsr.org/survey/polls/2011/p39efull.html#peaceprocess).

8. For more on the rationale behind the Palestinian UN strategy, see Mahmoud Abbas, "The Long Overdue Palestinian State," *New York Times,* May 17, 2011. See also Dan Ephron, "The Wrath of Abbas" (interview with Abbas), *Newsweek,* April 24, 2011.

9. In addition, the U.S. election calendar presents another important disincentive for tackling the Israeli-Palestinian question, given its high emotive value for several key domestic constituencies and the high probability that it will be exploited for partisan political purposes. Some of this was evident following Obama's Middle East speech, in which many of the president's partisan rivals sought to transform an otherwise uncontroversial reference to the "1967 lines" into a political "wedge" issue.

10. In a May 17, 2011, Pew Report, "Obama's Challenge in the Muslim World: Arab Spring Fails to Improve U.S. Image," the Obama administration's policies on the Israeli-Palestinian conflict received the lowest marks, with disapproval from at least eight in ten in Lebanon, Egypt, and Jordan and nearly seven in ten in Turkey (http://pewglobal. org/2011/05/17/arab-spring-fails-to-improve-us-image/2/#1-opinions-of-the-u-s-and-president-barack-obama).

11. The offer would have provided Israel with twenty F-35 fighter jets and unprecedented diplomatic and security guarantees in exchange for a ninety-day extension of a partial, temporary "moratorium" on settlement construction in the West Bank, though excluding East Jerusalem settlements, which account for some 40 percent of the total settler population. For details of the proposal, see David Makovsky, "Dear Prime Minister: U.S. Efforts to Keep the Peace Process on Track," Washington Institute for Near East Policy, PolicyWatch #1707, September 29, 2010 (www.washingtoninstitute.org/templateC05. php?CID=3256). See also Barak Ravid, "Netanyahu Rejects U.S. Guarantees in Exchange for Renewing Freeze," *Ha'aretz,* October 1, 2010 (www.haaretz.com/print-edition/news/ netanyahu-rejects-u-s-guarantees-in-exchange-for-renewing-freeze-1.316517).

12. See, for example, Editorial, "Egypt's New Foreign Policy," *Washington Post,* May 10, 2010 (www.washingtonpost.com/opinions/egypts-new-foreign-policy/2011/05/10/ AFEI53jG_story.html); Jeffrey Fleishman, "Egypt's New Foreign Policy Tests Old Alliances," *Los Angeles Times,* May 8, 2011 (http://articles.latimes.com/2011/may/08/world/ la-fg-egypt-diplomacy-20110508); Hassan Nafaa, "Egypt's Changing Foreign Policy," *Al-Masry Al-Youm,* May 3, 2011 (www.almasryalyoum.com/en/node/422298); Marwa Awad, "Palestinian Accord a Signal of Egypt Policy Shift," Reuters, April 29, 2011 (www.todays zaman.com/news-242376-palestinian-accord-a-signal-of-egypt-policy-shift.html); Doaa El-Bey, "Bowing to Popular Will," *Al-Ahram Weekly,* May 5-11, 2011 (http://weekly.ahram.org. eg/2011/1046/eg1.htm).

13. Prince Turki Al-Faisal, "Veto a State, Lose an Ally," *New York Times,* September 11, 2011 (http://www.nytimes.com/2011/09/12/opinion/veto-a-state-lose-an-ally.html).

14. The Quartet plan called for new negotiations within one month. The parties would then have three months to put forward "comprehensive proposals" on territory and security and six months to show "substantial progress." Agreement on all remaining issues would be reached no later than the end of 2012.

15. Minister of Foreign and European Affairs Alain Juppé, "Visit to Israel and the Palestinian Territories," statements at his joint press conference with Prime Minister Salam Fayyad of the Palestinian Authority, June 2, 2011 (http://www.ambafrance-uk.org/Alain-Juppe-outlines-proposals-for).

16. President Sarkozy Address to the UN General Assembly, September 21, 2011 (http:// www.consulfrance-atlanta.org/spip.php?article3093)

17. See Daniel Levy, "America's Attempted Quartet Sophistry," *Foreign Policy,* July 22, 2011 (http://mideast.foreignpolicy.com/posts/2011/07/22/palestine_israel_the_un_and_ america_s_attempted_quartet_sophistry).

CHAPTER SEVEN

1. James T. Quinlivan, "Coup-Proofing: Its Practice and Consequences in the Middle East," *International Security* 24 (Fall 1999).

2. On Turkish civil-military affairs, see Tuba Unlu Bilgic, "The Military and Europeanization Reforms in Turkey," *Middle Eastern Studies* 45 (September 2009): 803–24; Steven A. Cook, *Ruling but Not Governing: The Military and Political Development in Egypt, Algeria and Turkey* (Johns Hopkins University Press, 2007); Tanel Demirel, "Soldiers and Civilians: The Dilemma of Turkish Democracy," *Middle Eastern Studies* 40 (January 2004): 127–50; Metin Heper and Aylin Guney, "The Military and Democracy in the Third Turkish Republic," *Armed Forces and Society* 22 (Summer 1996): 619–42, and "The Military and Consolidation of Democracy: The Recent Turkish Experience," *Armed Forces and Society* 26 (Summer 2000): 635–57; Richard M. Lim, The Paradox of Turkish Civil Military Relations," *Journal of Applied Security Research* 6, no. 2 (2011): 255–72; Ergun Ozbudun, "Democratization Reforms in Turkey, 1993–2004," *Turkish Studies* 8 (June 2007): 179–96.

3. Sheri Berman, "Islamism, Revolution and Civil Society," *Perspectives on Politics* 1 (June 2003): 261; Theda Skocpol, *States and Social Revolutions: A Comparative Analysis of France, Russia and China* (Cambridge University Press, 1979), and *Social Revolutions in the Modern World* (Cambridge University Press, 1994).

4. While there are many theories of civil-military relations, all agree on the need for balance—although all believe that the balance is derived from differing sources. See, for instance, Peter D. Feaver, *Armed Servants: Agency, Oversight, and Civil-Military Relations* (Harvard University Press, 2003); Samuel E. Finer, *The Man on Horseback: The Role of the Military in Politics* (London: Pall Mall Press, 1962); Samuel P. Huntington, *The Soldier and the State: The Theory and Politics of Civil-Military Relations* (Harvard University Press, 1957); Rebecca L. Schiff, "Civil-Military Relations Reconsidered: A Theory of Concordance," *Armed Forces and Society* 22, no. 1 (1995): 7–24; Girotra Vinay, "Civil-Military Relations: Theoretical Explanation" (http://peterschifffan.oldschooleconomics.com/schiff/civil-military-relations [April 5, 2011]).

5. Kenneth M. Pollack, "The Influence of Arab Culture on Arab Military Effectiveness," Ph.D. dissertation, Massachusetts Institute of Technology, 1996.

6. On the critical role of political culture in civil-military affairs in a democracy, see, in particular, Douglas L. Bland, "A Unified Theory of Civil-Military Relations," *Armed Forces and Society* 26 (Fall 1999): 7–25, and "Patterns in Liberal Democratic Civil-Military Relations," *Armed Forces and Society* 27 (Summer 2001): 525–40.

7. On civil-military relations and the transition to democracy, see Singh Bilveer, "Civil-Military Relations in Democratizing Indonesia: Change amidst Continuity," *Armed Forces and Society* 26 (Summer 2000): 607–33; Andrew Cottey, Timothy Edmunds, and Anthony Forster, "The Second Generation Problematic: Rethinking Democracy and Civil Military Relations," *Armed Forces and Society* 29 (Fall 2002): 31–56; Aurel Croissant, "Riding the Tiger: Civilian Control of the Military in Democratizing Korea," *Armed Forces and Society* 30 (Spring 2004): 357–81; Aurel Croissant and David Kuehn, "Patterns of Civilian Control of the Military in East Asia's New Democracies," *Journal of East Asian Studies*, no. 9 (2009): 187–217; Gregory D. Foster, "Civil-Military Relations: The Postmodern Democratic Challenge," *World Affairs* 167 (Winter 2005): 91–100; Yong Cheol Kim, R. William Liddle, and Salim Said, "Political Leadership and Civilian Supremacy in Third Wave Democracies: Comparing South Korea and Indonesia," *Political Affairs* 79 (Summer 2006): 247–68; Ruth Stanley, "Modes of Transition v. Electoral Dynamics: Democratic Control of the Military in Argentina and Chile," *Journal of Third World Studies* 28 (Fall 2001): 71–91; Gregory Weeks, "Is the Mold Being Broken? Defense Ministries and Democracy in Latin America," *Journal of*

Political and Military Sociology 31 (Summer 2003): 23–37; Paul W. Zagorski, "Civil-Military Relations and Argentine Democracy: The Armed Forces under the Menem Government," *Armed Forces and Society* 20 (Spring 1994): 423–37.

8. For antecedents of the pressures on Arab militaries to democratize, see Kirk Campbell, "Civil-Military Relations and Political Liberalization: A Comparative Study of the Military's Corporateness and Political Values in Egypt, Syria, Turkey, and Pakistan," Ph.D. dissertation, George Washington University, 2009, esp. p. 31; Birthe Hansen and Carsten Jensen, "Challenges to the Role of Arab Militaries," in *Developments in Civil-Military Relations in the Middle East,* edited by Carsten Jensen (Copenhagen: Royal Danish Defense College University Press, 2008).

9. For more detailed recommendations, see Steven Cook, "The Unspoken Power: Civil-Military Relations and the Prospects for Reform," Analysis Paper 7 (Brookings Project on U.S. Policy toward the Islamic World, 2004).

10. Nathan G. Forbes, "Supplying Democracy? U.S. Security Assistance to Jordan, 1989–2002," Ph.D. dissertation, Naval Postgraduate School, 2003, esp. pp. 55–56.

11. On the dangers of this for democratic development, see Michael Desch, *Civilian Control of the Military: The Changing Security Environment* (John Hopkins University Press, 1999).

CHAPTER EIGHT

1. Roger Cohen, "Facebook and Arab Dignity," *New York Times,* January 24, 2011.

2. Stephen Glain, "Slow Death: Why Are Arab Economies on the Verge of Crisis?" *Newsweek,* October 7, 2002, p. 22.

3. "Creating Opportunities for Future Generations," *Arab Human Development Report,* (United Nations Development Program, 2002), p. 78.

4. Marcus Noland and Howard Pack, *The Arab Economies in a Changing World* (Washington: Peterson Institute for International Economics, 2007), p. 5.

5. "The Economics of Revolution," *Middle East,* March 2011, p. 19.

6. Glain, "Slow Death," p. 22.

7. See, for example, Jack A. Goldstone, Ted Robert Gurr, and Farrokh Moshiri, *Revolutions of the Late Twentieth Century* (Boulder, Colo.: Westview Press, 1991); Ted Robert Gurr, *Why Men Rebel* (Princeton University Press, 1970); Samuel Huntington, *Political Order in Changing Societies* (Yale University Press, 1968); Barrington Moore Jr., *Social Origins of Dictatorship and Democracy: Lord and Peasant in the Making of the Modern World* (Boston : Beacon Press, 1966); Theda Skocpol, *States and Social Revolutions: A Comparative Analysis of France, Russia and China* (Cambridge University Press, 1979); John Walton, *Reluctant Rebels: Comparative Studies of Revolution and Underdevelopment* (Columbia University Press, 1984); Nikki R. Keddie, ed., *Debating Revolutions* (New York University Press, 1995); Charles Tilly, *From Mobilization to Revolution* (Reading, Mass.: Addison-Wesley, 1978) and "Does Modernization Breed Revolution?" *Comparative Politics* 5 (April 1973). The 1979 Islamic Revolution in Iran contributed to a rethinking, including an effort by Skocpol to adapt her conclusions to the Iranian case, in "Rentier State and Shi'a Islam in the Iranian Revolution," *Theory and Society* 11 (1982): 265–83.

8. Omar S. Dahi, "Understanding the Political Economy of the Arab Revolts," *Middle East Report* 259 (Summer 2011): 2–6.

9. Edward Sayre and Samantha Constant, "Why the Middle East's 'Youth Bulge' Is Key to the Region's Stability," *National Journal,* February 17, 2011.

10. "Light, Dark and Muddle: Egypt's Economy," *The Economist,* June 25, 2011.

11. For the relevance of economic success to political outcomes in Turkey, see Steven Cook, "Is It The Economy, Stupid?" From the Potomac to the Euphrates blog (http://blogs. cfr.org/cook/2011/06/16/is-it-the-economy-stupid/ [June 16, 2011]).

12. See also Najmeh Bozorgmehr, "Business Reluctant to Cut Loose from Asad Regime," *Financial Times,* June 3, 2011, p. 8.

13. George T. Abed and others, "The Arab World in Transition: Assessing the Economic Impact," May 2, 2011, p. 3 (www.iif.com/emr/resources+1200.php).

14. For example, 36 percent of Turkish businesses reported that the Arab Spring had had a negative impact on their operations. "Global Firms Upbeat on Mideast Despite Unrest," *Khaleej Times,* June 23, 2011.

15. "The Economics of Revolution," *Middle East,* March 2011, p. 18.

16. Jumana Al Tamimi, "Campaign Encourages Tourists to Visit the Land of Peaceful Revolution," *Gulf News,* June 27, 2011.

17. Robert F. Worth and Laura Kasinof, "Chaos in Yemen Drives Economy to Edge of Ruin," *New York Times,* June 3, 2011, p. 1.

18. Abed and others, "The Arab World in Transition: Assessing the Economic Impact."

19. Bill Spindle, "Jordan, Too, Feels the Heat of Arab Spring Protests," *Wall Street Journal,* July 13, 2011.

20. "Algeria Govt Approves Big Hike in Public Spending," Reuters, May 3, 2011.

21. Niall Ferguson, "The Revolution Blows Up," *Newsweek,* June 13–20, 2011, p. 24.

22. Robert Powell, "The Economic Fallout of the Arab Spring (Part 1): Bad for Business?" *EIU Country Forecast Select,* June 20, 2011.

23. Interestingly, the Formula 1 case appears to be one in which celebrity activism within the sport itself helped persuade the race organizers to formally cancel the event. "Bahrain's Crash Course," *Wall Street Journal,* June 9, 2011.

24. Michael Peel, "Companies Feel the Heat in Mideast Revolution, *Financial Times,* June 29, 2011, p. 6.

25. "Global Firms Upbeat on Mideast Despite Unrest."

26. Pew Research Center, "Common Concerns about Islamic Extremism: Muslim-Western Tensions Persist" (Washington, July 21, 2011), pp. 54–55.

27. "Reform to Cost $25 Billion over 5 Years: Tunisia Finmin," Reuters, May 27, 2011.

28. Spindle, "Jordan, Too, Feels the Heat of Arab Spring Protests."

Chapter Nine

1. This chapter draws heavily on Daniel L. Byman, "Terrorism after the Revolutions," *Foreign Affairs* (May/June 2011) (www.foreignaffairs.com/articles/67697/daniel-byman/ terrorism-after-the-revolutions), and "Al Qaeda's Terrible Spring," *Foreign Affairs* (May 24, 2011) (www.foreignaffairs.com/articles/67864/daniel-byman/al-Qaedas-terrible-spring).

2. Ayman al-Zawahiri, "Message of Hope and Glad Tidings to Our People in Egypt," Episode 3, March 3, 2011.

3. See, for example, "Tsunami of Change," *Inspire* magazine, Spring 2011 (http://jihadology.net/2011/03/29/al-qa%E2%80%99idah-in-the-arabian-peninsula%E2%80%99s-al-mala%E1%B8%A5im-media-releases-inspire-magazine-issue-5/). See also al-Zawahiri, "Message of Hope and Glad Tidings to Our People in Egypt," Episode 5, April 14, 2011, and Episode 3, March 3, 2011; and Sheikh Abu Yahya al-Libi, "To our People in Libya," April 21, 2011(www.ansarullah.co.cc).

4. This quotation is from Brian Fishman, "At a Loss for Words," *Foreign Policy,* February 15, 2011 (www.foreignpolicy.com/articles/2011/02/15/at_a_loss_for_words).

5. See Zawahiri's "Questions and Answers" (www.nefafoundation.org/miscellaneous/.../nefazawahiri0408.pdf).

6. See the statement by Yahya Ibrahim in "Tsunami of Change," p. 1.

7. Zawahiri, "Message of Hope and Glad Tidings to Our People in Egypt," Episode 5, p. 3.

CHAPTER TEN

1. For more on the quantitative and qualitative evidence of support for democracy in the Middle East, see John L. Esposito and Dalia Mogahed, *Who Speaks for Islam: What a Billion Muslims Really Think* (New York: Gallup Press, 2008), pp. 31–32, 47–48, 57–58; Amaney A. Jamal, "Reassessing Support for Islam and Democracy in the Arab World? Evidence from Egypt and Jordan," *World Affairs* 169 (Fall 2006): 51–64; Thomas Carothers and Marina Ottaway, "The New Democracy Imperative," in *Uncharted Journey: Promoting Democracy in the Middle East,* edited by Thomas Carothers and Marina Ottaway (Washington: Carnegie Endowment for International Peace, 2005), p. 8; Abdou Filali-Ansary, "Muslims and Democracy," in *Islam and Democracy in the Middle East,* edited by Larry Diamond, Marc F. Plattner, and Daniel Brumberg (Johns Hopkins University Press, 2003), pp. 199–201; Amy Hawthorne, "The New Reform Ferment," in *Uncharted Journey,* edited by Carothers and Ottaway; Radwan A. Masmoudi, "The Silenced Majority," in *Islam and Democracy in the Middle East,* edited by Diamond and others, pp. 260–62; and Kenneth M. Pollack, *A Path Out of the Desert: A Grand Strategy for America in the Middle East* (New York: Random House, 2008), pp. 221–45.

2. Fareed Zakaria, "The Rise of Illiberal Democracy," *Foreign Affairs* 76 (November/December 1997).

3. See, for instance, Ted Robert Gurr, *People Versus States: Minorities at Risk in the New Century* (Washington: United States Institute of Peace, 2000).

4. The best-known work on this—although one that is not without considerable problems—is Edward D. Mansfield and Jack Snyder, *Electing to Fight: Why Emerging Democracies Go to War* (Harvard University, John F. Kennedy School of Government, 2005).

5. Farid E. Khazen, *The Breakdown of the State in Lebanon, 1967–1976* (London: I. B. Tauris, 2000).

6. On democratization and democratization in the Middle East, see Carothers and Ottaway, eds., *Uncharted Journey;* Thomas Carothers, "How Democracies Emerge: The 'Sequencing' Fallacy," *Journal of Democracy* 18 (January 2007): 13-27, and "The Democracy Crusade Myth," *National Interest,* no. 90 (July/August 2007); Diamond and others, eds., *Islam and Democracy in the Middle East;* Robert A. Dahl, *Democracy and Its Critics* (Yale University Press, 1989); John P. Entelis, "The Democratic Imperative vs. the Authoritarian Impulse: The Maghrib State between Transition and Terrorism," *Middle East Journal* 59 (Autumn 2005): 537–38; Michael C. Hudson, "After the Gulf War: Prospects for Democratization in the Arab World," *Middle East Journal* 45 (Summer 1991): 407–26; Barrington Moore Jr., *Social Origins of Dictatorship and Democracy: Lord and Peasant in the Making of the Modern World* (Boston: Beacon Press, 1966); Muhammad Muslih and Augustus Richard Norton, "The Need for Arab Democracy," *Foreign Policy* 83 (Summer 1991): 3; Tim Niblock, "Democratisation: A Theoretical and Practical Debate," *British Journal of Middle Eastern Studies* 25 (November 1998): 229; United Nations Development Programme (UNDP), Arab Fund for Economic and Social Development, *Arab Human Development Report, 2003* (New York, 2003), esp. pp. 151–57; Tamara Cofman Wittes, *Freedom's Unsteady March: America's Role in Promoting Arab Democracy* (Brookings, 2008).

7. On institutions, see Amy Hawthorne, "Is Civil Society the Answer?" in *Uncharted Journey,* edited by Carothers and Ottaway; Samuel P. Huntington, "Will Countries Become More Democratic?" *Political Science Quarterly* 99 (Summer 1984); Elie Kedourie, *Democracy and Arab Political Culture* (Washington: Institute for Near East Policy, 1992); James Kurth, "Ignoring History: U.S. Democratization in the Muslim World," *Orbis* 49 (Spring 2005): 30710.

8. Larry Diamond, ed., *The Return to Political Culture? Political Culture and Democracy in Developing Countries* (Boulder, Colo.: Lynne Rienner, 1993); Seymour Lipset, "The Social Requisites of Democracy Revisited," *American Sociological Review* 59 (February 1994): 1–22; Adam Przeworski and others, "What Makes Democracies Endure?" *Journal of Democracy* 7 (January 1996): 39–55.

9. For an interesting perspective on culture and democratization in the Arab world, see Lawrence Rosen, "Expecting the Unexpected: Cultural Components of Arab Governance," *Annals of the American Academy of Political and Social Science* 603 (January 2006): 163–78.

10. Steven Heydemann, "Upgrading Authoritarianism in the Arab World," Analysis Paper 13 (Brookings Saban Center for Middle East Policy, October 2007), p. 13.

11. See also Filali-Ansary, "Muslims and Democracy," in *Islam and Democracy in the Middle East,* edited by Diamond and others, pp. 202–03; John L. Esposito, "Political Islam and U.S. Foreign Policy," *Harvard International Review,* November 2, 2006; Graham Fuller, "Islamists and Democracy," in *Uncharted Journey,* edited by Carothers and Ottaway, pp. 37–55; Shadi Hamid, "The Rise of the Islamists: How Islamists Will Change Politics, and Vice Versa," *Foreign Affairs* 90 (May/June 2011): 40–48; Anwar Ibrahim, "Universal Values and Muslim Democracy," *Journal of Democracy* 17 (July 2006): 5–12; Farhad Kazemi, "The Inclusion Imperative," *Middle East Studies Association Bulletin,* December 1996; April Longley, "The High-Water Mark of Islamist Politics? The Case of Yemen," *Middle East Journal* 61 (Spring 2007): 240–45; Dalia Mogahed and Geneive Abdo, "Islam and Democracy," Special Report: Muslim World, Gallup World Poll, 2006, p. 3; Dalia Mogahed, "Understanding Islamic Democracy," *Europe's World,* no. 2 (Spring 2006), pp. 163–65; Jillian Schwedler, "Democratization, Inclusion and the Moderation of Islamist Parties," *Development* 50 (January 2007); David Smock, "Islam and Democracy," Special Report 93 (Washington: United States Institute of Peace, September 2002).

12. On the persistent threat of dictatorship, see Eva Bellin, "The Robustness of Authoritarianism in the Middle East: Exceptionalism in Comparative Perspective," *Comparative Politics* 36, no. 2 (2004); Marsha Pripstein Posusney and Michele Penner Angrist, eds., *Authoritarianism in the Middle East: Regimes and Resistance* (Boulder, Colo.: Lynne Rienner, 2005).

CHAPTER ELEVEN

1. U.S. State Department, "Remarks by the President on the Middle East and North Africa," Washington, May 19, 2011 (www.whitehouse.gov/the-press-office/2011/05/19/remarks-president-middle-east-and-north-africa [July 8, 2011]). Also see the remarks by Secretary of Defense Robert Gates on May 26, 2011, in "e-Newsletter: Why Iraq Still Matters" (Washington: Institute for the Study of War, June 2, 2011) (http://app.e2ma.net/app2/campaigns/archived/1409103/c8efa4d8280aad9561ea3b0ebd2e9525/ [July 8, 2011]).

2. For the best explanations and descriptions of the American mismanagement of the reconstruction of Iraq to date, see Larry Diamond, *Squandered Victory: The American Occupation and the Bungled Effort to Bring Democracy to Iraq* (New York: Times Books, 2005); James Fallows, "Blind into Baghdad," *Atlantic Monthly* 293 (January/February 2004); Michael Gordon and Bernard Trainor, *Cobra II: The Inside Story of the Invasion and Occupation of Iraq* (New York: Pantheon, 2006); George Packer, *The Assassin's Gate: America in*

Iraq (New York: Farrar, Straus and Giroux, 2005); David L. Phillips, *Losing Iraq: Inside the Postwar Reconstruction Fiasco* (Boulder, Colo.: Westview Press, 2005); Kenneth M. Pollack, "The Seven Deadly Sins of Failure in Iraq: A Retrospective Analysis of the Reconstruction," *Middle East Review of International Affairs* 10 (December 2006); Thomas E. Ricks, *Fiasco: The American Military Adventure in Iraq* (New York: Penguin, 2006).

3. This is a classic pattern for the onset of civil wars. See Barry Posen, "The Security Dilemma and Ethnic Conflict," *Survival* 35 (Spring 1993): 27–47; John Mueller, "The Banality of 'Ethnic War,'" *International Security* 25 (Summer 2002): 42–70.

4. On why and how the Surge succeeded in reversing Iraq's descent into civil war and creating a democratic outburst in Iraq, see Kimberly Kagan, *The Surge: A Military History* (New York: Encounter Books, 2008); Kenneth M. Pollack, "The Battle for Baghdad," *National Interest,* no. 103 (September/October 2009), pp. 8–18; Stephen Biddle, Michael E. O'Hanlon, and Kenneth M. Pollack, "Standing Down as Iraq Stands Up: Building on Progress," *Foreign Affairs* 87 (September/October 2008): 40–58.

5. For a fuller discussion of what Iraq needs to accomplish and how the United States should act to help bring this about, see Kenneth M. Pollack and others, *Unfinished Business: An American Strategy for Iraq Moving Forward* (Brookings, 2010). This section draws heavily on the recommendations of that book.

6. On the "commissarist" variant of politicization, see chapter 7.

Chapter Twelve

1. For more on civil-military relations in Egypt, see Steven Cook, *Ruling but Not Governing: The Military and Political Development in Egypt, Algeria and Turkey* (John Hopkins University Press, 2007).

2. The Solidarity Center, "Justice for All: The Struggle for Workers' Rights in Egypt" (Washington, February 2010), p. 14.

3. Abu Dhabi Gallup Center, "Egypt From Tahrir to Transition," June 2011 (www.abudhabigallupcenter.com/147896/Egypt-Tahrir-Transition.aspx).

4. See chapter 4.

5. Another analogy is with Iraq in 1958, when General 'Abd al-Karim Qasim and his own band of pan-Arab officers overthrew King Feisal. They, too, were hailed as liberators and revolutionaries by the Iraqi people who desperately sought the end of the hated monarchy.

6. A senior general said the women "were not like your daughter or mine. These were girls who had camped out in tents with male protesters."

7. Human Rights Watch, "Military Trials Usurp Justice System," April 29, 2011 (www.hrw.org/en/news/2011/04/29/egypt-military-trials-usurp-justice-system).

8. Noha El-Hennawy, "Brotherhood Divided over Friday Protests," *Al Masry al Youm* (www.almasryalyoum.com/en/node/452783).

9. For more on the Brotherhood's role in post-revolutionary Egypt, see chapter 4.

10. Joel D. Barkan, Paul J. Densham, and Gerard Rushton, "Space Matters: Designing Better Electoral Systems for Emerging Democracies," *American Journal of Political Science* 50 (October 2006): 926.

11. The vast majority of groups support a proportional system. Even the Brotherhood, the group most likely to benefit from a majoritarian system, has called for proportional representation.

12. Nazih N. Ayubi, "Government and the State in Egypt Today," in *Egypt under Mubarak,* edited by Charles Tripp and Roger Owen (New York: Routledge, 1989), p. 18.

13. A qualitative change in the regime's treatment of the opposition occurred in the early 1990s. See, for example, Hasanayn Tawfiq Ibrahim, *Al-Nizam al-Siyasi wa al-Ikhwan al-Muslimun fi Misr: Min al-Tasamuh ila al-Muwajaha, 1981–1996* [The Political System and the Muslim Brotherhood in Egypt: From Tolerance to Confrontation] (Beirut: Dar al-Tali'ah li al-Tiba'a wa al-Nashr, 1998), p. 6; Hesham al-Awadi, *In Pursuit of Legitimacy: The Muslim Brothers and Mubarak, 1982–2000* (London: Tauris Academic Studies, 2004), p. 193; Eberhard Kienle, "More than a Response to Islamism: The Political Deliberalization of Egypt in the 1990s," *Middle East Journal* 52 (Spring 1998): 221.

14. Pew Global Attitudes Project, June 17, 2010 (http://pewresearch.org/pubs/1630/obama-more-popular-abroad-global-american-image-benefit-22-nation-global-survey).

15. See Pew Global Attitudes Project, "Egyptians Embrace Revolt Leaders, Religious Parties and Military, as Well," April 25, 2011 (ttp://pewresearch.org/pubs/1971/egypt-poll-democracy-elections-islam-military-muslim-brotherhood-april-6-movement-israel-obama), "Osama bin Laden Largely Discredited among Muslim Publics in Recent Years," May 2, 2011 (http://pewresearch.org/pubs/1977/poll-osama-bin-laden-death-confidence-muslim-publics-al-Qaeda-favorability).

16. For more on the theory and its assumptions, see Alastair Smith, "Diversionary Foreign Policy in Democratic Systems," *International Studies Quarterly* 40 (March 1996): 133–53. See also Scott Bennett and Timothy Nordstrom, "Foreign Policy Substitutability and Internal Economic Problems in Enduring Rivalries," *Journal of Conflict Resolution* 44 (February 2000): 33–61.

17. For more on U.S.-Egypt relations during the Bush and Obama administrations, see Shadi Hamid, "Cairo Conundrum," *Democracy: A Journal of Ideas* (Winter 2010) (www.democracyjournal.org/15/6726.php); and Michele Dunne, "The Baby, the Bathwater and the Freedom Agenda in the Middle East," *Washington Quarterly,* January 2009, pp. 132–34.

18. Pew Global Attitudes Project, April 25, 2011.

19. International Monetary Fund, World Economic Outlook Database (www.imf.org/external/pubs/ft/weo/2011/01/weodata/index.aspx).

20. "Tourism to Egypt Down 46 Percent in First Quarter," Reuters, May 22, 2011 (http://af.reuters.com/article/investingNews/idAFJOE74L02G20110522).

21. Sarah Topol, "Egypt's Command Economy," *Slate,* December 15, 2010 (www.slate.com/id/2278044/).

Chapter Thirteen

1. For an explanation of why Ben Ali failed to follow through on his pledges, see Christopher Alexander, "Back from the Democratic Brink: Authoritarianism and Civil Society in Tunisia," *Middle East Report* 205 (October/December 1997): 34–38.

2. World Bank, "Doing Business 2009: Comparing Regulation in 181 Economies" (Washington, 2008), p. 79.

3. "About 300 People Killed in Original Tunisian Uprising, U.N. Reports," CNN, May 21, 2011 (http://articles.cnn.com/2011-05-21/world/tunisia.un_1_tunisian-uprising-human-rights-interim-government?_s=PM:WORLD).

4. Graham Usher, "The Reawakening of Nahda in Tunisia," Middle East Research and Information Project Online, April 30, 2011 (www.merip.org/mero/mero043011).

5. While the commission's decisions are not formally binding, they are effectively treated as such by the interim government. See Amine Ghali, "Tunisia's Moment of Opportunity" (Washington: Project on Middle East Democracy, January 28, 2011), p. 1.

6. Joel D. Barkan, Paul J. Densham, and Gerard Rushton, "Space Matters: Designing Better electoral Systems for Emerging Democracies," *American Journal of Political Science* 50 (October 2006): 926.

7. For an explanation of Tunisia's electoral system, see Jeff Fischer and Clement Henry, "Tunisia: Pre-election Technical Assessment" (Washington: International Foundation for Electoral Systems, January 31, 1994), p. 14.

8. This dynamic has surfaced in other countries in transition. During the Third Wave of democratization, Karen Remmer wrote that experiences under Latin American dictators generated "a willingness to compromise and moderate demands in the interest of avoiding relapses into authoritarianism." Karen Remmer, "New Wine or Old Bottlenecks? The Study of Latin American Politics," *Comparative Politics* 23 (July 1991). Ironically, then, authoritarianism can help create the very conditions that give rise to its opposite. It is often in democracy's absence—rather than its presence—that political actors realize just how important it is to the health of the political system. As the Chilean socialist Jorge Arrate once noted: "The loss of democracy and its denigration in the official discourse [of the dictatorship] induce a more profound appreciation of the value, meaning and contents of political democracy." Nancy Bermeo, "Democracy and the Lessons of Dictatorship," *Comparative Politics* 22 (April 1992): 278.

9. At around 1.5 percent of GDP, military spending in Tunisia has been significantly lower than in most other Arab countries.

10. For more on how pretransition legacies affect democratic transition, see Frances Hagopian, "After Regime Change: Authoritarian Legacies, Political Representation, and the Democratic Future of South America," *World Politics* 45 (April 1993).

11. For a discussion of MTI's origins and rise, see Marion Boulby, "The Islamic Challenge: Tunisia since Independence," *Third World Quarterly* 10 (April 1988): 590–614; and Emad Shahin, *Political Ascent: Contemporary Islamic Movements in North Africa* (Boulder, Colo.: Westview Press, 1997). For discussion of Islamists' relationship to trade unions and the left more generally, see Christopher Alexander, "Opportunities, Organizations, and Ideas: Islamists and Workers in Tunisia and Algeria," *International Journal of Middle East Studies* 32 (November 2000): 465–90.

12. For a sympathetic but informative biography of Ghannouchi as well as a broader discussion of Nahda's ideological evolution, see Azzam Tamimi, *Rachid Ghannouchi: A Democrat within Islamism* (Oxford University Press, 2001).

13. For Ghannouchi's first post-revolution interview, see "Interview Transcript: Rachid Ghannouchi," *Financial Times*, January 18, 2011 (www.ft.com/intl/cms/s/0/24d710a6-22ee-11e0-ad0b-00144feab49a.html).

14. Usher, "Reawakening of Nahda."

15. "Interview Transcript: Rachid Ghannouchi."

16. Usher, "Reawakening of Nahda."

17. U.S. Department of State, "Recent Protests and Website Hackings in Tunisia," January 7, 2011 (www.state.gov/r/pa/prs/ps/2011/01/154139.htm).

18. For a full transcript of Clinton's interview, see "Clinton Tackles Tunisia, Iran, Lebanon & Mideast Talks," Al Arabiya, January 12, 2011.

19. White House, "Statement by the President on Events in Tunisia," January 14, 2011.

20. Alexis Arieff, "Political Transition in Tunisia," Congressional Research Service Report for Congress, June 27, 2011, p. 10.

21. Stephen McInerney, "The Federal Budget and Appropriations for Fiscal Year 2012: Democracy, Governance and Human Rights in the Middle East" (Washington: Project on Middle East Democracy, July 2011).

22. "Declaration of the G8 on the Arab Spring," G8 Summit, Deauville, May 26–27, 2011 (www.g20-g8.com/g8-g20/g8/english/the-2011-summit/declarations-and-reports/declarations/declaration-of-the-g8-on-the-arab-springs.1316.html).

23. See the International Monetary Fund's World Economic Outlook Database (www.imf.org/external/pubs/ft/weo/2011/01/weodata/weoselgr.aspx).

24. Daphne Benoit, "Tunisia Seeks Way between Unrest and Uncertainty," Agence France-Presse, June 5 2011 (http://news.yahoo.com/s/afp/20110605/bs_afp/tunisiaeconomy tourismsocial_20110605055206).

25. "Tunisia Needs $125 Billion in Funding over 5 years: Report," Reuters, May 29, 2011 (www.reuters.com/article/2011/05/29/us-tunisia-economy-idUSTRE74S13O20110529).

26. See, for example, Adam Przeworski and Fernando Limongi, "Modernization: Theories and Facts," *World Politics* 49 (January 1997): 155–83; Seymour Martin Lipset, "Some Social Requisites of Democracy: Economic Development and Political Legitimacy," *American Political Science Review* 53 (March 1959). As Przeworski has noted, no democracy with a per capita income higher than $6,055 has ever collapsed: Adam Przeworski, "Why Do Political Parties Obey Results of Elections," in *Democracy and the Rule of Law*, edited by Jose Maria Maravall and Adam Przeworski (Cambridge University Press, 2003), p. 115. Accounting for inflation, Przeworski's threshold figure comes out to $12,656 in 2010 dollars. According to 2010 figures, Tunisia enjoys a per capita income of $9,483. On a purchasing power parity basis, see Charles Landow, "The Economic Approach to Middle East Democracy," CFR.org, June 8, 2011 (http://blogs.cfr.org/coleman/2011/06/08/the-economic-approach-to-middle-east-democracy/). Thus Tunisia is not quite there yet, but it is close.

27. Political development can spur economic growth, and not just the other way around. Moreover, it may be that income per capita is collinear with other noneconomic variables.

CHAPTER FOURTEEN

1. See "Laws of Associations," Programme on Governance in the Arab Region (www.undp-pogar.org/countries/theme.aspx?cid=10&t=2).

2. On the history and performance of the Libyan military in Uganda, Chad, and elsewhere, see Kenneth M. Pollack, *Arabs at War: Military Effectiveness, 1948–1991* (University of Nebraska Press, 2002), pp. 358–424.

3. International Crisis Group, "Popular Protest in North Africa and the Middle East (V): Making Sense of Libya," Middle East/North Africa Report 107 (Brussels, June 6, 2011), pp. 19–20 (www.crisisgroup.org/en/regions/middle-east-north-africa/north-africa/libya/107-popular-protest-in-north-africa-and-the-middle-east-v-making-sense-of-libya.aspx).

4. Human Rights Watch, "Libya: June 1996 Killings at Abu Salim Prison," June 28, 2006 (www.hrw.org/en/reports/2006/06/28/libya-june-1996-killings-abu-salim-prison).

5. According to some news accounts, Qadhafi actually said he would join the protesters, in an apparent attempt at co-opting the movement and directing anger at the government (namely, the prime minister) rather than at himself.

6. "Libya Revolt: Qadhafi in Crimes against Humanity Probe," *BBC News,* March 3, 2011 (www.bbc.co.uk/news/world-africa-12636798); Secretary-General's Remarks to the General Assembly on Libya," March 1, 2011 (www.un.org/apps/sg/sgstats.asp?nid=5116).

7. For two good accounts of the fall of Tripoli, see Nicolas Pelham, "Libya: How They Did It," *New York Review of Books* 58, no.14 (August 29, 2011) (www.nybooks.com/articles/archives/2011/sep/29/libya-how-they-did-it/?pagination=false); Anand Gopal, "The Tripoli Uprising," *Foreign Policy,* September 1, 2011 (www.foreignpolicy.com/articles/2011/09/01/the_tripoli_uprising?page=full)

8. For more on Islamists in Libya, see Christopher Boucek, "Dangerous Fallout from Libya's Implosion" (Washington: Carnegie Endowment for International Peace, March 9, 2011) (www.carnegieendowment.org/2011/03/09/dangerous-fallout-from-libya-s-implosion/6s9); International Crisis Group, "Popular Protest in North Africa and the Middle East (V): Making Sense of Libya," June 6, 2011; and Omar Ashour, "Ex-Jihadists in the New Libya," *Foreign Policy,* August 29, 2011.

9. As a result of the fighting, the country's borders are especially porous. For example, see Mohannad Sabry, "Arms Smuggling Explodes across Egypt-Libya Border," McClatchy Newspapers, September 8, 2011.

10. For more on the link between service delivery and legitimacy, see Derick W. Brinkerhoff, "Introduction—Governance Challenges in Fragile States: Re-establishing Security, Rebuilding Effectiveness, and Reconstituting Legitimacy," in *Governance in Post-Conflict Societies: Rebuilding Fragile States,* edited by Derick W. Brinkerhoff (New York: Routledge, 2007).

11. Roland Paris, *At War's End: Building Peace After Civil Conflict* (Cambridge University Press, 2004), p. 175.

12. Jeffrey M. Jones, "Americans Shift to More Negative View of Libya Military Action," Gallup, June 24, 2011 (www.gallup.com/poll/148196/americans-shift-negative-view-libya-military-action.aspx).

13. Qatar and the United Arab Emirates sent warplanes to participate in the air campaign, and Jordan provided only logistical support.

14. White House, "Remarks by the President in Address to the Nation on Libya," March 28, 2011 (www.whitehouse.gov/the-press-office/2011/03/28/remarks-president-address-nation-libya).

15. For an extensive study on establishing security after conflict, see Seth G. Jones, Jeremy M. Wilson, Andrew Rathmell, and K. Jack Riley, "Establishing Law and Order After Conflict" (RAND Corporation, 2005).

16. Paris, *At War's End,* and Edward D. Mansfield and Jack Snyder, "Prone to Violence: The Paradox of the Democratic Peace," *National Interest,* Winter 2005/2006.

17. For more on what the legacy of dictatorship means for democratization and post-transition civil society, see Michael Bernhard and Ekrem Karakoç, "Civil Society and the Legacies of Dictatorship," *World Politics* 59 (July 2007): 539–67.

18. For a brief description of the initiative, see U.S. Agency for International Development, "Transition Initiatives: Tunisia" (www.usaid.gov/our_work/cross-cutting_programs/transition_initiatives/country/tunisia/index.html [September 15, 2011]).

19. Roland Paris and Timothy D. Sisk, eds., *The Dilemmas of Statebuilding: Confronting the Contradictions of Postwar Peace Operations* (New York: Routledge, 2009).

CHAPTER FIFTEEN

1. At the peak of the Oslo process in 1999, the maximum area of PA jurisdiction did not exceed 40 percent of the West Bank—18 percent of this was in "Area A" (where it had full civil and security control) and 21 percent in "Area B" (where it had full civil control and joint control over security with Israel). For detailed and timely information on access and movement restrictions in the West Bank and Gaza Strip, see United Nations Office of Coordination for Humanitarian Affairs (OCHA) (www.ochaopt.org/).

2. For congressional threats, see, for example, Natasha Mozgovaya, "U.S. Lawmaker: Palestinians Must Return to Peace Talks or Suffer Possible Divestment," *Ha'aretz,* September 26, 2011 (http://www.haaretz.com/news/diplomacy-defense/u-s-lawmaker-palestinians-must-return-to-peace-talks-or-suffer-possible-divestment-1.386872). International donor

aid generally accounts for more than a third of the PA's budget. In 2010, it made up 37 percent of the PA budget. See Palestinian National Authority, "Building Palestine: Achievements and Challenges, Report of the Palestinian National Authority to the Ad Hoc Liaison Committee," April 13, 2011, p. 19. As a nonmember, non-state "entity" of the UN with only observer status, the PLO must rely on friendly member states to submit draft resolutions or to gain access to other international forums.

3. There are numerous examples of the contradictory and often competing roles of the PA, including the fact that PLO diplomatic missions abroad receive their instructions and budgetary support not from the PLO's foreign minister (a post currently held by Farouk Kaddoumi, who has now fallen out of favor with Abbas), but from the offices of the PA foreign minister and prime minister. Moreover, this is despite the fact that the Oslo Accords expressly prohibit the PA from conducting "international relations," which was the sole prerogative of the PLO.

4. The remaining 10 percent live in Israel as citizens of the state. In recognizing Israel in 1993 (within the pre-1967 borders), the PLO in effect relinquished claims to represent the Palestinian citizens of Israel.

5. The PLO was formally created by the Arab League in 1964 as a way for Arab regimes, particularly Egypt, to control (and often exploit) the Palestinian cause. After the crushing defeat of June 1967, however, Yasir Arafat's Fatah movement successfully led efforts by Palestinian resistance organizations to seize control of the PLO. For more on the history of the PLO and the Palestinian national movement, see Yezid Sayigh, *Armed Struggle and the Search for State: The Palestinian National Movement, 1949–1993* (Oxford University Press, 1999).

6. Karma Nabulsi, "The State-Building Project," in *Aid, Diplomacy and Facts on the Ground: The Case of Palestine,* edited by Michael Keating, Anne Le More, and Robert Lowe (London: Chatham House, 2006), pp. 117–28.

7. Jamil Hilal, "PLO Institutions: The Challenge Ahead," *Journal of Palestine Studies* 23 (Autumn 1993): 58. According to Hilal, "Each of the factions had a given number of seats in the PLO leadership bodies and a set representation in the mass organizations irrespective of its size, ideology, or influence or popularity among Palestinians."

8. Ibid., p. 58.

9. Anxiety among Palestinians of the occupied territories regarding the PLO's authoritarian tendencies was apparent from the moment the PA was formed. See, for example, Youssef Ibrahim, "Some Gazans Fearful Arafat Could Choke Off Democracy," *New York Times,* August 7, 1994.

10. Hilal, "PLO Institutions," p. 51.

11. See, for example, Nathan J. Brown, "Palestinian Civil Society in Theory and in Practice," paper prepared for the annual meeting of the Structure of Government Section, International Political Science Association, Washington, May 2003. See also Khalil Shikaki, "The Peace Process, National Reconstruction, and the Transition to Democracy in Palestine," *Journal of Palestine Studies* 25 (Winter 1996): 5–20.

12. See, for example, Anne Le More, "Killing with Kindness: Funding the Demise of a Palestinian State," *International Affairs* 81, no. 5 (2005): 981–99. See also Keating and others, eds., *Aid, Diplomacy and Facts on the Ground,* pp. 117–28.

13. For more on the limitations of state-building under occupation, see Raja Khalidi and Sobhi Samour, "Neoliberalism as Liberation: The Statehood Program and the Remaking of the Palestinian National Movement," *Journal of Palestine Studies* 40 (Winter 2011): 6–25. See also Yezid Sayegh, "Policing the People, Building the State: Authoritarian Transformation in the West Bank and Gaza," Carnegie Paper (Washington: Carnegie Endowment for International Peace, February 2011), p. 21 (http://carnegie-mec.org/publications/?fa=42924); and

Nathan J. Brown, "Are Palestinians Building a State?" (Washington: Carnegie Endowment for International Peace, June 2010) (www.carnegieendowment.org/files/palestinian_state1.pdf).

14. See "Hamas' Political Program" (crafted by newly elected Hamas parliamentarians following their election in January 2006), *Al Ayyam,* March 17, 2006, reprinted by Institute for Middle East Understanding (http://imeu.net/news/article002607.shtml).

15. Sayegh, "Policing the People, Building the State," p. 22.

16. Hilal, "PLO Institutions," p. 55.

17. See also Mazen Masri, "The PLO and the Crisis of Representation," *Muftah,* October 15, 2010 (http://muftah.org/?p=321).

18. For a sample of the current discourse among diaspora Palestinians regarding the PLO, see Naseer Aruri and others, "The PLO: A Positive Model or Doomed for Failure? Part II Roundtable on Palestinian Diaspora and Representation," *Jadaliyya,* May 25, 2011 (www.jadaliyya.com/pages/index/1681/the-plo_a-positive-model-or-doomed-for-failure-par).

19. That strict democratic governance may be less central than other Palestinian popular demands is also supported by recent opinion polls. According to one poll, just 10 percent of Palestinians identified the goal of building a democratic political system as the "most vital," coming in fourth after ending the occupation and building an independent state (45 percent), ensuring the refugees' right of return (27 percent), and building a more moral society (17 percent). See Palestinian Center for Policy Studies and Research (PCPSR), Palestinian Public Opinion Poll 39, April 10, 2011 (www.pcpsr.org/survey/polls/2011/p39efull.html#vital).

20. See Camille Mansour, "Toward a New Palestinian Negotiation Paradigm," *Journal of Palestine Studies* 40 (Spring 2011): 38–58.

21. See "Young Seek to End West Bank and Gaza Schism," *New York Times,* February 24, 2011.

22. Under the terms of the agreement, which has yet to be implemented, a new government of "national consensus" would be formed comprised of independents and technocrats not affiliated with either faction but approved by both. The government's mandate would be limited to preparing for new parliamentary and presidential elections, to be held after one year, and overseeing the reconstruction of Gaza. As of August 2011, progress appeared to be held up over the issue of who will serve as prime minister. Hamas has steadfastly refused the reappointment of Salam Fayyad, whom they view as too pro-Western, while Abbas believes Fayyad's retention is crucial to securing Western support for the new government. For a translation of the text of the agreement, see www.palestinemonitor.org/spip/spip.php?article1787.

23. For a Palestinian perspective on what a "Palestinian Spring" might look like and mean for the PLO and the Palestinian national movement, see Jamil Hilal, "Palestinian Answers in the Arab Spring," Al-Shabaka Policy Brief, May 6, 2011 (http://al-shabaka.org/policy-brief/politics/palestinian-answers-arab-spring). See also Adam Shatz, "Is Palestine Next?" *London Review of Books* 33 (July 14, 2011): 8–14.

24. See, for example, "Here Comes Your Non-violent Resistance, *The Economist,* May 17, 2011 (www.economist.com/blogs/democracyinamerica/2011/05/israel_and_palestine_0). See also Jesse Rosenfeld and Joseph Dana, "A Palestinian Revolt in the Making?" *The Nation,* May 26, 2011 (www.thenation.com/article/160975/palestinian-revolt-making).

25. There is some evidence to suggest that the Syrian regime supported or encouraged the Palestinian protesters in a bid to deflect attention away from its growing repression of its own people.

26. Quoted in Tovah Lazaroff, "The Window for a Negotiated Peace Ends in September," *Jerusalem Post,* March 23, 2011 (www.jpost.com/MiddleEast/Article.aspx?id=213386).

27. For most Palestinians, nearly two decades of on-and-off negotiations have brought them no closer to statehood, while the peace process itself has presided over increased settlement construction and land confiscations, home demolitions, internal movement restrictions, a crippling blockade on Gaza, and a debilitating political division between their two largest factions. A recent Palestinian opinion poll found that two-thirds of Palestinians believe the chances of a Palestinian state being created alongside Israel in the coming five years are slim to none. An even higher proportion (69 percent) oppose America's role in the peace process. See PCPSR, Palestinian Public Opinion Poll 39.

28. For more on the rationale behind the Palestinian UN strategy, see Mahmoud Abbas, "The Long Overdue Palestinian State," *New York Times,* May 17, 2011. See also Khaled Elgindy, "Palestine Goes to the UN: Understanding the New Statehood Strategy," *Foreign Affairs* (September/October 2011): 102–13; Dan Ephron, "The Wrath of Abbas" (interview with Abbas), *Newsweek,* April 24, 2011.

29. According to a poll conducted just before Abbas's UN gambit, 83 percent of Palestinians said they supported the move. In addition, "About 70 percent of Israelis think that if the UN recognizes a Palestinian state Israel should accept the decision." Palestinian Center for Policy and Survey Research, Joint Israeli-Palestinian Poll, September 21, 2011 (www.pcpsr. org/survey/polls/2011/p41ejoint.html)

CHAPTER SIXTEEN

1. "Revolution Death Toll Was 846," United Press International, April 21, 2011 (www. upi.com/Top_News/World-News/2011/04/20/Revolution-death-toll-was-846/UPI-60871303299902/[May 12, 2011]).

2. This section draws on Kenneth M. Pollack, *A Path Out of the Desert: A Grand Strategy for America in the Middle East* (New York.: Random House, 2008), pp. 221–24.

3. Alan Richards, "Economic Reform in the Middle East: The Challenge to Governance," in Nora Bensahel and Daniel L. Byman eds., *The Future Security Environment in the Middle East: Conflict, Stability and Political Change* (Santa Monica, Calif.: RAND, 2004), p. 59. Eva Bellin notes that early successes in Jordan, Morocco, Tunisia, and Turkey employing this strategy provide some confirmation that it can work in the Middle East. Eva Bellin, "The Political-Economic Conundrum," in *Uncharted Journey: Promoting Democracy in the Middle East,* edited by Thomas Carothers and Marina Ottaway (Washington: Carnegie Endowment for International Peace, 2005), pp. 144–45.

4. Bellin, "The Political-Economic Conundrum," pp. 135, 144–45; Thomas Carothers, "Choosing a Strategy," in *Uncharted Journey,* edited by Carothers and Ottaway, p. 199; Marcus Noland and Howard Pack, *The Arab Economies in a Changing World* (Washington: Peterson Institute for International Economics, 2007), p. 274; Richards, "Economic Reform in the Middle East," p. 128.

5. Crane Brinton, *The Anatomy of Revolution* (New York: Vintage Books, 1965); Barrington Moore Jr., *Social Origins of Dictatorship and Democracy: Lord and Peasant in the Making of the Modern World* (Boston: Beacon Press, 1966); Theda Skocpol, *States and Social Revolutions: A Comparative Analysis of France, Russia and China* (Cambridge University Press, 1979), and *Social Revolutions in the Modern World* (Cambridge University Press, 1994); Caroline Ziemke, "Perceived Oppression and Relative Deprivation: Social Factors Contributing to Terrorism," in *"In The Same Light As Slavery": Building a Global Antiterrorist Consensus,* edited by Joseph McMillan (Washington: National Defense University Press, 2006).

6. For arguments that Middle Eastern countries should be encouraged to reform their economies first, see Richard N. Haass, *The Opportunity: America's Moment to Alter History's Course* (New York: Public Affairs, 2005), esp. pp. 72, 119; Fareed Zakaria, *The Future of Freedom: Illiberal Democracy at Home and Abroad* (New York: Norton, 2003), pp. 69–73. For arguments that political reform must accompany (not follow) economic reform, see Thomas Carothers, "How Democracies Emerge: The 'Sequencing' Fallacy," *Journal of Democracy* 18 (January 2007): 13–27; Tamara Cofman Wittes, *Freedom's Unsteady March: America's Role in Promoting Arab Democracy* (Brookings, 2008), pp. 59–66.

7. James Zogby, "Arab Attitudes, 2011" (Washington: Arab American Institute Foundation, July 2011) (http://aai.3cdn.net/5d2b8344e3b3b7ef19_xkm6ba4r9.pdf [July 30, 2011]).

8. Thomas Carothers and Marina Ottaway, "The New Democracy Imperative," in *Uncharted Journey,* edited by Carothers and Ottaway, pp. 6–7; Saad Eddin Ibrahim, "A Dissident Asks: Can Bush Turn Words into Action?" *Washington Post,* December 23, 2003; Marina Ottaway, "The Problem of Credibility," in *Uncharted Journey,* edited by Carothers and Ottaway, pp. 173–92; Barry Rubin, *The Long War for Freedom: The Arab Struggle for Democracy in the Middle East* (New York: John Wiley and Sons, 2006), esp. pp. 38–54, 123–78; Wittes, *Freedom's Unsteady March,* pp. 26–28.

9. Paul Collier, *The Bottom Billion: Why the Poorest Countries Are Failing and What Can Be Done about It* (Oxford University Press, 2007), esp. pp. 99–123.

10. International Crisis Group, *The Challenge of Political Reform: Jordanian Democratization and Regional Instability,* Middle East Briefing (Amman/Brussels, October 8, 2003), p. 2 (www.crisisgroup.org/library/documents/middle_east___north_africa/jordan_political__ reform08_10_03.pdf [July 2007]); International Crisis Group, *Can Saudi Arabia Reform Itself?* Middle East Report 28 (Cairo/Brussels, July 14, 2004), pp. 20–26.

Chapter Seventeen

1. See, for example, Tamara Cofman Wittes and Sarah E. Yerkes, "What Price Freedom? Assessing the Bush Administration's Freedom Agenda," Analysis Paper 10 (Brookings Saban Center for Middle East Policy, September 2006).

2. Shadi Hamid, "Cairo Conundrum," *Democracy: A Journal of Ideas* 15 (Winter 2010).

3. John P. Entelis, "The Democratic Imperative vs. the Authoritarian Impulse: The Maghrib State between Transition and Terrorism," *Middle East Journal* 59 (Autumn 2005): 543–45.

4. Eva Bellin, "The Robustness of Authoritarianism in the Middle East: Exceptionalism in Comparative Perspective," *Comparative Politics* 36 (2004): 144–45.

5. Ibid., pp. 147–49; F. Gregory Gause III, "The Persistence of Monarchy in the Arabian Peninsula: A Comparative Analysis," in *Middle East Monarchies: The Challenge of Modernity,* edited by Joseph Kostiner (Boulder, Colo.: Lynne Rienner, 2000), pp. 167–85.

6. Tamara Cofman Wittes, *Freedom's Unsteady March: America's Role in Promoting Arab Democracy* (Brookings, 2008), pp. 19–21.

7. Shadi Hamid, "Arab Elections: Free, Sort of Fair . . . and Meaningless," *Foreign Policy,* October 27, 2010 (http://mideast.foreignpolicy.com/posts/2010/10/27/arab_ elections_free_sort_of_fair_and_meaningless).

8. For a discussion of how a Helsinki-like process could be developed for the Arab world, see Michael McFaul, "A Helsinki Process for the Middle East," *Democracy,* no. 8 (Spring 2008) (ww.democracyjournal.org/8/6590.php [July 30, 2011]).

9. S. Abdallah Schleifer, "The Impact of Arab Satellite Television on the Prospects for Democracy in the Arab World" (Philadelphia: Foreign Policy Research Institute, May 12,

2005). See also Jon B. Alterman, "Arab Media: Tools of the Government; Tools for the People?" (Washington: United States Institute of Peace, August 2005); Jon B. Alterman, "The Information Revolution and the Middle East," in *The Future Security Environment in the Middle East: Conflict, Stability and Political Change,* edited by Nora Bensahel and Daniel L. Byman (Santa Monica, Calif.: RAND, 2004), pp. 227–52; Michael Kraig and Kathy Gockel, "Open Media and Transitioning Societies in the Middle East: Implications for U.S. Security Policy" (Muscatine, Iowa: Stanley Foundation, 2005–06), esp. p. 23.

10. Parts of this section are based on Sarah E. Yerkes, "Civil Society and Elections in the MENA Region," paper presented at the annual conference of the Middle East Studies Association, Washington, 2008.

11. Marina Ottaway and Thomas Carothers, eds., *Funding Virtue: Civil Society Aid and Democracy Promotion* (Washington: Carnegie Endowment for International Peace, 2000); Marina Ottaway and Julia Choucair-Vizoso, eds., *Beyond the Façade: Political Reform in the Arab World* (Washington: Carnegie Endowment for International Peace, 2008); Steven Heydemann, "Upgrading Authoritarianism in the Arab World,"Analysis Paper 13 (Brookings Saban Center for Middle East Policy, October 2007); Thomas Carothers, William Barndt, and Mustapha Kamel Al-Sayyid, "Civil Society," *Foreign Policy* 117 (1999/2000): 18–30; Omar G. Encarnación, *The Myth of Civil Society: Social Capital and Democratic Consolidation in Spain and Brazil* (New York: Palgrave Macmillan, 2003); David Rieff, "The False Dawn of Civil Society," *The Nation,* February 22, 1999.

12. See, for example, Larry Diamond, *Developing Democracy: Toward Consolidation* (Johns Hopkins University Press, 1999); Richard Gunther, P. Nikiforos Diamandouros, and Hans-Jürgen Puhle, eds., *The Politics of Democratic Consolidation: Southern Europe in Comparative Perspective* (Johns Hopkins University Press, 1995); John Higley and Richard Gunther, eds., *Elites and Democratic Consolidation in Latin America and Southern Europe* (Cambridge University Press, 1992); Juan J. Linz and Alfred Stepan, *Problems of Democratic Transition and Consolidation* (Johns Hopkins University Press, 1996); Scott Mainwaring, Guillermo O'Donnell, and J. Samuel Valenzuela, eds., *Issues in Democratic Consolidation: The New South American Democracies in Comparative Perspective* (University of Notre Dame Press, 1992); Guillermo O'Donnell, Philippe C. Schmitter, and Laurence Whitehead, eds., *Transitions from Authoritarian Rule: Prospects for Democracy* (Johns Hopkins University Press, 1986).

13. Diamond, *Developing Democracy;* Linz and Stepan, *Problems of Democratic Transition and Consolidation.*

14. Marc Morjé Howard and Philip Roessler, "Liberalizing Electoral Outcomes in Competitive Authoritarian Regimes," *American Journal of Political Science* 50, no. 2 (2006): 365–81.

15. Interviews with donors and civil society organizations by Sarah Yerkes, Cairo, Egypt, June 2011.

16. Sarah E. Yerkes, "The Nature of Oppositional Civil Society in Hybrid Regimes in the MENA Region," paper presented at the annual conference of the American Political Science Association (APSA), Washington, September 2010.

17. According to the 2009 Arab Human Development Report, at that time 44 percent of Egypt's population lived on less than $2 a day. That number was 7 percent in Jordan and 14 percent in Morocco, the two monarchies most likely to reform. United Nations Development Program, Regional Bureau for Arab States, "Arab Human Development Report 2009: Challenges to Human Security in the Arab Countries" (www.arab-hdr.org/contents/index. aspx?rid=5).

18. For an argument that the United States should pull the Fifth Fleet headquarters from Bahrain, see Toby Jones, "Time to Disband the Bahrain-Based U.S. Fifth Fleet," *Atlantic*

Monthly, June 2011 (www.theatlantic.com/international/archive/2011/06/time-to-disband-the-bahrain-based-us-fifth-fleet/240243/ [July 30, 2011]).

19. See, for instance, Paul K. Huth, *Extended Deterrence and the Prevention of War* (Yale University Press, 1988); Paul Huth and Bruce Russett, "What Makes Deterrence Work? Cases from 1900 to 1980," *World Politics* 36 (July 1984); Robert Jervis, "Deterrence Theory Revisited," *World Politics* 31 (January 1979): 289–324; Kathleen MacInnis, "Extended Deterrence: The U.S. Credibility Gap in the Middle East," *Washington Quarterly* 28 (Summer 2005): 169–86; Thomas Schelling, *Arms and Influence* (Yale University Press, 1966); Glenn H. Snyder, *Deterrence and Defense: Toward a Theory of National Security* (Princeton University Press, 1961).

CHAPTER EIGHTEEN

1. Toby Craig Jones, "Saudi Arabia Moves to Maintain Regime Stability," *CTC Sentinel,* vol. 4 (Combating Terrorism Center at West Point, April 2011).

2. Natana J. Delong-Bas, *Wahhabi Islam: From Revival and Reform to Global Jihad* (Cairo: American University Press, 2005).

3. Neil MacFarquhar, "Saudis Arrest Woman Leading Right to Drive Campaign," *New York Times,* May 24, 2011.

4. See Bruce Riedel, "Introduction," in *The Battle for Yemen: Al Qaeda and the Struggle for Stability* (Washington: Jamestown Foundation, 2010).

5. See Bruce Riedel, *The Search for al Qaeda: Its Leadership, Ideology and Future,* rev. ed. (Brookings, 2010).

6. "ISI Asked Saudis to Stop Funding Nawaz's Campaign," *Express Tribune* (Pakistan), May 31, 2011.

7. Sultan Abdallah, "Bandar bin Sultan Draws Red Gulf Lines in Tour to East," Saudi-owned Elaph website, March 24, 2011; and "Pakistani Soldiers on Gulf Duty Alert," Paris Intelligence Online, March 31, 2011.

8. Leigh Nolan, "Managing Reform? Saudi Arabia and the King's Dilemma," Policy Briefing (Brookings Doha Center, May 2011).

9. Yousef Gamal El-Din, "Turmoil in the Middle East: Will Saudi Arabia be Next?" CNBC, February 20, 2011 (www.cnbc.com/id/41690671/Turmoil_in_the_Middle_East_Will_Saudi_Arabia_be_Next [July 8, 2011]).

10. For much information on Saudi regional animosities, see John R. Bradley, *Saudi Arabia Exposed: Inside a Kingdom in Crisis* (New York: Palgrave, 2005).

11. For a brilliant analysis of the al-Qaeda challenge, see Thomas Hegghammer, *Jihad in Saudi Arabia: Violence and Pan-Islamism since 1979* (Cambridge University Press, 2010).

CHAPTER NINETEEN

1. Jeremy M. Sharp, "Jordan: Background and U.S. Relations," Congressional Research Service (April 21, 2011), p. 16 (www.fas.org/sgp/crs/mideast/RL33546.pdf).

2. Ibid., p. 18.

3. Bahrain, Israel, Morocco, and Oman also have free trade agreements with the United States.

4. "Jordan's King Abdullah Open to Constitutional Monarchy," *ABC News* (March 15, 2005) (http://abcnews.go.com/WNT/story?id=583538&page=1).

5. Economist Intelligence Unit, *Country Report—Jordan* (London: January 2011).

6. "Transcript: Obama's Speech in Amman, Jordan," *New York Times,* July 22, 2008 (www.nytimes.com/2008/07/22/us/politics/22text-obama.html?pagewanted=1).

7. Morton Valbjorn, "Post-democratization Lessons from the Jordanian 'Success Story,'" *Foreign Policy,* June 16, 2011 (http://mideast.foreignpolicy.com/articles/2010/06/15/post_democratization_lessons_from_the_jordanian_success_story).

8. Shadi Hamid, "A New Security Strategy, but Not Necessarily a New Gulf Cooperation Council," *The National,* May 16, 2011 (www.brookings.edu/opinions/2011/0516_gulf_cooperation_council_hamid.aspx).

9. Glenn E. Robinson, "Defensive Democratization in Jordan," *International Journal of Middle East Studies* 30 (August 1998): 394.

10. *Jordan Times,* March 6, 2005.

11. In response to the protests, on January 20, Prime Minister Rifai announced a $230 million package in the 2011 budget to provide bread subsidies, decrease fuel prices, and help create jobs. When this measure failed to deter protesters, the prime minister offered a $550 million subsidy package for fuel and staple products like rice and sugar. When this measure also failed to quell unrest, Rifai was sacked.

12. "Jordan King Pledges Parliamentary Reform," Agence Presse-France, June 13, 2011 (www.google.com/hostednews/afp/article/ALeqM5jmt3tlMCgrWaq5roDpOWs13v2jyg?docId=CNG.cd4577a43425ef99e756265e3cb55023.7c1).

13. Randa Habib, "Jordan Islamists: 'Nothing New' in King's Speech," Middle East Online, June 13, 2011 (www.middle-east-online.com/english/?id=46663).

14. Mohammad Ben Hussein, "Opposition Parties 'Disappointed' at Suggested Elections Law," *Jordan Times,* June 8, 2011 (www.jordantimes.com/?news=38280).

15. On the proposal, see Cory Eldridge, "A Complicated Dialogue," JO Online, June 30, 2011 (www.jo.jo/index.php?view=article&catid=81:politics&id=2125:a-complicated-dialogue&tmpl=component&print=1&layout=default&page=&option=com_content&Itemid=197 [July 30, 2011]).

16. Thameen Kheetan, "Newly Launched National Front for Reform Seeks Rule of Law," *Jordan Times,* May 22, 2011 (www.jordantimes.com/index.php?news=37695).

17. Nathan Brown, "Jordan and Its Islamist Movement: The Limits of Inclusion?" Carnegie Papers Middle East Series 74 (Washington, 2006) (www.carnegieendowment.org/files/cp_74_brown_final.pdf).

18. Hashemite Kingdom of Jordan Department of Statistics, "11.9% the Unemployment Rate during the Fourth Quarter of 2010" (Amman: December 28, 2010) (www.dos.gov.jo/dos_home_e/archive/emp_12_2010.pdf).

19. World Bank, "Doing Business 2011: Ease of Doing Business in Jordan" (Washington, 2011) (www.doingbusiness.org/data/exploreeconomies/jordan/).

20. Sufyan Alissa, "Rethinking Economic Reform in Jordan: Confronting Socioeconomic Realities" (Washington: Carnegie Middle East Center, August 2007) (http://carnegie-mec.org/publications/?fa=19465).

21. Suleiman al-Khalidi, "Tribal Feuds Threaten Jordan's Stability," Reuters, January 13, 2011 (www.reuters.com/article/2011/01/13/us-jordan-tribes-idUSTRE70C2XT20110113).

22. Khaled Abu Toameh, "Jordanian Beduin Tribal Leaders Demand Political Reforms," *Jerusalem Post,* February 9, 2011.

23. "Jordanians Want 'Corrupt, Oppressive' Govt Sacked," Agence France-Presse, May 20, 2011 (www.google.com/hostednews/afp/article/ALeqM5hPYmnVwvw8rErYvUNuJoor_cB7tA?docId=CNG.6a78e6071d24e298f016ac597ed2a84f.481).

24. "Jordan Islamists, Leftists Unite against Corruption," AFP News, June 1, 2011 (www.google.com/hostednews/afp/article/ALeqM5jzoUJXVidHPreA0rq5VGwlu0ZXJA?docId=CNG.1a110a4a421a7358125f6f5f221a6179.41).

25. Shadi Hamid, "Jordan: The Myth of the Democratizing Monarchy," in *The Struggle over Democracy in the Middle East,* edited by Nathan Brown and Emad Shahin (New York: Routledge, 2009).

CHAPTER TWENTY

1. Doha's vigorous campaign to host the World Cup included the construction of a 500-person scale model of a carbon-neutral, air-conditioned stadium. Kevin Brass, "Summer, and Controversy, Reignite Debate over Qatar World Cup Plan," *The National,* June 10, 2011. More recently, Qatar has come under scrutiny after press reports alleging that a Qatari official tried to use bribes to win the presidency of the sport's governing authority. Roger Blitz, "Fifa Faces Fresh Corruption Crisis," *Financial Times,* May 25, 2011; Sam Wallace, "Qatar May Be Stripped of World Cup, Says Blatter," *The Independent,* May 20, 2011.

2. "Airport Blocked by Oman Pay Protests," *The Gulf,* April 1, 2011.

3. Michael Birnbaum, "Battle to Oust Kuwaiti Premier Gains Urgency," *Washington Post,* March 7, 2011.

4. B. Izzak, "Amir Accepts Sheikh Jaber's Resignation," *Kuwait Times,* February 7, 2011; Kristian Coates Ulrichsen, "Old Problems, New Rules," *The Gulf,* May 1, 2011.

5. Hussain Al-Qatari, "Activists to Stage Protest on Feb 8," *Kuwait Times,* February 3, 2011; "Youths in Kuwait to Challenge Government with Unauthorized Protests," *International Business Times News,* March 8, 2011; Ulrichsen, "Old Problems, New Rules."

6. "Guantanamo Jab Sparks Fistfight among Kuwait MPs," Reuters, May 18, 2011 (http://in.reuters.com/article/2011/05/18/idINIndia-57106020110518).

7. Ulf Laessing, "Kuwaitis Protest, Demand Prime Minister Resign," Reuters, June 4, 2011 (http://in.reuters.com/article/2011/06/03/idINIndia-57491120110603).

8. Emily Meredith, "Kuwait: Diversity Factor," *Energy Compass,* April 15, 2011.

9. "Kuwait Emir Warns against Political Chaos," Agence France-Presse, June 15, 2011.

10. Meris Lutz, "Al Jazeera Faces Tough Questions as Doha Backs Saudi Troops in Bahrain," *Los Angeles Times* Babylon and Beyond Blog, March 15, 2011 (http://latimesblogs.latimes.com/babylonbeyond/2011/03/qatar-bahrain-saudi-arabia-protests-troops-security.html).

11. See www.arabyouthsurvey.com/files/AYS_2010_white_paper.pdf.

12. Sultan Sooud Al-Qassemi, "Hunkering Down Is the Worst Option for Gulf Leaderships," *Daily Star* (Lebanon), June 29, 2011.

13. Ulrichsen, "Old Problems, New Rules."

14. Gala Riani, "Omani Sultan Aims to End Protests with Major Government Reshuffle," *Global Insight,* March 8, 2011.

15. "Jobless Omani Activists Vow to Hold More Protests," Reuters, May 17, 2011.

16. "UAE Boosts Military Pensions, Unveils Bonus Scheme," ArabianBusiness.com (Reuters), March 24, 2011; Erika Solomon, "Youth in UAE Question Cost of Political Silence but Back Benign Government," Al Arabiya.net (Reuters), May 12, 2011.

17. "UAE Economy Minister Urges Retailers to Keep Lid on Prices," *Daily Star* (Lebanon), March 28, 2011; Solomon, "Youth in UAE Question Cost."

18. Samuel Ciszuk, "Gulf States Pledge Aid for Bahrain and Oman, Await Saudi Protests Anxiously," *Global Insight,* March 11, 2011.

19. Gwenn Okruhlik, "Rentier Wealth, Unruly Law, and the Rise of Opposition: The Political Economy of Oil States," *Comparative Politics* 31 (April 1999): 295–315.

20. "Reshuffle Fails to Quell Omani Protests," Agence France-Presse, March 8, 2011; "Oman Frees 57 Detainees Following Unrest," Associated Press, April 3, 2011.

21. "UAE to Elect New Advisory Body Members," Agence France-Presse, March 17, 2011.

22. Solomon, "Youth in UAE Question Cost."

23. "Hundreds Arrested in Oman as Security Forces Disperse Protesters," AlArabiya.net, May 13, 2011; Fahad Al Ghadani, "117 People Sign Statement Condemning 'Abductions,'" *Times of Oman*, April 12, 2011; "'Sinbad Hometown' Puts Genie Back in Bottle," Agence France-Presse, April 10, 2011; "Oman Set to Prosecute Protests' 'Ringleader,' 25 Others," Reuters, April 9, 2011; "Oman Arrests Protesters Preparing Weapons," Associated Press, April 5, 2011; "Oman Arrests Six as Protesters Call for More Jobs, Higher Salaries," *Daily Star* (Lebanon), May 10, 2011; "Amnesty Asks Oman to Clarify Protest Arrests," Agence France-Presse, May 18, 2011; "Oman Continues Crackdown on Activists," Agence France-Presse, May 17, 2011.

24. "Kuwait's Stateless Demand Citizenship," AlArabiya.net, March 12, 2011; "50 Stateless Arabs Arrested in Protests in Kuwait," AlArabiya.net, February 18, 2011.

25. "Kuwait to Settle Illegal Residents' Issue Soon—MoI," Kuwait News Agency (KUNA), March 10, 2011.

26. Barbara Surk, "UAE Quiet on Streets but Web Reformers Face Heat," Associated Press, April 27, 2011; Hannah Gurman, "Break the Silence in the UAE,"*Foreign Policy in Focus*, April 27, 2011; "UAE Confirms Five Activists Held in Custody," Agence France-Presse, April 25, 2011.

27. Anna Louie Sussman, "Repression in the United Arab Emirates," *The Nation*, June 1, 2011 (www.thenation.com/article/161058/repression-united-arab-emirates).

28. Mark Mazzetti and Emily B. Hager, "Secret Desert Force Set Up by Blackwater's Founder," *New York Times*, May 14, 2011.

29. Sussman, "Repression in the United Arab Emirates."

30. Portia Walker, "Qatari Military Advisers on the Ground, Helping Libyan Rebels Get into Shape," *Washington Post*, May 12, 2011.

31. "Qatar Gains Global Limelight as Arab Standout in U.N.-Backed Coalition in Libya," Associated Press, March 28, 2011.

32. "Obama meets Abu Dhabi Crown Prince," Agence France-Presse, April 26, 2011.

CHAPTER TWENTY-ONE

1. Up to that point, Hamad had been emir, the traditional title of the ruler of Bahrain until Hamad proclaimed himself king.

2. White House, "Remarks by the President on the Middle East and North Africa," May 19, 2011.

3. Nathan Hodge, "U.S. Says Iran is Meddling in Bahrain," *Wall Street Journal*, April 7, 2011 (http://online.wsj.com/article/SB10001424052748703280904576247230001105602.html). Interviews with U.S. officials by the author, Washington, DC, March–April 2011.

4. "U.S. Embassy Cables: Bahrain's Relations with Iran," Cable from Manama, August 8, 2008, published in "The U.S. Embassy Cables: The Documents," *The Guardian*, February 15, 2001 (www.guardian.co.uk/world/us-embassy-cables-documents/164906).

5. Justin Gengler, "How Radical are Bahrain's Shia? The Real Source of Unrest in the Kingdom," *Foreign Affairs* (May 15, 2011) (www.foreignaffairs.com/articles/67855/justin-gengler/how-radical-are-bahrains-shia?page=show).

6. "Remarks by the President on the Middle East and North Africa."

7. The British system is the oldest and clearest example of a constitutional monarchy, in which the monarch acts as head of state, while the prime minster, as the head of government, exercises effective political power. Other variations on this model include the

European political systems in the Netherlands, Sweden, and Norway. It may be the current French political system, however, with its periods of "cohabitation," that may be the most interesting and realistic example for Bahrain. In the French system, the president (head of state) shares executive power with his or her appointed prime minister. The president heads the armed forces, appoints the prime minister, has the power to dismiss the National Assembly, chairs the Council of Ministers, appoints the senior most judges, and negotiates all foreign treaties. However, all domestic decisions must be approved by the prime minister, who manages the daily affairs of government and is responsible for national defense. The prime minister also must be supported by the majority of the directly elected lower house of parliament. In periods of "cohabitation," the president and prime minister have come from the opposing sides of French politics. The requirement for two sides to work together despite their political differences could be an inspiration for Bahrain's current political schism.

CHAPTER TWENTY-TWO

1. James Sater, "Reform in Morocco: Caught between Terror and the King," *National Conversation,* May 6, 2011 (www.thenational.ae/thenationalconversation/comment/reform-in-morocco-caught-between-terror-and-the-king?pageCount=0 [May 15, 2011]).

2. World Bank, "World Bank President Supports Further Moroccan Reforms and Civic Participation," press release (Washington, May 5, 2011).

3. Jay Martin, "Pressure on Moroccan Government Spikes over Bombing," CNN, May 9, 2011.

4. For example, the Arab Barometer survey instrument found that 75 percent of Moroccans surveyed had either "not very much" trust or "none at all" in political parties, while 57 percent held the same view of the courts, 68 percent the parliament, and 56 percent the prime minister. In the same survey, 74 percent of Moroccans said that either "most officials" or "almost everyone" is corrupt. Arab Barometer, "Comparative Findings of All Arab Barometer Surveys in Jordan, Palestine, Morocco, Algeria and Kuwait," 2006 (www.arabbarometer.org/).

5. Molly Hennessy-Fiske, "Morocco: Protest Violence Could Escalate, Intelligence Analyst Says," *Los Angeles Times,* May 23, 2011.

6. Sarah E. Yerkes, "Oppositional Civil Society and Democratization: How Democratic is Moroccan Civil Society?" paper presented at the annual conference of the American Political Science Association, Boston, September 2008.

7. Adam Tanner, "Moroccan Rights Watchdog Defends Protest Crackdown," Reuters, May 24, 2011.

8. Emma Rosen, "Morocco's Uprising and All the King's Men," Al Jazeera, June 5, 2011 (http://english.aljazeera.net/indepth/features/2011/06/20116512125272326.html [June 6, 2011]).

9. In 1998 King Hassan II asked Abderrahmane Youssoufi, head of the Socialist Union of Popular Forces (USFP), an opposition party that received a plurality of seats in the parliamentary elections, to form a new government. This event is called the *alternance* and is significant both because it was the first and only time the opposition took power in Morocco and because Youssoui was a major and outspoken regime opponent.

10. Voter turnout in Morocco peaked at 82 percent in 1977 and then steadily declined, reaching a bare 37 percent in the most recent elections in 2007. While estimates for the voter turnout for the July 1 referendum have reached as high as 98 percent, these figures are suspect.

11. Siham Ali, "Morocco to Hold Early Legislative Vote," *Magharebia,* May 31, 2011 (www.magharebia.com/cocoon/awi/xhtml1/en_GB/features/awi/features/2011/05/31/feature-03).

12. Ursula Lindsey, "Morocco Suppresses Poll Despite Favorable Results for King," *Christian Science Monitor,* August 5, 2009.

13. "The Opinion of the Moroccan People: Release Rachid Nini," *Al-Akhbar* (Lebanon), May 3, 2011 (www.al-akhbar.com/node/11250 [June 1, 2011]).

14. Anouar Boukhars, "Does Morocco Have a Place in the GCC?" *Arab Reform Bulletin,* May 25, 2011.

Chapter Twenty-Three

1. Camille Tawil, *Brothers in Arms: The Story of al Qaida and the Arab Jihadists* (London: Saqi, 2010), p. 66.

2. Andrew Pierre and William Quandt, *The Algerian Crisis: Policy Options for the West* (Washington: Carnegie Endowment for Peace, 1996).

3. Anthony Faiola, "In Algeria, a Chill in the Arab Spring," *Washington Post,* April 8, 2011.

4. Dario Cristiani, "Algeria's Response to Revolt in Libya Is Complicated by Volatile Relationship with Qadhafi Regime," Jamestown Foundation Terrorism Monitor, May 2011.

5. Tawil, *Brothers in Arms,* p. 195.

Chapter Twenty-Four

1. For a review of definitional issues regarding what constitutes a civil war, see Nicholas Sambanis, "What Is Civil War? Conceptual and Empirical Complexities of an Operational Definition," *Journal of Conflict Resolution* 48 (December 2004): 814–58.

2. For a discussion of spillover from civil wars and its various manifestations, see Daniel L. Byman and Kenneth M. Pollack, *Things Fall Apart: Containing the Spillover from an Iraqi Civil War* (Brookings, 2007), pp. 17–59.

3. See, among others, Sheri Berman, "Islamism, Revolution and Civil Society," *Perspectives on Politics* 1 (June 2003): 261; Theda Skocpol, *States and Social Revolutions: A Comparative Analysis of France, Russia and China* (Cambridge University Press, 1979), and *Social Revolutions in the Modern World* (Cambridge University Press, 1994); Mark R. Thompson, "To Shoot or Not to Shoot: Posttotalitarianism in China and Eastern Europe," *Comparative Politics* 34 (October 2001): 63–83.

4. For a statement of this problem, see Barry Posen, "The Security Dilemma and Ethnic Conflict," *Survival* 35 (Spring 1993): 27–47; for a critique, see John Mueller, "The Banality of 'Ethnic War,'" *International Security* 25 (Summer 2002): 42–70.

5. See, in particular, Stathis Kalyvas, "Warfare in Civil Wars," in *Rethinking the Nature of War,* edited by Isabelle Duyvesteyn and Jan Angstrom (Abingdon, U.K.: Frank Cass, 2005), pp. 88–108; Stathis Kalvas, "Promises and Pitfalls of an Emerging Research Program: The Microdynamics of Civil War," in *Order, Conflict, Violence,* edited by Stathis N. Kalyvas, Ian Shapiro, and Tarek Masoud (Cambridge University Press, 2008), pp. 397–421.

6. Benjamin Valentino, Paul Huth, and Dylan Balch-Lindsay, "'Draining the Sea': Mass Killing and Guerrilla Warfare," *International Organization* 58 (Spring 2004): 375–407; Macartan Humphreys and Jeremy M. Weinstein, "Handling and Manhandling Civilians in Civil War," *American Political Science Review* 100 (August 2006): 429–47.

7. Chaim Kaufmann, "Possible and Impossible Solutions to Ethnic Civil Wars," *International Security* 20 (Spring 1996): 136–75.

8. Paul Collier and Anke Hoeffler, "Greed and Grievance in Civil War" (Washington: World Bank, Development Research Group, 2001); James D. Fearon, "Primary Commodity Exports and Civil War," *Journal of Conflict Resolution* 49, no. 4 (2005): 483–507; James D. Fearon and David D. Laitin, "Ethnicity, Insurgency, and Civil War," *American Political Science Review* 97, no. 1 (February 2003): 75–90; James D. Fearon and David Laitin, "Violence and the Social Construction of Ethnic Identity," *International Organization* 54, no. 4 (2002): 845–77; James D. Fearon, "Why Do Some Civil Wars Last So Much Longer than Others?" *Journal of Peace Research* 41 (May 2004): 275–302; Michael Ross, "What Do We Know about Natural Resources and Civil War?" *Journal of Peace Research* 41 (May 2004); Barbara Walter and Jack Snyder, eds., *Civil Wars, Insecurity, and Intervention* (Columbia University Press, 1999); Barbara Walter, "Does Conflict Beget Conflict? Explaining Recurring Civil War," *Journal of Peace Research* 41 (May 2004): 371–88.

9. This section draws on Byman and Pollack, *Things Fall Apart.*

10. Thomas Hegghammer, "The Rise of Muslim Foreign Fighters," *International Security* 35 (Winter 2010/11): 53–94.

11. On terrorist learning, see Michael Horowitz, "Nonstate Actors and the Diffusion of Innovations: The Case of Suicide Terrorism," *International Organization* 64 (Winter 2010).

12. Barbara Walter, "Information, Uncertainty and the Decision to Secede," *International Organization* 60 (Winter 2006): 105–36.

13. Barry R. Posen, "Military Responses to Refugee Disasters," *International Security* 21 (Summer 1996): 72–112.

14. For a discussion of these and other issues, see Sarah Lischer, "Collateral Damage: Humanitarian Assistance as a Cause of Conflict," *International Security* 28 (2003): 79–109.

15. Barbara Walter, "The Critical Barrier to Civil War Settlement," *International Organization* 51 (1997): 335–64; Kelly Greenhill and Solomon Major, "The Perils of Profiling: Civil War Spoilers and the Collapse of International Peace Accords," *International Security* 31 (Winter 2006/07): 7–40; Alexander Downes, "The Problem with Negotiated Settlements to Ethnic Civil Wars," *Security Studies* 13 (Summer 2004): 230–79.

16. Virginia Page Fortna, "Does Peacekeeping Keep Peace? International Intervention and the Duration of Peace after Civil War," *International Studies Quarterly* 48 (June 2004): 269–92.

Chapter Twenty-Five

1. See also Charles Schmitz, "Yemen's Tribal Showdown," *Foreign Affairs,* June 3, 2011.

2. "Yemen, Civil War and Political Unrest," Britannica Online Encyclopedia.

3. Husain Badr al-Din al-Huthi founded the movement in the 1980s as "Believing Youth" (*al-shabab al-mu'min*) mainly to promote religious education in the Saada governorate. In the mid-1990s it had between 1,000 and 3,000 followers. See Sarah Phillips, "Cracks in the Yemeni System," Middle East Report Online, July 28, 2005 (www.merip.org/mero/mero072805.html).

4. Human Rights Watch, "Invisible Civilians" (ww.hrw.org/en/node/76086/section/5#_ftn15).

5. See Barak A. Salmoni, Bryce Loidolt, and Madeleine Wells, "Regime and Periphery in Norther Yemen: The Huthi Phenomenon" (Santa Monica, Calif: RAND National Defense Research Institute, 2010) (www.rand.org/pubs/monographs/2010/RAND_MG962.pdf).

6. For a timeline of events in the Yemen uprising, see Al Jazeera English (http://aljazeera.com/news/middleeast/2011/03/20113211104457102860.html).

7. Yemen has 60 guns per 100 people, the second highest in the world behind only the United States, according to the Small Arms Survey, a Geneva-based independent research project. Laura Kassinoff, "Yemen, Awash in Guns, Wary of Unrest," *Christian Science Monitor,* February 18, 2011.

8. "Yemen's Weapon Culture," *BBC News,* January 22, 2002 (http://news.bbc.co.uk/2/hi/middle_east/1775938.stm).

9. Shatha al-Harazi, "Tribes Reconcile as President Threatens Civil War," Reliefweb, April 21, 2011.

10. See www.al-tagheer.com and the Friends of Yemen website (http://yemenfriends.org/Federal.php).

11. *Al-Wasat,* May 11, 2011 (www.alwasat-ye.net/index.php?action=showNews&id=555).

12. Indeed, elite strategies and goals tend to be far more influential than public opinion in creating and sustaining civil wars. See Paul Collier, Anke Hoeffler, and Måns Söderbom, "On the Duration of Civil War," *Journal of Peace Research* 41, no. 3 (2004): 253–73; Steven R. David, "Internal War: Causes and Cures," *World Politics* 49 (July 1997): 552–76; James D. Fearon, "Why Do Some Civil Wars Last So Much Longer than Others?" *Journal of Peace Research* 41, no. 3 (2004): 275–302; Stuart J. Kaufman, "Symbolic Politics or Rational Choice? Testing Theories of Extreme Ethnic Violence," *International Security* 30 (Spring 2006): 45–86; David Keen, "Incentives and Disincentives for Violence," in *Greed and Grievance: Economic Agendas in Civil Wars,* edited by Mats Berdal and David Malone (Boulder, Colo.: Lynne Rienner, 2000).

13. Author's interview and discussion with Robert Burrowes, president of the American Institute for Yemeni Studies and author of *A Historical Dictionary of Yemen,* May 2011.

14. Andrew Lee Butters, "Is Yemen the Next Afghanistan?" *Time* magazine, October 5, 2009 (www.time.com/time/magazine/article/0,9171,1926015,00.html).

15. Figures are for 2003. See U.S. Central Intelligence Agency, *The World Factbook* (Washington, regularly updated).

16. Ibid.

17. Andrew Lee Butters, "Is Yemen Chewing Itself to Death?" *Time* magazine, August 25, 2009 (www.time.com/time/world/article/0,8599,1917685,00.html).

18. Author's interview with Ambassador Barbara Bodine, May 2011.

19. Charles Schmitz, "Yemen's Tribal Showdown," *Foreign Affairs,* June 3, 2011. However, there is another possibility. In the context of civil war, tribes have the potential to function as a "stabilizing factor," if dealt with properly. The fact that tribes are heavily militarized may be a deterrent to violence and create a situation in which there is a balance of power and an incentive for compromise. In addition, because tribes are not monolithic entities, and their leaders are not always fully in control of their actions, power is diffused and there are opportunities for negotiations and conflict resolution.

20. The governorate of Dali' in the South, for example, has witnessed numerous violent attacks in the past years against the government and even vehicles carrying North plates.

21. Bruce Riedel, interview with Kristina Wong, "Yemen: 'Major Staging Base for Al Qaeda: Q and A with Former CIA Official and Al Qaeda Expert Bruce Riedel," *ABC News,* January 6, 2010 (http://abcnews.go.com/Politics/yemen-major-staging-base-al-Qaeda/story?id=9478552).

22. For AQAP being "fragmented," see Sarah Philips, "What Comes Next in Yemen? Al-Qaeda, the Tribes, and State-Building" (Carnegie Endowment for International Peace, March 2010), p. 7. Gregory Johnsen suggests that "AQAP poses a security threat but not the most serious threat." Gregory Johnsen, interview on Al Jazeera, May 30, 2011.

23. Author's interview with Izzedine al-Asbahi, Yemeni expert and civil rights activist, May 2011. Other interviews with Yemeni experts in May 2011 have also informed this section.

24. In fact, the UN High Commissioner for Refugees (UNHCR) estimates that as of June 2011 some 300,000 Yemenis have been displaced because of the crisis. See "Martina Fuchs, UNHCR Sees Growing Refugee Crisis in Yemen," Reuters, June 6, 2011 (http://uk.reuters.com/article/2011/06/06/uk-yemen-unhcr-idUKTRE7554TV20110606).

25. Jeremy M. Sharp, "Yemen: Background and U.S. Relations," Congressional Research Service, June 8, 2011 (www.fas.org/sgp/crs/mideast/RL34170.pdf).

26. Interview with al-Asbahi, May 2011.

Chapter Twenty-Six

1. Hugh Macleod, "Inside Deraa," Al Jazeera, April 19, 2011 (http://english.aljazeera.net/indepth/features/2011/04/201141918352728300.html).

2. For a detailed account of the siege of Dara'a, see "'We've Never Seen Such Horror': Crimes against Humanity by Syrian Security Forces," Human Rights Watch, June 1, 2011 (www.hrw.org/node/99366).

3. John Kifner, "Syria Said to Raze Part of Rebel City," New York Times, February 21, 1982.

4. On the role of Alawites in the Syrian state, see Nikolaos van Dam, The Struggle for Power in Syria: Politics and Society under Asad and the Ba'th Party (New York: I. B. Tauris, 1996).

5. Ian Black, "Six Syrians Who Helped Bashar al-Asad Keep Iron Grip after Father's Death," The Guardian, April 28, 2011 (www.guardian.co.uk/world/2011/apr/28/syria-bashar-Asad-regime-members>).

6. Adnan al-Suwadi, "'Al-Shabbiha," al-Arabiya, March 27, 2011 (www.alarabiya.net/articles/2011/03/27/143208.html); and Tony Badran, "Who Are the Shabbiha?," Weekly Standard Blog, April 12, 2011 (www.weeklystandard.com/blogs/who-are-shabbiha_557329.html).

7. "Numair al-Asad Is Stealing the Syrians," YouTube, December 24, 2006 (www.youtube.com/watch?v=NyXrru5zQA4).

8. Liz Sly, "Sectarian Violence in Syria Raises Fears," Washington Post, July 19, 2011.

9. For a revealing analysis of the Asad regime, see Shmuel Bar, "Bashar's Syria: The Regime and Its Strategic Worldview," Herzliya Conference, 2006 (www.herzliyaconference.org/_Uploads/2590Bashars.pdf).

10. Suleiman al-Khalidi and Simon Cameron-Moore, "Syria Opposition Group Form Council to Counter Assad," Reuters, July 16, 2011 (www.reuters.com/article/2011/07/16/us-syria-opposition-council-idUSTRE76F1W320110716).

11. See, for example: "President Asad Receives a Delegation . . . ," al-Thawra, June 22, 2011 (http://thawra.alwehda.gov.sy/_archive.asp?FileName=598676337201106222015946).

12. Khaled Yakoub Oweis, "32 Killed in Syria Protests, Damascus Moves: Activists," Reuters, July 15, 2011 (www.reuters.com/article/2011/07/16/us-syria-idUSTRE76D7NP20110716). See also www.youtube.com/watch?v=PnEdb6I70DQ.

Chapter Twenty-Seven

1. Iraq, of course, is a major oil producer and has also started down the path of democratization. However, it is the exception that proves the rule in that it only began to democratize because the United States—not the Iraqi people—overthrew its autocratic regime and instituted a democratic transition.

Chapter Twenty-Eight

1. This chapter draws heavily on Daniel Byman, "Israel's Pessimistic View of the Arab Spring," *Washington Quarterly,* Summer 2011 (www.twq.com/11summer/index.cfm?id=447).

2. Prime Minister Benjamin Netanyahu, "Speech to a Joint Meeting of the U.S. Congress," May 24, 2011 (www.pmo.gov.il/PMOEng/Communication/PMSpeaks/speech congress240511.htm).

3. Aluf Benn, "Overcoming Fear and Anxiety in Tel Aviv," *Foreign Affairs* (February 8, 2011) (www.foreignaffairs.com/articles/67353/aluf-benn/overcoming-fear-and-anxiety-in-tel-aviv).

4. Eli Lake, "Muslim Brotherhood Seeks End to Israel Treaty," *Washington Times,* February 3, 2011 (www.washingtontimes.com/news/2011/feb/3/muslim-brotherhood-seeks-end-to-israel-treaty/).

5. Janine Zacharia, "Israel Wary of Transition in Egypt, Concerned about Regional Stability," *Washington Post,* February 1, 2011.

6. Jason Burke, "Amr Moussa, Secretary General of the Arab League," *The Guardian,* March 21, 2011 (www.guardian.co.uk/world/2011/mar/21/amr-moussa-secretary-general-arab-league).

7. Steven Erlanger, "Upheaval Jolts Israel and Raises New Worry," *New York Times,* February 23, 2011 (www.nytimes.com/2011/02/24/world/middleeast/24arabs.html).

8. Pew Research Center, "U.S. Wins No Friends," April 25, 2011.

9. See www.bbc.co.uk/news/world-middle-east-13660311.

10. Benn, "Overcoming Fear and Anxiety in Tel Aviv."

11. Netanyahu, speech to Congress, May 24, 2011.

12. University of Maryland and Zogby International, "2010 Arab Public Opinion Poll," August 5, 2010 (www.brookings.edu/~/media/Files/rc/reports/2010/08_arab_opinion_poll_telhami/08_arab_opinion_poll_telhami.pdf).

13. Isabel Kershner, "Egypt's Upheaval Hardens Israel's Stance on Peace," *New York Times,* February 2, 2011 (www.nytimes.com/2011/02/03/world/middleeast/03israel.html?scp=56&sq=Isabel+Kershner&st=ny).

14. Erlanger, "Upheaval Jolts Israel and Raises New Worry."

15. Elior Levy, "Egypt to Open Rafah Crossing," *Yedioth Ahronoth* (Tel Aviv), April 29, 2011 (www.ynetnews.com/articles/0,7340,L-4062118,00.html).

16. Yossi Klein Halevi, "Israel's Neighborhood Watch," *Foreign Affairs* (February 1, 2011).

17. Aaron David Miller, "2011: The Year of the (Bad) Initiative," *New York Times,* March 11, 2011 (www.nytimes.com/2011/03/12/opinion/12iht-edmiller12.html).

Chapter Twenty-Nine

1. See, for example, Karam Mohammadi, "Bashar al-Asad and Suppressing the People of Syria, *Mardom-e Salari* (Tehran), June 12, 2011.

2. "Syria in Its Interaction with People Should Solve the Problems: Mottaki," *Siyasat-e Ruz* (Tehran), April 19, 2011.

3. Nawaf Obaid, "Amidst the Arab Spring, a U.S.-Saudi Split," *Washington Post,* May 15, 2011 (www.washingtonpost.com/opinions/amid-the-arab-spring-a-us-saudi-split/2011/05/13/AFMy8Q4G_story.html).

4. Khamenei speech on the occasion of Noruz (New Year), given in Mashhad on March 21, 2011.

5. "Iranian MP Calls for Pilgrim Boycott against S. Arabia," Reuters, April 26, 2011 (http://af.reuters.com/article/energyOilNews/idAFPOM63074720110426).

6. The Comprehensive Iran Sanctions and Divestment Act, which was signed by President Obama in July 2010, exempts hardware or software necessary for Internet services from U.S. economic sanctions. See www.treasury.gov/resource-center/sanctions/Documents/hr2194.pdf. The 2009 Victims of Iranian Censorship (VOICE) Act authorized a $20 million fund for development of technology to facilitate Internet access in Iran.

CHAPTER THIRTY

1. Thomas Friedman, "Letter from Istanbul," *New York Times,* June 15, 2010.
2. For an analysis of these new dynamics, see Ömer Taşpinar, "The Three Strategic Visions of Turkey," *U.S.-Europe Analysis,* no. 50 (March 8, 2011).
3. In 2009 Albania was admitted to NATO as the second Muslim member state.

CHAPTER THIRTY-ONE

1. U.S. Energy Information Administration (USEIA), "International Energy Statistics" (www.eia.gov/cfapps/ipdbproject/IEDIndex3.cfm?tid=5&pid=53&aid=1 [July 15, 2011]).
2. Rachel Bronson, *Thicker than Oil: America's Uneasy Partnership with Saudi Arabia* (Oxford University Press, 2006), p. 22.
3. USEIA, "Short-Term Outlook: OPEC Oil Production," March 2007; Matthew Simmons, "Shock to the System: The Impending Global Energy Supply Crisis," *Harvard International Review,* Fall 2006, p. 63. Simmons estimates that Saudi Arabia has less than 1 million bpd in spare production capacity.
4. Robert L. Hirsch, Roger Bezdek, and Robert Wendling, "Peaking of World Oil Production: Impacts, Mitigation, and Risk Management," February 2005, p. 8 (ww.netl.doe.gov/publications/others/pdf/Oil_Peaking_NETL.pdf [April 6, 2007]). Statistics from Department of Transportation, Bureau of Transportation Statistics, "Ending the Energy Stalemate: A Bipartisan Strategy to Meet America's Energy Challenges," December 2006, p. 3.
5. USEIA, "Petroleum Products" (www.eia.doe.gov/neic/infosheets/petroleumproducts.htm [April 5, 2007]).
6. Shaul Bakhash, *The Reign of the Ayatollahs: Iran and the Islamic Revolution,* rev. ed. (New York: Basic Books, 1990), p. 230; Central Intelligence Agency, *World Factbook* (Washington: Government Printing Office, 1989); Michael M. J. Fischer, *Iran: From Religious Dispute to Revolution* (University of Wisconsin Press, 1980), p. 224.
7. Alan Greenspan, "Monetary Policy and the Economic Outlook," testimony before the Joint Economic Committee, U.S. Congress, April 17, 2002 (www.federalreserve.gov/BoardDocs/Testimony/2002/20020417/default.htm [April 5, 2007]).
8. Jad Muawad, "Rising Demand for Oil Provokes New Energy Crisis," *New York Times,* November 9, 2007.

CHAPTER THIRTY-TWO

1. George Joffé, "The European Union, Democracy and Counter-Terrorism in the Maghreb," *Journal of Common Market Studies* 46, no. 1 (January 2008): 147–71.
2. Richard Youngs, "Democracy Promotion as External Governance?" *Journal of European Public Policy* 16, no. 6 (2009): 895–915.
3. Federica Bicchi, "Dilemmas of Implementation: EU Democracy Assistance in the Mediterranean," *Democratization* 17, no. 5 (2010): 976–96.
4. Nathalie Tocci and Jean-Pierre Cassarino, "Rethinking the EU's Mediterranean Policies Post 1/11," IAI Working Paper 11|06 (Istituto Affari Internazionali, March 2011).

Chapter Thirty-Three

1. One representative analysis is Mikhail Margelov, "After Stability," *Russia in Global Affairs,* April 19, 2011 (www.globalaffairs.ru/number/Posle-stabilnosti-15176). The Russian Foreign Ministry journal published a critical commentary on Obama's speech; see Sergei Filatov, "The U.S. Ultimatum to the Middle East," *Mezhdunarodnaya zhizn,* May 21, 2011 (http://interaffairs.ru/read.php?item=7661).

2. For a particularly insightful analysis of the trajectory of current political development in Russia, see Carnegie Moscow Center, "Russia 2020" (http://russia-2020.org/ru/). My research on the dynamics of revolutions in the post-Soviet era is presented in Pavel Baev, "Re-Examining the 'Color Revolutions,'" *Comparative Social Research* 27 (2010): 249–76.

3. See "Khodorkovsky Unabridged," *Wall Street Journal,* June 15, 2011; for my reflections, see Pavel Baev, "Medvedev Speaks against Putinism and Fails to Disprove Khodorkovsky," *Eurasia Daily Monitor,* June 20, 2011.

4. Official translation of the remarks at the meeting of the National Anti-Terrorist Committee on February 22, 2011 (http://eng.kremlin.ru/transcripts/1804).

5. Deputy Prime Minister Igor Sechin spelled out the accusations against "high-level managers of Google" in an interview with *Wall Street Journal* (February 22, 2011), much to the entertainment of Russian bloggers. For an example of the analysis, see Sergei Pechurov, "The Controlled Chaos Technology Works in the Arab East," *Nezavisimoe voennoe obozrenie,* March 25, 2011.

6. Official translation of the remarks at the press conference in Denmark, April 26, 2011 (http://premier.gov.ru/eng/visits/world/14991/events/14996/).

7. See, for instance, Evgeny Satanovsky, "Revolution and Democracy in the Arab World," *Russia in Global Affairs,* February 14, 2011 (www.globalaffairs.ru/number/Revolyutciya-i-demokratiya-v-islamskom-mire-15101).

8. One sharp Russian analysis is Fedor Lukyanov, "The War with No Aims," Gazeta.ru, March 24, 2011 (www.gazeta.ru/column/lukyanov/3563673.shtml).

9. Putin's remarks at a meeting with workers of Votkinsk plant on March 21, 2011 (http://premier.gov.ru/eng/events/news/14542/). For an official translation of Medvedev's press conference on May 18, 2011, see http://eng.kremlin.ru/news/2223. For one noteworthy comment, see Nikolai Zlobin, "Why Russia Is Not Libya," *Vedomosti,* March 28, 2011; see also Ellen Barry, "Leaders' Spat Tests Skills of Survival in the Kremlin," *New York Times,* March 24, 2011.

10. For one revisionist assessment of NATO's declining capabilities, see Aleksandr Khramchihin, "NATO Is Scary in Its Weakness," *Nezavisimoe Voennoe Obozrenie,* April 15, 2011.

11. The Kremlin, "News Conference by President of Russia," May 18, 2011 (http://eng.kremlin.ru/news/2223).

12. *The Economist,* February 24, 2011 (http://www.economist.com/node/18239804).

13. My reading of the failed Russian attempt to draw a "road map" for solving this conflict at the trilateral summit in Kazan appears in Pavel Baev, "Medvedev Fails in Mediating a Compromise between Armenia and Azerbaijan," *Eurasia Daily Monitor,* June 27, 2011.

14. Precise analysis can be found in Aleksei Malashenko, "Russia-2020: The Future of the North Caucasus," *Vedomosti,* April 13, 2011.

15. Sound analysis can be found in "Tajikistan: The Changing Insurgent Threats," *Asia Report* 205 (Brussels: International Crisis Group, May 24, 2011).

16. On the scope of preemptive measures, see Muhammad Tahir, "Governments Move to Thwart 'Arab Spring' in Central Asia," RFE/RL Features, April 28, 2011 (www.rferl.org/content/governments_move_to_thwart_arab_spring_in_central_asia/16796618.html).

17. Medvedev had perfectly friendly telephone conversations with President Asad on April 6 and May 24, 2011. According to the official records, Asad expressed his commitment

to reforms and to ensuring "the peaceful free expression of Syrian citizens' will" (http://eng. kremlin.ru/news/2264).

18. This idea is spelled out in Dmitri Trenin, "Ankara as a Geopolitical Partner for Moscow," InoSMI.ru, April 29, 2011 (http://inosmi.ru/op_ed/20110429/168896495.html).

CHAPTER THIRTY-FOUR

1. "China Says It Suffers 'Large-Scale' Economic Losses in Libya," Reuters, February 24, 2011 (http://af.reuters.com/article/libyaNews/idAFTOE71N06L20110224?pageNumber=1& virtualBrandChannel=0).

2. Sun Liping, "Social Order Is Currently a Severe Challenge," Economic Observer, February 25, 2011 (http://opinion.hexun.com/2011-02-25/127571301.html). There are understandable questions about how to define and measure these incidents, but the scope of such activity is beyond dispute. For more on this, see Will Freeman, "The Accuracy of China's 'Mass Incidents,'" Financial Times, March 2, 2010 (www.ft.com/intl/cms/s/0/9ee6fa64-25b5-11df-9bd3-00144feab49a,s01=1.html#axzz1SCTI2xlj).

3. "China-Egypt 10-Year Strategic Cooperation—Mutual Benefit and Win-Win Cooperation," interview with China's Ambassador to Egypt, August 6, 2009 (www.focac.org/eng/ jlydh/sjzs/t619121.htm).

4. For relevant data, see Erica Downs, "China-Gulf Energy Relations," in China and the Persian Gulf, edited by Bryce Wakefield and Susan L. Levenstein (Washington: Woodrow Wilson International Center for Scholars, 2011), pp. 63–65.

5. "No Pastoral Idyll: Turbulence in Inner Mongolia Makes Managing China No Easier," The Economist, June 2, 2011 (www.economist.com/node/18775303). See also Jamil Anderlini, "Unrest Spreads among China's Migrant Masses," Financial Times, June 17, 2011 (www.ft.com/intl/cms/s/0/e0696f2c-98f9-11e0-acd2-00144feab49a.html#axzz1SCTI2xlj); Liang Chen and Li Qian, "Deadly Blast Hits Govt Office in Jiangxi," Global Times (China), May 27, 2011 (http://china.globaltimes.cn/society/2011-05/659581.html).

6. "Wen Jiabao: Comparing China to North Africa and Other Politically Unstable Countries is Incorrect," Global Times, March 14, 2011 (http://china.huanqiu.com/lhbd/ gdxw/2011-03/1561300.html).

7. On the immediate suppression of public protests in Beijing, see James Fallows, "Arab Spring, Chinese Winter," The Atlantic, September 2011 (www.theatlantic.com/magazine/ archive/2011/09/arab-spring-chinese-winter/8601/).

8. Fiona Hill, "How Russia and China See the Egyptian Revolution," Foreign Policy, February 15, 2011 (http://www.foreignpolicy.com/articles/2011/02/15/how_russia_and_china_ see_the_egyptian_revolution?print=yes&hidecomments=yes&page=full); Andrew Jacobs and Jonathan Ansfield, "Catching Scent of Revolution, China Moves to Snip Jasmine," New York Times, May 10, 2011 (www.nytimes.com/2011/05/11/world/asia/11jasmine.html?_r=2).

9. Sharon LaFraniere and Edward Wong, "Even With Protests Averted, China Turns to Intimidation of Foreign Journalists," New York Times, March 6, 2012 (http://www.nytimes. com/2011/03/07/world/asia/07china.html?pagewanted=all).

10. See, in particular, Ye Qing, "Debating the Arab Uprisings: Views from China" (Washington: Center for Strategic and International Studies, June 2011), pp. 1–2 (http://csis.org/ files/publication/fr11n06.pdf).

11. Huang Jingjing, "China Counting Financial Losses in Libya," Global Times (China), March 4, 2011 (http://china.globaltimes.cn/diplomacy/2011-03/629817.html).

12. "China Evacuates Nationals from Chaotic Libya," People's Daily, February 23, 2011 (http://english.peopledaily.com.cn/90001/90776/90883/7296633.html).

13. Yun Sun, "China's Acquiescence on UNSCR 1973, No Big Deal," PacNet 20, March 31, 2011 (http://csis.org/files/publication/pac1120.pdf).

14. "Transcript of PRC FM Spokesman News Conference on June 9, 2011" (opensource. gov [June 10, 2011]).

15. See comments by Minister of Foreign Affairs Yang Jiechi to Mahmoud Jibril, chairman of the National Transitional Council, then visiting Beijing, in Li Lianxing, "Libyan Opposition 'Important Dialogue Partner,'" *China Daily,* June 23, 2011 (www.chinadaily. com.cn/cndy/2011-06/23/content_12756584.htm).

16. Though there are major differences in estimated losses calculated by different Chinese sources, comments by officials from the Ministry of Commerce and the China International Contractors Association acknowledge that the losses were severe. See Huang, "China Counting Financial Losses in Libya."

17. See the comments of Foreign Affairs spokesman Ma Zhaoxu, *Xinhua,* August 22, 2011 (www.china.org.cn).

18. A subsequent official estimate placed the total number of Chinese projects in Libya at fifty, with a total worth of $18.8 billion. See Zheng Yangpeng and Wang Yan, "NTL Recognized as Ruling Authority," *China Daily,* September 13, 2011.

19. Yun Sun, "China's Acquiescence on UNSCR 1973."

20. Keith Bradsher, "China Moves Closer to Libyan Opposition," *New York Times,* June 22, 2011 (http://www.nytimes.com/2011/06/23/world/asia/23beijing.html?_r=1). "Senior PRC Diplomat Visits Libyan Opposition Base, Urges Political Solution," *Xinhua,* July 6, 2011 (http://news.xinhuanet.com/english2010/china/2011-07/07/c_13969784.htm).

21. For additional details, see Gabe Collins and Andrew Erickson, "Implications of China's Military Evacuation of Citizens from Libya," *China Brief* 11 no. 4 (March 10, 2011) (www.jamestown.org/programs/chinabrief/single/?tx_ttnews%5Btt_news%5D=37633&c Hash=7278cfd21e6fb19afe8a823c5cf88f07).

CHAPTER THIRTY-FIVE

1. Fareed Zakaria, *The Post-American World* (New York: W. W. Norton, 2008).

2. Laura Rozen, "U.S. Scrambles to Respond as Egypt Protests Intensify," *Politico,* January 28, 2011; Phil Stewart and David Morgan, "ElBaradei Urges U.S. to Abandon Mubarak," Reuters, January 30, 2011; Evan Hill, "Egypt Protesters Consolidate Gains," Al Jazeera, February 5, 2011; Kirit Radia, Huma Khan, and Alexander Marquardt, "President Mubarak Tells Defiant Egyptians That Government Will Resign," *ABC News,* January 28, 2011. For audiences parsing statements, see Shadi Hamid, "Values Added: Euphoria in Cairo," Brookings Video, February 13, 2011.

3. On China, see Geoffrey Kemp, *The East Moves West: India, China, and Asia's Growing Presence in the Middle East* (Brookings, 2010); Chietigj Bajpaee, "China Stakes Its Middle East Claim," *Asia Times,* March 14, 2006; Simon Henderson, "China and Oil: The Middle East Dimension," PolicyWatch 898 (Washington Institute for Near East Policy, September 15, 2004). On Russia, see Hannah Carter and Anoushiravan Ehteshami, eds., *The Middle East's Relations with Asia and Russia* (New York: Routledge, 2004); Igor Khrestin and John Elliot, "Russia and the Middle East," *Middle East Quarterly* 9, no. 1 (2007): 21–27; "Country Overview," *Iran Investment Monthly,* August 2010, p. 5; Marat Terterov, *Russian and CIS Relations with the Gulf Region: Current Trends in Political and Economic Dynamics* (Dubai: Gulf Research Center, November 2009). On energy relationships, see Simon Shen, "Qualitative Energy Diplomacy in Central Asia: A Comparative Analysis of the Policies of the United States, Russia and China," Brookings Research and Commentary, April 2011.

4. On India-Iran ties, see Ronak D. Desai and Xenia Dormandy, "India-Iran Relations: Key Security Implications" (Harvard University, Belfer Center for Science and International Affairs, March 24, 2008); C. Christine Fair, "India and Iran: New Delhi's Balancing Act," *Washington Quarterly* 30, no. 3 (2007): 145–59; Donald L. Berlin, "India-Iran Relations: A Deepening Entente" (Honolulu: Asia-Pacific Center for Security Studies, October 2004); Sujata Ashwarya Cheema, "India-Iran Relations: Progress, Challenges and Prospects," *India Quarterly* 66, no. 4 (2010): 383–96. For commercial relationships, see "'New Era' for Saudi-Indian ties," *BBC News,* January 27, 2006.

5. "Brazil and Turkey Urge UN Security Council against Iran Sanctions," *The Telegraph* (U.K.), May 20, 2010; "Iran, Turkey and Brazil Declaration," Al Jazeera, May 17, 2010.

6. Jay Solomon, "Sarkozy Tries to Revive Middle East Peace Process," *Wall Street Journal,* June 8, 2011.

7. "Indonesia's President: 'We Can Be Model for Islam and Democracy,'" *CNN News,* June 15, 2011; Robin Bush, "Lessons from Indonesia's Democratic Transition," Asia Foundation, May 4, 2011; Joshua Kurlantzick, "Middle East Revolutions Only Aspire to Indonesia's Success," *The National,* February 20, 2011; Karen Brooks, "Indonesia's Lessons for Egypt" (New York: Council on Foreign Relations, February 17, 2011).

8. Author's notes, American University of Cairo; and World Bank, Conference on World Development Report 2011, Egypt, May 8–10, 2011; Doha Global Forum, Doha, Qatar, May 10–12, 2011.

9. Hong Kong's figure of trade as a percentage of GDP was 415 percent in 2008. World Bank World Development Indicators: Trade (percent of GDP); European Commission Globalization Indicators; World Trade Organization Statistics Database Trade Profiles; Organization for Economic Cooperation and Development (OECD), "Trade as a Percentage of GDP," in *Measuring Globalisation: OECD Economic Globalisation Indicators 2010* (Paris, 2010).

10. Kenneth M. Pollack, *A Path Out of the Desert: A Grand Strategy for America in the Middle East* (New York: Random House, 2008), pp. 5–23.

11. Robert Kaplan, *Monsoon: The Indian Ocean and the Future of American Power* (New York: Random House, 2010), and "Center Stage for the 21st Century: Power Plays in the Indian Ocean," *Foreign Affairs* (March/April 2009); "China Builds Up Strategic Sea Lanes," *Washington Times,* January 17, 2005; Bernard D. Cole, *The Great Wall at Sea: China's Navy Enters the Twenty-first Century* (Annapolis: U.S. Naval Institute, 2001).

12. Statistical Review of World Energy 2011 (BP, June 2011).

13. See Pollack, *A Path Out of the Desert,* pp. 419–30.

14. United Nations Human Rights Council, *United Nations Resolution S-15/2: Situation of Human Rights in the Libyan Arab Jamahiriya,* Fifteenth Special Session of the Council, February 25, 2011 (adopted without a vote). See also "General Assembly Suspends Libya from Human Rights Council" (UN Department of Public Information, March 1, 2011).

15. United Nations, *United Nations General Assembly Resolution 65/265,* Sixty-Fifth Session of the General Assembly, March 3, 2011.

16. White House, "Remarks by the President to Parliament in London, United Kingdom," May 25, 2011.

Chapter Thirty-Six

1. For a more detailed explanation of such a strategy, see, for instance, Kenneth M. Pollack, *A Path Out of the Desert: A Grand Strategy for America in the Middle East* (New York: Random House, 2008), esp. pp. 215–29; and Tamara C. Wittes, *Freedom's Unsteady March: America's Role in Building Arab Democracy* (Brookings, 2008).

2. James Zogby, "Arab Attitudes toward Iran, 2011," Arab-American Institute Foundation, July 28, 2011 (http://aai.3cdn.net/fd7ac73539e31a321a_r9m6iy9y0.pdf [July 30, 2011]).

Appendix Part 1

1. Data for all countries in "Algeria Country Review," CountryWatch, Inc., 2011, pp. 24–30.

2. "Freedom in the World Country Report," Freedom House, last modified 2011 (http://www.freedomhouse.org/template.cfm?page=21&year=2011).

3. "Corruption Perceptions Index 2010 Results," Transparency International, last modified 2010 (www.transparency.org/policy_research/surveys_indices/cpi/2010/results).

4. "Worldwide Tracking System," National Counterterrorism Center, 2011 (https://wits.nctc.gov/FederalDiscoverWITS/index.do?t=Reports&Rcv=Incident&Nf=p_Incident Date%7CGTEQ+20100101%7C%7Cp_IncidentDate%7CLTEQ+20101231&N=0).

5. "Map of Press Freedom 2010," Freedom House, last modified 2010 (www.freedom house.org/template.cfm?page=251&year=2010).

6. "International Human Development Indicators," United Nations Development Programme, last modified February 2, 2011 (http://hdrstats.undp.org/en/indicators/49806.html).

7. "World Development Indicators 2010," World Bank, 2010, pp. 114–15 (http://elibrary.worldbank.org/content/book/9780821382325).

8. "2011 Country Operations Profile," United Nations High Commissioner for Refugees (www.unhcr.org/pages/49c3646c2.html).

9. "ICT Data and Statistics (IDS)," International Telecommunication Union (www.itu.int/ITU-D/ict/statistics/).

10. "World Development Indicators & Global Development Finance," World Bank (http://databank.worldbank.org/ddp/home.do).

11. "Bahrain Country Review," CountryWatch, Inc., 2011, p. 58.

12. "Kuwait Country Review," CountryWatch, Inc., 2011, p. 60.

13. "World Development Indicators & Global Development Finance," World Bank.

14. CountryWatch, Inc., 2011, "Algeria Country Review," p. 49; "Bahrain Country Review," p. 40; "Egypt Country Review," p. 49; "Iran Country Review," p. 118; "Iraq Country Review," p. 164; "Jordan Country Review," p. 42; "Kuwait Country Review," p. 43; "Libya Country Review," p. 43.

15. "World Development Indicators 2010," World Bank, April 2010, pp. 98–99 (http://elibrary.worldbank.org/content/book/9780821382325).

16. "World Development Indicators 2010," p. 108.

17. "World Development Indicators 2010," pp. 316–17.

18. "U.S. Overseas Loans and Grants, Ten-year Country Report," United States Agency for International Development (http://gbk.eads.usaidallnet.gov/query/do?_program=/eads/gbk/countryReport&unit=R).

19. "Conventional Arms Transfers to Developing Nations, 2002-2009," Congressional Research Service, 2010, pp. 57–58 (www.fas.org/sgp/crs/weapons/R41403.pdf).

Appendix Part 2

1. Data for all countries in "Algeria Country Review," CountryWatch, Inc., 2011, pp. 24–30.

2. "Freedom in the World Country Report," Freedom House, last modified 2011 (http://www.freedomhouse.org/template.cfm?page=21&year=2011).

3. "Corruption Perceptions Index 2010 Results," Transparency International, last modified 2010 (www.transparency.org/policy_research/surveys_indices/cpi/2010/results).

4. "Worldwide Tracking System," National Counterterrorism Center, 2011 (https://wits.nctc.gov/FederalDiscoverWITS/index.do?t=Reports&Rcv=Incident&Nf=p_Incident Date%7CGTEQ+20100101%7C%7Cp_IncidentDate%7CLTEQ+20101231&N=0).

5. "Map of Press Freedom 2010," Freedom House, last modified 2010 (www.freedom house.org/template.cfm?page=251&year=2010).

6. "International Human Development Indicators," United Nations Development Programme, last modified February 2, 2011 (http://hdrstats.undp.org/en/indicators/49806. html).

7. "World Development Indicators 2010," World Bank, 2010, pp. 114–15 (http://elibrary.worldbank.org/content/book/9780821382325).

8. "2011 Country Operations Profile," United Nations High Commissioner for Refugees (www.unhcr.org/pages/49c3646c2.html).

9. "ICT Data and Statistics (IDS)," International Telecommunication Union (www.itu. int/ITU-D/ict/statistics/).

10. "World Development Indicators & Global Development Finance," World Bank (http://databank.worldbank.org/ddp/home.do).

11. "Oman GDP—Real Growth Rate," IndexMundi (www.indexmundi.com/oman/gdp_real_growth_rate.html).

12. "World Development Indicators & Global Development Finance," World Bank.

13. CountryWatch, Inc., 2011, "Saudi Arabia Country Review," p. 47; "Tunisia Country Review," p. 44; "United Arab Emirates Country Review," p. 40; Yemen Country Review," p. 57.

14. "Oman," U.S. Central Intelligence Agency, *The World Factbook* (Washington, regularly updated) (www.cia.gov/library/publications/the-world-factbook/geos/mu.html).

15. "Gaza Strip," U.S. Central Intelligence Agency, *The World Factbook* (Washington, regularly updated) (www.cia.gov/library/publications/the-world-factbook/geos/gz.html).

16. "West Bank," U.S. Central Intelligence Agency, *The World Factbook* (Washington, regularly updated) (www.cia.gov/library/publications/the-world-factbook/geos/we.html).

17. "Qatar," U.S. Central Intelligence Agency, *The World Factbook* (Washington, regularly updated) (www.cia.gov/library/publications/the-world-factbook/geos/qa.html).

18. "Syria," U.S. Central Intelligence Agency, *The World Factbook* (Washington, regularly updated) (www.cia.gov/library/publications/the-world-factbook/geos/sy.html).

19. "World Development Indicators 2010," World Bank, April 2010, p. 100 (http://elibrary.worldbank.org/content/book/9780821382325).

20. "World Development Indicators 2010," p. 108.

21. "World Development Indicators 2010," pp. 317–18.

22. "U.S. Overseas Loans and Grants, Ten-year Country Report," United States Agency for International Development (http://gbk.eads.usaidallnet.gov/query/do?_program=/eads/gbk/countryReport&unit=R).

23. "Conventional Arms Transfers to Developing Nations, 2002–2009," Congressional Research Service, 2010, pp. 57–58 (www.fas.org/sgp/crs/weapons/R41403.pdf).

About the Authors

Kenneth M. Pollack
Kenneth M. Pollack is a Senior Fellow at the Brookings Institution, where he is Director of the Saban Center for Middle East Policy. Previously, he was Director for Persian Gulf Affairs at the National Security Council and spent seven years in the CIA as a Persian Gulf military analyst.

Daniel L. Byman
Daniel L. Byman is Research Director of the Saban Center for Middle East Policy at Brookings and a professor at Georgetown University's School of Foreign Service. Previously, he served as a staff member on the 9/11 Commission and worked for the U.S. government.

Akram Al-Turk
Akram Al-Turk is the Publications Manager and Senior Research Assistant in the Project on U.S. Relations with the Islamic World at the Saban Center for Middle East Policy at the Brookings Institution.

Pavel K. Baev
Pavel K. Baev is a Nonresident Senior Fellow at the Brookings Institution, where he is affiliated with the Center on the United States and Europe. He holds the position of Research Professor at the Peace Research Institute, Oslo (PRIO). He writes extensively on Russia's foreign and energy policy, Russian military reform, and conflict management in the Caucasus.

Michael S. Doran
Michael S. Doran is the Roger Hertog Senior Fellow with the Saban Center for Middle East Policy at Brookings, where he specializes in Middle East security issues. He has held several academic positions and has served as a Deputy Assistant Secretary of Defense and a Senior Director at the National Security Council.

Khaled Elgindy

Khaled Elgindy is a Visiting Fellow with the Saban Center for Middle East Policy at Brookings. He most recently served with the Negotiations Support Unit in Ramallah as an adviser to the Palestinian leadership on permanent status negotiations with Israel (2004–09) and was a key participant in the negotiations launched at Annapolis in November 2007.

Stephen R. Grand

Stephen R. Grand is a Fellow and Director of the Project on U.S. Relations with the Islamic World, which is housed within the Saban Center for Middle East Policy at Brookings. Previously, he was the Director of the Aspen Institute's Middle East Strategy Group and Director of Programs at the German Marshall Fund of the United States.

Shadi Hamid

Shadi Hamid is Director of Research at the Brookings Doha Center and a Fellow at the Saban Center for Middle East Policy at the Brookings Institution. He is an expert on democratization and the role of Islamist parties in the Arab world.

Bruce Jones

Bruce Jones is Director of the Managing Global Insecurity initiative, a Senior Fellow at Brookings, and Director of the Center on International Cooperation at New York University. His research focuses on U.S. policy on global order and transnational threats, international conflict management, and fragile states.

Suzanne Maloney

Suzanne Maloney is a Senior Fellow with the Saban Center for Middle East Policy at Brookings, where she studies Iran, the political economy of the Persian Gulf, and Middle East energy policy. A former U.S. State Department policy adviser, she has also counseled private companies on Middle East issues and is the author of *Iran's Long Reach: Iran as a Pivotal State in the Muslim World* (2008).

Jonathan D. Pollack

Jonathan D. Pollack is a Senior Fellow in the John L. Thornton Center at Brookings, where he specializes in Chinese foreign and security policy, U.S.-China relations, and East Asian political-military affairs. Prior to joining Brookings in December 2010, he was Professor of Asian and Pacific Studies at the U.S. Naval War College. His most recent publication is *No Exit: North Korea, Nuclear Weapons and International Security* (2011).

Bruce O. Riedel

Bruce Riedel is a Senior Fellow with the Saban Center for Middle East Policy at Brookings and a professor at Johns Hopkins School of Advanced International Studies. He served in the CIA for thirty years with assignments at the White House, Pentagon, and overseas. He is the author of *The Search for al Qaeda: Its Leadership, Ideology and Future* (2008) and *Deadly Embrace: Pakistan, America and the Future of the Global Jihad* (2011).

Ruth Hanau Santini

Ruth Hanau Santini is a Visiting Fellow at the Center on the United States and Europe at Brookings, where she deals with European foreign policy toward the Middle East and North Africa. She was previously coordinator of Italian foreign policy dialogue, an initiative based at Johns Hopkins School of Advanced International Studies in Bologna. She has been a Visiting Fellow in several European think tanks.

Salman Shaikh

Salman Shaikh is Director of the Brookings Doha Center and a Fellow at the Saban Center for Middle East Policy at Brookings. He has held posts at the United Nations and the Office of Her Highness Sheikha Mozah Bint Nasser Al Missned in Qatar. He also held the position of Special Representative in Europe to the Muslim West Facts Project.

Ibrahim Sharqieh

Ibrahim Sharqieh is Deputy Director of the Brookings Doha Center. He previously served as Senior Project Director at the Academy for Educational Development (AED), managing development projects in Yemen and Qatar, and as an adjunct professor of International Conflict Resolution at George Washington University, George Mason University, and Catholic University.

Ömer Taşpınar

Ömer Taşpınar is a Nonresident Senior Fellow with the Center on the United States and Europe at Brookings. He is a professor at the National War College and an adjunct professor at Johns Hopkins School of Advanced International Studies.

Shibley Telhami

Shibley Telhami is the Anwar Sadat Professor for Peace and Development at the University of Maryland and a Nonresident Senior Fellow at the Saban Center for Middle East Policy at Brookings. He is the Principal Investigator for the Annual

Arab Public Opinion Poll, which he has been conducting for more than a decade, and the author of a forthcoming book on Arab public opinion and media.

SARAH E. YERKES

Sarah E. Yerkes is a former Research Analyst at the Saban Center for Middle East Policy at Brookings. She is an adjunct faculty member in the Department of Political Science at George Washington University and a Ph.D. candidate in the Department of Government at Georgetown University, where she focuses on state-society relations in the Arab world.

INDEX

Surnames starting with al- or el- are alphabetized under the following part of the name.

CPSIA information can be obtained
at www.ICGtesting.com
Printed in the USA
LVHW031346231118
598061LV00001B/143/P